CRIMES AG<

Crimes Against the State
From Treason to Terrorism

MICHAEL HEAD
University of Western Sydney, Australia

Routledge
Taylor & Francis Group

LONDON AND NEW YORK

First published 2011 by Ashgate Publishing

2 Park Square, Milton Park, Abingdon, Oxon OX14 4RN
711 Third Avenue, New York, NY 10017, USA

Routledge is an imprint of the Taylor & Francis Group, an informa business

First issued in paperback 2016

British Library Cataloguing in Publication Data
Head, Michael, LL.B.
 Crimes against the state : from treason to terrorism.
 1. Political crimes and offences--Great Britain.
 2. Political crimes and offences--United States.
 3. Political crimes and offences--Canada. 4. Political
 crimes and offences--Australia.
 I. Title
 345'.0231-dc22

Library of Congress Cataloging-in-Publication Data
Head, Michael, LL.B.
 Crimes against the state : from treason to terrorism / by Michael Head.
  p. cm.
 Includes bibliographical references and index.
 ISBN 978-0-7546-7819-9 (hardback)
 1. Political crimes and offenses--English speaking countries. I. Title.

 K5250.H43 2011
 345'.0231--dc22

                                                                    2011007781

ISBN 978-0-7546-7819-9 (hbk)
ISBN 978-1-138-26035-1 (pbk)

Contents

Preface   *vii*

Introduction: What are 'Crimes against the State'?   1

1   A Controversial History   21

2   The United States: Free Speech in 'War' and 'Peace'   37

3   Insurrection, Rebellion and Unlawful Associations   65

4   Treason and Mutiny   95

5   Espionage, Official Secrets and Sabotage   125

6   Sedition and Politically Motivated Violence   147

7   Terrorism   181

8   Riot, Affray and Unlawful Assembly   221

9   Emergency Powers, Martial Law and Official Lawlessness   247

10   Conclusions   273

Bibliography   *281*
Index   *293*

Preface: Completing an Unfinished Task

In 1979, as a young law lecturer at the Australian National University, I published an article on the inglorious history of the crime of sedition (Head 1979). The article described sedition as the quintessence of the fundamental role of the criminal law – the maintenance of the prevailing political order. Sedition, I wrote, took to the 'highest and clearest point' the punishment of perceived threats to the tranquillity of that order. My survey concluded that the law of sedition, despite falling from prominence for a number of decades, was in an unsatisfactory state. It was ripe for revival and manipulation by governments to utilise against political opponents in periods of turmoil. The article ended by drawing attention to the need for a wider inquiry:

> I have left undiscussed the wider range of statutory and common law provisions which can be used to stifle dissent. Sedition is, or should be, merely the 'pure' form in which the question is raised. In the light of the state of law presented it is important that a more complete picture be assembled. (Head 1979: 107)

This book, somewhat belatedly, attempts to address that unfinished business. It seeks to assemble and analyse the law devoted to the basic task of protecting the existing order from political dissent and destabilisation. Generally, I have approached the law historically and examined first the British provisions and then their American and Australian applications, with some references to other English-based legal systems. Not all aspects of the law are covered uniformly. There are differences in the degree of detail in the treatment of different offences, and various jurisdictions. The primary focus is on relevant historical experiences of how the most significant legal measures have been applied in practice.

Hopefully, the book makes an initial contribution toward a wider and more insightful understanding of the interaction between the law of crimes against the state and economic, social and political atmosphere in which it operates.

As will become apparent, the outcomes of many of the cases examined in this volume cannot be explained by a purely legal approach. In English-derived legal systems there is a supposed principle that the law is applied neutrally and independently by the appropriate police, intelligence and law enforcement agencies, without government interference. Frequently, however, decisions on whether to prosecute or not, and for which offences, were made for political reasons. In some instances, documentary evidence now exists of cabinet-level determinations to proceed, or not to proceed. In other cases, laws that had lain dormant for decades were revived to confront perceived political threats. Moreover, verdicts and sentences were often shaped more by political considerations than the precise terms of the law.

Many events have intervened since my 1979 article on sedition. Nevertheless, the resumption of this work has been timely. The global economic breakdown that first began to erupt in 2007 and 2008 has again highlighted the problems, contradictions and underlying instability of the present socio-economic system. It has also heightened the likelihood of civil unrest and political opposition that will challenge governments and possibly call into question the capitalist structure of society itself. These are not idle speculations. There is clear evidence that such concerns have been felt within the security apparatuses.

Testifying before the United States Senate Committee on Intelligence in 2009, the American national intelligence director Dennis Blair warned that the deepening world crisis posed the paramount threat to US national security and warned that its continuation could trigger a return to the 'economic turmoil', 'instability' and 'violent extremism' of the 1920s and 1930s. Blair also referred to the damage that had been done to the global credibility of American capitalism, declaring that the 'widely held perception that excesses in US financial markets and inadequate regulation were responsible has increased criticism about free market policies, which may make it difficult to achieve long-time US objectives' (Blair 2009: 2–3). Likewise, Australian Federal Police Commissioner Mick Keelty delivered an address to a 2009 national security conference in which he noted that if the global financial crisis continued, 'it could create levels of social unrest and political instability that could undermine security in some parts of the world' (Keelty 2009).

The historical record reviewed in this book suggests that such a period of turmoil and discontent is likely to produce renewed resort by governments and prosecuting authorities to arrests for crimes against the state.

As always, my thanks go to my colleagues at the University of Western Sydney for the intellectual encouragement and nourishment, without which this research would not be possible. Above all, I am deeply grateful to my partner Mary and our four sons and daughter, Clayton, Lincoln, Tom, Daniel and Kathleen, for their love and forbearance during the long months of labour.

Introduction:
What are 'Crimes against the State'?

Why this book? It aims to meet an unfilled need for a thorough and critical examination of the wide range and essential nature of the criminal offences created to protect the established economic, political and legal order. It examines who has been affected by these laws in the past and who might be prosecuted in the future. It does so in the post-2001 context of the 'war on terrorism' and rising international and domestic tensions.

This volume reviews in some detail what are generally classified as crimes against the state or against the nation – subversion, rebellion, treason, mutiny, espionage, sedition, terrorism, riot and unlawful assembly – in several comparable countries with English-derived legal systems, primarily the United Kingdom, the United States and Australia. It does not cover a broader variety of offences that affect government, but arguably not existentially, such as bribery and corruption, tax evasion, money-laundering and economic crimes, petty offences, perjury, interference with the judicial system, smuggling, 'people smuggling' and infringements of official sexual standards.

Rather than an abstract approach, the relevant laws are placed in their historical and political context. Leading cases, including some of the most controversial prosecutions in history, are critically probed. That is because the character and implications of these laws cannot be grasped in isolation, outside their application. Throughout modern history – from the summary trial and execution of Charles I in 1649 for 'high treason and other high crimes', and the summary trial and execution of his prosecutors in 1660 for treason for 'compassing and imagining' the King's death, through to the 'anti-terrorism' cases of the first decade of the twenty-first century – prosecutions of crimes against the state have been intimately bound up with the political agendas and requirements of those wielding power, both legal and socio-economic.

The major cases demonstrate that the precise words and concepts of the relevant statutes and common law rules, while important in some circumstances, are not usually decisive in determining arrests, prosecutions, convictions and sentences. Rather, the substantial calculations are political, not legal. The many complex and often interlocking legal provisions invariably offer considerable choices to the prosecuting authorities. Moreover, the historical record provides many examples of direct intervention in these decisions by the governments of the day.

To some extent, these factors have been acknowledged officially. In a 2006 report on the law of sedition, the Australian Law Reform Commission observed that 'the development and use of sedition laws have been influenced strongly by the changing political climate and the degree of citizen support for existing state institutions; theories about the relationship between citizen and state, and evolving notions of the relationship between action, idea, association and responsibility' (ALRC 2006: 48). The same report also noted that 'the breadth of the law of treason has fluctuated throughout history' (ALRC 2006: 49 fn 11).

Such offences are at the heart of the criminal law of each country. Chapter 115 of Title 18 of the United States Code, entitled 'Treason, Sedition, and Subversive Activities' provides for penalties of up to execution for treason. In Australia, chapter five of the Criminal Code Act 1995 (Cth) is devoted to 'The security of the Commonwealth'. Part 5.1 covers treason and urging violence, part 5.2 covers espionage and similar activities and part 5.3 covers terrorism. Those offences regarded as the most serious – treason and some terrorist-related offences – are punishable by life imprisonment, the most severe penalty currently available under Australian law, a penalty that is otherwise reserved for murder. The other offences carry lengthy prison sentences, ranging from 7 to 25 years.

This volume will closely examine the laws themselves, their judicial interpretation and their political use and abuse. It will also trace the manner in which these measures have been used against political opponents, particularly during periods of economic and social convulsion (for instance, the 1792 sedition prosecution of Thomas Paine in England for publishing *Rights of Man*, in defence of the French Revolution).

These provisions essentially relate to political activities that are regarded as a threat to the established political system, public order or the existence of the nation-state itself. Some of the offences involve violence or plans for violence, but others not necessarily so (for example, treason and espionage). Ironically, in some instances, the proscribed activities could be regarded as laudable if conducted in support of the nation-state, rather than against it. Advocating support for an existing constitution, rather than urging its abolition, would not be seditious. Rather, it would be treated as praiseworthy. Sabotage or espionage conducted in the interests of one's country would be officially rewarded, not punished. It is the political or ideological content of the conduct that is generally of concern, not the nature of the activities per se.

Totalitarian governments are notorious for punishing their political opponents for 'crimes against the state', but history shows that governments regarded as democratic have also strenuously prosecuted these offences. These offences have become more prominent and frequently used under conditions of escalating economic and military tensions between rival nation-states, financial turmoil and growing social and political tensions domestically.

Although the most serious offences generally have been rarely used since World War II and the post-war 'Cold War' in the developed Western countries, prosecutions for insurrection and sedition have been launched in the twenty-first century by governments against their political opponents in numbers of countries, including Thailand and Malaysia. While in recent decades these kinds of cases have occurred primarily in less wealthy countries, there is reason to believe that similar trends could appear in the developed states as well in the coming period, particularly under conditions of economic breakdown and popular discontent.

As an example of how apparently moribund laws can be brought forward, and put to fresh use, in late 2010, US Attorney General Eric Holder confirmed there was 'a very serious, active ongoing investigation that is criminal in nature' in relation to WikiLeaks' disclosure of classified State Department cables. Holder said the Justice Department was looking to prosecute WikiLeaks founder Julian Assange under the Espionage Act. Section (c) of the Espionage Act (18 USC § 793) makes it a felony when a person 'receives or obtains or agrees or attempts to receive or obtain from any person, or from any source whatever, any document' ... 'respecting the national defense with intent or reason to believe that the information is to be used to the injury of the United States, or to the advantage of any foreign nation'. Those found guilty of 'conspiring' to engage in any action found to violate the Act can also be convicted. It appeared that the government was planning to show that Assange induced someone in the government to provide him with secret information, making both Assange and his alleged partner guilty of a conspiracy of espionage.

According to a report by the Congressional Research Service (CRS), the nonpartisan research arm of the US Congress, it would be almost unprecedented to prosecute Assange for making classified information public. US criminal statutes covering such information, the report noted, 'have been used almost exclusively to prosecute individuals with access to classified information (and a corresponding obligation to protect it) who make it available to foreign agents, or to foreign agents who obtain classified information unlawfully while present in the United States'. No one other than government employees had been successfully prosecuted under the Espionage Act for receiving and passing on secret documents (Congressional Research Service 2010: ii).

Since the turn of the century, a number of governments, including those of the US, Britain and Australia, have increased their powers to deal with subversion, espionage and alleged threats of insurrection, as well as terrorism. Some of these measures have been controversially extended since 2001 under the banner of the 'war on terrorism'.

One of this book's main theses is that offences against the state have been used for all manner of political purposes in the past, and can be readily so used in the future. At the same time, these laws and their application reveal the ultimate character of the state itself, as a defender of the established order, behind the façades of freedom and democracy. Both the use and abuse of these laws is examined. By that is meant the following:

(1) Historically, these provisions have been exploited for purposes beyond, or even in defiance of, their stated functions. Measures purportedly directed against existential threats to society or the established order have been utilised to pursue a variety of agendas, notably to suppress dissent, intimidate political opponents, poison public opinion, prevent official embarrassment

and divert attention from government or systemic failures. Prosecutions for these offences, even if ultimately unsuccessful, have had wider impacts in chilling dissent. For example, they have given rise to intensive police raids, multiple arrests and property seizures that can seriously disrupt political organisations, damage reputations and shred basic democratic rights, such as freedom of expression.

(2) Even where these laws have been 'properly' used, that is, to arrest, prosecute and punish acts genuinely directed at de-stabilising, undermining or overturning the socio-political system, or at causing fundamental damage to society or members of the public, these offences are inherently anti-democratic and designed to uphold the interests of the economically and politically powerful.

These issues must be assessed in a definite contemporary context. It is widely acknowledged that the world economy has plunged into its deepest and most systemic breakdown since the Great Depression of the 1930s. As in the 1930s, this economic turmoil can be expected to generate not only serious social and class tensions, but also political discontent and challenges to the established order.

Under these conditions, there were also indications of a shift, with the advent of the Obama Administration in the United States in 2009, to broaden the concept of 'security'. Instead of terrorism, economic and political instability was becoming the primary focus of concern. In 2009, America's director of national intelligence, retired admiral Dennis Blair, told Congress that the financial crisis, rather than terrorism, was the foremost security threat to the US (Sevastopulo 2009). Commenting on this testimony in a 2009 address to a national security conference, Australian Federal Police Commissioner Mick Keelty noted:

> This is a major shift in thinking, especially after ten years in which it could be argued that the term 'National Security' was more often than not used as a synonym for 'counter-terrorism'…This approach means that 'national security' now encompasses a broad range of principles – which include economic stability and a peaceful international environment. (Keelty 2009)

If maintaining 'economic stability' and 'a peaceful international environment' are now regarded as essential to national security, and perhaps to the existence of the state itself, we could see considerably more use of 'crimes against the state' than we have since World War II.

This book seeks to fill a noticeable gap: no books cover this field in English-derived law and it is badly neglected in standard criminal law texts. Various books deal with more minor 'public order' offences or with terrorism, but none examine the range of crimes against the state. In the present climate of economic turmoil and political instability, it is important to subject this field to long overdue examination, and encourage informed debate.

Conceptualising Crimes Against the State

The most essential laws of any state are those relating to self-preservation, or to the upholding of the power and stability of the state itself. Beneath whatever appearance is given of liberty and democracy, there always exist those crimes – indeed often the 'highest' or most heavily punishable crimes – that are directed against any conduct deemed to threaten the state itself.

After tracing the history of the rise of the modern state, Frederick Engels concluded that, as a rule, it represented the interests of the most powerful, economically dominant class that 'through the medium of the state, becomes also the politically dominant class, and thus acquires new means of holding down and exploiting the oppressed class' (Engels 1977: 168). He described the emergence, at the heart of the state, of bodies of 'armed men' alongside 'material adjuncts, prisons and institutions of coercion of all kinds, of which gentile [clan] society knew nothing'. He noted that this apparatus of force grew stronger as class antagonisms within the state became more acute and as tensions grew between rival international powers (Engels 1977: 167).

In his work, *The Origin of the Family, Private Property, and the State,* Engels traced the disintegration of primitive communities and the emergence of class societies based on the accumulation of surpluses and, eventually, private property. He probed the essential origins of the state in rising labour productivity, the exploitation of the labour power of others and the consequent rise of class antagonisms. These fundamentally irreconcilable antagonisms led to the establishment of a state apparatus whose function was to simultaneously suppress the class conflict, in the interests of the ruling class, and to seemingly stand above the conflict, so as to legitimise the prevailing socio-economic order. This 'special, public power' no longer consisted of the population organising itself as an armed force, because 'a self-acting armed organisation of the population has become impossible since the split into classes'. Engels concluded:

> The state is, therefore, by no means a power forced on society from without; just as little is it 'the reality of the ethical idea', 'the image and reality of reason', as Hegel maintains. Rather, it is a product of society at a certain stage of development; it is the admission that this society has become entangled in an insoluble contradiction with itself, that it has split into irreconcilable antagonisms which it is powerless to dispel. But in order that these antagonisms, these classes with conflicting economic interests, might not consume themselves and society in fruitless struggle, it became necessary to have a power, seemingly standing above society, that would alleviate the conflict and keep it within the bounds of 'order'; and this power, arisen out of society but placing itself above it, and alienating itself more and more from it, is the state. (Engels 1977: 177–8)

Thus, according to Engels, the state apparatus is an organ of class rule, an organ for the oppression of one class by another; it is the creation of 'order' that legalises and perpetuates this oppression by moderating the conflict between classes, while depriving the oppressed classes of definite means and methods of struggle to overthrow the oppressors.

Drawing on the work of Engels, Vladimir Lenin observed that behind the democratic façade of modern capitalist states, with their formal undertakings to uphold freedom of assembly, freedom of the press and 'equality of all citizens before the law', there existed provisions allowing for all these guarantees to be swept aside to suppress threats from below during periods of crisis:

> There is not a single state, however democratic, which has no loopholes or reservations in its constitution guaranteeing the bourgeois the possibility of dispatching troops against the workers, of proclaiming martial law, and so forth, in case of a 'violation of public order,' and actually in case the exploited class 'violates' its position of slavery and tries to behave in a non-slavish manner. (Tucker 1975: 468)

Lenin's colleague Leon Trotsky observed that in times of economic advancement, the capitalist class preferred, and could afford, to govern democratically, displaying tolerance toward political and industrial opposition in order to better stabilise and legitimise its rule. But in periods of economic stagnation or decline, such as the 1930s, the political safety valves of democracy gave way. In 1929, examining the breakdown of democratic institutions that was starting to unfold in Europe, giving way to fascism or dictatorship in major countries such as Italy, Germany and Spain, Trotsky explained that the move toward totalitarianism flowed from the fact that parliamentary democratic institutions could not stand the pressure of the class tensions internally, and the international political conflicts.

> By analogy with electrical engineering, democracy might be defined as a system of safety switches and circuit breakers for protection against currents overloaded by the national or social struggle. No period of human history has been – even remotely – so overcharged with antagonisms such as ours. The overloading of lines occurs more and more frequently at different points in the European power grid. Under the impact of class and international contradictions that are too highly charged, the safety switches of democracy either burn out or explode. That is what the short circuit of dictatorship represents. (Trotsky 1997: 53–4)

In 1936, Trotsky again drew attention to the use of 'detachments of armed men in defence of property':

> The bourgeoisie was able to tolerate the freedom of strikes, of assembly and of the press only so long as the productive forces were mounting upwards, so long as the sales markets were being extended, the welfare of the popular masses, even if only partially, was rising and the capitalist nations were able to live and let live. It is otherwise now. (Trotsky 1975: 15, 17)

Perhaps the best-known early Soviet jurist, Evgeny Pashukanis, contended that the capitalist state was bound up with the principle of commodity exchange, and hence the protection of dominant private interests (Head 2007b). These interests required, as far as possible, limits on the power of the state, and an avoidance of dictatorial methods that could threaten personal and property rights. Thus, the character of the state as a seemingly independent apparatus standing above society was not a purely ideological construct for duping ordinary people; the appearance was rooted in the reality of maintaining an *impersonal* guarantor of *personal* rights. To best achieve that end, the state could not be the plaything of this or that tycoon or even dictator. Pashukanis quoted Marx and Engels' famous characterisation of the bourgeois state as a 'committee for managing the common affairs of the whole bourgeoisie' (Pashukanis 1978: 149). However, in times of crisis, particularly when capitalist interests as a whole were threatened from below, the ideal of the constitutional state would be dispensed with:

> For the bourgeoisie has never, in favour of purity of theory, lost sight of the fact that class society is not only a market where autonomous owners of commodities meet, but is at the same time the battlefield of a bitter class war, where the machinery of state represents a very powerful weapon... The more the hegemony of the bourgeoisie was shattered, the more compromising these corrections became, the more quickly the 'constitutional state' was transformed into a disembodied shadow, until finally the extraordinary sharpening of the class struggle forced the bourgeoisie to discard the mask of the constitutional state altogether, revealing the nature of state power as the organised power of one class over the other. (Pashukanis 1978: 149–50)

Other scholars have pointed to the importance of the ideology of justice in camouflaging the essential character of the legal system. One example is Douglas Hay, in his study of eighteenth century English criminal justice, and the operation of the 'Bloody Code' under which an increasing number of offences were made felonies punishable by death. In his view, the ruling class manipulated the ideology of law, to use it as 'an instrument of authority and a breeder of values' in order to maintain the legitimacy of the existing social order. Since fear alone could not establish deference to the law, the structures of the law itself had to be used ideologically, to establish deference without force, to legitimate the class structure, and to maintain the domination of the holders of property. Elements of majesty, justice and mercy, embodied in the practices of the criminal law, served these ends (Hay 1975: 17).

Many scholars, and not only those influenced by Marxism, have observed that law is ultimately a reflection of the interests of the most powerful in society. In his work on political crime, Jeffrey Ian Ross observed: 'The ability to treat the other's actions as crime (whether street crime or political crime) begins with power. The ability to evade having the criminal label applied to oneself likewise depends on power' (Ross 2003: x). Ross referred to the example of terrorism, which has been defined differently over time to cover certain organisations and countries, but not others.

Ross elaborated the concept of 'oppositional political crimes' as a subset of 'crimes against the administration of government'. The broader category included treason, misprision of treason, rebellion, espionage, sedition, suborning of perjury, false swearing, bribery, contempt, obstruction of justice, resisting arrest, escape and misconduct in office. Ross nominated treason, misprision of treason, criminal syndicalism, rebellion, espionage, sedition and bribery as traditionally considered to be political crimes (Ross 2003: 32).

Definitions of political crime have varied over time. The competing definitions highlight the difficulties involved in distinguishing crimes against the state from other forms of crime, some of which may also be politically-motivated.

Sagarin said a political crime is 'any violation of law which is motivated by political aims – by the intent, that is, of bringing about (or preventing) a change in the political system, in the distribution of political power or in the structure of the political-governmental bodies' (Sagarin 1973: viii). This definition is too broad for the current purpose; it could go beyond perceived existential threats to the state to cover acts of political dissent or civil disobedience that seek only to pressure or demand change from the occupants of political office.

Turk more narrowly defined political crime as 'whatever is recognised or anticipated by authorities to be resistance threatening the established structure of differential resources and opportunities' (Turk 1984: 120). This definition still includes offences, such as tax evasion, draft dodging and civil disobedience, that may have political overtones without being necessarily regarded as directed against the state itself.

Packer subdivided oppositional political crimes into 'conduct inimical to the very existence of government, and offenses which affect the orderly and just administration of public business' (Packer 1962: 77). Treason, sedition, advocacy of overthrow and espionage were examples of the former; while perjury, bribery, corruption and criminal libel belonged in the latter. This distinction comes closer to the concept of crimes against the state.

Most nation-states in the Anglo-American tradition have corresponding criminal law classifications.

In Canada, a 1986 Law Reform Commission report examined 'Crimes Against the State'. The principal categories were treason, intimidating Parliament, sedition and sabotage (then found in Part II of the Criminal Code), and espionage and leakage, which were then dealt with by the Official Secrets Act (Canada 1986). The report explained, in traditional terms, the particular importance attached to these offences:

> Though rarely committed and even more rarely charged, crimes against the State are some of the most serious offences in the whole Criminal Code. This is because such conduct jeopardizes the security and well-being of the whole nation and its inhabitants. (Canada 1986: 1)

The Law Reform Commission of Canada distinguished those offences from 'offences against society', such as riot and unlawful assembly, which 'generally threaten law and order' (Canada 1986: 1). That distinction, however, is not borne out by history. As will be seen, the development and use of the offences of riot, affray and unlawful assembly has been intimately bound up with, and frequently overlapping, the 'state' crimes. These serious 'law and order' offences are best understood as ancillary weapons in the hands of the authorities to deal with conduct deemed threatening to the existence of the state itself.

Recent times have seen additions to the range of offences that might be considered crimes against the state. Most notable are the anti-terrorism laws, considered in Chapter 7. Other provisions include US laws (18 USC 2332a) that impose penalties of up to life imprisonment for the use, threat or attempt or conspiracy to use a weapon of mass destruction. These measures have been applied to individuals who threatened anthrax attacks (see, for example, *United States v. Davila* 461 F.3d 298). However, these and other similar offences, such as damaging, derailing, setting fire to or disabling a mass transportation vehicle, require a detailed examination that is beyond the ambit of this book.

Confusion, Complexity and Arbitrariness

Although this book necessarily examines the main offences separately in turn, they must be viewed in their totality. They form a continuum of often overlapping categories, with the boundaries frequently blurred. The Canadian Law Reform Commission demonstrated that that country's provisions were marked by overlapping, inconsistency, excessive complexity and detail, and uncertainty as to scope and meaning, as well as out-of-date features, over-criminalisation and possible violations of the *Canadian Charter of Rights and Freedoms* (Canada 1986: 25). The Australian Law Reform Commission's 2006 report on sedition found significant overlaps between the offences of sedition, treason and treachery.

Considerable official and prosecutorial discretion exists in selecting which offence or offences to pursue. These decisions can be as much influenced by political calculations as legal distinctions. The historical record points to certain offences being elevated to prominence under various circumstances, usually related to the level and nature of popular discontent. Another observed phenomenon is the replacement over a period of time of prosecutions for one offence by arrests for another once legal or political impediments emerged to the initial prosecutions. Different centuries, and even decades, produced different responses by prosecuting authorities.

Furthermore, both the scope of all the offences and the arbitrariness of choosing which to prosecute are magnified by the extending mechanisms of incitement, conspiracy, attempt and complicity. Other measures, such as those outlawing 'providing material support', concealment or harbouring suspects, widen the field.

Historically, conspiracy laws, in the form of both legislative and common law provisions, have played a particularly significant role. As will be explored in more detail in some of the cases examined in the following chapters, these provisions can permit prosecutions on the basis of little or no evidence of a specific criminal plan or plot. Instead, alleged vague agreements or understandings, or mere expressions of political or religious opinion, can suffice to convict. It may not even be necessary to prove that any proposed action by the alleged conspirators would have amounted to a specified offence; merely that something unlawful or potentially harmful was intended.

Justifications

'The Constitution is not a suicide pact' is a rhetorical phrase in American political and legal discourse. The phrase expresses the belief that constitutional restrictions on governmental power must give way to urgent practical needs. It is most often attributed to Abraham Lincoln, as a response to charges that he was violating the United States Constitution by suspending habeas corpus during the American Civil War. As will be discussed in Chapter 2, this attribution distorts Lincoln's stance. Despite the existence of battlefield conditions amid a civil war, rather than suspending the constitution, Lincoln temporarily suspended habeas corpus, insisting that this was consistent with the constitution, which provided for such a measure in cases of 'rebellion'. Although the phrase 'suicide pact' echoes statements made by Lincoln, and although the sentiment has been enunciated on several other occasions in American history, the precise phrase 'suicide pact' was first used by Justice Robert H. Jackson in his dissenting opinion in *Terminiello v. Chicago* (337 US 1), a 1949 free speech case decided by the US Supreme Court. The phrase also appears in the same context in *Kennedy v. Mendoza-Martinez* (372 US 144), a 1963 US Supreme Court decision written by Justice Arthur Goldberg.

In 2006, Judge Richard Posner of the United States Court of Appeals for the Seventh Circuit and professor at the University of Chicago Law School, published *Not a Suicide Pact: The Constitution in a Time of National Emergency* (Posner 2006). Posner argues that because of terrorism and the threat of weapons of mass destruction, the scope of constitutional rights must be adjusted. Using a so-called cost-benefit analysis to balance the harm that new security measures would inflict on personal liberty against the increased security those measures would provide, Posner came down, almost in every respect, on the side of increased government power. To this end, Posner argued that the United States should reinterpret the principle of habeas corpus to allow for the indefinite detention of suspected terrorists (Posner 2006: 56); reinterpret the Fourth Amendment to the US Constitution to deny its applicability to suspected terrorists (Posner 2006: 88–91); allow torture for purposes of intelligence-related information gathering (Posner 2006: 86–7); allow unlimited electronic surveillance (and perhaps physical searches) without warrants or probable cause (Posner 2006: 99–101); and reinterpret the First Amendment to allow for the censorship of 'hate speech' by and against Muslims (Posner 2006: 124).

The extraordinary scope of these proposals illustrates that the underlying logic of defending the status quo knows few, if any, bounds. The utilisation of alleged terrorist threats to overturn traditional civil liberties raises disturbing historical experiences. It should never be forgotten that Adolf Hitler cited the 1933 Reichstag Fire, which the Nazis falsely attributed to communists, as the reason for insisting that the parliament agree to rule by decree (Kershaw 1998: 456–60). The morning after the fire, Hitler's cabinet adopted the emergency decree, 'For the Protection of the People and State'. In the words of historian Ian Kershaw:

> With one brief paragraph, the personal liberties enshrined in the Weimar Constitution – including freedom of speech, of association and of the press, and privacy of postal and telephone communications – were suspended indefinitely...
> The hastily constructed emergency decree amounted to the charter of the Third Reich. (Kershaw 1998: 459)

A month later, on 23 March 1933, the Nazi-controlled Reichstag passed 'enabling' legislation declaring that the executive had the power to make laws. 'The Act to Relieve the Distress of the People and the Reich' cemented dictatorial power in Germany under Hitler. It essentially transformed into legislation legal opinions previously prepared by the leading Nazi jurist Carl Schmitt. These opinions authorised executive rule because of the 'state of exception' in Germany, namely its economic and political crisis and the alleged threat of revolution. Schmitt published a 'legal defence' of the enabling legislation, in which he opined that the executive prerogative was unlimited at a time of national crisis (Neumann 1942).

Some liberal critics of the arbitrary use of political offences have justified the ultimate power of the established order to defend itself, even at the expense of basic civil liberties such as freedom of expression and organisation. During 2009, for example, three Australian academics published a law review article advocating that the state should have the power to ban organisations deemed to be terrorist. Moreover, in the face of criticism of that power, they recommended that it be exercised by the executive, not the parliament or the courts. The authors contended that the federal Attorney-General, as the representative of the executive, should retain the power of proscription, first introduced by the post-2001 counter-terrorism legislation (Lynch, McGarrity and Williams 2009).

The authors argued that the state must have the right, for symbolic purposes, to impose criminal sanctions in a manner designed to 'send a message', even if there were no evidence that the measures have any practical effect:

> We believe that the State should be able to identify and condemn particular organisations on the basis of their activities while, at the same time, sending a message through the use of criminal sanctions to its citizens to avoid implicating themselves with these groups. The symbolic value of doing so may outweigh the practical, in light of what both research and experience appears to confirm

about how modern terrorism is practiced, but this does not render the exercise
meaningless. (Lynch, McGarrity and Williams 2009: 39)

The authors insisted that the fundamentally political function of this power
did not render it illegitimate, regardless of whether the power was exercised
undemocratically. 'Inescapably,' they wrote, 'the power of the State to brand
some movements as "terrorist" while leaving others free of that taint is a political
judgment' and it remained valid even if made 'with scant regard for democratic
considerations'(Lynch, McGarrity and Williams 2009: 40).

   Ironically, the authors argued that the very *political* character of the proscription
power, and the calculations involved in exercising it, made it appropriate for the
executive to hold that power. They conceded the notoriously arbitrary content of
affixing the label 'terrorist' to groups:

> It is hard to think of two more politically charged decisions than to designate
> a group as one within the definition of a 'terrorist organisation', and then to
> determine whether the group poses a sufficient threat to Australia and/or the
> international community to justify its proscription. The making of these two
> decisions occurs in a highly contested and subjective arena, due to a confluence
> of factors: the multi-faceted and intersecting definitions of 'terrorist act' and
> 'terrorist organisation'; the absence of detailed criteria for the decision-maker
> to apply and the inability to precisely calculate the source, scope and nature
> of the terrorist threat posed by a particular organisation to Australia. (Lynch,
> McGarrity and Williams 2009)

Remarkably, this proposition also rests upon the vagueness of the counter-terrorism
legislation; specifically the far-reaching definitions of 'terrorist act' and 'terrorist
organisation'. As will be discussed in Chapter 7, the very breadth and arbitrariness
of these definitions are causes for immense concern. Under the Australian definition,
given by section 100.1 of the Criminal Code Act 1995 (Cth), terrorism extends
to acts or threats that advance 'a political, religious or ideological cause' for the
purpose of 'coercing or influencing by intimidation' any government or section of
the public. 'Advocacy, protest, dissent or industrial action' is exempted but not if
it involves an intention to cause harm to a person, 'serious damage' to property,
'serious risk' to public health or safety, or 'serious interference' with an information,
telecommunications, financial, essential services or transport system.

   Given that the purpose of many protests and strikes is to apply pressure
to a government, employer or other authority, this definition could cover any
demonstration or strike action in which a person was injured or felt endangered.
Nurses taking strike action that shuts down hospital wards in support of a political
demand for greater health spending, for example, could be accused of endangering
public health and thus be charged as terrorists. Terrorist offences could apply to
a wide range of political activity, such as planning a protest outside government
buildings or facilities where damage may occur. Demonstrators who prepared to

block roads or entrances to financial institutions, such as the stock exchange, could be charged as terrorists, as could computer hackers.

Under section 102.1 of the Criminal Code, 'terrorist organisation' means: 'an organisation that is directly or indirectly engaged in, preparing, planning, assisting in or fostering the doing of a terrorist act (whether or not a terrorist act occurs)' or an organisation listed in regulations. To list an organisation, the Attorney-General 'must be satisfied on reasonable grounds' that the organisation meets the above definition or 'advocates the doing of a terrorist act (whether or not a terrorist act has occurred or will occur)'. 'Advocates' is defined to include 'counsels', 'urges' and 'praises'. Proscription orders may have far-reaching implications. Any person who directs or provides support to the activities of a terrorist organisation, knowing it to be terrorist, can be jailed for 25 years or, if they are 'reckless' as to whether the organisation is terrorist or not, for 15 years. A member of a group banned under a regulation faces up to 10 years imprisonment. Membership is defined to include 'informal membership' or taking 'steps to become a member'. It is a defence to have taken 'reasonable steps' to cease membership 'as soon as practicable' after knowing the organisation was terrorist, but the burden of proof lies on the defendant.

Thus, any organisation that 'advocates', 'praises' or 'counsels' a terrorist act can be outlawed, automatically exposing its members, supporters and financial donors to imprisonment as well. 'Praising' terrorism could mean merely justifying or expressing sympathy for a hypothetical terrorist act, or even calling for an understanding of terrorism's social and economic roots. Members, even if 'informal', of an organisation could be prosecuted if someone in their organisation praised terrorism, even if the organisation has no other involvement in terrorism; even if the praise did not result in a terrorist act; and even if the person praising terrorism did not intend to cause terrorism. This is a sweeping extension of criminal liability, since it can collectively punish members of groups for the actions of their associates beyond their control.

Nevertheless, the three authors contended that this potentially vast proscribing and criminalising power should exist, and remain vested in the hands of the executive, effectively beyond the scrutiny of the courts. 'The executive has greater experience than the judiciary in making policy-based decisions involving such a clear mix of political considerations', they argued. Their article added another argument: that of secrecy. 'While scrutiny of decisions affecting national security is always inhibited by the need to protect information, it may be that continuing accountability and more effective oversight of decisions to proscribe organisations will be facilitated if the power is retained by the Attorney-General rather than ceded to the courts'(Lynch, McGarrity and Williams 2009: 23).

The authors claimed high-level judicial support for their approach, citing the English House of Lords in *A v. Secretary of State for the Home Department* (2004), where Lord Nicholls of Birkenhead stated:

> All courts are very much aware of the heavy burden, resting on the elected government and not the judiciary, to protect the security of this country and all who live here. All courts are acutely conscious that the government alone is able

to evaluate and decide what counter-terrorism steps are needed and what steps will suffice. Courts are not equipped to make such decisions, nor are they charged with that responsibility. ([2004] UKHL 56, [79])

While purporting to offer support for the proposition that executive government should be left to determine what is necessary for the 'security' of the state, this heavy judicial deference to the executive raises increased concern about the effectively unfettered power held by the executive, largely free of legal or judicial scrutiny. The ruling in *A v. Secretary of State for the Home Department* demonstrates that the courts have given executive governments considerable scope to make decisions that they regard as essential to the 'security' or survival of the national state.

The House of Lords, with Lord Hoffman dissenting, accepted that indefinite detention without trial of foreign national terrorist suspects, unable to be prosecuted or deported, could be permissible under the 'public emergency' clause of the European Convention on Human Rights and Fundamental Freedoms, as incorporated by the UK Human Rights Act 1998. However, the majority ultimately declared the provisions to be discriminatory and disproportionate to the exigencies of the public emergency. In his controversial dissent on the threshold issue of whether the threat of terrorism constituted a 'public emergency threatening the life of the nation', Lord Hoffman stated:

> The real threat to the life of the nation, in the sense of a people living in accordance with its traditional laws and political values, comes not from terrorism but from laws such as these. ([2004] UKHL 56, [94–7])

Nonetheless, the eight-to-one majority view was that the courts had to defer heavily to the views of the executive government. In the words of Baroness Hale:

> Assessing the strength of a general threat to the life of the nation is, or should be, within the expertise of the Government and its advisers ... If a Government were to declare a public emergency where patently there was no such thing, it would be the duty of the court to say so. But here we are considering the immediate aftermath of the unforgettable events of 11 September 2001. The attacks launched on the United States on that date were clearly intended to threaten the life of the nation. ([2004] UKHL 56, [226])

International Law and Human Rights

The ruling in *A v. Secretary of State for the Home Department* also highlights the extent to which international law reserves to the national state the power to override even the most basic legal and democratic rights in alleged emergencies or dire challenges to the stability of the state. In the Universal Declaration of Human Rights, the International Covenant on Civil and Political Rights (ICCPR), and other related instruments, such as the European Convention on Human Rights and Fundamental Freedoms and the UK Human Rights Act, the listed civil and legal rights are mostly subject to far-reaching exemptions, including 'national security' and 'public safety'– leaving considerable leeway for draconian measures, such as the forms of detention without trial and other provisions imposed in the name of fighting the 'war on terrorism'. Thus, Article 4 of the ICCPR states:

(1) In time of public emergency which threatens the life of the nation and the existence of which is officially proclaimed, the States Parties to the present Covenant may take measures derogating from their obligations under the present Covenant to the extent strictly required by the exigencies of the situation, provided that such measures are not inconsistent with their other obligations under international law and do not involve discrimination solely on the ground of race, colour, sex, language, religion or social origin.

(2) No derogation from articles 6, 7, 8 (paragraphs I and 2), 11, 15, 16 and 18 may be made under this provision.

These exceptions to derogation relate to killing, torture, slavery, trial by law and freedom of religion. Under the European Convention on Human Rights and Fundamental Freedoms even the right to life is carefully circumscribed to permit killing by state forces in order to make arrests, prevent escapes from detention and quell riots and insurrections (Article 2). Governments can derogate from most obligations under the European Convention 'in time of war or other public emergency threatening the life of the nation' (Article 15). Particularly since the declaration of the 'war on terrorism' in 2001, courts have tended to give executive governments much leeway to use these provisions.

Thus, international human rights law provides little reliable protection against the application of offences against the state, regardless of any violation of basic democratic rights. In any case, because the nation-state system still prevails globally, international law is not legally binding domestically unless it is incorporated into national legislation. Moreover, with some exceptions, such as the US Constitution's Bill of Rights and the Canadian Charter of Rights and Freedoms, domestic human rights measures are not constitutionally entrenched, and can therefore be abridged, amended or repealed by legislatures.

Some provisions simply require courts to interpret all legislation, where possible, consistently with enumerated human rights, generally drawn from the International Covenant on Civil and Political Rights. If the legislation under consideration cannot be interpreted consistently with a human right, the court may only declare that an incompatibility exists, and report the issue to the legislature. Such a declaration does not affect the validity of the legislation in question.

Furthermore, under provisions like the UK Human Rights Act, the courts are instructed to permit reasonable limits to human rights if the limit is 'demonstrably justified in a free and democratic society'. This proviso, which English House of Lords judges have described as one of proportionality, leaves scope for governments to brush aside or whittle down democratic rights of minorities in the name of upholding the democratic rights of the majority.

Executive and Emergency Powers

This volume does not attempt to deal in detail with emergency powers – the range of executive and prerogative powers, emergency legislation, martial law provisos and modifications to criminal law processes that the countries under examination have in place, or have adopted in periods of war or alleged emergency. These provisions are strictly speaking outside the scope of crimes against the state, in the sense that they are extraordinary measures of a semi-legal or extra-legal character, typically suspending or overriding the traditional criminal law, as well as basic or constitutional protections of legal and democratic rights. Precisely because of the far-reaching nature of these powers, however, it would be artificial and misleading to discuss the law without at least reviewing them in outline form. That is done in Chapter 9.

One theme that runs through the troubled history of crimes against the state is the readiness of governments and other authorities to exploit vague and elastic phrases such as 'emergency', 'essential' and 'security' to intervene militarily, or to act without clear legal authorisation and, if necessary, obtain retrospective indemnity. No less than seven Indemnity Acts were passed in Ireland between 1796 and 1800 to protect the British authorities against legal liability for their unlawful acts (Lee 1984: 222). Whelan traced this trend and gave some examples, one of which was the British government's media announcement during the 1926 General Strike:

> All ranks of the Armed Forces of the Crown are hereby notified that any action which they may find is necessary to take in an honest endeavour to aid the Civil Power will receive, both now and afterwards, the full support of His Majesty's Government. (Whelan 1985: 289–90)

Another instance was English Attorney General Sir Hartley Shawcross's advice during the 1949 docks strike about the doubtful legal enforceability of the emergency regulations:

> I do not think that matters ... I have advised that this risk should be taken and that the Regulations should cover matters on which action is required without due regard to the niceties of the law. In an emergency the Government may have, in matters admitting of legal doubt, to act first and argue about the doubts later, if necessary obtaining an indemnification Act. (Whelan 1985: 289–90)

Shawcross's phrase, 'without due regard for the niceties of the law', illustrates the propensity and capacity of governments to dispense with the finer points of the 'rule of law' when confronted by serious political, social or industrial challenges to the established order.

Similar issues arose in 1974, when the British military conducted exercises at London's Heathrow airport during a period when the Conservative government of Edward Heath was in danger of being forced from office by a wave of industrial action. Although the 1974 Heathrow operation was officially justified as a precaution against terrorism, the legal authority of the government to use the army was not clear (Lee 1984: 211). The editor of the *Criminal Law Review* proposed that resort be had to the royal prerogative to address the legal vacuum: 'If on a future occasion the legal powers of police and soldier prove inadequate, reliance may, in the last resort, have to be placed on the Royal Prerogative governing emergencies. That power, with its requirements of compensation, may be an acceptable means of filling in gaps in statutory and common law powers' (Lee 1984: 211–12).

The 'War on Terrorism'

In the opening years of the twenty-first century, numbers of governments have used the threat of terrorism as a pretext to erode such vital principles as free speech, freedom of political association, prevention of arbitrary detention, and the right to seek asylum. Governments in many countries followed the lead of the George W. Bush administration in the United States by declaring that the 11 September 2001 terrorist attacks in the US required an indefinite 'war' against terrorism abroad, accompanied by curtailment of legal rights at home. Despite criticisms by civil liberties groups, governments introduced severe anti-terrorism measures, including detention without trial and proscription of organisations (for a comparison of the US and British legislation see Hancock 2002: 2–8). Amnesty International condemned the Bush administration, for example, for breaching the International Covenant on Civil and Political Rights and other international protocols against arbitrary detention and inhuman treatment of prisoners (Amnesty International 2002).

The 'war on terror' has also provided the justification for greater powers to deploy the military domestically, overturning long-standing constitutional or legal taboos on the internal use of the armed forces (Head and Mann 2009). Some scholars have argued that concerns about these developments are exaggerated or even unwarranted because one must trust elected governments. For example, Norman Laing, an Australian barrister with military experience, has suggested that a domestic callout of the Australian Defence Force (ADF) would not be 'the end of civilisation' because 'the ADF will only ever be deployed for a legitimate purpose' and 'one must have faith in those elected representatives to undertake such a responsibility' (Laing 2005: 521). Ironically, Laing's article began by recalling the protests against the Vietnam War and President Richard Nixon's invasion of Cambodia, and the use of the Ohio National Guard to shoot down four innocent students at Kent State University in 1970 (Laing 2005: 507–8).

Is it safe to simply say 'one must have faith' in elected governments? The opening years of the twenty-first century have already seen troops dispatched to invade a country and put down domestic resistance – in Iraq – on the basis of information supplied by intelligence agencies, security services and government leaders that was subsequently acknowledged to have been false. After the collapse of the falsifications used to justify the United States-led invasion – 'weapons of mass destruction', 'nuclear stockpiles' and Saddam Hussein's supposed links to terrorism – one is entitled, perhaps even obliged, to approach the entire 'war on terror' with considerable scepticism.

Moreover, a 'war' of indefinite duration has been declared on vaguely defined 'enemies' whose only identifiable characteristic is that they pursue a set of tactics, tactics of acts of individual violence that can attract an array of disoriented and disaffected political, religious and ethnic currents. It is beyond the scope of this book to investigate the root causes of terrorism, but it must be said that the label is notoriously open to political dispute and abuse. After all, today's primary 'terrorist' targets – Al Qaeda-linked groups – were yesterday's 'freedom fighters' in the guerrilla war against the Soviet-backed regime in Afghanistan (Blum 2002: 155). Likewise, Saddam Hussein was once a close ally of Washington, particularly during the fratricidal Iran–Iraq war of the 1980s (Blum 2002: 133–4, 145–6).

The outrages in New York and Washington on 11 September 2001were reprehensible but there is ample evidence that they provided the pretext for the implementation of plans prepared in certain Washington political circles much earlier – during the 1990s – for the conquest of Afghanistan and Iraq (Bacevich 2002). The Middle East and Central Asia, as is well known, contain the largest proven concentrations of oil and natural gas reserves in the world. For all their claims to be exporting democracy to the Middle East, Washington and its allies have for decades financially, diplomatically and military supported dictatorial regimes like the Saudi monarchy and the Gulf kingdoms (and previously the Shah of Iran), in the interests of dominating the resource-rich and strategically critical region (Shalom 1993: 63–88). The latest US-led interventions in the region, followed by the establishment of US military bases throughout Central Asia, have added weight to the evidence that Washington's underlying ambition is to secure hegemony over this entire vital expanse.

Domestically, there is no more reason to believe that the same US-allied governments are primarily motivated simply by the need to protect ordinary people from terrorism. On the face of it, none of the new powers were necessary for that purpose. In most jurisdictions, any conceivable terrorist activity, such as murder, bombing, hijacking, kidnapping and arson, was already a serious crime under existing law. Moreover, the police and intelligence services hardly needed new powers to detect terrorists. They already had powers to tap phones, install listening devices in offices and homes, intercept telecommunications, open people's mail, monitor on-line discussion, break into computer files and databases, seize computers and use personal tracking devices (for details see Head 2004b).

The official rationale for the anti-terrorism measures asserts that the 'war on terrorism' requires a 'new framework' for considering civil liberties and the rule of law. For instance, in 2004, Australian Attorney General Philip Ruddock stated:

> The war on terror is like no other war in living memory. This is a war which may have no obvious conclusion, no armistice and no treaty. Victory in this war will not necessarily be measured by territory gained or regimes toppled. In this war victories will be measured by disasters averted and democracy strengthened. This war's victories will be measured by citizens feeling safe in their homes. This war's victories will be measured in the steadfastness and resolve of Australians to be cognisant of, but not to fear, a potential terrorist threat... Our Constitution, one of the world's oldest and most stable, provides us with a mechanism to protect our country and at the same time protect civil liberties through human security laws. In enacting such laws we are not only preserving traditional notions of civil liberties and the rule of law, but we are recognising that these operate in a different paradigm. If we are to preserve human rights then we must preserve the most fundamental right of all – the right to human security. (Ruddock 2004)

While insisting that the government was upholding the constitution, civil liberties and the rule of law, the minister asserted that these now operate in a new paradigm: the right to human security, which is said to be the most fundamental right of all. Ruddock loosely defined 'human security' as encompassing human rights, good governance, access to education and health care and opportunities for individuals to fulfill their potential. All these, the minister asserted, depended upon a secure environment. Thus, in the name of defending civil liberties and the rule of law, basic rights are said to no longer have any independent or absolute existence. Instead, they have been subsumed under another concept, human security. Making 'citizens feel safe in their homes' has become the chief criterion for the unknown duration of the current 'state of war'. This line of argument could justify far-reaching resort to prosecutions for crimes against the state, or to other extraordinary measures, including emergency and military operations.

Chapter 1
A Controversial History

> He that addresses himself to a crowded auditory of the poorer class, without
> employment or occupation, and brooding at the time over their wrongs; whether
> imaginary or real, will not want ready hearers ... (Chief Justice Tindal in *R v.*
> *Vincent* (1842) Car & M 661n)

Chief Justice Tindal's reference to the 'poorer class' provides a clue to the central
motivation behind a recurring historical pattern with crimes against the state.
He was defining seditious speech. Why should it matter whether the audience
of an allegedly seditious address is poor or wealthy? The Chief Justice referred
to crowds 'brooding at the time over their wrongs'. In essence, the concern is
that the unemployed and others of the working class – who in the 1840s were
demanding, and being denied, the basic right to vote – would be most receptive
to anti-establishment appeals. As will be seen, the fear of revolt from below, and
ultimately of social revolution, is what has animated the historical development of
the law in this sphere. In judicial judgements one finds contemptuous references
to the alleged gullibility or stupidity of poorer people. On other occasions, judges
have warned that members of the lower classes are particularly susceptible to
criticisms of governments and the existing order.

The history of crimes against the state is inglorious. In every epoch, the offences,
both common law and statutory, have become more draconian, far-reaching
and severely punished whenever the ruling establishment has felt threatened by
domestic opposition, particularly from the plebeian masses, or by foreign rivals,
especially once war loomed or armed hostilities broke out. Far from being fixed,
or clearly defined by legal criteria, offences evolved and sharp shifts occurred in
the frequency of prosecution of various offences, in response to perceived political
dangers.

Numbers of empirical studies have demonstrated such patterns. One study of
the English law from the late eighteenth century to the mid-nineteenth century, for
example, detected a marked turn from the use by the authorities of seditious libel
to prosecutions for unlawful assembly. The scholar traced this shift to a fear of the
rising level of mass political consciousness after the Peterloo Massacre of 1819
and in the development of the Chartist movement, which demanded the right to
vote. Michael Lobban concluded:

> Until the end of the eighteenth century, when riotous activity was relatively
> common, the ruling classes were not as frightened of crowds as they would later
> become—indeed, the idea of national police force scared them more. The fear of
> the crowd grew as the crowd was seen as a threat to the established order; and
> paradoxically, this occurred when the crowds were becoming less turbulent, but

more organized. The fact that they were *political* crowds made them a threat: the fact that they might pose a public order threat allowed the authorities to clamp down on them. (Lobban 1990: 352) (italics in original, footnotes removed)

A related trend has been for the authorities to utilise different offences after others have become unusable, commonly for political reasons. An earlier historical study, for example, found that the eighteenth century English reliance on the offence of seditious libel to control the printed press had arisen out of seventeenth century political and legal difficulties in using the laws of treason, heresy, licensing and *Scandalum Magnatum*. Philip Hamburger sums up the process as follows:

> In the mid-sixteenth century, the Crown possessed a wide variety of means for dealing with the printed press, including the laws of treason, *Scandalum Magnatum,* heresy, and licensing. Legal restraints and public opinion, however, gradually forced the Crown to abandon one method after another until in the late seventeenth century it had great difficulty finding a law with which it could defend itself against printed criticism. The sole remaining law that the Crown could rely upon for prosecuting the printed press was one that during the previous century had not been considered suitable for the purpose. It was, however, the Crown's only alternative, and, after doctrinal adjustments, it became the chief means of prosecuting the printed press in the eighteenth century. This was the law of seditious libel. (Hamburger 1985: 662–3)

The authorities and the courts have regarded perceived threats to the established order to be far more serious when they (1) involve the working class and (2) call into question the right or ability of the state to mobilise armed force, including the military, to put down civil unrest. As cited above at the beginning of the chapter, Chief Justice Tindal declared that if an audience came from the 'poorer class', that could make an otherwise lawful statement a seditious one. His ruling was delivered in the context of the mass trials conducted at the height of the Chartist movement, during which large crowds of people demanded the right to vote (Lobban 1990: 350–1). Similar judicial sentiments were commonly expressed during the trials that followed the 1819 Peterloo Massacre. Instructing the jury in the trial of Henry Hunt and other organisers of the St Peter's Fields meeting, Justice Bayley said the banners carried by participants, objecting to 'taxation without representation' and being 'sold like slaves' were evidence of a seditious conspiracy and unlawful assembly. 'Is the telling a large body of men they are sold like slaves likely to make them satisfied and contented with their situation in society?' he asked rhetorically (*R v. Hunt* (1820) 1 St Tr NS, at 479, cited in Lobban 1990: 344).

The aftermath of Peterloo also provided demonstrations of the critical importance attached by judges to punishing any challenge to the authority of the armed forces to intervene violently against popular disturbances. In one trial, Sir Francis Burdett was charged with seditious libel for urging his constituents to join protests against the massacre in St Peter's Field. Burdett had written to his electors that

> They must join the general voice, loudly demanding justice and redress, and head public meetings throughout the United Kingdom to put a stop in its commencement to a reign of terror and of blood. (Lobban 1990: 330)

Justice Best directed the jury that the letter was a libel, for while the government did not rest on the military, where there was an insurrection, soldiers were needed to aid the magistracy. 'Therefore, at a moment like this, to put them in mind of circumstances likely to paralyse them in the discharge of their duty, is the most dangerous libel that could be circulated' (*R v. Burdett* (1820) 1 St Tr NS 1, 55, cited in Lobban 1990: 330).

Scholarly analyses of the history of crimes against the state have generally not identified these recurring patterns, even though numbers of studies have empirically established connections between political imperatives and the evolution of the law in finite periods. An examination of the history, even if only in outline, demonstrates the need for a new systemic method of approach: one that critically examines the changing legal doctrines and their application in the context of socio-economic tensions and conflicts.

This approach is essential to gauge accurately the propensity of the ruling establishments to resort to legal repression in times of turmoil. It provides a reminder that laws such as sedition and treason that may have been little used, or even lain dormant, for decades, can be resuscitated in periods of acute economic, social and political stress. An examination of the historical record also provides an antidote to the views of those who suggest that the public can and should trust governments and security agencies to make decisions about what is necessary to combat 'terrorism' or 'political violence' or to otherwise protect 'national security'.

In the early twenty-first century, judicial deference to executive decision-making about national security became almost axiomatic. In *A v. Secretary of State for the Home Department* ([2005] 2 AC 68), Lord Nicholls of Birkenhead stated: 'All courts are acutely conscious that the government alone is able to evaluate and decide what counter-terrorism steps are needed and what steps will suffice' ([2005] 2 AC 68 at 128 [79]). Academics, even those with civil libertarian reputations, have similarly expressed faith in governments. As discussed in the Introduction, three Australian academics declared their support for executive power to proscribe organisations as terrorist, even though proscription immediately exposes alleged members (and 'informal members') to serious criminal prosecutions. They contended: 'The executive has greater experience than the judiciary in making policy-based decisions involving such a clear mix of political considerations' (Lynch, McGarrity and Williams 2009: 23).

History demonstrates, however, that the nature of this 'experience' is not one conducive to reliable judgements or to respect for basic legal and democratic rights. On the contrary, the 'clear mix of political considerations' has produced no shortage of legally dubious and politically-motivated decisions, including outright abuse of the extensive surveillance, investigatory, detention, prosecution and punitive powers available to the authorities.

This chapter briefly reviews the ancient sources of the law, and then the historical record in Britain and Australia. The following chapter considers the evolution of crimes against the state in the United States, from the American Declaration of Independence to the post-2001 'war on terrorism'.

Ancient Origins

Although the history of crimes against the state evidently can be traced back to the early Germanic law of treason, the origins of the modern law can be found in the forms imposed by Rome on the vanquished Germanic peoples (Canada 1986: 3). The more complex and absolutist Roman law, or *crimen laesae majestatis*, was adopted once the Roman Republic had degenerated into the autocratic Roman Empire. The concept of *crimen laesae majestatis* corresponded to the requirements of the imperial state, effectively established by the anointment of Augustus as the first emperor (initially known as Princeps or 'first citizen') in 27 BC (Gibbon 2003).

The Roman law of treason developed into an extensive doctrine, protecting both the person and authority of the Emperor. It included major offences such as taking up arms against the state, delivering provinces or towns from Roman rule, sedition or insurrection, plotting against the life of the Emperor or his principal officers, and lesser acts such as destroying the statutes of the Emperor or insulting the memory of a deceased Emperor (Canada 1986: 3).

After the fall of Rome, *crimen laesae majestatis* was lost to the West for hundreds of years. Treason re-emerged initially in feudal clothes, focused on feudal notions of obligation. Early Germanic treasons of assisting the enemies of one's tribe and betraying one's lord were revived and modified to cover serious breaches of the vassal's pledge of fealty. The terms 'treason' and 'sedition' were used interchangeably, and mere treasonable or seditious words were considered sufficient for punishment. In the feudal system, treason could be committed against one's lord, regardless of whether he was king, but feudal law also recognised an entitlement of vassals (and lords) to rebel if the lord (or king) persistently denied justice to them (Canada 1986: 4).

Roman legal doctrines were reincarnated in Western Europe after the eleventh century, as power was consolidated in the hands of absolute or near-absolute monarchs. These kings adapted the Roman concept of *crimen laesae majestatis* for their offences against the state, and in France the outcome was the broad crime of lèse-majesté, which was employed until the French Revolution of 1789 (Canada 1986: 4). This consolidation of socio-economic power found reflections in the writings of the Dominican, St Thomas Aquinas, who contended that subjects were obliged to obey even unjust laws if disobedience would create civil disorder (Wacks 2009: 19).

The English law evolved to protect the king only, not the lesser lords, and included not just acts against him but also endeavouring, plotting or compassing such acts (the general law categories of attempt and conspiracy had not yet developed; in fact they have their origins in the early law of treason, in compassing the king's death). To assassinate the monarch was considered so serious that even an intent or attempt to kill the king was itself treason (Canada 1986: 4).

While traces of Germanic, feudal and Roman law can be detected in the 1351 Statute of Treasons – the first English codification – it consolidated the transformation of the crime of treason into one against the person and authority of the sovereign, who embodied the state, and abolished the feudal right of the vassal to wage war on an unjust lord. The Statute contained three main offences: (1) compassing the death of the monarch; (2) levying war against the king in his realm; and (3) adhering to the king's enemies in his realm or elsewhere. The enactment also established various ancillary crimes, such as violating the king's companion, counterfeiting the king's seal and killing the chancellor or the king's justices (Canada 1986: 5).

Over the following centuries, at times of crisis, English monarchs added more detailed and oppressive laws to the Statute. Judicial interpretations also enlarged the legislation. Thus, 'compassing the king's death' was held to apply where the king was in no actual physical danger and included plotting to depose him, conspiring with a foreign prince to levy war on the realm and intending anything that might expose the king to personal danger or deprivation of any authority. 'Levying war' was interpreted to cover any amount of violence with a political object, from riot to revolution (Canada 1986: 6)

As the struggle between the emerging capitalist class and the monarchy began to develop in the lead up to the English Revolution of the seventeenth century, sedition arose as a crime distinct from treason. Although a 1275 statute had already codified the offence of defaming public figures through the dissemination of 'false news' (*scandalum magnatum*), the invention of the printing press drove the monarchy's interest in prohibiting the expression and dissemination of critical ideas (Canada 1986: 6, Hamburger 1985: 662–762, Lobban 1990: 307–14). On behalf of the monarchy, the Star Chamber fashioned the offence of seditious libel as a terrible weapon against the rising parliamentarians, with punishments that could, according to the 1606 case of *De Libellis Famosis* ((1606) 77 ER 250) include pillory and loss of ears. The notorious Star Chamber asserted its jurisdiction at the expense of the ordinary courts, which resisted the conviction of individuals for disrespectful utterances against the king (Head 1979: 93–5 and Chapter 4). Following the abolition of the Star Chamber by the Long Parliament in 1641, however, the ordinary courts developed the offence further.

A turning point came during the politically fragile years after the 1688 'Glorious Revolution'. Anxious to secure its position, the new regime under William III and Mary adopted a harsh policy toward political dissent, and the courts followed suit in 1704 by holding that it was a crime to defame the government, as well as to libel an individual figure associated with the establishment. In effect, in the case of *Tutchin* ((1704) 91 Eng Rep 1224; 14 St Tr (OS) 1096), the judges reversed a century of common law precedents that confined seditious libel to the defamation of some particular person (Hamburger 1985: 725–53). Defending the ruling, Lord Chief Justice Holt declared:

But this is a very strange doctrine, to say, it is not a libel, reflecting on the
Government ... If men should not be called to account for possessing the people
with an ill opinion of the Government, no Government can subsist; for it is very
necessary for every Government, that the people should have a good opinion of
it. And nothing can be worse to any Government, than to endeavour to procure
animosities as to the management of it. This has always been looked upon as
a crime, and no Government can be safe unless it be punished. (90 Eng Rep at
1133–4)

In both its political content ('it is very necessary for every Government, that
the people should have a good opinion of it') and its vague formulations
('procure animosities as to the management of it'), Holt's utterance epitomises
the quintessential role of sedition, and indeed, all crimes against the state. The
common law, as well as statutory variations, is designed to intimidate and punish
any conduct considered to be a threat to the tranquillity of the prevailing political
and economic order.

Britain: From the French Revolution to Peterloo

In response to the French Revolution of 1789 and rising demands for political
reform in Britain, the authorities responded with political repression, featuring the
sedition trials of 1792 and 1793 and the treason trials of 1794. Vigorous political
debate had been sparked by the publication in 1790 of Edmund Burke's *Reflections
on the Revolution in France*. Burke, who had supported the American Revolution of
1776, vehemently condemned the French Revolution and the British radicals who
had welcomed its early stages. While the radicals saw the revolution as analogous
to the 1688 Glorious Revolution, which had restricted the powers of the monarchy,
Burke argued that the appropriate historical analogy was the English Civil War of
1642–51, in which Charles I had been executed in 1649. He declared the French
Revolution to be the violent overthrow of a legitimate government. In *Reflections* he
argued that citizens did not have the right to revolt against their government, because
civilizations, including governments, are the result of social and political consensus.
If a culture's traditions were challenged, the result would be endless anarchy.

There was an immediate response from the British supporters of the French
revolution, most notably Thomas Paine in his *Rights of Man*. In this heated
pamphlet war, writers addressed topics ranging from representative government to
human rights and the separation of church and state (Butler 1984, Barrell and Mee
2006: xi-xii). Paine posited that popular political revolution was permissible when
a government did not 'safeguard its people, their natural rights, and their national
interests':

The fact, therefore, must be that the individuals, themselves, each, in his own
personal and sovereign right, entered into a compact with each other to produce

a government: and this is the only mode in which governments have a right to arise, and the only principle on which they have a right to exist.

Rights of Man concluded by proposing practical reformations of English government: a written Constitution composed by a national assembly, in the American mould; the elimination of aristocratic titles, because democracy is incompatible with primogeniture, which leads to the despotism of the family; a national budget without allotted military and war expenses; lower taxes for the poor, and subsidised education for them; and a progressive income tax weighted against wealthy estates to prevent the emergence of a hereditary aristocracy. Paine dedicated *Rights of Man* to General George Washington and to the Marquis de Lafayette, acknowledging the importance of the American and the French revolutions in his formulating the principles of modern democratic governance.

As a result of the publication of *Rights of Man,* radical associations began to proliferate. The government issued a royal proclamation against seditious writings in 1792, and there were over 100 prosecutions for sedition in the 1790s alone (Barrell and Mee 2006: xiii). Accompanied by an increasing number of political arrests, government also infiltrated the radical groups; threatened to 'revoke the licences of publicans who continued to host politicised debating societies and to carry reformist literature'; seized the mail of 'suspected dissidents'; and supported groups that disrupted radical events and attacked radicals in the press (Keen 1999: 54). Radicals decried 'the institution of a system of terror, almost as hideous in its features, almost as gigantic in its stature, and infinitely more pernicious in its tendency, than France ever knew' (Barrell and Mee 2006: xxi).

Paine's publisher, J.S. Jordan, was indicted for sedition for publishing *Rights of Man* in May 1792, although Paine himself was not charged until the royal proclamation was promulgated. Even then, Paine's trial was delayed until late in the year and he fled to France in the intervening months, apparently with the government's blessing, which was afraid that Paine might use his trial as a political platform (Barrell and Mee 2006: xviii). When the trial finally took place, its outcome was a foregone conclusion. The government had been lambasting Paine for months and the trial judge had negotiated the prosecution's arguments with them ahead of time.

The radical lawyer Thomas Erskine represented Paine, arguing that his pamphlet was part of an honourable English tradition of political philosophy that included the writings of John Milton, John Locke and David Hume. The Attorney General displayed the authorities' fear that subversive ideas might reach the disenfranchised working layers of society, arguing that the pamphlet was clearly aimed at readers 'whose minds cannot be supposed to be conversant with subjects of this sort' and cited its cheap price as evidence of its lack of serious intent (Barrell and Mee 2006: xix). The prosecution did not even have to rebut Erskine's arguments; the jury informed the judge they had already decided Paine was guilty (Barrell and Mee 2006: xix).

Rights of Man represented an entirely new form of political writing for a mass audience. It was in a highly colloquial style, and directed at men of Paine's own background – ordinary artisans and labouring people. For that reason, it became an international bestseller. By the time he was declared guilty, Paine was in France. Nevertheless, crowds of supporters greeted Paine's lawyer as he emerged from the court after the verdict and pulled his carriage through the streets of London. Across the Channel, Paine himself was feted as a hero, granted citizenship and made a representative to the National Convention. He remained in France until 1802, returning to the United States at President Thomas Jefferson's invitation.

The rise of the Chartist movement triggered one of the most notorious invocations of crimes against the state: the Peterloo Massacre of 1819. Cavalry troops charged into a crowd of 60,000 to 80,000 people gathered at St Peter's Field, Manchester, for a public meeting, which had been declared illegal, to demand parliamentary representation. Shortly after the meeting began, local magistrates called on the military to arrest the speakers on the platform and to disperse the crowd. Soldiers on horses charged in with sabres drawn, killing 15 people and injuring 400–700, including women and children (Reid 1989). Whereas the arrested speakers were charged with sedition, found guilty and jailed, a test case against four members of the armed forces ended in acquittal, because the court ruled that their actions had been justified to disperse an illegal gathering (Reid 1989: 204–5). In the meantime, nine days after the massacre, the Home Secretary, Lord Sidmouth, had conveyed to the magistrates the thanks of the Prince Regent for their action in 'preservation of the public peace' (Farrer and Brownbill 2003, Babington 1990: 46–58). Lord Sidmouth's public congratulations displayed scant regard for legal neutrality or the right to a fair trial.

Citing a range of sources and authorities, one scholar noted the alacrity with which both the parliament and the judiciary were prepared to cast aside concerns about domestic military intervention in the face of rising social unrest, which reached new heights during the Chartist movement for voting and other basic rights.

> Civil libertarian reservations about the increasing use of the army in riots seem to have been overwhelmed by the general establishment view that what was good for the maintenance of public order was desirable and, therefore, legal. The fear of disorder had by this stage largely replaced the spectre of military intervention in civil affairs as the *bete noir* of the status quo. (Greer 1983: 583)

Following the defeat of the 1831 parliamentary reform bill, riots broke out in Bristol, which soldiers dispersed, killing 12 people and wounding about 100 (Babington 1990, 75–84). These riots gave rise to the last English case in which calling out the troops was directly examined. In *R v. Pinney* ((1832) 5 Car & P 254; 170 ER 962), the mayor of Bristol and nine aldermen were prosecuted by the Attorney General for breaching their common law duty to assemble a sufficient force to put down three days of riots, during which thousands of people, some allegedly armed with 'iron bars, iron crows, pickaxes, hammers, pieces of wood, and bludgeons' broke open a jail and forced the release of prisoners. A military major advised the mayor that it would be 'imprudent to put arms in the hands of young troops'. The jury found the defendants not guilty.

The law report of *R v. Pinney* also records Tindal LCJ's *Charge to the Bristol Grand Jury* after the riots. Lord Tindal insisted that soldiers had a duty, as citizens, on their own authority, to do their utmost to 'put down riot and tumult'. Two officers who had refused to order the troops to fire without a magistrate's sanction were found guilty of neglect of duty, causing one to commit suicide. The third officer, who had fatally shot a boy during an incident, was acquitted of manslaughter. Lord Tindal instructed the Grand Jury that if the shot was 'discharged in the fair and honest execution of his duty, in endeavouring to disperse the mob', the killing was justified and amounted to accidental death only (170 ER 962, 969, Babington 1990: 84). As late as 1888, the Secretary of State for War listed 'the effective support of the civil power in all parts of the United Kingdom' as the principal duty of the British army.

Suppressing Industrial and Socialist Agitation

The rise of the trade union movement during the final years of the nineteenth century and the emergence of the socialist movement, particularly after the 1917 Russian Revolution, produced further legal repression, accompanied by a shift from military to police intervention. An episode that illustrated the continuing power of magistrates to call out the troops was the Featherstone Colliery Riots of September 1893. Four people, including two bystanders, were killed when an infantry captain ordered soldiers to fire on striking coal miners and their supporters after a local magistrate had read the proclamation from the Riot Act 1714.

The 1893 *Report of the Select Committee on the Featherstone Riots* exonerated the captain and his troops, saying 'The necessary prevention of such outrage on person and property justifies the guardians of the peace in the employment against a riotous crowd of even deadly weapons' (Whelan 1985: 272). However, the committee warned that 'officers and soldiers are under no special privileges and subject to no special responsibilities as regards this principle of the law'. The taking of life must be shown to be necessary and resort to military assistance must be the 'last expedient' of the civil authorities, but when such a call was made, 'to refuse such assistance is in law a misdemeanour' (United Kingdom Parliamentary Papers 1893: 381, Babington 1990: 122–32).

From the beginning of the twentieth century, the creation of larger police forces meant that troops were deployed less frequently to control riots. Nevertheless, military interventions continued, and so did fatalities. In mid-1906, a detachment of infantry was sent to patrol the Belfast docks to protect strike-breakers. After a mutiny in police ranks in sympathy with the strikers, soldiers patrolled city streets throughout the summer and opened fire on a pro-strike rally, killing two people and wounding at least five (Babington 1990: 133–4).

A parliamentary select committee in 1908 was told that during the previous 30 years, the military had been called out on 24 separate occasions in England and Wales (Babington 1990: 135, Jeffery 1985: 52). While insisting that the power to call out the troops must continue, the committee recommended that police forces should be 'so organised and administered as to obviate to the utmost possible extent any necessity for resorting to military aid' (Jeffery 1985: 53).

Even so, in 1910 troops were called out at Tonypandy, South Wales, during a coal strike, and a miner was killed by a baton blow. The Home Secretary, Winston Churchill, took personal charge of the operation, issuing an unprecedented order placing all the police and army forces under the command of an army general (Babington 1990: 137–40). The next year, troops were mobilised in Cardiff, London and Liverpool to help suppress strikes by seamen and dockers, and opened fire on striking workers at Liverpool, killing two. Two naval gunboats and a cruiser were sent to the Mersey and large contingents of soldiers took up positions in the city (Babington 1990: 140–1). During a rail strike later that year, the Riot Act was read a number of times, troops charged a crowd at Chesterfield with bayonets fixed and at Llanelli in Wales, soldiers killed two men when a scab train was held up (Babington 1990: 141). After telling the House of Commons that an unprecedented challenge to government authority existed, Churchill sent out telegrams to police chief constables in all the affected areas informing them that the procedures for requesting military assistance via a magistrate had been suspended and that army commanders had a complete discretion to use their troops as they saw fit. Churchill came under criticism for instituting a type of martial law, yet the law officers contended that his measures were justified under the circumstances as the soldiers were merely exercising their rights and duties as ordinary citizens (Babington 1990: 142).

After World War I, armed military units were called out when half the Liverpool police force went on strike in 1919. Four battalions and a troop of tanks were deployed. After a magistrate read the Riot Act, two alleged rioters were shot, one fatally. At the height of the confrontation, HMS Valiant steamed up the Mersey, carrying 8 x 15 inch guns (Bramall 1985: 79–80). At the subsequent inquest into the death, the coroner's jury returned a verdict of 'justifiable homicide' (Babington 1990: 146).

During this period, an Act that had lain dormant for more than 100 years, the Incitement to Mutiny Act 1797, was resuscitated to target the rise of socialist-led militancy in the working class. The first prosecution was launched in 1912. Tom Mann, an internationally-known socialist and trade union leader, and four other syndicalists were jailed for six to nine months for issuing an open letter, appealing to British soldiers not to shoot striking workers (Ewing and Gearty 2000: 119ff). As the historical circumstances illustrated, this plea to the soldiers was hardly an exaggerated one. The judges ruled that Mann and his co-thinkers could be convicted without any proof that a single soldier was actually approached by the defendants or seduced by the letter. By contrast, while the syndicalists were jailed, there were no prosecutions in 1914 of the Tory politicians who urged army officers to mutiny, and army officers who did so, in order to defeat the Home Rule Bill for Ireland. These cases are examined in more detail in Chapter 4.

The next phase of invoking crimes against the state focused on the young Communist Party of Great Britain (CPGB), which had been founded in response to the October 1917 Russian Revolution. As also discussed in Chapter 4, this phase began in 1922 and continued through the 1930s. In October 1925, police raided the national and London headquarters of the CPGB, the Young Communist League, the National Unemployed Workers Movement and the CPGB's newspaper, *Workers' Weekly*. Twelve of the CPGB's leaders were arrested, including almost the entire political bureau. They were imprisoned and charged with sedition and inciting others to mutiny under the 1797 Act. They remained in jail for six months or a year, and most were still incarcerated when the May 1926 general strike began.

In 1934, the 1797 Act was superseded by the Incitement to Disaffection Act, which substantially reproduced its language but provided for summary prosecutions to make prosecutions easier, both legally and politically. In moving the bill, the Attorney General cited passages from Communist Party publications, including one that urged servicemen to turn any war into 'a civil war against the capitalist war-mongers and their bankrupt system' (Ewing and Gearty 2000: 242). Such anti-war statements are clearly ones of political program, not an immediate call for mutiny.

During World War II, the Emergency Powers (Defence) Act 1939 effectively supplanted the 1934 Act, outlawing wider anti-war activities, including endeavouring to incite people not to obey conscription notices or to enlist voluntarily (despite the latter being a legal right). Numbers of pacifists and anarchists were prosecuted (Young 1976: 77–80).

There was no further prosecution under the 1934 Act until 1972, when it began to be used against groups appealing to soldiers to desert and join the Irish Republican Army. The dispatch of troops to the British-ruled enclave of Northern Ireland in 1969 had provoked considerable public opposition. The early 1970s was also a period of considerable industrial and political turbulence. In 1972–3, the British government declared a state of emergency to combat a coal miners' strike and drew up a list of 16 key industries and the possibility of using military labour in the event of strikes (Hennessy 1985: 99–100). During the 1974 miners' strike, which triggered the fall of the conservative Heath government, military exercises were conducted, involving the SAS, at London's Heathrow Airport, and it was later admitted that senior officers had discussed plans for a military takeover in the midst of that political crisis (Vallely 2002).

After 2001, as examined in Chapter 7, sweeping anti-terrorism laws were adopted in Britain, providing for lengthy imprisonment for politically-motivated acts classified as 'terrorist'. The Civil Contingencies Act of 2004 also empowered the government to issue sweeping emergency regulations in any event that 'threatens serious damage to human welfare' or 'war or terrorism, which threatens serious damage to the security of the United Kingdom'. These regulations could, inter alia, 'enable the Defence Council to authorise the deployment of Her Majesty's armed forces' (Walker and Broderick 2006: 63–80, 153–88).

Thus, in every period of military, economic and political fragility, legal measures have been adopted, or unexpectedly revived, to provide for prosecutions or other forms of police or military intervention, with far-reaching implications for basic civil liberties and political free speech.

Australia

A similar pattern has occurred in Australia. Among those subjected to sedition prosecutions have been John Macarthur, founder of the Australian merino wool industry, for challenging the authority of Governor Bligh in 1807–8; Henry Seekamp, the editor and owner of the *Ballarat Times* during the Eureka Stockade in 1854; anti-conscriptionists who opposed Australia's involvement in World War I; and Fred Paterson, who later became Australia's first Communist MP, for expressing support for workers' struggles against capitalism at a public meeting in 1930 (ALRC 2006: 53).

The Eureka Stockade, which was an actual armed rebellion, albeit on a small and local scale, provided a case study in the political factors affecting prosecutions and outcomes. Henry Seekamp was convicted of sedition for publishing a series of anti-government articles in the weeks before the Stockade, and sentenced to six months' imprisonment (he served only three). However, much to the chagrin of the colonial authorities, such was the popular support for the rebels that juries refused to convict the 13 miners charged with high treason, an offence that carried the death penalty (see Chapter 3).

During the twentieth century, three significant cases occurred during periods of acute political tension – in World War I, the 1930s Great Depression and the post-World War II 'Cold War'.

In what became known as the 'Sydney Twelve' case, during World War I, 12 members of the syndicalist International Workers of the World (IWW) were accused of setting Sydney factories, warehouses and stores alight to force the federal Labor government to drop its plans to introduce conscription. They were arrested against a backdrop of emerging disquiet over the horrific losses of life during World War I, widespread opposition to an ultimately defeated referendum on conscription and increasing working class militancy, which was to culminate in 1917 in a virtual general strike in New South Wales (Turner 1969: 3, 20, 90–1).

As explained in Chapter 4, they were originally charged with 'treason felony' for endeavouring, among other things, to 'intimidate or overawe' parliament (Turner 1969: 36). Before their trial began, however, that charge was replaced by three counts of conspiracy: to commit arson, to defeat the ends of justice and seditious conspiracy (Rushton 1973: 53–4). It was widely believed in the labour movement that the men were framed or railroaded for their anti-war views and opposition to conscription. That belief was reinforced by the fact that the charges were laid in the lead-up to a referendum on conscription called by the Prime Minister, Billy Hughes. Hughes sought to discredit the IWW, which agitated against conscription, and hence undermine the 'no' campaign. While the 12 were still awaiting trial, in highly prejudicial comments, he declared: 'The IWW not only preach but they practise sabotage ... They are to a man anti-conscriptionist' (Turner 1969: 47–8). In this political atmosphere, a jury found seven men guilty of all three counts, four guilty of conspiracy to commit arson and seditious conspiracy, and one guilty of seditious conspiracy.

Ultimately, after a legal appeal and two judicial inquiries, the convictions unravelled, but not before two of the men had served five years in custody and the IWW had been effectively dismantled. After an active public campaign for the release of the Sydney Twelve, a Royal Commission was convened in 1920, which concluded that six of the men were not 'justly or rightly' convicted of any offence, and the others had been excessively punished. Ten men were released in August 1920 and two late in 1921, but were never compensated (Turner 1969: 247–50).

At the beginning of the Great Depression, Fred Paterson, a prominent member of the Communist Party of Australia (CPA), was arrested in January 1930 on sedition charges. Under conditions of economic breakdown, rapidly growing unemployment and acute social unrest, the media depicted the CPA as a poisonous threat to Australian society (Fitzgerald 2002: 49). Paterson was arrested for having addressed a lunchtime gathering in Brisbane's Domain on the subject of 'the law and the working class'. He was alleged to have urged workers to 'take the law into their own hands' in order to be 'emancipated'. However, Paterson, who represented himself in court, convinced the jury that the two police witnesses could not have recalled, word for word, the 'seditious words' in his hour-long speech (for the details of those words see Chapter 5). The two police officers both recounted over 200 words, without a word of difference and without the aid of notes. Paterson dubbed the pair 'the Siamese twins of the Queensland police force'. After retiring for less than 15 minutes, the jury returned a verdict of not guilty (Fitzgerald 2002: 50–2).

The political use of sedition laws in Australia was revived during the opening years of the so-called Cold War, from the late 1940s to the early 1950s. Successive governments, both Labor and Coalition, exploited sedition prosecutions to harass, disrupt, vilify and, in some instances, jail, political dissenters. The best known twentieth century cases occurred in 1948 and 1949. The High Court upheld the jailing of two leaders of the Communist Party, Gilbert Burns and Lance Sharkey, who both made statements refusing to support Australia militarily in response to hypothetical questions about a war against the Soviet Union (*Burns v. Ramsley* (1949) 79 CLR 101; *R v. Sharkey* (1949) 79 CLR 121).

On each occasion, the majority of High Court judges ruled that the prosecution need not prove that the accused subjectively intended to 'excite disaffection' (Head 1979: 99–105). The majority decisions rejected the distinction made at times by the US Supreme Court between exhortations that create a 'clear and present danger' of violence or disorder, and 'mere doctrinal justification or prediction of the use of force under hypothetical conditions' (Head 1979: 101).

As legal scholar Laurence Maher has demonstrated in some detail, these prosecutions, and other threatened prosecutions, became vehicles for wider political, surveillance and prosecutorial campaigns against the Communist Party, and for permitting extensive operations by the intelligence and police services, including frequent search and seizure raids on party members (Maher 1992, Maher 1994). These efforts reached crescendos during Prime Minister Robert Menzies' 1950–1 bid to ban the Communist Party and in the lead-up to the mid-1950s Petrov Royal Commission.

Drawing on the official archives, Maher showed that decisions were taken to launch the sedition prosecutions, which required the approval of the Attorney General, for purely political purposes. Under pressure from the United States government to 'get tough with' the Communist Party, Prime Minister Ben Chifley sent the head of the Defence Department to Washington, where he 'made as much as he could of the prosecutions of Burns, Sharkey and Healy as one important indication of the Chifley Government's anti-communist resolve' (Maher 1992: 305). The Labor government also had its own domestic reasons to harass the Communist Party. As Maher explained, citing another archive document:

> [T]hese three cases were part of the overall political struggle of the time which, for example, saw the Chifley Government crush the CPA-inspired coal strike in June–August 1949 and take a variety of other measures in 1948–49 to strengthen Australia's internal security apparatus in the face of increasing anxiety about communist disruption of Australia's industry and defence preparedness. (Maher 1992: 304–5)

In the case of Burns, Maher noted that the Acting Attorney General Nicholas McKenna 'discussed the case with [Prime Minister Ben] Chifley before making his decision' (Maher 1992: 300). The Labor government claimed it was doing no more than enforcing the criminal law, and dishonestly denied that the proceedings were directed against the Communist Party. In court, prosecution counsel echoed these claims, making statements that were 'all false, and hypocritical in the extreme' (Maher 1992: 303). These practices, which involve clear and deliberate abuses of the legal system, are a chilling reminder of the extent to which the extraordinary powers given to the intelligence and security agencies can be misused to trample over fundamental legal rights, political freedoms and civil liberties.

Another Cold War prosecution of a Communist Party leader, that of William Fardon Burns in 1950, arose from articles published in the party newspaper, *Tribune*, urging 'resistance' to Australia's involvement in the Korean War. After examining the archive record, Roger Douglas established that although Burns was ultimately convicted, and jailed for six months, on one of three counts of publishing seditious words, it was a 'classical political trial', conducted by the Liberal government of Prime Minister Robert Menzies, that coincided with the passage of the Communist Party Dissolution Act 1950. Douglas concluded that while 'sedition laws are weapons which are used sparingly', such prosecutions, whether legally successful or not, serve a wider purpose. Douglas referred to the 'more subtle, more ubiquitous, and more effective forms of repression which typically accompany prosecutions for political crimes' (Douglas 2005: 248).

Douglas suggested that in the light of the problematic prosecution of Burns, and the subsequent experiences of the Vietnam War, federal governments subsequently pursued the war against communists by less legally perilous means, including surveillance (Douglas 2005: 248, Douglas 2001, Douglas 2002). Yet, as Maher's 1994 article noted, one further 'particularly ill-conceived' sedition prosecution was conducted in 1953, arising out of a *Communist Review* article criticising the royal family. Moreover, the High Court upheld yet another anti-communist sedition conviction in 1961, in which a former junior officer in the Australian colonial administration of Papua New Guinea was charged with 'exciting disaffection against the government' for remarks he made during a series of informal lunchtime meetings encouraging local people to demand independence (Head 2007). And as Maher recorded in his 1992 article, calls were made for sedition prosecutions against anti-war groups during the 1990–1 Gulf War (see also ALRC 2006: 59). These cases are examined in Chapter 6. They may have serious implications in the light of the Howard government's inclusion of modified sedition provisions in the anti-terrorism legislation in 2005, and the subsequent Labor government's partial meeting of a 2007 election promise to repeal those provisions. These issues are also considered in Chapters 6 and 7.

Canada and New Zealand

Both Canada and New Zealand, two other former British colonies, provide illustrations of the political factors affecting the introduction and prosecution of offences against the state.

In Canada, following the 1917 Russian Revolution and the 1919 Winnipeg general strike, legislation was introduced to declare unlawful any organisation whose purpose was to bring about any governmental, industrial or economic change by force, violence or physical injury. The criminalisation extended to teaching, advocating, advising or defending such a purpose. Anyone convicted of being a member of, or defending such an organisation or possessing its literature could be jailed for 20 years. The law was used throughout the 1920s and early 1930s to break up meetings, raid offices and seize literature. In 1931, eight leaders of the Communist Party of Canada were convicted and sentenced to up to five years in prison. The severity of the sentences, however, began to turn public opinion against the law. It was repealed in 1936, but the law of sedition was simultaneously reinforced. Similar unlawful association provisions later re-emerged in the War Measures Act, which was used during World War II and the October 1970 Quebec crisis (see Chapter 3).

In New Zealand, sedition charges were brought forward during World War I to deal with a general strike and an anti-conscription campaign. Strike leaders were jailed for sedition and inciting violence after they advised striking waterside workers to resist the police and troops who were dispatched with machine guns to break their strike. Three anti-conscription campaigners were also prosecuted for sedition. Nearly a century later, after lying mostly dormant, the sedition offence was used against someone who urged acts of civil disobedience against foreshore and seabed legislation that sought to annul traditional Maori land claims (see Chapter 6).

Chapter 2

The United States: Free Speech in 'War' and 'Peace'

The United States offers a significant insight into the history of crimes against the state. One study of free speech in the US concludes that the country has attempted to punish individuals for criticising government officials or policies only during six war-related episodes: the conflict with France at the end of the eighteenth century, the Civil War, World Wars I and II, the Cold War and the Vietnam War. In each of those periods, 'the United States went too far in sacrificing civil liberties – particularly the freedom of speech' (Stone 2004: 12–13).

There is no doubt that during these years, severe measures were taken to punish political dissent and shore up official authority. In 1798, on the brink of war with France, Congress enacted the Sedition Act, which made it an offence for anyone to publish or utter any disloyal statement against the US government, the Congress or the president, with the intent to bring them into contempt or disrepute. During the Civil War, President Abraham Lincoln suspended the writ of habeas corpus and military tribunals imprisoned or exiled political opponents who publicly condemned the president, the emancipation of slaves, conscription and the war. In World War I, about 2,000 people were prosecuted for opposing the war and the draft. Those convicted under the 1917 Espionage Act and the 1918 Sedition Act were routinely sentenced to 10 to 20 years' imprisonment, including Eugene Debs, who had received nearly a million votes as the Socialist Party candidate for the presidency in 1912.

During World War II, 120,000 people of Japanese descent were interned and President Franklin Roosevelt sought to stifle criticism by having the authorities prosecute, denaturalise or deport opponents of the war. The leaders of the Trotskyist Socialist Workers Party were jailed. As part of the Cold War of the late 1940s to the early 1960s, the McCarthyite witch hunts led to abusive loyalty programs, congressional investigations and criminal prosecutions of alleged communists. During the Vietnam War of the 1960s and 1970s, the FBI sought to disrupt dissident political activities, anti-war protesters were prosecuted for expressing contempt for the American flag and burning draft cards, and National Guard troops shot demonstrating students at Kent State University (Stone 2004: 12–13).

A closer examination of that history indicates, however, that one would be ill-advised to accept that these developments were merely wartime aberrations or that such repression could not happen again. The fact that neither the Cold War nor the Vietnam War was a true wartime situation is another cause for consideration. Moreover, the adoption of the term 'war on terrorism' in 2001 to justify measures such as detention without trial, demonstrates how fragile fundamental legal and constitutional rights can be in times of political stress. These dangers are intensified by the fact that this 'war' was proclaimed to be indefinite. President George W. Bush declared that 'the war on terrorism will never end' (Stone 2004: 554).

The study cited above contends that the war on terrorism has lacked the arrests of anti-war dissenters and government critics that characterised the earlier wars. It asserts that 'American values, politics and law have reached a point where such prosecutions seem almost unthinkable' (Stone 2004: 551). Yet, the author concedes a series of 'problematic' practices, such as the indefinite detention without trial of more than 1,000 non-citizens; secret deportations; the incarceration of a citizen without trial for two years; and expanded eavesdropping, surveillance and infiltration powers. These measures included the USA PATRIOT Act, which 'smuggled into law several investigative practices that have nothing to do with fighting terrorism' and expanded unchecked executive power. Guidelines imposed on the FBI to restrict its authority to investigate political and religious activities – after its Vietnam War domestic spying and disruption programs were exposed – were effectively dismantled (Stone 2004: 552–7). In 2010, the Obama administration and Congress extended the PATRIOT Act unamended.

The Sedition Act of 1798

A brief historical review reveals a pattern of resort to criminal prosecutions or other repressive measures in every period of political turmoil. The 1776 Declaration of Independence proclaimed the right to revolution and the inalienable rights to life, liberty and the pursuit of happiness. Just two decades later, however, the US Congress passed the Sedition Act of 1798, citing a potential war with France. The Act prohibited any person from writing, publishing or uttering anything of a 'false, scandalous and malicious' nature against the US government, the Congress or the President with intent to defame them or bring them into 'contempt or disrepute'.

Within months, a congressman, Matthew Lyon, was indicted for accusing President Adam's administration of 'a continual grasp for power ... an unbounded thirst for ridiculous pomp, foolish adulation and selfish avarice'. Lyon was jailed for four months, but successfully campaigned for re-election from his prison cell (Stone 2004: 20–54). The administration had argued that the legislation liberalised the common law by requiring malicious intent, making truth a defence and specifying that juries must decide whether an utterance had a seditious effect (Stone 2004: 43–4). These reforms, however, proved illusory.

By 1801, when the Act expired, 25 well-known Republicans had been arrested under it. Ten cases went to trial, all resulting in convictions, and some ended in jail terms of up to nine months. In addition, the majority Federalists initiated several common law prosecutions for seditious libel. Under the Sedition Act, the most severe sentence was imposed on David Brown, a vagabond radical who agitated in the name of liberty against the Sedition Act and other legislation, such as the

Stamp Act and the Aliens Bill. The presiding judge, Justice Samuel Chase, branded Brown a 'wandering apostle of sedition' and sentenced him to a fine of $450 and 18 months in prison (Brown served 20 months because he could not pay the fine) (Stone 2004: 64).

Stone concludes that 'although the Sedition Act was purportedly enacted as a war measure to strengthen the nation in its impending war with France, it served primarily as a political weapon to strengthen the Federalists in their "war" with the Republicans' (Stone 2004: 67). The Act was designed to expire on the last day of President Adams's term of office. While the Act therefore had a distinctly partisan motivation, it demonstrated how concerns about wartime security could be exploited more generally as a pretext for political repression. Moreover, the judiciary provided no protection against the abuse. Although the Supreme Court did not rule on the constitutionality of the Sedition Act, other judges were unanimous in upholding it. Justice James Iredell told a grand jury the Act made sense because if you 'take away from a Republic the confidence of the people ... the whole fabric crumbles into the dust' (Stone 2004: 68).

It is true that in 1801, the incoming President Thomas Jefferson pardoned all those who had been convicted under the Sedition Act, and 40 years later Congress repaid all the fines imposed under it. More than 150 years further on, the Supreme Court declared, in *New York Times v. Sullivan* (376 US 254 (1964)), that the lesson to be drawn from the debate over the 1798 Sedition Act was that debate on public issues should be 'uninhibited, robust and wide-open'. The judges suggested that although the Act was never tested in the court, it had been held invalid by 'the court of history'. Nonetheless, belated declarations of commitments to free speech do not alter the record of what actually happened, and constitute no guarantee against similar practices in the future. Indeed, Stone warns that one lesson from this experience is that 'in times of national crisis, judges will not always be inclined or able to preserve civil liberties when they are under assault' (Stone 2004: 75).

The Civil War

The next 'perilous time' for civil liberties was the Civil War of the 1860s. This was the period in which the existence of the United States was most genuinely at risk, directly confronted by a military challenge from the slave-owning states. In many ways, the Civil War was the completion of the American Revolution, abolishing slavery, confiscating slave-derived wealth and clearing the way for the industrial development of American capitalism (McPherson 1990). Quite validly, some measures adopted in this 'war' period can be regarded as a necessary suspension of aspects of civil law in a battlefield context. A civil war necessarily produces conditions in which it may be difficult, if not impossible to maintain civil law. As historian James McPherson observes: 'Martial law prevails over large parts of a country wracked by civil war; newspapers and other media of communication are often muzzled; enemy partisans and sympathisers are arbitrarily arrested and jailed, sometimes tortured and murdered (McPherson 1990: 57).

Rather than suspending the constitution, President Abraham Lincoln suspended habeas corpus and permitted military commissions to try those accused of damaging the war effort. One of his first wartime orders was to suspend habeas corpus in portions of Maryland affected by guerrilla activities and mob attacks. Lincoln eventually extended the suspension to the entire country in cases of what he defined as 'disloyal persons [who] are not adequately restrained by the ordinary processes of law from … giving aid and comfort in various ways to the insurrection' (McPherson 1990: 57).

The US Constitution specifies that the privilege of the writ of habeas corpus (that is, freedom from detention without trial) 'shall not be suspended, except when in cases of rebellion or invasion the public safety may require it'. Lincoln argued that the southern rebellion was precisely the kind of exception crisis that the framers had in mind. Lincoln insisted that suspension of the writ was also an emergency measure that had to be exercised by the president acting in executive capacity, not Congress. Many constitutional scholars then and since have supported that position. The nation itself was threatened, Lincoln maintained. At stake was the survival of that nation 'conceived in liberty and dedicated to the proposition that all men are created equal' (McPherson 1990: 59). In his first message to Congress on 4 July 1861, Lincoln said the temporary suspension of habeas corpus was a small price to pay for the preservation of the republican liberty established in 1776. He asserted that most of the military arrests of civilians were for military crimes such as sabotage, espionage and guerrilla warfare. As for the few conspicuous cases of arrests of politicians like former congressman Clement Vallandigham, or of newspaper editors for speaking out against the war or conscription, Lincoln argued that their utterances discouraged enlistment in the army or encouraged desertions from it, thereby 'damaging the army, upon the existence of which the life of the nation depends' (McPherson 1990: 59–60).

Vallandigham was arrested by a military general for a speech in which he described the war as 'wicked, cruel and unnecessary', blamed it on Lincoln and the Republicans and called it a war 'for the freedom of the blacks and the enslavement of the whites'. Charged with making 'treasonable utterances', he was tried and convicted by a military commission, which sentenced him to imprisonment for the remainder of the war (Stone 2004: 82). Despite considerable protests against Vallandigham's arrest, Lincoln refused to intervene. Generally in such cases, he deferred to the judgement of military commanders, although he issued stern instructions to limit arrests. In one instance, in 1863, he stipulated to a general: '[Y]ou will only arrest individuals and suppress assemblies, or newspapers, when they may be working *palpable* injury to the Military' and 'in no other case will you interfere with the expression of opinion in any form' (Stone 2004: 125).

It is not known exactly how many civilians were arrested by military authorities during the Civil War. Estimates range from 13,000 to 38,000. Most of the arrests occurred in states where the fighting was taking place, and most were for offences such as draft evasion, trading with the enemy, bridge burning and other forms of sabotage. Phrases and words like 'treasonable language', 'Southern sympathiser', 'disloyalty' and 'inducing desertion' appear occasionally in the prison records but relatively few people were arrested for their political beliefs or expressions (Stone 2004: 124). Lincoln has been accused of tyranny. On the whole, however, there was limited use of criminal prosecutions to stifle political expression during the war. The Lincoln administration enacted no sedition legislation, left most dissenters alone and quickly released those speakers arrested for seditious remarks (Stone 2004: 133).

It was not until after the Civil War that the Supreme Court had occasion to consider the constitutionality of the use of military commissions to try civilians. In *Ex parte Milligan* 71 US (4 Wall) 2 (1866), which concerned a man sentenced to death for conspiring to engage in criminal acts to aid the Confederacy, the court held that such tribunals were unconstitutional, even in times of war or insurrection, if the civil courts were open and functioning (Stone 2004: 126).

World War I and the 'Red Scare'

The United States' controversial entry into the final stages of World War I in 1917 produced an almost immediate resort to politically repressive measures. Less than three weeks after voting for war, the US Congress began debate on what became the Espionage Act of 1917. In seeking a declaration of war by the Congress, President Woodrow Wilson confronted objections that the intervention was motivated by mercenary commercial considerations, and warnings that the introduction of conscription would provoke opposition that would have the streets of America 'running red with blood' (Stone 2004: 137). Wilson countered by declaring that disloyalty would be met with a 'firm hand of stern repression'. Proposing the Espionage Act, he declared that disloyalty was 'not a subject on which there was room for ... debate' and disloyal individuals had 'sacrificed their right to civil liberties' (Stone 2004: 137). Among those who were to be imprisoned were anti-capitalist defenders of the 1917 Russian Revolution like Mollie Steimer, the prominent pacifist Jane Addams, the Socialist Party presidential candidate Eugene V. Debs and the internationally-famous anarchist Emma Goldman (Stone 2004: 138–44).

Although directed at espionage and the protection of military secrets, the original bill included press censorship, 'disaffection' and postal banning provisions. After heated debates, the press censorship clauses were dropped, the 'disaffection' wording was narrowed and the phrase 'treasonable or anarchistic character' was removed from the postmaster general's powers to exclude political materials from the mails. The relevant part of the final act made it a crime, when the nation is at war, for any person to wilfully (a) 'make or convey false reports or false statements with intent to interfere' with the military success of the US or promote the success of its enemies; (b) 'cause or attempt to cause insubordination, disloyalty, mutiny, or refusal of duty' in the US military; or (c) 'obstruct the recruitment or enlistment service of the United States'. Violations were punishable by up to 20 years' imprisonment. The postmaster general could also ban the mailing of any material 'advocating or urging treason, insurrection or forcible resistance to any law' of the US (Stone 2004: 146–52).

These laws were applied in an atmosphere of war hysteria stirred by government propaganda. At the government's direct instigation, vigilante groups accused thousands of people of disloyalty, often on the basis of hearsay, gossip and slander. The attorney general boasted that with the assistance of these volunteer groups, the government had 'scores of thousands of persons under observation' (Stone 2004: 156–8). Altogether, more than 2,000 dissenters were prosecuted for allegedly disloyal, seditious or incendiary speech (Stone 2004: 170).

Some lower court judges took a stand against the sweeping use of the act. For instance, a Montana man was acquitted after stating, in a small rural village, that 'the United States was only fighting for Wall Street millionaires'. The judge said these were statements of belief or opinion, not 'false reports' and were made in such a remote location that they were unlikely to interfere with the war effort. In the more prominent case of *Masses Publishing v. Patten* (244 F 535 (SD NY 1917)), Judge Learned Hand ruled that the *Masses*, a monthly 'revolutionary' journal whose editors included John Reed and Max Eastman, was wrongly prohibited by the postmaster general. In essence, Hand argued that the cited cartoons, poems and text in the magazine did not expressly advocate unlawful conduct. He avoided considering whether the ban infringed the US Constitution's First Amendment on free speech by interpreting the Espionage Act as not intended to outlaw all criticism that could arouse discontent and disaffection. However, after the attorney general charged that Hand had gutted the act, the court of appeals emphatically reversed the ruling (Stone 2004: 164–70)

Most judges and juries were 'swayed by wartime hysteria'. They were determined to impose severe sentences on those charged with disloyalty, regardless of the niceties of statutory interpretation or the First Amendment. For example, a man was sentenced to 10 years in prison for producing a movie about the American Revolution that depicted soldiers of Britain, now a wartime ally, as brutal. The judge ruled that regardless of historical fact, 'this is no time' for 'sowing … animosity or want of confidence between us and our allies' (Stone 2004: 170–3). A wide range of publications were excluded from the mails, the Pittsburgh Symphony was even forbidden to perform Beethoven and Los Angeles public schools were prohibited from discussing the virtues of peace. Leaders of the newly-formed National Civil Liberties Bureau were threatened with prosecution for challenging Espionage Act prosecutions and offering legal support to those charged under it (Stone 2004: 181–3).

Before the war ended, Congress also passed the Alien Act of 1918, which authorised the government to deport any non-citizen, or even a naturalised citizen, who was a member of an anarchist organisation. The entire process was administrative, with no right of appeal, semi-secret proceedings and limited right to counsel. In 1918 alone, 11,625 people were deported under this act (Stone

2004: 181). Equally repressive was the Sedition Act of 1918, which was adopted to counter the handful of acquittals under the Espionage Act. It became an offence, when the US is in war, to

- wilfully utter, print, write or publish any disloyal, profane, scurrilous or abusive language about the form of government, Constitution, military forces, flag or military uniforms of the US, or
- use any language intended to bring form of government, Constitution, military forces, flag or military uniforms of the US into contempt, scorn, contumely or disrepute, or
- wilfully display the flag of any foreign country, or wilfully urge, incite or advocate any curtailment of production necessary for the war, or wilfully advocate, teach, defend or suggest the doing of any of the above acts, or by word or act support or favour the cause of any country with which the US is at war, or by word or act oppose the cause of the US. (Stone 2004: 186)

An amendment saying that 'nothing in this act shall be construed as limiting the liberty ... of any individual to publish or speak what is true, with good motives and for justifiable ends' was defeated. The passage of the act led to 'a large increase' in the number of prosecutions under the Espionage Act, although there were relatively few under the Sedition Act (Stone 2004: 190–1).

The Supreme Court's embrace of the repression, particularly directed against socialists, was displayed in *Schenck v. United States* (249 US 47 (1919)). Led by Justice Oliver Wendell Holmes, the court unanimously upheld the conviction of Socialist Party supporters who had been charged with conspiring to obstruct the recruiting and enlistment service by circulating a pamphlet to men who had been conscripted. The pamphlet argued that the draft was unconstitutional and a 'monstrous wrong' designed to further the interests of Wall Street. It urged readers to join the Socialist Party, write to their congressmen and petition for the repeal of the act. Although few inductees received the leaflet and there was no evidence that any were influenced by it, the defendants were convicted at trial because the 'natural and probable tendency' of the pamphlet was to dampen the willingness of men to serve in the armed forces and because the jury could reasonably infer that the defendants intended to cause the natural and probable consequences of their actions (Stone 2004: 192).

Justice Holmes agreed, saying 'the document would not have been sent unless it had been intended to have some effect' (249 US 47 (1919) at 51). In a famous passage, he enunciated the rather vague 'clear and present danger' doctrine for testing whether the speech was protected by the First Amendment:

> The question in every case is whether the words used are used in such circumstances and are of such a nature as to create a clear and present danger that they will bring about the substantive evils that Congress has a right to prevent. It is a question of proximity and degree. When a nation is at war many

things that might be said in time of peace are such a hindrance to its efforts that their utterance will not be endured so long as men fight and no Court could regard them as protected by any constitutional right ... (249 US 47 (1919) at 52)

In effect, as Geoffrey Stone suggests, that test was another version of the 'bad tendency' standard applied by the trial court (Stone 2004: 195–6). The capacity of the test to be used to punish political dissent was amply demonstrated in two cases handed down by the Supreme Court a week later. Justice Holmes spoke for a unanimous court in both. In *Frowerk v. United States* (249 US 204 (1919)), a publisher of anti-war, anti-draft articles in a German-language newspaper was sentenced to 10 years' jail under the Espionage Act. One of the articles described the war as 'outright murder without serving anything practical'. Justice Holmes brushed aside the First Amendment issue, saying the newspaper was circulated in quarters where 'a little breath could be enough to kindle a flame' (249 US 204 (1919) at 208–9).

Debs v. United States (249 US 211 (1919)) was a more prominent case. Eugene V. Debs was an internationally-renowned figure, who had won almost one million votes as the Socialist Party's 1912 presidential candidate. He was sentenced to 10 years in prison for making a speech near a prison after visiting three Socialist Party members who had been jailed for violating the Espionage Act. His address, delivered to some 1,200 listeners, praised the three 'martyrs for freedom' and said:

> They have come to realise, as many of us have, that it is extremely dangerous to exercise the constitutional right of free speech in a country fighting to make democracy safe in the world ... [Our three comrades] are simply paying the penalty, that all men have paid in all the ages of history for standing erect, and for seeking to pave the way to better conditions for mankind. (Stone 2004: 197)

Debs was charged with two offences under the Espionage Act. One count alleged that in his speech he intentionally caused and incited and attempted to cause and incite insubordination, disloyalty, mutiny and refusal of duty in the military and naval forces. The second alleged that by the same speech he intentionally obstructed and attempted to obstruct the recruiting and enlistment service. On appeal to the Supreme Court, Justice Holmes again roundly rejected the First Amendment argument. While acknowledging that the main theme of the speech was to celebrate socialism, he added, if 'one purpose of the speech, whether incidental or not does not matter, was to oppose [the] war, ... and if, in all the circumstances, that would be its probable effect, it would not be protected' (249 US 211 (1919) at 212–15). Holmes, one of America's most celebrated jurists, often described as one of the most dominant intellectual forces in American law, proved to be one of the most draconian when facing a perceived threat to the political order. Debs defiantly ran his 1920 presidential campaign from prison, as 'Convict No. 9653', and again received nearly a million votes (Stone 2004: 198).

Equally instructive was the next major case, *Abrams v. United States* (260 US 616 (1919)). The Supreme Court upheld jail terms of up to 20 years imposed on socialists and anarchists who protested against the dispatch of US marines to Vladivostok and Murmansk as part of Western efforts to overturn the 1917 Russian Revolution. They distributed leaflets condemning the expedition as an attempt to 'crush the Russian Revolution' and calling for a general strike. One leaflet denounced the 'plutocratic gang in Washington' and declared there was 'only one enemy of the workers of the world and that is CAPITALISM'. The defendants were arrested by the military police. Their highly public and controversial trial featured an anti-foreigner, anti-Semitic and anti-Bolshevik diatribe from the judge. His remarks included notorious slanders, declaring, 'we are not going to help carry out the plans mapped out by the Imperial German Government, and which are being carried out by Lenine [sic] and Trotsky (Stone 2004: 206).

The Supreme Court affirmed the convictions on two counts; one charging conspiracy 'to incite, provoke or encourage resistance to the United States' and the other alleging conspiracy to urge curtailment of production of war materials with intent to 'cripple or hinder the United States in the prosecution of the war'. Justice Holmes dissented, joined by Justice Louis Brandeis, but insisted he saw no reason to doubt the First Amendment rulings in *Schenck, Frohwerk* and *Debs*. Instead, he concluded that the 'silly leaflet' presented no 'immediate danger that its opinions would hinder the success of the government arms or have any appreciable tendency to do so'. Justice Holmes restated the 'immediate and present danger' test as requiring an imminent threat of 'immediate interference with the lawful and pressing purposes of the law [such that] an immediate check is required to save the country' (260 US 616 (1919) at 629–31). Notwithstanding this robust language, the test was left hinging on a curial assessment of the likelihood of success of the supposedly subversive material. Any serious threat to the political establishment would remain criminal.

In several post-*Abrams* decisions, the Supreme Court, despite dissents by Justices Holmes and Brandeis, consistently upheld convictions under the Espionage and Sedition Acts. In one notable instance, *Pierce v. United States* (254 US 325 (1920)), four Albany socialists were punished for expressing opinions that pointed to the economic and strategic calculations behind Washington's belated entry into World War I. They were convicted of violating the 'false statement' clause of the Espionage Act for distributing a pamphlet that asserted that, despite all President Wilson's rhetoric about democracy, 'this war began over commercial routes'. The court held that 'common knowledge ... sufficed to show' that the 'statements as to the causes that led to the entry of the United States into the war ... were grossly false'. In his dissenting judgement, Justice Holmes noted that the causes of war are complex and that even 'historians rarely agree' about such matters. Such statements were necessarily 'matters of opinion and judgement, not matters of fact to be determined by a jury'. Justice Brandeis added that to outlaw such statements would deny to those who dissent from government policy all 'freedom of criticism and of discussion in times when feelings run high' (254 US 325 (1920) at 246–7, 251, 269).

How far the legislation could be used to suppress political dissent and thwart the results of elections is demonstrated by the saga of Victor Berger, the first member of the Socialist Party elected to Congress, serving from 1911 to 1913. Later, in September 1917, just after he was nominated as the Socialist candidate in Wisconsin for the US Senate, he was indicted under the Espionage Act for publishing several editorials in the *Milwaukee Leader*, an anti-war German American newspaper. The editorials said, among other things, that the US was in the war because the Allies were washed up. Despite the criminal charges against him, and denunciations by both Democrat and Republican members of Congress, he received more than 100,000 votes. Before his trial began, he was re-elected to Congress in November 1918, easily defeating both the Democrat and Republican candidates. The next month, he was convicted and sentenced to 20 years' imprisonment. While his appeal was pending, the House of Representatives refused to seat him. In December 1919, the governor of Wisconsin ordered a special election for a replacement for Berger, but Berger was again elected, and by an ever greater margin than before. The House still refused to seat him. A year later, in *Berger v. United States* (255 US 22 (1921)), the Supreme Court reversed Berger's criminal conviction because the trial judge had made a series of highly inflammatory and prejudicial pre-trial statements about Germans and German Americans. It must be noted that the court did not reject the outlawing of the content of the editorials. With Justices Holmes and Brandeis dissenting, it had earlier upheld the exclusion of the *Milwaukee Leader* from the mail, in *Milwaukee Social Democratic Publishing Co v. Burleson* (255 US 407 (1920)). Ultimately, the Department of Justice dropped the charges against Berger and he was finally permitted to take his seat in the House in December 1923, four years after he was elected (Stone 2004: 211–12).

The Berger affair continued for five years after the war ended in November 1918. The backdrop was the vicious Red Scare of 1919–20. This episode illustrates that the repressive measures were not simply wartime exceptions, directed only against opponents of the war. Rather, they were aimed at crushing political dissent, particularly that inspired by the Russian Revolution. That revolution produced a sharp polarisation. The media was consumed with stories depicting Bolshevik rule as a descent into slaughter, confiscations and disorder. But Socialist Party membership grew by a third in 1918–19, and then many prominent members broke away to form the Communist Labor Party, advocating the overthrow of capitalist rule. During 1919, the discontent of returning soldiers helped fuel a series of major strikes – a Seattle general strike, a Boston police strike, a national steelworkers' strike and a mineworkers' strike. Bombs exploded in numbers of cities, some targeting administration officials, and May Day riots broke out in several cities. Attorney General A. Mitchell Palmer declared the bombings an attempt to 'terrorise the country', the *New York Times* ran a front-page headline, 'Mass Terror of Bolsheviki!' and the *New York Tribune* warned that strikers, 'red-soaked in the doctrines of Bolshevism,' sought to start 'a general red revolution in America' (Stone 2004: 220–2).

Mass arrests followed. Attorney General Palmer appointed J. Edgar Hoover to head a new General Intelligence Division within the Bureau of Investigations. It placed more than 200,000 people under surveillance and disseminated fabricated charges that communists and radicals had instigated violent strikes and race riots. By January 1920, more than 4,600 people had been arrested – virtually every known communist – and some 3,000 non-citizens were soon deported. The *Washington Post* declared: 'There is no time to waste on hairsplitting over infringement of liberty.' With the encouragement of Palmer, who described those arrested in the police raids as having 'sly and crafty eyes ... lopsided faces, sloping brows and misshapen features', states enacted criminal anarchy or criminal syndicalism statutes prohibiting advocacy of overthrowing the government. Thirty-two states outlawed displays of the Red Flag. In 1919–20, at least 1,400 people were arrested under such legislation, with at least 300 convicted and sentenced to jail terms of up to 20 years. In April 1920, the New York legislature expelled its five Socialist Party members on the grounds of being unpatriotic and disloyal. Five months later, all five were re-elected, signalling growing public opposition to the political witchhunt, which then began to collapse (Stone 2004: 223–5). At the end of 1920, Congress quietly repealed the Sedition Act of 1918, but the Espionage Act of 1917 remained in effect. Only in December 1923 were the last of the 200 prisoners in jail for Espionage or Sedition Act convictions finally released, on the orders of President Coolidge (Stone 2004: 231–2).

Stone observes that the Supreme Court dismissed First Amendment arguments in all nine cases in which they were mounted from 1919 to 1927 – a performance he describes as 'simply wretched' (Stone 2004: 228). He suggests that there was then a more permissive shift which lasted until World War II. However, in the two cases that purportedly demonstrate the shift, *Gitlow v. New York* (268 US 652 (1925)) and *Whitney v. California* (274 US 357 (1927)), the court upheld the constitutionality of state laws making it a crime to advocate the overthrow of the government. The judges stated that the laws only outlawed the express advocacy of using 'unlawful means' to overthrow organised government. While extolling the virtues of liberty and the framers of the Constitution for championing it, Justice Brandeis, for example, still gave great leeway to governments, saying: 'Only an emergency can justify repression ...' (274 US 357 (1927) at 377).

In *Gitlow*, the majority upheld the constitutional validity of a New York statute on 'criminal anarchy', which punished those who advocated overthrowing or overturning organised government by force, violence, or any unlawful means. The court ruled that the statute did not penalise the utterance or publication of abstract doctrine or academic discussion having no quality of incitement to any concrete action, but denounced the advocacy of action for accomplishing the overthrow of organized government by unlawful means. The majority said the statute was constitutional as applied to a printed manifesto issued by the Left Wing Section of the Socialist Party, advocating and urging mass action. According to the court, the manifesto sought to 'progressively foment industrial disturbances and, through political mass strikes and revolutionary mass action, overthrow and destroy organised parliamentary government; even though the advocacy was in general terms, and not addressed to particular immediate acts or to particular person' (268 US 652, 654).

World War II

In 1941, on the eve of US entry into World War II, the court stated that 'before utterances can be punished' the 'substantive evil must be extremely serious and the degree of imminence extremely high' (*Bridges v. California*, 314 US 252, 266 (1941)). Far from being a qualitative departure from *Debs* and the other World War I cases, this formulation still left ample scope for repression of opinions that were regarded as a serious threat to the official order. The scene was set for another wave of repression during and after World War II.

One early indicator of what was to come was President Roosevelt's secret 1936 decision to authorise the J. Edgar Hoover-led FBI to investigate suspected fascists and communists in the US. Hoover regarded the assignment as an invitation to resume many of the activities he supervised during the Red Scare of 1919–20 (Stone 2004: 248). During 1940, before the US entered the war against Germany, the Congress re-enacted the Espionage Act of 1917, making its provisions applicable for the first time in peacetime. It then went further, passing the Alien Registration Act of 1940 (the Smith Act), which required all resident non-citizens to register with the government, streamlined deportation procedures and forbade any person 'knowingly or wilfully' to 'advocate, abet, advise, or teach the duty, necessity, desirability, or propriety of overthrowing or destroying any government in the United States by force or violence'. Roosevelt declined to veto the Act, claiming that its advocacy provisions 'hardly ... constitute an improper encroachment on civil liberties in the light of present world conditions' (Stone 2004: 252).

The first prosecution under the Smith Act came even before the December 1941 Japanese attack on Pearl Harbor provided the pretext for Roosevelt administration to enter the war. The accused were 29 leaders of the Socialist Workers Party (SWP), the Trotskyist party, which opposed World War II as an inter-imperialist conflict waged in the interests of the business elites. The SWP had been involved in several major work stoppages that affected the military industry in Minneapolis. Before instigating the prosecution, Attorney General Francis Biddle advised Roosevelt that bringing some prosecutions might have a 'salutary effect' (Stone 2004: 255). Eighteen of the defendants were convicted and jailed for conspiring to advocate the forceful overthrow of the government, and the Supreme Court denied review (for a detailed examination of this case see Chapter 3).

During 1942, the conviction of an American fascist, William Pelley, under the Espionage Act of 1917 for making 'false statements with intent to interfere with the operation or success of the military or naval forces' set a far-reaching precedent. Pelley was convicted on the basis of critical statements published in his movement's magazine. A US Court of Appeals readily brushed aside the 'with intent' requirement, asserting that the 'argument that proof of intent is lacking hardly needs consideration'. The court stated that 'in time of war, when success depends on unified national effort', an individual who reported the country's 'failure in battle', asserted that the nation was 'bankrupt', claimed that it had 'incompetent leadership' and extolled the virtues of its enemies could not plausibly deny a criminal intent to interfere with the operation or success of the military forces. The ruling effectively reversed the onus of proof, placing the burden on the accused to disprove intent. Yet, the Supreme Court declined to review the case, and Pelley spent 10 years in prison before being paroled on the condition that he not participate in any 'political activities' (Stone 2004: 265–6). Another trial of 26 American fascist leaders – dubbed by the media as the 'Great Sedition Trial' – languished after the trial judge died. The defendants were charged under both the Espionage Act of 1917 and the Smith Act of 1940. Following a four-year saga, the case was finally abandoned in December 1945, three months after the war ended. It thus set no legal precedent, but chilled political opinion during the war and set a political precedent for Smith Act prosecutions of communists during the Cold War (Stone 2004: 272–5).

Stone suggests that two wartime Supreme Court rulings placed some curbs on prosecutions for 'subversive' advocacy. In *Taylor v. Mississippi* (319 US 583 (1943)), three Jehovah's Witnesses were charged, under a Mississippi statute, with advocating refusal to salute the flag and making statements 'calculated to encourage violence, sabotage, or disloyalty to the government of the United States, or the state of Mississippi'. One defendant had said 'it was wrong for our President to send our boys ... to be shot down for no purpose at all'. After emphasising the defendants' religious motivations, the court held: 'What these appellants communicated were their beliefs and opinions concerning domestic measures and trends in national and world affairs. Under our decisions criminal sanctions cannot be imposed for such communication' ((319 US 583, 590). This ruling seems to provide some protection for religious beliefs, but not anti-establishment politics. In *Hartzel v. United States* (322 US 680 (1944)), the defendant, an avowed anti-Semite, pro-fascist and anti-communist, was convicted under the Espionage Act for distributing pamphlets that, in the court's words, depicted the war as a gross betrayal of America, assailed the patriotism of the President and called for the conversion of the war into a racial conflict. The court reversed the conviction on the narrow basis that there was inadequate evidence of the necessary intent. 'There is nothing on the face of the three pamphlets in question to indicate that the petitioner intended specifically to cause insubordination, disloyalty, mutiny, or refusal of duty in the military forces, or to obstruct the recruiting and enlistment service' (322 US 680, 687). Far from issuing any general defence of free speech, the court cautiously concluded: 'Unless there is sufficient evidence from which a jury could infer beyond a reasonable doubt that he intended to bring about the specific consequences prohibited by the Act, an American citizen has the right to discuss these matters, either by temperate reasoning or by immoderate and vicious invective, without running afoul of the Espionage Act of 1917 (322 US 680, 689).

During World War II, almost 5 million non-citizens were registered under the Smith Act, about 900,000 Japanese, German and Italian nationals were classified as 'enemy aliens' and more than 9,000 were detained. Another 120,000 people of Japanese descent, two-thirds of whom were US citizens, were ordered to leave their West Coast homes to live in detention camps, even though there was not one documented act of espionage, sabotage or treason committed by anyone of Japanese descent residing on the West Coast (Stone 2004: 283–303). The Supreme Court sanctioned these internments in *Korematsu v. United States* (323 US 214 (1944)), commenting that 'hardships are part of war' (Stone 2004: 300).

The Cold War

The next period of 'war' – the Cold War – did not involve a genuine war mobilisation at all. While it partly encompassed the Korean War, it was a wider political confrontation. Internationally, it was a struggle for US global dominance, directed against the Soviet Union, and domestically it was aimed against communists and alleged 'fellow travellers'. The Cold War produced 'one of the most repressive periods in American history' (Stone 2004: 312). It was a period of red-baiting, black-listing and McCarthyism, conducted under the long shadow of the House Un-American Activities Committee (Stone 2004: 312–426). Alongside the Communist Control Act of 1954, which 'outlawed' the Communist Party and stripped it of all rights, privileges and immunities, there were loyalty programs, emergency detention plans, undercover surveillance, legislative investigations and criminal prosecutions. As well as federal law, numbers of states enacted anti-communist laws, with Tennessee even authorising the death penalty for members of the party (Stone 2004: 340). In this atmosphere, the Supreme Court again proved to be no protector of civil liberties.

In 1949, 11 leaders of the Communist Party were charged under the Smith Act. The charge was that 'they conspired ... to organise as the Communist Party and willfully to advocate and teach the principles of Marxism-Leninism'. This was equated with meaning 'overthrowing and destroying the government of the United States by force and violence' at some unspecified future time. They were also accused of conspiring to 'publish and circulate ... books, articles, magazines, and newspapers advocating the principles of Marxism-Leninism'. The *Communist Manifesto*, Lenin's *State and Revolution*, and Stalin's *Foundation of Leninism* were introduced as evidence for the prosecution. More than 400 police officers and detectives surrounded the court on the opening day of the trial. According to one account, the trial was 'circuslike from the opening bell' and the subject of incessant media headlines (Stone 2004: 396).

The charges were inherently problematic. They did not allege an attempt to overthrow the government, or even a conspiracy to do so, just a conspiracy to advocate the overthrow of the government. How could it be said that there was a 'clear and present danger'? The defendants themselves argued that Marxism eschewed any resort to violence unless the ruling class prevented a peaceful transition to socialism, and that no such issue could arise until the majority of Americans had been persuaded of the merits of socialism (Stone 2004: 397). Nevertheless, after a marathon nine-month trial, ten defendants were given sentences of five years and fined $10,000; an eleventh defendant, an armed forces veteran, was sentenced to three years as an act of gratitude. The US Court of Appeals for the Second Circuit upheld the convictions, with the judgement written by Chief Judge Learned Hand, often described as a champion of free speech. He insisted that no government had to wait for a 'probable danger' to become 'clear and present' (Stone 2004: 401). In *Dennis v. United States (341 US 494 (1951)), t*he Supreme Court upheld the convictions by a vote of six to two with Justices Hugo Black and William O. Douglas dissenting. Speaking for four of the majority judges, Chief Justice Fred Vinson adopted the 'clear and present danger' test and interpreted it thus:

> Obviously, the words cannot mean that before the Government must act, it must wait until the putsch is about to be executed, the plans have been laid and the signal is awaited. If the Government is aware that a group aiming at its overthrow is attempting to indoctrinate its members and to commit them to a course whereby they will strike when the leaders feel the circumstances permit, action by the Government is required. (*341 US 494,* 508–9)

By reasoning backward from the perceived putsch plot, this test opens immense scope for repression of ideas, long before any actual threat arises. Justice Black wrote that the government's indictment was 'a virulent form of prior censorship of speech and press' and a violation of the First Amendment. He suggested that his fellow judges had succumbed to 'present pressures, passions and fears' produced by the Cold War (341 US 579–81).

One scholar concludes that, given the McCarthyite witch hunting, Stalin's domination of Eastern Europe, the Soviet atomic bomb, the fall of China and the Korean War, it was simply 'no wonder' that even 'such sophisticated and experienced judges' bowed to the prevailing hysteria (Stone 2004: 410–11). Again, this is hardly a reassuring picture of the judiciary in times of political stress. It should be noted that the 'liberal' media performed no better. The *New York Times* applauded the court for affirming that 'liberty shall not be abused to its own destruction' (Stone 2004: 411). And the legal profession proved no more principled – the American Bar Association called for the expulsion of all Communist Party members and many lawyers, including the prominent Abe Fortas, refused to represent current or former party members (Stone 2004: 420–1).

The Supreme Court's ruling paved the way for a wave of arrests, which began two weeks after the decision. Soon, 23 other leaders of the party were indicted, and by 1957, over 140 leaders and members of the Communist Party had been charged. Of these, by one calculation, 108 were convicted, only 10 were acquitted and the rest were still awaiting trial in 1957 (Stone 2004: 411).

The prosecutions finally ceased in the early 1960s, in the wake of the Supreme Court rulings in *Yates v. United States* (354 US 298 (1957)) and three other decisions handed down on the same day. According to Stone, the decisions 'reversed the course of constitutional history' (Stone 2004: 413). Likewise, commenting on *Yates,* Gellhorn states:

> The aftermath of the *Yates* case is interesting. By the end of 1956, convictions of Communist leaders under the Smith Act had numbered 114. Many of these cases were still pending in the appellate courts when the *Yates* decision was announced in June of 1957. On one ground or another, convictions were set aside and new trials were granted to many of these defendants. The Department of Justice itself dropped the prosecution of a considerable number, on the ground that they could not properly be convicted on the basis of the evidence now available. Most significantly of all, the cases against the nine remaining defendants in *Yates,* as to whom the Supreme Court had refused to dismiss the charges, were abandoned by the prosecution because there was insufficient evidence that they had advocated action, as distinct from opinion. After all the clamor, after all the expressed alarm about the peril into which the United States was being plunged by this handful of misguided fanatics, the prosecution felt itself unable to show persuasively that the Communist spokesmen had engaged in the forbidden incitements to illegality.(Gellhorn 1960: 232)

It would be a false comfort, however, to conclude that the lack of cases since 1961 was the result of the Supreme Court rulings. The historical context suggests that the end of prosecutions had more to do with the waning of the anti-communist red-baiting of the McCarthyite period, and the Communist Party's return to advocacy of a 'peaceful road to socialism' in keeping with the Kremlin's doctrine. A closer examination suggests that the decision in *Yates*, followed by that in *Scales v. United States* (367 US 203 (1961)), leaves potential scope for the use of 'advocating overthrow of government' against those considered dangers to political stability in times of unrest.

In *Yates*, the 14 petitioners, leaders of the Communist Party in California, were indicted in 1951 in a Federal District Court under § 3 of the Smith Act and 18 USC § 371 for conspiring (1) to advocate and teach the duty and necessity of overthrowing the Government of the United States by force and violence, and (2) to organise, as the Communist Party of the United States, a society of persons who so advocate and teach, all with the intent of causing the overthrow of the Government by force and violence as speedily as circumstances would permit. The indictment charged that the conspiracy originated in 1940 and continued down to the date of the indictment, and that, in carrying it out, petitioners and their co-conspirators would (a) become members and officers of the Communist Party, with knowledge of its unlawful purposes, and assume leadership in carrying out its policies and activities, (b) cause to be organised units of the Party in California and elsewhere, (c) write and publish articles on such advocacy and teaching, (d) conduct schools for the indoctrination of Party members in such advocacy and teaching, and (e) recruit new Party members, particularly from among persons employed in key industries. It also alleged 23 overt acts in furtherance of the conspiracy. Petitioners were convicted after a jury trial, and their convictions were sustained by the Court of Appeals.

By a majority, the Supreme Court judges reversed the convictions, but only five of the petitioners were acquitted; the remaining nine were to be retried. In essence, the rulings hinged on issues of evidence, rather than constitutional principles. The majority found that the three-year statute of limitations had run out on the 'organising' charge. Applying the rule that criminal statutes are to be construed strictly, the court said the word 'organise' as used in the Smith Act referred only to acts in creating a new organisation, and not to acts thereafter performed in carrying on its activities.

The court further interpreted the Smith Act as not prohibiting advocacy and teaching of the forcible overthrow of the government as an abstract principle, divorced from any effort to instigate action to that end. Distinguishing the court's 1951 decision in *Dennis*, the judges said that the District Court appeared to have been led astray by the holding in *Dennis* that advocacy of violent action to be taken at some future time was enough. The majority insisted that *Dennis* had not obliterated the 'traditional dividing line between advocacy of abstract doctrine and advocacy of action' (354 US 320). However, the majority stated its agreement with the verdict in *Dennis*, arguing that in that case, although the defendant's advocacy was not directed at, or created any danger of, immediate overthrow, it was aimed at building up a seditious group and maintaining it in readiness for action at a propitious time (354 US 321).

The *Yates* majority said the 'essential distinction' was that 'those to whom the advocacy is addressed must be urged to *do* something, now or in the future, rather than merely to *believe* in something (354 US 235). Thus, advocacy of future action, even action in the indefinite future, is sufficient for a conviction; there is no need to prove that the advocacy represents a 'clear and present danger' of subversion. This was despite strenuous dissents by Justices Black and Douglas, who argued that all the convictions should be overturned, not just five of them. Justice Black pointed to the political arbitrariness involved in such prosecutions:

> The kind of trials conducted here are wholly dissimilar to normal criminal trials. Ordinarily, these 'Smith Act' trials are prolonged affairs lasting for months. In part, this is attributable to the routine introduction in evidence of massive collections of books, tracts, pamphlets, newspapers, and manifestoes discussing Communism, Socialism, Capitalism, Feudalism and governmental institutions in general, which, it is not too much to say, are turgid, diffuse, abstruse, and just plain dull. Of course, no juror can or is expected to plow his way through this jungle of verbiage. The testimony of witnesses is comparatively insignificant. Guilt or innocence may turn on what Marx or Engels or someone else wrote or advocated as much as a hundred or more years ago. Elaborate,

refined distinctions are drawn between 'Communism,' 'Marxism,' 'Leninism,' 'Trotskyism,' and 'Stalinism.' When the propriety of obnoxious or unorthodox views about government is in reality made the crucial issue, as it must be in cases of this kind, prejudice makes conviction inevitable except in the rarest circumstances. (354 US 339).

Moreover, the majority stated that 'distinctions between advocacy or teaching of abstract doctrines, with evil intent, and that which is directed to stirring people to action, are often subtle and difficult to grasp' (354 US 327). To illustrate the difficulty of making the distinction, the majority referred to Justice Holmes's dissent in *Gitlow v. People (*268 US 652 (1925)), where he said: 'Every idea is an incitement' (268 US 673). These observations point to the wide discretions left in the hands of governments and courts to convict on the basis of ideas alleged to be inciting revolutionary action, even in general terms.

In *Yates*, the court also took an extraordinary view of the conduct that could constitute 'overt acts' as required for conviction for conspiracy under 18 USC § 371. Only two overt acts were proved. Each was a public meeting held under Communist Party auspices at which speeches were made by one or more of the petitioners extolling leaders of the Soviet Union and criticising various aspects of the foreign policy of the United States. At one of the meetings, an appeal for funds was made. The government conceded that nothing unlawful was shown to have been said or done at these meetings, but the court ruled in its favour, saying: 'It is not necessary that an overt act be the substantive crime charged in the indictment as the object of the conspiracy' (354 US 334).

Despite claims that the indictments and trials ended in 1957 as the result of *Yates*, in 1961 the Supreme Court upheld by 5–4 the conviction and jailing for six years of Junius Scales under the 'membership clause' of the Smith Act. Scales was convicted because he was an 'active' member of the Communist Party, which advocated the overthrow of the government 'as speedily as circumstances would permit'. Challenging his felony charge, Scales claimed that the Internal Security Act of 1950 stated that membership in a Communist organisation shall not constitute a per se violation of any criminal statute. The court held that the Smith Act goes beyond 'per se' participation by targeting those whose membership in an organisation entails their knowing and deliberate participation in criminal activity.

Furthermore, the majority adopted a narrow view of *Yates*, interpreting it as a decision on the insufficiency of the evidence only, and asserting that evidence of advocacy of 'abstract' doctrine could be relevant in establishing illegal advocacy of action. The judges stated that Yates had shown what type of evidence was not, in itself, sufficient to show illegal advocacy:

This category includes evidence of the following: the teaching of Marxism-Leninism and the connected use of Marxist 'classics' as textbooks; the official general resolutions and pronouncements of the Party at past conventions; dissemination of the Party's general literature, including the standard outlines on Marxism; the Party's history and organizational structure; the secrecy of meetings and the clandestine nature of the Party generally; statements by officials evidencing sympathy for and alliance with the U.S.S.R. (*Scales v. United States* 367 US 203, 232 (1961))

However, the majority insisted that this kind of evidence, while insufficient, is not irrelevant. 'Such evidence, in the context of other evidence, may be of value in showing illegal advocacy' (367 US 233). This ruling leaves the door open for governments to introduce potentially prejudicial material in efforts to sway juries to convict, precisely as warned by Justice Black in *Yates*. The judges also concluded that *Yates* indicated at least two patterns of evidence sufficient to show illegal advocacy:

(a) the teaching of forceful overthrow, accompanied by directions as to the type of illegal action which must be taken when the time for the revolution is reached, and (b) the teaching of forceful overthrow, accompanied by a contemporary, though legal, course of conduct clearly undertaken for the specific purpose of rendering effective the later illegal activity which is advocated. (367 US 234)

The majority distinguished *Yates* on the basis that the evidence in that case had been insufficient because the incidents of illegal advocacy were infrequent, sporadic, not fairly related to the period covered by the indictment, and not sufficiently tied to officials who spoke for the party as such. Further, the judges warned that party pronouncements, if taken out of context, might appear harmless and peaceable without in reality being so. While they described the distinction drawn in *Yates* between theoretical advocacy and advocacy of violent action as 'of course, basic', they warned that when teaching was carried out in a 'special vocabulary', knowledge of that vocabulary was relevant to an understanding of the quality and tenor of the teaching (367 US 234–5). These vague formulations undermine the distinction drawn in *Yates* and permit governments and courts to claim that abstract literature, combined with 'context', frequency and 'special vocabulary', can constitute illegal advocacy, even if no illegal action is actually canvassed.

These sweeping propositions were adopted despite strongly-worded dissents, notably by Justices Black and Douglas, who objected that it was a violation of the First Amendment to outlaw membership in a political party merely because one of the philosophical tenets of the party is that the existing government should be overthrown by force at some distant time in the future when circumstances may permit. Justice Black accused the majority of rewriting the statute to justify their stance by importing requirements of 'activity' and 'specific intent' as implicit in words that plainly do not include them. More broadly, he denounced the 'freedom-destroying' nature of the 'balancing test' approach being applied by the court to permit 'the informed exercise of a valid government function' to override First Amendment freedoms. 'This doctrine, to say the very least, is capable of being used to justify almost any action government may wish to take to suppress First Amendment freedoms.' Black pointed out that Scales was being jailed for the express reason that he had associated with people who had entertained unlawful ideas and said unlawful things (367 US 261–2).

Justice Douglas declared that the Smith Act had imported into American law the 'alien' and 'abhorrent' doctrine of guilt by association. 'Not a single illegal act is charged to petitioner. That is why the essence of the crime covered by the indictment is merely belief—belief in the proletarian revolution, belief in Communist creed' (367 US 265). Invoking Spinoza and Montesquieu, he cautioned that 'free people should not venture again into the field of prosecuting beliefs' (367 US 267). Douglas cited the right of revolution articulated in the Declaration of Independence and warned of a return to the dark pre-revolutionary days when governments could determine what was 'dangerous' talk and suppress it. However, he insisted that a government had 'the right of self-preservation' and could 'move against those who take up arms against it' (367 US 270).

As Justice Douglas later noted in the 1969 case of *Brandenburg* (see below), the *Scales* doctrine left the door wide open for governments and law enforcement agencies to harass government opponents, by way of investigation and threats to prosecute. Douglas commented:

> Out of the 'clear and present danger' test came other offspring. Advocacy and teaching of forcible overthrow of government as an abstract principle is immune from prosecution. *Yates v. United States*. But an 'active' member, who has a guilty knowledge and intent of the aim to overthrow the Government by violence (*Noto v. United States*) may be prosecuted. *Scales v. United States*. And the power to investigate, backed by the powerful sanction of contempt, includes the power to determine which of the two categories fits the particular witness. *Barenblatt v. United States*. And so the investigator roams at will through all of the beliefs of the witness, ransacking his conscience and his innermost thoughts. (*Brandenburg v. Ohio* (395 US 444, 453–4 (1969) (citations omitted)

The Vietnam War

Compared to the Cold War, the Vietnam War tested the legal order more acutely, and led to a somewhat different response, primarily because as the war dragged on to ultimate defeat for the United States, powerful domestic opposition began to develop to it. In Stone's words, 'Over more than a decade of conflict, the war in Vietnam provoked increasingly bitter dissent and increasingly furious repression' (Stone 2004: 428). Contrary to the commonly held view, the opposition to the war was not confined to students but spread to the working class, and also intersected with a worldwide period of anti-government upheavals. As a result of the deepening anti-war sentiment, as early as 1968, President Lyndon B. Johnson was forced to withdraw from his re-election campaign. Days later, the assassination of Martin Luther King triggered riots in more than a hundred cities, despite more than 200,000 arrests (Stone 2004: 545).

Already, at the height of the urban riots by African-American workers and youth in the 1960s, troops had been sent into Detroit and other cities (Hammond 1997). Another turning point came when four students were shot dead during an anti-war protest at Kent State University in 1970. Ohio Governor James A. Rhodes had sent National Guard troops to the campus at the request of the local mayor (Bills 1998, Caputo 2005). The Kent State killings were part of a wave of repression in the aftermath of the television announcement by President Richard Nixon that US forces had crossed the border from Vietnam and invaded Cambodia. By then, the war had been raging at full force for more than five years, with US casualties mounting into the tens of thousands and Vietnamese casualties into the millions. The invasion of Cambodia triggered mass protests across the country, and the Kent State shootings had a politically galvanising effect upon millions of young people. On the following weekend, at short notice, well over 100,000 people demonstrated in Washington, DC. An unprecedented nationwide student strike developed, involving an estimated 4.3 million students, shutting down or disrupting more than 900 college campuses. The National Guard was dispatched to 21 campuses, while police battled students at another 26. University officials closed down 51 campuses for the remainder of the term (Stone 2004: 465–6).

The year 1970 saw the greatest number of strikes in two decades. Just weeks before Kent State, the first-ever national postal strike had led the Nixon administration to call out the National Guard to move the mail. Earlier, General Electric had been shut down by a militant and protracted strike. Later in the year, General Motors workers walked out. Within four years, amid escalating hostility to the war and its social cost, Nixon was forced to resign, ultimately as a result of the Watergate burglary. The following year, his unelected successor, Gerald Ford, was compelled to withdraw all US troops from Vietnam, conceding defeat. In the meantime, the Watergate affair began to reveal the unprecedented extent of illegal bugging, wire-tapping and surveillance conducted by the White House and the security agencies in their efforts to suppress the anti-war movement (Stone 2004: 471).

Once again, in this climate, Congress and the Supreme Court readily embraced the shredding of civil liberties, including First Amendment free speech. In 1965, both chambers of Congress overwhelmingly voted for a law to make the wilful destruction or mutilation of a military draft card a criminal offence. In *United States v. O'Brien* (391 US 367 (1968)), the Supreme Court upheld a conviction under this legislation, ruling that such a law could override First Amendment rights so long as it furthered a 'substantial governmental interest'. Chief Justice Earl Warren said the government had such an interest in requiring individuals to be in possession of their draft cards at all times. The judges ruled that the law had only an incidental effect on free speech, and declined to examine the actual congressional purpose, despite evidence that it was indeed to suppress anti-war opinion (Stone 2004: 474–7). That ruling opened the door to a prosecution for conspiracy to advocate draft resistance. Four men, including the famous paediatrician Dr Benjamin Spock, were sentenced to two years' jail in the Boston Five conspiracy trial, although their convictions were later overturned by a federal appeals court on technical grounds (*United States v. Spock* 416 F2d 165 (1st Cir 1969), Stone 2004: 477–82).

A series of other conspiracy trials were later directed against anti-war activists, but the prosecutions failed because of lack of evidence, unlawful government surveillance or reversal on appeal. Politically, these cases backfired because they gave invaluable publicity and moral authority to the defendants (Stone 2004: 482–3). Similarly, the most prominent conspiracy trial, against the leaders of the demonstrations outside the 1968 Chicago Democratic Convention, transformed the defendants into national celebrities. Ultimately, sentences of up to nine years in jail for inciting a riot were overturned by the court of appeals because the 'deprecatory and often antagonistic attitude' of the trial judge had prevented a fair trial (Stone 2004: 483–7).

Throughout the Vietnam War, the FBI ran an expanded illegal counter-intelligence program (COINTELPRO) that went beyond surveillance to active political harassment, infiltration, disruption, provocations, smear campaigns and frame-ups. Originally directed against the Communist Party in the 1950s, COINTELPRO was extended to the Trotskyist Socialist Workers Party, civil rights organisations and, prodded by the Johnson administration, the anti-war movement. The FBI's operation was accompanied by equally unlawful domestic operations by the CIA, in blatant violation of its legislative charter, which expressly forbid it from undertaking any 'internal security' role, by Army intelligence, which mobilised 1,500 undercover agents to collect information on groups seeking significant change in the US, and by the National Security Agency. According to a subsequent Senate committee report, the FBI alone compiled more than half a million domestic intelligence files (Stone 2004: 488–500).

The Supreme Court, however, effectively gave a green light to these activities. In *Laird v. Tatum* (408 US 1 (1972)), the court, while invoking a principle against 'military intrusion into civilian affairs', ruled that the plaintiffs, who suspected they had been placed under Army intelligence surveillance, lacked standing to challenge the infringement of their freedom of expression. The court found that they had not shown any direct injury and that mere knowledge of military investigative activity fell short of a 'chilling' of their First Amendment free speech rights. In what amounted to a 'Catch-22' situation, the judges refused to order the military to stop collecting information about civilians unless plaintiffs could prove that they had been harmed by what the military was doing. On this basis, the court declined to rule on the constitutionality of Army domestic intelligence activity (Stone 2004: 499, fn 311). This decision established a far-reaching precedent, as was seen 20 years later when a US District Court, in *New Alliance Party v. Federal Bureau of Investigations* (858 F Supp (SD NY 1994)), issued a similar ruling to strike down a challenge to FBI surveillance activities (Stone 2004: 499, fn 311).

Despite this record, Stone argues that the courts, including the Supreme Court, played a critical role in ensuring there was no wholesale effort to stifle dissent through criminal prosecutions during the Vietnam War, unlike 1798, 1861, 1917,

1941 and 1951. At the same time, he admits that throughout the Vietnam War era, the government relied much more than in the past on indirect and surreptitious means of quelling opposition. He also concedes that one reason for the lesser use of criminal prosecutions was the unpopularity of the war, which drove two presidents from office (Stone 2004: 499–500). In other words, it was the strength of the anti-government movement, rather than the law or the courts, that prevented greater resort to repressive prosecutions.

Even so, in 1971 the Nixon administration invoked the Espionage Act of 1917 to attempt to stop the release of the Pentagon Papers. It filed an injunction alleging that by publishing an initial article disclosing previously secret contents of the leaked documents, the *Washington Post* had violated the Espionage Act by wilfully communicating information 'it knew or had reason to believe ... could be used to the injury of the United States ... to persons not entitled to receive such information' (Stone 2004: 507).

The Pentagon Papers, which had been handed to the media by former Defense Department and Rand Corporation researcher, Daniel Ellsberg, contained a damning historical review of America's involvement in Vietnam since 1945. The documents showed that successive US governments had repeatedly lied to the American people, carried out secret illegal operations in Vietnam, militarily intervened on blatantly false pretences and killed tens of thousands of Vietnamese civilians. The papers demonstrated that Washington had consistently violated international law and committed the most serious war crimes. A 47-volume study, commissioned in 1967 by Secretary of State Robert McNamara, documented, for example, that at the end of World War II, President Truman had rejected urgent appeals from Vietnamese leader Ho Chi Minh for US assistance; that while the 1954 Geneva peace conference was in session, the US was planning paramilitary operations against the North; that President Kennedy's 'advisers' in Vietnam had participated directly in military operations; that the US government had knowingly publicised false South Vietnamese intelligence reports about the extent of Communist infiltration; that the Gulf of Tonkin resolution that officially justified US military intervention had falsely accused the North of attacking a US warship; and the US government had concealed from the American public the fact that extensive bombing of North Vietnam had done little to impair the North's military capacity but had killed tens of thousands of civilians (Stone 2004: 500).

By the time that the Nixon administration's injunction was considered by the Supreme Court, some 20 newspapers had published material from the Pentagon Papers (Stone 2004: 508). In that context, the court ruled 6 to 3 that the government had not met the 'heavy burden of showing justification' for a prior restraint on the press. One member of the majority, Justice Byron White, warned that the ruling did not mean that a criminal prosecution for publishing information that endangered national security would necessarily also be unconstitutional (Stone 2004: 511). In the meantime, Ellsberg and an associate, Anthony Russo, were indicted on a range of charges, including conspiracy to violate the Espionage Act of 1917, carrying possible total sentences of 125 years in prison. These charges were never put to the test, however. Two years later, they were dismissed as a result of the Watergate burglary – White House-organised 'plumbers' had broken into the offices of Ellsberg's psychiatrist in an effort to obtain information to smear Ellsberg and the anti-war movement in the media. In 1973, the trial judge ruled that the 'unprecedented' government misconduct had 'incurably infected the prosecution of this case' (Stone 2004: 515).

In a series of cases during the latter phases of the Vietnam War, from 1969 onward, the Supreme Court upheld First Amendment free speech rights in circumstances involving relatively minor expressions of anti-war protest. These included high school students wearing black armbands (*Tinker v. Des Moines Independent Communist School District*, 393 US 503 (1969)), actors wearing a US military uniform in a theatrical production (*Schacht v. United States*, 398 US 58 (1970)), a protestor disrespectfully displaying a small replica of the American flag (*Smith v. Goguen*, 415 US 566 (1974)) and an anti-war resident displaying a US flag with a peace symbol attached (*Spence v. Washington*, 418 US 405 (1974)).

Similar judgements were also handed down in two cases that were closer to the issue of subversive advocacy. In *Bond v. Floyd* (385 US 116 (1966)), the court unanimously held that the Georgia House of Representatives could not constitutionally refuse to seat a duly elected representative because he had endorsed statements criticising the war and conscription. Although the statements had opposed the draft and 'supported' those who refused to serve, they stopped short of express advocacy of law violation. The landmark decision is said to be that in *Brandenburg v. Ohio* (395 US 444 (1969)). However, this was not an anti-war case, but one involving the prosecution of a Ku Klux Klansman for threatening racial violence. The relevant Ohio statute made it unlawful to advocate sabotage, violence or terrorism to achieve industrial or political change. In order to invalidate the Ohio law, and acquit the Klansman, the court revisited all its prior decisions about subversive advocacy and finally, unambiguously adopted the Holmes-Brandeis version of the 'clear and present danger' test.

As a result of the *Bond* and *Brandenburg* rulings, the Supreme Court's approach seemed to permit the punishment of subversive advocacy if three conditions were met: there must be express advocacy of law violation, a call for immediate law violation, and the immediate violation must be likely to occur (Stone 2004: 523). Nevertheless, scholars have warned against any reliance on this degree of tolerance in the face of a perceived serious challenge to the security of the United States. As one constitutional lawyer noted, 'just about every time the country has felt seriously threatened the First Amendment has retreated' (Lee Bollinger cited in Stone 2004: 523). Looking back, in World War I the Supreme Court enunciated the 'clear and present danger' test but interpreted it in a manner that upheld the convictions of those who protested the war. In subsequent decades too, successive benches of the court likewise expressed regret at earlier repressive rulings, but nonetheless upheld the convictions of those regarded as contemporary threats. Judge Richard Posner observed that 'when the country feels very safe the Justices ... can ... plume themselves on their fearless devotion to freedom of speech' but 'they are likely to change their tune when next the country feels endangered' (Stone 2004: 524). The historical record also demonstrates that once one method of silencing dissent proves unsuccessful – such as prosecutions for espionage or sedition – governments turn to other means, including surveillance, harassment, disruption and secrecy.

The 'War on Terrorism'

That record was again in evidence in the wake of the terrorist attacks in the United States on 11 September, 2001. As noted in the Introduction, there is much evidence and many good reasons to doubt the official verdict of 9/11, which quickly became the trigger for previously-prepared plans to invade Afghanistan and Iraq. Domestically, the Bush administration swiftly moved to assert far-reaching powers and introduce draconian legislation that, in the name of protecting ordinary people against terrorism, violated basic civil liberties.

According to one summary, the measures included indefinite detention, with no access to judicial review, of more than a thousand non-citizens who were lawfully in the US and had not been charged with any crime; blanket secrecy concerning the identity of these detainees; refusal to permit many of these detainees to communicate with an attorney; an unprecedented assertion of authority to eavesdrop on constitutionally-protected attorney-client communications; secret deportation proceedings; the incarceration of an American citizen, incommunicado, with no access to a lawyer, solely on the basis of an executive determination that he was an 'enemy combatant'; new limitations on the Freedom of Information Act; expanded authority to conduct undercover infiltration and surveillance of political and religious groups; increased power to wiretap, engage in electronic eavesdropping, and covertly review Internet and email communications; new powers to secretly review financial records; and expanded authority to conduct clandestine property searches (Stone 2004: 552).

To that list must be added the USA PATRIOT Act, which 'smuggled into law several investigative practices that have nothing to do with fighting terrorism, but that law enforcement officials had for years tried unsuccessfully to persuade Congress to authorise' (Stone 2004: 553). Perhaps most egregious of all was the indefinite detention, without trial, of hundreds, if not thousands, of foreign citizens in military camps at Guantánamo Bay and elsewhere, including secret locations in allied countries, where detainees were 'rendered' for torture. These detainees were designated 'enemy combatants', an arbitrary classification that violates the Geneva Conventions, and subjected to brutalities that made a mockery of the international Convention Against Torture (Sands 2006: 143–223).

In addition, the limited guidelines promulgated in 1976 – after the exposure of the COINTELPRO and other programs in violation of the First Amendment – restricting the FBI's authority to investigate political and religious activities, were effectively dismantled. The FBI was authorised to monitor a wide range of constitutionally protected activities without having to show that any unlawful conduct might be afoot. Anti-war demonstrators were soon targeted, together with what the FBI termed 'anarchists' and 'extremist elements' (Stone 2004: 555–6).

While all these measures were ostensibly aimed at terrorists, or would-be terrorists, they set in place mechanisms for wider use in suppressing dissent, as well as defining terrorism in terms that can extend to many traditional forms of anti-government sentiment and activity. The pattern was a familiar one. Stone comments:

> [A]s in past episodes, the Bush administration may have seriously misled the American people in order to heighten the public's insecurity and build support for escalating the war. Just as the Federalists exaggerated the risk of a French invasion in 1798 to justify a military buildup, and Lyndon Johnson exaggerated the events surrounding the Tonkin Gulf incident in order to justify a more aggressive strategy in Vietnam, George Bush exaggerated the evidence that Saddam Hussein had weapons of mass destruction in order to justify his invasion of Iraq. (Stone 2004: 555)

It must be said that more than exaggeration was involved in the fabrications that provided the pretexts for the Vietnam and Iraq wars. It must also be said that Bush's successor, Barack Obama, maintained the US military presence in Iraq, Afghanistan and Pakistan on the equally false pretences of fighting terrorism, and retained all the essential features of the domestic war against basic legal and democratic rights.

Moreover, the Supreme Court has again proven no fundamental obstacle. In 2008, just as it did in 1973 in *Laird v. Tatum*, the court refused to hear an appeal brought by the American Civil Liberties Union and other groups challenging the Bush administration's warrantless domestic wiretapping program, conducted by the National Security Agency (NSA), a military agency (ACLU 2008). The wiretapping program began in 2001 but was first revealed to the public through a media leak in 2005. The program, the full details of which are still not known, included domestic spying in breach of the Foreign Intelligence Surveillance Act (FISA).

In 2006, a US District Court judge had ruled that the program violated the First and Fourth Amendments, the separation of powers and FISA. When that ruling in *ACLU v. NSA* was overturned on appeal, the challengers were caught in another 'Catch-22' situation. The government refused to identify the individuals targeted by the NSA program, on the grounds that this information was secret. However, the appellate court upheld the government's argument that only those who could prove they had been specifically targeted by the program could have standing to sue. The Supreme Court rejected a further appeal without comment.

In 2004, the Supreme Court, by a 6–3 majority, ruled that Guantánamo Bay detainees could seek writs of habeas corpus in US courts. The majority judgement, delivered by Stevens J, suggested that at stake were democratic conceptions dating back nearly 800 years to the Magna Carta of 1215 (*Rasul v. Bush*; *Al Odah v. United States,* 542 US 466 (2004)). Nevertheless, no detainees were released as a direct result of the decision. Four years later, in *Boumediene v. Bush* (553

US 723 (2008)), the Supreme Court ruled 5–4 that Guantánamo detainees could immediately file habeas corpus petitions in US district courts challenging the legality of their confinement. Most had been held at the US naval base under brutal conditions, often enduring solitary confinement, water-boarding and other coercive techniques or torture, for more than six years, without having the merits of their cases reviewed by a court of law. However, the ruling did not question the executive branch's ability to declare someone an 'enemy combatant', a power the Supreme Court had upheld four years earlier in *Hamdi v. Rumsfeld* (542 US 507 (2004)).

Later in 2008, a 5-to-4 decision by the US Court of Appeals for the 4th Circuit backed the Bush administration's contention that the President has such power. In *Al-Marri v. Pucciarelli* (4th Cir. July 15, 2008), the court effectively overturned a decision reached by a three-judge panel of the same court in 2007, which compared the assumption of such sweeping powers to military rule and the oppression of the American colonies by King George III. The appellate ruling denied habeas corpus to Al-Marri, a legal resident of the US, before the White House declared him an enemy combatant in 2003 and ordered the military to detain him in a Navy brig in South Carolina. The government claimed that the Authorization to Use Military Force (AUMF) resolution passed by Congress in 2002 gave the president the power to carry out such detentions. Alternately, it asserted that the Commander in Chief has unchallengeable authority to imprison anyone without charges for the duration of a global war on terror.

Lest it be thought that the post-9/11 practices were simply the product of the Bush administration or the Republican Party, it must be noted that little changed after the advent of the Obama Democratic administration in 2009. While the terminology of the 'war on terror' was initially modified, the substance remained. For example, in 2010, the Obama administration and Congress extended the USA PATRIOT Act unamended. This continuity was maintained under conditions of the global financial crisis that erupted to the surface in 2008. The greatest economic breakdown since the Great Depression of the 1930s soon produced severe unemployment, budgetary and fiscal crises at federal, state and local levels and substantial discontent. Once more, in line with the recurring pattern seen in US history, 'wartime' and 'exceptional' measures that can target serious political dissent have been retained.

Chapter 3
Insurrection, Rebellion and Unlawful Associations

This right of revolution has been and is a part of the fabric of our institutions. (Justice Douglas in *Scales v. United States*, 367 US 203, 269 (1961))

Of course, the constituted authority has the right of self-preservation. (Justice Douglas in *Scales v. United States*, 367 US 203, 270 (1961)).

Arguably, the most essential crimes against the state are those specifically directed at protecting the political establishment from individuals or organisations seeking to overthrow the current order, or the socio-economic system underpinning it. Historically, however, social revolutions have played an indispensable role in human progress. Revolutions were needed to end absolutism and feudalism. It took the English Civil War of the 1640s and the overthrow of the absolutist monarchy, which was ultimately sealed by the 'Glorious Revolution' of 1688–9, to clear the path for the rise of British capitalism. That revolution was accompanied by legal and political theories that recognised the right to overthrow a dictatorial or abusive regime. Notably, John Locke, a seminal figure in Western political and legal philosophy, declared a right to rebellion against a tyrannical government, or one that had violated the people's trust (Freeman 2001: 114–5).

The American Revolution of 1776 was necessary for the formation of the United States, which was to replace the United Kingdom as the ascendant capitalist power in the twentieth century. Reflecting its purposes, the American Declaration of Independence proclaimed the right of revolution to secure the 'inalienable' rights to life, liberty and the pursuit of happiness:

> whenever any Form of Government becomes destructive of these Ends, it is the Right of the People to alter or abolish it, and to institute new Government, laying its Foundation on such Principles, and organizing its Powers in such Form, as to them shall seem most likely to effect their Safety and Happiness.

Indeed, that declaration stated that revolution can become the *duty* of the people, insisting that 'when a long train of abuses and usurpations, pursuing invariably the same Object evinces a design to reduce them under absolute Despotism, it is their right, it is their duty, to throw off such Government'.

Nonetheless, over time, the new states created by these social revolutions increasingly adopted legal measures designed to suppress any further or future such overturns. In particular, the emergence of the industrial working class and its struggles for political and social emancipation produced laws and powers designed to answer the perceived threat from below. These measures have been especially directed against socialists, above all revolutionary Marxists who strive for a further social revolution. Such revolutions are arguably needed to liberate humanity from the wars, inequality and irrationality of the capitalist private profit system. This author has argued elsewhere that the October 1917 Bolshevik-led revolution in Russia did, despite the subsequent Stalinist degeneration, demonstrate the possibility of a truly democratic, egalitarian and participatory polity and society (Head 2007b, Head 2010).

The range of offences invoked to combat social revolutions includes many of those examined in subsequent chapters, such as treason, mutiny and sedition. As previously noted, none of the crimes against the state can be assessed in isolation, and their application often involves defendants being prosecuted for a variety of offences. Before turning to this broader range of offences, it is essential to focus on the crimes that directly and specifically target revolutionaries or would-be revolutionaries. This chapter therefore reviews the various measures enacted or adopted against those involved in preparing or attempting revolutions, insurrections or rebellions. It also considers 'unlawful associations' and similar provisions designed to outlaw political or industrial organisations that are regarded as inherently subversive.

The Right to Revolution

Does there remain, politically or legally, a right to revolution? That question substantially exceeds the remit of this book, but some of the most influential thinkers throughout English-derived political history have accepted such a fundamental right, with varying degrees of amplitude.

The right may be traced back to the 1215 Magna Carta, which required the English king to renounce certain rights and accept that his will could be bound by the law. It included a 'security clause' that gave the right to a committee of barons to overrule the will of the king through force if needed. In that period, of course, the right of revolt was reserved for barons, members of the feudal aristocracy. By the seventeenthcentury, the century of the English Revolution, the right had become associated with broader layers of the population, primarily through doctrines of social contract.

Even Thomas Hobbes, who wrote his principal work, *Leviathan*, in 1651, in reaction against the civil war and Cromwellian revolution in Britain, postulated that the obligation to obey ceases when the sovereign fails to maintain the peace and order that is the fundamental term of the social contract. Then the individual right of self-defence could abrogate the duty of obedience owed to the ruler (Freeman 2001: 111–12).

Hobbes was writing after the execution of a king, the establishment of a parliamentary dictatorship and the emergence of radical egalitarian tendencies such as the Levellers and Diggers. Hobbes argued that the proper purpose of government and law was primarily to guarantee peace and order. Otherwise, in a time of war, he famously wrote, 'the life of man is solitary, poor, nasty, brutish and short' (Freeman 2001: 147). One of his two basic principles was that everyone should strive for peace but may resort to self-defence when the endeavour proves impossible. Despite his bleak and authoritarian view of humanity, his writing contained the germs of a concept of natural rights (Freeman 2001: 111–12).

Whereas Hobbes was the theorist of the post-Cromwell Restoration, John Locke provided the theoretical underpinning for the 1688 'Glorious Revolution' in which the parliament and the emergent capitalist class re-established their supremacy by overthrowing James II and replacing him with Protestants, William II and Mary II of Orange. Locke's rationale for the Settlement between the monarchy and the parliament had two key planks: (1) the rejection of any 'absolute' power in favour of a limited sovereign, and (2) all individuals had 'natural rights' to life, health, liberty and property.

If these principles were transgressed, 'the people have the right to resume their original liberty'. In some cases, Locke deemed revolution an obligation, as a safeguard against tyranny. Although he proclaimed a right of revolution, however, he was not an enemy of political authority. He postulated the existence of 'tacit and scarce consent' as well as express consent (Freeman 2001: 114–15). Merely by remaining within a state, people tacitly consented to obey its laws because they benefited from the actions of its sovereign. Locke declared that to disturb government was also to breach the law of nature – it could only be justified when the sovereign had betrayed this trust.

At the same time, Locke helped forge the necessary ideological weapons for the emergence of a new capitalist society. One of the most important battles in the development of capitalism was the establishment of *exclusive* property rights, above all in land, over the common property rights which had played such a central role in the lives of the peasantry under feudalism. This new form of property had to establish itself against the conception that land should be held in common and its fruits available to all. The forms of property, based on exclusion, which are considered as emanating from human nature today, were once regarded as so 'unnatural' that they had to be argued for. Locke could be characterised as the advocate of propertied revolution. By insisting on the inviolability of property against tyranny, his was the classic bourgeois outlook. This notion found its way into judicial judgements. Take, for example, the remark of Pratt CJ in *Entinck v. Carrington* ((1765) 19 How St Tr 1029) that: 'The great end for which men entered into society was to secure their property.'

Nevertheless, Locke's conception of property was more complex than simply privately held assets. It included the right to the fruits of one's own labour. He deplored the growth of inequality and espoused a right to physical subsistence, even where it cut across property rights. Locke argued that if a man insisted on the market price for food for a man dying of hunger, he was guilty of murder (Freeman 2001: 116–17).

Even as late as the 1760s, on the eve of the American and French revolutions, William Blackstone's *Commentaries on the Laws of England* stated that English law included 'the law of redress against public oppression' (Blackstone 2001: I: 238). Like the right of revolution, this constitutional law of redress justified the people resisting the sovereign, and arose from a contract between the people and the king to preserve the public welfare.

The law of redress, as with the right of revolution, was not an individual right. It belonged to the community as a whole, as one of the parties to the original constitutional contract. It was not a means of first resort, or response to trivial or casual errors of government. Blackstone's *Commentaries* suggested that using the law of redress would be 'extraordinary'. for example if the king broke the original contract, violated 'the fundamental laws' or abandoned the kingdom (Blackstone 2001: I: 243 and 238).

In his *Commentaries*, Blackstone appealed to natural law to sanctify the English common law. For this, Jeremy Bentham, one of the founders of legal positivism, denounced Blackstone because the natural law doctrine tends to legitimise, and even encourage people to rise up against laws they opposed. Natural law, Bentham insisted, was 'nonsense on stilts'. In his *A Fragment on Government,* he wrote: '[T]he natural tendency of such doctrine is to impel a man, by the force of conscience, to rise up in arms against any law whatever that he happens not to like' (Bentham 1967: ch.4, para. 19). This was written in 1776, the year of the American Revolution, and 13 years before the French Revolution, which confirmed Bentham's fears.

By their very origins – arising out of revolutions themselves – post-revolutionary societies and legal systems have an inbuilt contradiction. They cannot easily renounce the right to revolution that they have just exercised, but they inevitably seek to defend themselves against counter-revolution, and future revolutions. This can be seen acutely in the evolution of the concept following the American Revolution. Justice Douglas, in his dissenting judgement, cited at the beginning of this chapter, in *Scales v. United States,* quoted an 1848 address by Abraham Lincoln before the US House of Representatives, where Lincoln stated:

> Any people anywhere, being inclined and having the power, have the *right* to rise up, and shake off the existing government, and form a new one that suits them better. This is a most valuable – a most sacred right – a right, which we hope and believe, is to liberate the world.

Douglas, however, immediately commented: 'Of course, government can move against those who take up arms against it. Of course, the constituted authority has the right of self-preservation' (*Scales v. United States* at 269–70). In an appendix to his judgement, Douglas noted that the constitutions of 15 states of the United States had, at one time or another, made specific provision for the right of revolution by reserving to the people the right to 'alter, reform or abolish' the existing frame of government, and some 24 other states had adopted slightly varying forms of the same provision. He added that the older constitutions often added a clause that showed the roots of these provisions in the right of revolution:

> The doctrine of nonresistance against arbitrary power and oppression is absurd, slavish, and destructive of the good and happiness of mankind. (*Scales v. United States* at 276–8)

Douglas disassociated himself from the following language in the Supreme Court decision in *Dennis v. United States* (341 US 494, 501), which suggested that the right to revolution only applied where no official mechanism existed for political change:

> Whatever theoretical merit there may be to the argument that there is a 'right' to rebellion against dictatorial governments is without force where the existing structure of the government provides for peaceful and orderly change.

Citing a Pennsylvania state court decision (*Wells v. Bain,* 75 Pa St 39), Douglas argued that the right of revolution had always meant more than this. The state court had acknowledged three recognised modes by which the whole people, the state, can give their consent to an alteration of an existing lawful frame of government, viz.:

> 1. The mode provided in the existing constitution.
>
> 2. A law, as the instrumental process of raising the body for revision and conveying to it the powers of the people.
>
> 3. A revolution.
>
> The first two are peaceful means through which the consent of the people to alteration is obtained, and by which the existing government consents to be displaced without revolution. The government gives its consent, either by pursuing the mode provided in the constitution or by passing a law to call a convention. If consent be not so given by the existing government, the remedy of the people is in the third mode – revolution. (*Scales v. United States* at 276–8)

Thus, Douglas upheld the right to rise up, even in defiance of official procedures for 'peaceful and orderly change'. However, he emphasised that this does not mean the helplessness of the established government in the face of armed resistance, 'for that government has the duty of maintaining existing institutions'. Even so, Douglas maintained that the right of revolution is ultimately reserved to the people themselves, 'whatever formal, but useless, remedies the existing government may offer'. He concluded that while legislatures and governments have the right to protect themselves, and may judge as to the appropriate means of meeting force directed against them, the propriety of the exercise of the ultimate right of revolution, remained the prerogative of the population. 'As John Locke says, "The people shall be judge." (*Second Treatise on Civil Government* § 240)' (*Scales v. United States* at 276–8).

As reviewed in Chapter 2, these propositions seek to distinguish between advocacy of the abstract right to revolution, which is arguably protected by the American constitution, and actually engaging in, or even urging, revolution. In effect, the US Constitution, while it may recognise a 'right' to revolution, also recognises the 'right' and 'duty' of governments to put down actual rebellions. As we shall see, the same kind of prohibition on attempting a physical overthrow of the existing order is contained in all the English-derived legal systems.

In a study of the idea of rule by the people in the American Revolution and in early post-revolutionary America, legal historian Christian Fritz argues that the logic of a revolution that would erect a government by the people, not a king, also served to 'impl[y] the irrelevance of a right of revolution' in post-revolutionary America:

> This did not develop instantly or uniformly after the establishment of American governments. Some of the first state constitutions included 'alter or abolish' provisions that mirrored the traditional right of revolution ... Increasingly, as Americans included it in their constitutions, the right of revolution came to be seen as a constitutional principle permitting the people as the sovereign to control government and revise their constitutions without limit. In this way, the right broke loose from its traditional moorings of resistance to oppression. The alter or abolish provisions could now be interpreted consistent with the constitutional principle that in America, the sovereign was the people. (Fritz 2008: 24–5)

This argument is predicated on the questionable assumption that the American polity became, and has remained, truly democratic, with the people as sovereign. Socialists have pointed out that the US political system has effectively become a plutocracy, governed by the wealthy, for the wealthy. By 2001, the richest 1 per cent of the population controlled 33 per cent of the national wealth. One Marxist writer commented: 'The concentration of political power in the hands of the two bourgeois parties complements the concentration of national wealth in the very small social strata that constitute the American ruling elite' (North 2004: 80, 84).

International law offers no more effective protection of the right to overthrow a government. Far from recognising any right to revolution, the third paragraph in the preamble to the Universal Declaration of Human Rights states that the upholding of the human rights enunciated in the declaration provide an alternative to revolution: 'Whereas it is essential, if man is not to be compelled to have recourse, as a last resort, to rebellion against tyranny and oppression, that human rights should be protected by the rule of law'.

'Revolutionary Legality' and Necessity

There is a related question. Over the past few centuries, the courts have developed the doctrines of revolutionary legality and necessity to distinguish between 'successful' revolutions that become new legal orders and those that fail or are regarded as illegitimate. It is also far beyond the scope of this book to explore these doctrines, let alone their applications over the years, but a brief examination is needed, given the diametrically opposite legal results that can ensue, depending on whether a revolution succeeds, and is thus deemed lawful, or not.

Unsurprisingly, the doctrine of revolution was primarily shaped by the English and American revolutions of the seventeenth and eighteenth centuries. In these revolutions, the British and American courts recognised the legitimacy of the victorious side and generally sanctioned acts done in the name of their revolutions, dating back to the dates on which their rebellions commenced (see *Mokotso* [1989] LRC (Const) 24, 96). These revolutions were fundamentally progressive eruptions, breaking up the old feudal-monarchical forms of rule and signalling the rise to ascendancy of the emerging capitalist classes.

During the second half of the twentieth century, however, the doctrine of revolution was utilised to justify anti-democratic, military-backed coups, at least so long as the new regime accommodated the interests of British and global capital. Much of this modern history draws upon a 1951 parliamentary speech by the British Secretary of State for Foreign Affairs, Herbert Morrison, setting out the practice of the British Government in deciding whether to recognise the outcome of a coup d'état (United Kingdom, 1951). The speech, cited in the leading House of Lords decision (*Carl-Zeiss Stiftung v. Rayner & Keeler Ltd (No 2)* [1966] 2 All ER 536, 548) stipulates that a new regime must have 'effective control' over most of the state's territory, where that control 'seems likely to continue' and is 'firmly established'.

This approach has been used to uphold the legality of various military or military-backed coups, including those in Pakistan (1958), Uganda (1966), Lesotho (1986 and 1989), the Seychelles (1977) and Grenada (1979) (Head 2001: 545). In Pakistan, the Supreme Court has validated successive alternations between civilian rule and military coups, including the October 1999 coup by General Pervez Musharraf (Head 2001: 545). For example, in a 1958 case, Chief Justice Munir stated:

> If the revolution is victorious in the sense that the persons assuming power under the change can successfully require the inhabitants of the country to conform to the new regime, then the revolution itself becomes a law-creating fact because thereafter its own legality is judged not by reference to the annulled Constitution but by reference to its own success. (*State v. Dosso* ([1958] 2 PLD SC (Pak) 533)

Little regard was paid to democratic rights in these cases. In the 1989 Lesotho case of *Mokotso*, after exhaustively reviewing the authorities, Chief Justice Cullinan concluded that a military coup was legal because,

> [i]f the judge is satisfied that the new regime is firmly established and there is no opposition thereto, and that the people are acting by and large in conformity with the new legal order, signifying their acceptance thereof, for whatever reason, I

> do not see that the judge can hold that regime to be other than legitimate ... If
> the people ultimately acquiesce, then the new regime is entitled to recognition
> by the courts. (*Mokotso* [1989] LRC (Const) 24, 131–3)

By contrast, where the usurpation of power cut across Britain's strategic interests, as happened when Rhodesia's Ian Smith unilaterally declared independence from Britain in 1965, the Privy Council judges ruled that the regime failed the test of 'successful revolution'. They insisted that Britain remained the lawful power, ready and willing to resume control over Rhodesia, a stance backed by British economic and diplomatic sanctions designed to bring Smith to the bargaining table (*Madzimbamuto v. Lardner-Burke* [1969] 1 AC 645, 725, 722–3, 725).

In most post-World War II cases on coups d'état, the courts made reference to the 'principle of effectiveness' enunciated by Austrian legal philosopher Hans Kelsen in his work *General Theory of Law and State* (Kelsen 1946: 118–19). In essence, Kelsen's theory justified the seizure of power by force. Quoting his writings, judges ruled that coups did not need to command 'universal adherence', simply 'a minimum of support'. Kelsen applied a purely legal positivist approach to revolutions, arguing that a successful revolution creates its own legitimacy (Kelsen 1946: 117–19, 220).

To justify his entire theoretical framework, Kelsen postulated the existence of a 'basic norm' or Grundnorm which formed the foundation of the legal order of a nation. Kelsen's concept of the basic norm was vague – it could be a written constitution or an unwritten principle of government. But if such a Grundnorm is overthrown by a successful revolution, then a new Grundnorm is established that forms the foundation of all subsequent law. Thus, 'a national legal order begins to be valid as soon as it has become – on the whole – efficacious; and it ceases to be valid as soon as it loses this efficacy' (Kelsen 1946: 220). By this effectiveness doctrine, if a revolutionary government is successful enough to destroy the existing Grundnorm and put its own legal order into effect, then it becomes the de jure government. This applies no matter what the motivation of the revolutionary government was in seizing power, or whether its rule can be considered just or unjust according to conventional standards of morality. Ironically, Kelsen developed this amoral theory in an attempt to devise a 'pure theory of law', devoid of all the moral, ethical, political and sociological factors that Kelsen considered 'impure'.

Courts that have adopted Kelsen's principle of effectiveness have generally required proof of two elements. First, the revolution must be successful. It must be in unchallenged control of the country with no pre-existing legitimate government contending for power. Second, it must be effective, in that it commands the obedience of the bulk of the population (Edelstein 2002: 61). Even where judges expressed concern about the authoritarian conclusions of Kelsen's principle, they ultimately drew similar conclusions. In the 1989 Lesotho case, Chief Justice Cullinan denied any requirement for a usurping regime to prove popular acceptance, stating:

Throughout the course of history there have been regimes, indeed dynasties, holding sway for many years, indeed centuries, whose rule could not be said by any manner of means to be popular and could even be described as oppressive; but who is going to say that a new legal order was not created with their coming and going? (*Mokotso* [1989] LRC (Const) 24, 130)

The Privy Council made a similar observation in the Rhodesian case:

It is an historical fact that in many countries – and indeed in many countries which are or have been under British Sovereignty – there are now régimes which are universally recognised as lawful but which derive their origins from revolutions or coups d'état. The law must take account of that fact. (*Madzimbamuto* [1969] 1 AC 645, 724)

Likewise, the doctrine of necessity – the history of which can also be traced back to the British and American revolutions of the seventeenth and eighteenth centuries – has predominantly become a means of justifying the suspension of legal rights. Most of the early cases on necessity arose from the American Civil War, in which the northern industrialists defeated the secessionist southern governments based on a slave-owning form of capitalism.

The US Supreme Court upheld the legality of measures taken by the southern states to maintain order and economic life, even though these governments were engaged in rebellion against the US Government. In 1868, the Court declared that

acts necessary to peace and good order among citizens ... which would be valid if emanating from a lawful government, must be regarded in general as valid when proceeding from an actual, though unlawful government. (*Texas v. White* (1868) 7 Wallace 700, 733)

These acts therefore had to be obeyed, even if they infringed the US Constitution.

In 1969, in the Rhodesian case, the Privy Council applied this doctrine to rule on the legality of the Smith regime's indefinite detention of political opponents under emergency powers. With Lord Pearce dissenting, a majority of the Court held the detention invalid – but only on the ground that Britain remained the only legal authority. In principle, the law lords were prepared to sanction the use of emergency powers to override democratic rights, observing that '[u]nder pressure of necessity the lawful Sovereign and his forces may be justified in taking action which infringes the ordinary rights of his subjects' (*Madzimbamuto* [1969] 1 AC 645, 721–2, 726, 731).

Some scholars have argued that, since the 1970s, numbers of courts have expressed discomfort at Kelsen's separation of law and justice. One commentator drew attention to a 1986 Grenada Court of Appeal ruling, where the court stated:

> ... the Court called upon to decide the question [of the legality of a coup] should take into consideration both the reason why the old constitutional government was overthrown and the nature and character of the new legal order. Was the motivation mere power grabbing or was it a rebellion for example against oppression or corruption or ineptitude? And is the new legal order a just one? (*Mitchell v. Director of Public Prosecutions* [1986] LRC (Const) 35, 67)

The author mentioned that the decision followed the US invasion of Grenada (Edelstein 2002: 62). However, he failed to explain that the court was upholding the legality of the regime that was installed by that invasion, which overthrew the nationalist New Jewel movement. This context suggests that overthrow of an existing order is more likely to be legalised by a court if the outcome accords with the strategic objectives of the US or another major power.

A similar point must be made about the 2001 ruling of the Fiji Court of Appeal in the *Prasad* case (*Republic of Fiji v. Prasad* [2001] FJCA 1), which the same writer contended represents 'a fusion of the indestructible Grundnorm with Western democratic thought'. According to this view, the court rejected Kelsen's theories in unequivocal terms, noting that they 'might too readily reward a usurper' (Edelstein 2002: 64). Likewise, another scholar argued that Prasad was a 'legal landmark' that would 'make it extremely difficult for a tyrannical regime which violates basic human rights recognised at international law to gain judicial recognition' (Williams 2001: 149–50).

It is certainly true that the court declared that a military-appointed Interim Government failed to establish that it was the legal government. It ruled that the 1997 Fijian Constitution remained the supreme law of the country and had not been lawfully abrogated by the military commander, Commodore Frank Bainimarama, when he effectively took power in 2000. In reality, however, the judgement in *Prasad* does not substantiate the claims made above. Rather, the court left the way open for the military's administration to remain in office, at least until it re-organised itself by conducting stage-managed elections. Moreover, the judges rejected the argument that a usurping regime must be judged by its acceptance of international human rights obligations and declined to require observance of democratic norms.

Arguably, the most significant new criterion suggested by the court was acceptance of a new regime by the 'international community' which, in the context, referred to the stance taken by major Western nations, notably Australia, New Zealand, Britain and the United States. The judgement may have set an international precedent for assessing repressive military regimes and their actions — but a precedent that will primarily assist the major powers to impose their requirements with the assistance of local elites, not one that will defend the democratic rights of ordinary people (Head 2001: 535–49).

Prosecutions for Insurrection and Rebellion

Britain

The great trials arising out of the English Civil War illustrate the intensely political character of prosecutions of participants in revolutions and counter-revolutions. Placing Charles I on trial raised innumerable legal problems, not least rewriting the law of treason to prosecute the monarch (Robertson 2005: 135–50). Nevertheless, having conducted a revolutionary war for seven years and defeated the king on the battlefield, the forces of parliament were not deterred by legal niceties. The 1649 indictment, headed 'A Charge of High Treason and Other High Crimes' and drafted by prosecutor John Cooke, impeached Charles Stuart as a 'tyrant, traitor, murderer and a public and implacable enemy to the Commonwealth of England'. It charged that he had 'traitorously and maliciously levied war against the present parliament and the people therein represented'. Charles was held responsible for 'insurrections within this land' and 'invasions from foreign parts'. He was 'the occasioner, author and continuer of the said unnatural, cruel and bloody wars, and therein guilty of all the treasons, murders, rapines, burning, spoils, desolations, damages and mischiefs to this nation' (Robertson 2005: 148–9). When Charles refused to plead to the charge and objected that the 70 judges empanelled to try him lacked any power to do so, his claim was simply overruled (Robertson 2005: 152–9).

Even so, the trial, conviction and execution of Charles was a model of moderation and due process compared to the trials of the 'regicides'. John Cooke, who had prosecuted the king, and the others were summarily tried, convicted and hung drawn and quartered by the restored British monarchy in 1660 for their part in the 1649 trial. The regicide trials were carefully choreographed, from the rigging of the jury to the rigging of the law. The handpicked judges advised the prosecutors not to charge the defendants with murdering the King, because not all were directly involved. Instead, the charge was treason by 'compassing and imagining' the King's death, which meant no more than doing or saying something that might lead to regicide. The ancient rule that treason had to be established by overt acts, each proved by sworn testimony from two witnesses, was swept aside. The rules of evidence were discarded. Legal representation was denied – on the grounds that it would be treasonous for a barrister to argue that the King had been tried by a legitimate government. Pleas that the court lacked jurisdiction over acts commissioned by parliament were quickly dismissed. The grand jury was instructed that 'the King can do no wrong: that is a rule of law' (Robertson 2005: 295). The jurors were warned that if they refused to indict the men guilty of shedding the King's blood they would themselves be guilty of treason (Robertson 2005: 296). Parliamentary privilege was overturned so that MPs could be executed for words spoken in the House of Commons (Robertson 2005: 306).

Overall, Geoffrey Robertson's account of the despotic and barbaric retribution inflicted on Cooke and his colleagues is chilling. It illustrates the violent methods that historically-doomed regimes are capable of unleashing (Robertson 2005: 291–338).

Another regicide trial was that of Daniel Axtell in 1660. Axtell, the Commander of the Guard at the trial of Charles I, sought to defend himself under the long-standing principle of English law that obedience to the 'King for the time being' was not treason. The court, however, held that 'this defence did not avail one who served a *de facto* government that was not monarchical' (Williams 1961: 298).

Other notable British trials, such as that of Thomas Paine for proselytising in favour of the French Revolution, and of communists accused of seeking to follow the example of the 1917 Russian Revolution, are considered in other chapters.

United States

Two explicit US provisions outlawing revolution are the Smith Act, now codified as 'advocating overthrow of government' in 18 USC 2385, and the accompanying 18 USC 2383, headed 'rebellion or insurrection'. The former, first enacted in 1940, on the eve of the American entry into World War II, provides:

> Whoever knowingly or willfully advocates, abets, advises, or teaches the duty, necessity, desirability, or propriety of overthrowing or destroying the government of the United States or the government of any State, Territory, District or Possession thereof, or the government of any political subdivision therein, by force or violence, or by the assassination of any officer of any such government; or

> Whoever, with intent to cause the overthrow or destruction of any such government, prints, publishes, edits, issues, circulates, sells, distributes, or publicly displays any written or printed matter advocating, advising, or teaching the duty, necessity, desirability, or propriety of overthrowing or destroying any government in the United States by force or violence, or attempts to do so; or

> Whoever organizes or helps or attempts to organize any society, group, or assembly of persons who teach, advocate, or encourage the overthrow or destruction of any such government by force or violence; or becomes or is a member of, or affiliates with, any such society, group, or assembly of persons, knowing the purposes thereof—

> Shall be fined under this title or imprisoned not more than twenty years, or both, and shall be ineligible for employment by the United States or any department or agency thereof, for the five years next following his conviction.

> If two or more persons conspire to commit any offense named in this section, each shall be fined under this title or imprisoned not more than twenty years,

or both, and shall be ineligible for employment by the United States or any department or agency thereof, for the five years next following his conviction.

As used in this section, the terms 'organizes' and 'organize', with respect to any society, group, or assembly of persons, include the recruiting of new members, the forming of new units, and the regrouping or expansion of existing clubs, classes, and other units of such society, group, or assembly of persons.

§ 2383 on 'Rebellion or insurrection' states:

Whoever incites, sets on foot, assists, or engages in any rebellion or insurrection against the authority of the United States or the laws thereof, or gives aid or comfort thereto, shall be fined under this title or imprisoned not more than ten years, or both; and shall be incapable of holding any office under the United States.

On their face, these provisions are sweeping, and leave extraordinary scope for a government to prosecute political opponents of the existing order, far beyond those engaged in actual revolution or insurrection. In essence, the statutes permit persecution of the mere espousal of ideas. The words 'advocates, abets, advises, teaches, incites and assists' and the terms 'desirability or propriety' are capable of extending the offences to those who assert or defend the right of revolution itself. The measures relating to dissemination and organising further widen the net. How to reconcile this breadth with the American Revolution's declaration of the right to revolution and with the US Constitution's First Amendment, which upholds freedom of speech? As discussed in Chapter 2, the US Supreme Court has placed some constitutional limits on the use of these measures, but its rulings nevertheless leave substantial room for governments to engage in outright political persecution.

Originally also known as the Alien Registration Act in 1940, the Smith Act required all non-citizen adult residents to register with the government; within four months, 4,741,971 aliens had registered under the Act's provisions. The statute, first used to prosecute the Socialist Workers Party (SWP), the American Trotskyist party, became a vehicle for a concerted wave of cases against the pro-Moscow Communist Party in the 1940s and 1950s. Prosecutions continued until Supreme Court decisions in 1957 made them more difficult, but the court upheld a major conviction in 1961, and the statute remains on the books.

The focus of twentieth century American governments on suppressing revolutionary Marxism in periods of upheaval is illustrated by the World War II prosecution of the SWP. On 27 June 1941, FBI agents raided the SWP's St. Paul-Minneapolis offices and seized large quantities of literature and party documents. Less than three weeks later, on 15 July, a federal grand jury indicted 28 members of the SWP, including national secretary James P. Cannon and virtually all the party leaders in Minneapolis, on two counts. The first count, based on the 1861 Sedition Act, charged that the defendants conspired 'to overthrow, put down and to destroy by force the Government of the United States of America, and to oppose by force the authority thereof ... The defendants would seek to bring about, whenever the time seemed propitious, an armed revolution ...'

The second count, based on the Smith Act, charged the defendants with advocating the overthrow of the government by force and violence and urging insubordination in the armed forces. They were charged, among other things, with 'conspiracy to *advocate* the overthrow of the government by force and violence' (North 1998: 55).

During the trial, which began in the Federal District Court in Minneapolis on 27 October 1941, the prosecution was unable to produce any proof of conspiracy. Its 'evidence' consisted mainly of public statements by the party and its leaders, as well as the *Communist Manifesto* by Marx and Engels and writings by Vladimir Lenin and Leon Trotsky. The evidence regarding insubordination of the armed forces consisted of oral testimony by two government witnesses to the effect that one or two defendants had told them that soldiers should be induced to 'kick' (complain) about food and living conditions.

After 56 hours of deliberation, the jury found the 23 defendants then remaining not guilty on the first count and five were found not guilty on the second count also. It found 18 defendants guilty on the second but added a recommendation for leniency. Twelve of the defendants received 16-month sentences and the rest 12-month terms. The 18 convicted Trotskyists included Albert Goldman, the SWP's lawyer who conducted the courtroom defence. The appeals of the defendants were eventually denied, with the Supreme Court refusing to hear an ultimate appeal (North 1998: 56).

At the trial, Cannon denied the government's charges, which effectively threatened the illegalisation of the SWP, and defended the party's opposition to the world war and its program for socialist revolution. His testimony was published in the pamphlet *Socialism on Trial,* which became a basic text of the Trotskyist Fourth International. It provided a guide to the movement's stance of exposing the war as an inter-imperialist one, while calling for the unity of the working class of all sides to defeat fascism and militarism and overthrow the capitalist system responsible for the conflagration. Cannon explained the SWP's trial strategy as follows:

> Naturally, we decided to utilise to the fullest extent each and every legal protection, technicality and resource available to us under the law and the Constitution. A party leadership hesitating or neglecting to do this would frivolously jeopardise the legality of the party and show a very wasteful attitude indeed toward party cadres. Such a leadership would deserve only to be driven out with sticks and stones.

> On the other hand, we planned to conduct our defence in court not as a 'criminal' defence but as a propaganda offensive. Without foolishly disregarding or provoking the jury or needlessly helping the prosecutor, it was our aim to use

the courtroom as a forum to popularise the principles of our movement. We saw in this second proposition our main duty and opportunity and never for a moment intended to let purely legalistic considerations take precedence over it. Therefore we sternly rejected the repeated advice of attorneys—some who assisted Goldman in the trial of the case as well as others who were consulted about participation—to eliminate or play down our 'propaganda' program and leave the defence policy to the lawyers. (Cannon 1999, Part V)

Throughout the trial, the SWP insisted that its activities consisted of preparing the working class for revolutionary struggle through propaganda and agitation. Applying a classic Marxist analysis of the root causes of social revolutions, it denied that the SWP artificially fomented discontent or created disorder. Cannon testified:

The real revolutionary factors, the real powers that are driving for socialism, are the contradictions within the capitalist system itself. All that our agitation can do is to try to foresee theoretically what is possible and what is probable in the line of social revolution, to prepare people's minds for it, to convince them of the desirability of it, to try to organize them to accelerate it and to bring it about in the most economical and effective way. That is all agitation can do. (North 1998: 59)

In response to the questions of the government prosecutor, Cannon defended the anti-war line of the SWP as follows:

Q: And you will seek to utilize war, during the war, to destroy the present form of government, will you not?

A: Well, that is no secret, that we want to change this form of government.

Q: And you look forward, do you not, to the forthcoming war as the time when you may be able to accomplish that?

A: Yes, I think the forthcoming war will unquestionably weaken the imperialist governments in all countries.

Q: You said, I believe, that you will not support the war? You do not believe in national defense at all, do you?

A: Not in imperialist countries, no.

Q: I am speaking of this country.

A: I believe 100 per cent in defending this country by our own means, but I do not believe in defending the imperialist governments of the world —

Q: I am speaking about the government of the United States as it is now constitutionally constituted. You do not believe in defending that, do you?

A: Not in a political sense, no.

Q: You do not believe in defending it in any sense, do you?

A: I explained the other day, that if the majority of the people decide on war, and participate in the war, our people and the people under our influence will also participate in the war. We do not sabotage the war, we do not obstruct it, but we continue to propagate our ideas, calling for a cessation of the war and calling for a change in government. (North 1998: 71)

When the SWP refused to be silenced despite the jailing of its main leaders, the Roosevelt administration moved to block the distribution of the party's newspaper, *Militant*, through the post office by revoking its second-class mailing rights. In a letter dated 28 December 1942, addressed to the Postmaster General, the Attorney General of the United States, Francis Biddle, explained the reasons for his punitive action:

Since December 7, 1941 this publication has openly discouraged participation in the war by the masses of the people. It is permeated with the thesis that the war is being fought solely for the benefit of the ruling groups and will serve merely to continue the enslavement of the working classes. It is urged that this war is only an imperialistic clash for spoils at the expense of the lives and living standards of the people who should, therefore, not support it. The lines in the publication also include derision of democracy and the 'four freedoms' as hypocritical shams, anti-British attacks, charges of Fascist collaboration by the United States, stimulation of race issues and other material deemed divisionary in character and appearing to be calculated to engender opposition to the war effort as well as to interfere with the morale of the armed forces. I am enclosing a memorandum consisting solely of excerpts taken from *The Militant* since December 7, 1941.

I suggest that you may wish to consider the issuance of an order to show cause why *The Militant* should not be denied the second-class mailing privilege. In this connection you will recall that in previous cases I called your attention to Section 3 of Title I of the Espionage Act of 1917 and to the decision of the United States Supreme Court in the case of *Milwaukee Publishing Company* v. *Burleson*, 255 US 407 (1921), upholding the right of the Postmaster General to suspend or revoke the second-class mailing privilege of a publication which, over a period of time, consistently publishes seditious matter. This department offers you its complete cooperation in any action which you may deem advisable. (North 1998; 83–5).

In other words, the Roosevelt administration acted on the premise that it was seditious to oppose the war and point to the material class interests motivating it. Political advocacy, seeking to convince a majority of people of the inevitable need for a new social revolution in America to overcome the root causes of imperialist war, was equally intolerable.

The pro-Kremlin Communist Party supported the trial and conviction of Trotskyists under the Smith Act; however, its leaders were to face a wave of similar prosecutions from 1949, during the Cold War (see Chapter 2). Although the wave of prosecutions ended in the early 1960s, as argued in Chapter 2, the leading Supreme Court cases in *Yates* (1957) and *Scales* (1961) provide considerable scope for 'advocating the overthrow of government' charges against anyone perceived to be a threat to the political order during periods of upheaval. In *Scales*, as noted in the quotations given at the start of the current chapter, even Justice Douglas, one the two dissentients, emphasised that a government could 'move against those who take up arms against it' (367 US 270).

Australia

The only trials for actual rebellion conducted in Australia arose from the Eureka Stockade of 1854. One legal study of the Eureka trials summed up the result as follows:

> Thirteen rebel diggers were prosecuted for treason. All were acquitted by stalwart juries who refused to be intimidated by a government – supported by the judiciary – intent upon securing convictions. (Fricke 1997: 59)

The trials were the culmination of a miners' rebellion on the goldfields of the Ballarat region in the then British colony of Victoria, which was met with bloody repression that resulted in the deaths of 28 people (including 6 soldiers). It was the most significant conflict in the colonial history of Australia and remains the only armed uprising since the early convict rebellions. The miners, drawn to the country from all over the world by the gold rush, had erected a stockade and armed themselves. They were objecting to heavily priced mining items, the expense of a miner's licence, taxation (via the licence) without political representation and the actions of the government, the police and military (Molony 1989).

When the soldiers and police, numbering 288, including 176 infantry and 100 cavalry, made their attack, the stockade was defended by about 120 miners. The battle was brief and brutal. There was no reading of the Riot Act, or call for surrender. After 10 minutes of sustained firing, there was hand-to-hand fighting around the stockade with miners shot, bayoneted and gouged by sabres. When the rebels were overcome, a bloodbath occurred. Police and troops went on a rampage, bayoneting the wounded, burning tents and shooting at non-combatants. Twenty-four miners were killed, about half of them after the fortification had been overrun and their Southern Cross flag pulled down. An official inquiry later concluded that mounted police made a 'needless as well as ruthless sacrifice of human life indiscriminative of innocent or guilty, and after all resistance had disappeared'. A picture of brutal killing of some of the rebels emerges from various reports (Fricke 1997: 61, Clark 1978: 78–9).

The first trial relating to the rebellion was a charge of sedition against Henry Seekamp, editor of the *Ballarat Times*. He had, in the weeks before the Stockade, printed a series of allegedly inflammatory articles. The day before the bloody attack, his paper carried the following:

> Instead therefore of the diggers looking for remedies where none can be found let them strike deep at the root of rottenness and reform the Chief Government. What if we lop off the branches from an unwholesome trunk. Only unwholesome branches can spring. We must undermine the tree and burn it off. The voice of the people must be raised for a free and British constitution and their wishes enforced by the strongest means. (Brief for the Prosecution 1854)

Seekamp was tried and convicted of seditious libel by a Melbourne jury and, after a series of appeals, sentenced to six months' imprisonment. However, he was released from prison three months early.

Of the approximately 120 miners detained after the rebellion, 13 were tried for high treason, an offence that carried the death penalty (for the law of treason, see Chapter 4). The cases against all the others were dismissed due to lack of evidence. Fearing that Ballarat juries might acquit, the authorities decided to conduct the trials in Melbourne (Fricke 1997: 61). Before the individual trials commenced, the prisoners were placed at the bar, and a summary of the charges against them was read:

> Prisoners at the bar, the charge against you in the first count of the information to which you are now called to plead is, that you did, on the 3rd December, 1854 (being at the time armed in a warlike manner), traitorously assemble together against our Lady the Queen; and that you did, whilst so armed and assembled together, levy and make war against our said Lady the Queen, within that part of her dominions called Victoria, and attempt by force of arms to destroy the Government constituted there and by law established, and to depose our Lady the Queen from the kingly name and her Imperial Crown.
>
> In the second count you are charged with having made war, as in the first count mentioned, and with attempting at the same time to compel by force our said Lady the Queen to change her measures and counsels.

In the third count the charge against you is, that having devised and intended to deprive our said Lady the Queen of the kingly name of the Imperial Crown in Victoria, you did express and evince such treasonable intention by the four following overt acts:

Ist That you raised upon a pole, and collected round a certain standard, and did solemnly swear to defend each other, with the intention of levying war against our said Lady the Queen.

2nd That being armed with divers offensive weapons, you collected together and formed troops and bands under distinct leaders, and were drilled and trained in military exercise, to prepare for fighting against the soldiers and other loyal subjects of the Queen.

3rd That you collected and provided arms and ammunition, and erected divers fences and stockades, in order to levy war against our said Lady the Queen.

4th That being armed and arrayed in a warlike manner, you fired upon, fought with, wounded, and killed divers of the said soldiers and other subjects then fighting in behalf of our said Lady the Queen, contrary to duty and allegiance. In the fourth count the charge against you is, that [you did] levy war against the Queen, in order to compel her by force and constraint her measures and counsels, you did express and evince such treasonable and divers acts, which overt acts are four in number, and the same as those described in the third count. (Public Record Office 2003)

All 13 pled not guilty. The first to stand trial was John Joseph, a black American from New York City, one of three Americans arrested at the stockade. The prosecution was handled by Attorney General William Stawell before Chief Justice William à Beckett. In his argument, the Attorney General emphasised what he considered to be the heinous nature of the offences and their wider implications for the newly formed colony. He argued that 'if men were allowed to organize such a conspiracy as this, there is no saying how many wrong-headed men, acting with zeal – but misguided zeal – might be led into the commission of the most dreadful crimes and outrages'. He defined treason as 'an insurrection, and that insurrection must be accompanied with force – it must be not merely the outburst of a moment, but must have been planned and arranged by previous concert; and the conspiracy must be with a general object' (Public Record Office 2003).

A general overview of the events leading up to the stockade in Ballarat was then described to the court. The Attorney General made particular reference to the drilling of diggers, and the oath taken by them to fight for their rights and liberties under the flag of the Southern Cross. John Joseph, it was argued, had been seen 'distinctly' in the stockade while the battle was occurring, armed with a double-barrelled gun. One witness, Stawell argued, had seen Joseph firing this gun in the direction of Captain Wise, who later died from wounds incurred at the stockade. Witnesses also testified to Joseph being drilled on the days leading up to the battle. The Attorney General concluded with the summation that the evidence presented would be enough to convict the prisoner on all counts (Public Record Office 2003).

The defence counsel attacked the quality and reliability of the identification evidence, having regard to the early hour of the day, the distances, the poor opportunities for making observations and the witnesses' lack of familiarity with his client. He denied that the mental element of the offence had existed, arguing that Joseph had not sought to overthrow the monarchy or British rule, or even to challenge the government's measures as a whole. He asked the jury, 'do you suppose that there was any intention in his mind to induce Her Majesty to change her measures?' (Fricke 1997: 64–5).

In his directions to the jury, Chief Justice à Beckett denounced many 'erroneous principles' advanced by the defence and insisted that the authorities had a duty to suppress meetings that caused alarm to the neighbourhood and which manifested an intention to commit acts of violence. He said the prisoner's intentions could be inferred from his acts in attending meetings and being present at the stockade. The Chief Justice declared there was 'no doubt' about the identification evidence. He effectively reversed the onus of proof by stating that it rested upon the prisoners to show that he was not present at the stockade for a treasonous object. In what one scholar called 'an attempt at theological intimidation', à Beckett exhorted the jury to 'think only of Him on whose Gospel you are sworn to give a true verdict'. (This became a theme of the Eureka trials, with another judge Redmond Barry later warning a jury that the 'eye of Heaven' was upon their deliberations (Fricke 1997: 65–6, 68–9).)

Within half an hour, however, the jury returned a not guilty verdict, with the courtroom audience erupting in wild cheering. The Chief Justice reacted by sentencing two members of the public to a week's imprisonment for contempt of court (Fricke 1997: 66). John Joseph was carried around the streets of Melbourne in a chair in triumph by over 10,000 people – a substantial crowd for a town with a population of 100,000.

There was a similar result in the second trial, that of John Manning, who claimed to be the author of some of the 'seditious' material in the *Ballarat Times*. The 'State Trials', as they were commonly labelled in newspapers, were then suspended while jury lists were redrawn, a 'gross perversion of justice revealing the fixity of purpose of the Governor and his judiciary'. Lieutenant Governor Hotham reported to England that the trials did not bring about the outcome he had sought. There was widespread resentment throughout the Victorian community, with even the *Argus* joining in the condemnation (Molony 1989: 183–5).

The empanelling of new juries backfired. Despite trials conducted with 'unseemly haste' (11 trials in less than 10 sitting days) and with 'disquieting' features prejudicial to the prisoners, juries rapidly acquitted each of the other 11 accused men (Fricke 1997: 67–9). With each not guilty verdict announced the courtroom erupted into celebration, much to the chagrin of the Attorney General and Justice Barry, the presiding judge (Molony 1989). After three months in prison, the men were released. Historian Stuart Macintyre summarised the outcome:

> Juries in Melbourne refused to convict the leaders put on trial for high treason; a royal commission condemned the goldfields administration; the miners' grievances were remedied and even their demands for political representation were soon conceded. (Macintyre 1999: 90)

A study of the cases by Graham Fricke, a former judge, concluded that 'there seems little doubt that the outcomes would have been very different if the question of guilt had been left to the judiciary' (Fricke 1997: 69). Fricke used the trials to argue that the jury system, which has been under attack, served especially well in 'turbulent times, when the establishment and popular viewpoints have diverged' and the trials 'demonstrate the system's capacity to defuse conflict' (Fricke 1997: 59).

A different conclusion should be drawn. Both the bloody suppression of the Eureka Stockade and the ensuing Eureka Trials demonstrate the lengths to which the political and legal establishment, including the police, military and the judiciary, will go to put down and punish rebels. For all the myths of an independent legal system and judiciary, the prosecutions were directed by the government and vigorously pursued by the judges, trampling over basic legal principles in the process. That the juries refused to be browbeaten is clearly related to the groundswell of popular hostility triggered by the Eureka massacre and the blatantly vindictive treatment of the survivors, including the politically loaded character of the trials. Ultimately, the establishment settled the conflict by making political and economic concessions, as Macintyre indicates. During that period, the burgeoning wealth of the young colony, based on the gold discoveries, the rich pastoral lands seized from the Aboriginal population and the raw material needs of industrial Britain, made such concessions possible. But once the class struggle re-emerged, during the industrial strikes of the 1890s and the battles over conscription in World War I, the same repressive tendencies reappeared, as seen in the 1916 frame-up of International Workers of the World members in the 'Sydney Twelve' case, discussed in Chapter 4.

Unlawful Associations

Another means of punishing subversion is via legislation proscribing, or permitting the government to proscribe, organisations. Such measures may have the effect of automatically, or semi-automatically, criminalising members, supporters and financial donors of the banned organisations. Those proven to have such links become guilty of serious crimes, without being convicted of any substantive offence. This can mean de facto retrospective punishment for involvement with an organisation whose outlawed status is subsequently declared. This danger is heightened where legislation gives an executive government a general power to proscribe. Such measures have been adopted characteristically in periods of war and political crises, often designed to overcome legal or political problems in prosecuting targeted individuals for subversive conduct.

Since the declaration of the 'war on terror' in 2001, many governments involved, including those in the US, Britain and Australia, have adopted measures allowing executive governments to proscribe alleged terrorist organisations. Given the wide official definitions of terrorism, these powers could also be used against supposedly seditious political opponents. Those laws, and that issue, are explored in Chapter 6.

Legislation proscribing associations has long been used as a political tool. In the United Kingdom, the Combination Acts of 1799 and 1800 prohibited collective bargaining over wages or conditions by 'journeymen, manufacturers or other persons'. The rise of the working class, and the emergence of any form of workplace organisation, was regarded from the outset as a subversive threat. The Parliament led by William Pitt the Younger intended by these laws to put an end to any behaviour that might resemble the activities of the republicans during the French Revolution and thus lead to rioting and the holding of the government to ransom (Deane 1979). Any workman who entered into an agreement, written or unwritten, for the purpose of collective bargaining, or had a meeting for that purpose, or who tried to induce others to enter into 'a combination' (a group) for that purpose, was guilty of an offence the penalty for which, under the 1800 Act, was three months' imprisonment, or two months' imprisonment with hard labour.

However, the laws were ineffective to put an end to trade unions, merely serving to drive them underground. Recognising this, and that asserting that the laws had 'a tendency to ... give violent character to the combinations and to render them highly dangerous to the peace of the community' (Select Committee of the House of Commons 1824, quoted in Deane 1979: 161), the government repealed them in 1824. A new Combination Act was passed in 1825 that allowed labour unions to exist but narrowly defined their rights. The fact that such unions were now legal did not, however, protect the 'combination' that later became known as the Tolpuddle Martyrs. In 1834, a 1797 law against administering unlawful oaths was used to arrest and prosecute six men who two years earlier had founded the Friendly Society of Agricultural Labourers in Dorset in order to protest against the ongoing lowering of wages for agricultural workers. With the tacit approval of the Whig government, whose members feared a continuation of agricultural agitation, they were sentenced to transportation to Australia for seven years, but the public uproar that ensued resulted in pardons once they had suffered in the penal colony for several months (Deane 1979).

Over time, the trade unions became legally recognised and incorporated into the official mechanisms, such as arbitration tribunals, for restraining industrial action. Unlawful associations legislation did not reappear in Britain during the twentieth century. Rather, as reviewed in Chapter 1, use was made of other provisions, such as sedition, mutiny and unlawful assembly. Following the 1917

Russian Revolution, more than a dozen communists were imprisoned during the 1920s and 1930s, accompanied by raids and property seizures directed against the Communist Party. Some countries with English-derived legal institutions, including India and Burma (Myanmar) do retain unlawful associations legislation.

Australia

Despite calls for their repeal by official inquiries in 1991 and 2006, Australia retained far-reaching unlawful associations provisions until 2010. Even so, they were essentially replaced by executive powers to outlaw groups as 'terrorist organisations' (examined in Chapter 7). According to the official memorandum of the National Security Legislation Amendment Bill 2010, the old provisions were 'no longer relevant in the current security environment, and offences within the Criminal Code relating to terrorist organisations adequately address associating with a terrorist organisation'.

The old powers had been contained in 16 sections gathered together in Part IIA of the Crimes Act 1914 (Cth), under the heading, 'Protection of the Constitution and other services'. The origins of these measures went back to World War I and the 1917 Russian Revolution, when similar provisions were adopted as part of a wider government campaign against militant syndicalists, and anti-war and anti-conscription activists (Turner 1969: 69–70, 86–9). In their ultimate form they were inserted in 1926, apparently in response to federal government concerns about radical trade unionism, the rise of communism and the potential for revolutionary socialist activity (Douglas 2001: 259). A 2005 amendment added a definition of 'seditious intention' as part of a revamp of sedition law in the name of combatting terrorism via the Anti-Terrorism Act (No 2) 2005 (Cth).

Section 30A of the Crimes Act automatically declared the following to be unlawful associations:

(a) any body of persons, incorporated or unincorporated, which by its constitution or propaganda or otherwise advocates or encourages:

(i) the overthrow of the Constitution of the Commonwealth by revolution or sabotage;

(ii) the overthrow by force or violence of the established government of the Commonwealth or of a State or of any other civilized country or of organized government; or

(iii) the destruction or injury of property of the Commonwealth or of property used in trade or commerce with other countries or among the States;

or which is, or purports to be, affiliated with any organization which advocates or encourages any of the doctrines or practices specified in this paragraph;

(b) any body of persons, incorporated or unincorporated, which by its constitution or propaganda or otherwise advocates or encourages the doing of any act having or purporting to have as an object the carrying out of a seditious intention (see subsection (3)).

(2) Any branch or committee of an unlawful association, and any institution or school conducted by or under the authority or apparent authority of an unlawful association, shall, for all the purposes of this Act, be deemed to be an unlawful association.

(3) In this section:

seditious intention means an intention to use force or violence to effect any of the following purposes:

(a) to bring the Sovereign into hatred or contempt;

(b) to urge disaffection against the following:

  (i)   the Constitution;

  (ii) the Government of the Commonwealth;

  (iii) either House of the Parliament;

(c) to urge another person to attempt to procure a change, otherwise than by lawful means, to any matter established by law of the Commonwealth;

(d) to promote feelings of ill-will or hostility between different groups so as to threaten the peace, order and good government of the Commonwealth.

Alternatively, under section 30A(IA) a body was deemed to be unlawful if so declared by the Full Court of the Federal Court, following an application by the Attorney General pursuant to section 30AA. That section set out a procedure for nominated organisations to be required to show cause, 'to the satisfaction of the Court', why they should not be declared unlawful. In other words, the onus was placed on the organisation to prove that it was not unlawful. Thus, a body could be outlawed in two ways: it could be so declared by the Full Court, or it could be found by a court to be unlawful when someone was arrested and prosecuted for one of the various criminal offences created by Part IIA. These offences included:

- failure to provide information relating to an unlawful association upon the request of the Attorney-General;
- being an officer, member, representative or teacher of an unlawful association;
- giving money or goods to, or soliciting donations for, an unlawful association;
- printing, publishing or selling literature issued by an unlawful association;
- allowing meetings of an unlawful association to be held on property owned or controlled by a person.

Maximum jail terms for these offences ranged between six and twelve months. In addition, all goods and chattels belonging to an unlawful association, or held on its behalf, were to be forfeited. Moreover, executive members were disqualified from voting in federal elections for seven years. Proof of membership could consist of merely attending a meeting of the association, or speaking publicly in advocacy of it, or distributing its literature, unless there was proof to the contrary. Likewise, unless the defendant proved otherwise, literature that purported to be issued by, on behalf of, or in the interests of, the association was deemed to be issued by it (sections 30AB–30R).

Further offences were created for advocating or encouraging any of the political objects outlawed by section 30A, punishable by up to two years' imprisonment (section 30C), and for participating in or encouraging strikes, lockouts or boycotts, punishable by up to one year's jail (sections 30J–K). (The latter provisions, which interlocked with industrial relations laws, are beyond the scope of this book. Nonetheless, their inclusion in Part IIA was revealing of the perceived connection between industrial action and subversion. The two sections were adopted as a result of a 1925 seamen's strike and government fears of alleged revolutionary motives for industrial action (Douglas 2001: 260–1).)

Numerous issues were raised by the breadth and vagueness of these provisions. In a detailed examination of them, Douglas described the definition of unlawful association as both 'puzzling and difficult'. The 'seditious intention' criterion did not contain any defence of good faith, as some other Australian sedition offences did. Many other key terms were undefined. It was unclear whether 'overthrow by revolution' required violence. According to a typical dictionary definition, 'sabotage' could extend to laziness and disruptiveness on the job. Did 'advocate' and 'encourage' apply where no overthrow or revolution was imminent? Did anyone in the intended audience have to be actually encouraged? Did an alleged member have to know of the political stance that made the association unlawful? (Douglas 2001: 263–5).

Beyond the criticisms made by Douglas, further objections arose. 'Seditious intention' was defined so broadly (for example, 'promote feelings of ill-will' that threaten 'peace, order and good government') that it covered civil disobedience and protest marches (ALRC 2006: 90). Even where good faith arguments apply, sedition is a notoriously vague and value-laden concept (see Chapter 6). What was meant by 'other civilized government'? Would it be unlawful to encourage the overthrow of a dictatorship or undemocratically-installed government? 'Injury of property' was likewise unclear and could extend to minor damage. Serious criminal consequences flowed for members and supporters of unlawful associations. Yet the traditional criminal burden of proof – beyond a reasonable doubt – was effectively reversed by compelling a group to show cause why it should not be declared unlawful.

Despite these obvious flaws, Part IIA of the Crimes Act remained on the books for eight decades. Its repeal was recommended by the 1991 Gibbs Committee and the 2006 Australian Law Reform Commission's *Fighting Words* report (ALRC 2006: 89–98). The latter contended that the provisions were no longer needed because of the powers to proscribe terrorist organisations in the post-2001 counter-terrorism legislation (see Chapter 7). Only one prosecution had been mounted under the non-industrial provisions of Part IIA, in 1932, and that conviction was overturned on appeal (see below). Douglas suggested that attempts to enforce Part IIA would be likely to politically backfire and be difficult to prove (Douglas 2001: 294–7). Nevertheless, one can only conclude that governments retained Part

IIA for use in periods of political crisis, and that similar powers have since been introduced, in the name of combatting terrorism. Those conclusions are reinforced by the historical record.

That record dates back to 1916, when, following the convictions and jailing of International Workers of the World (IWW) members in the Sydney Twelve seditious conspiracy case (see Chapters 4 and 5), conservative voices called for the IWW itself to be outlawed. The *Sydney Morning Herald* declared there was strong public opinion favouring a ban. The issue was not the right to free speech of 'visionaries intent upon bringing in the millennium' but of incitement to anarchy and destruction. The newspaper said the demands of war made the task even more urgent, because IWW sedition was undermining the national solidarity needed to confront the enemy (Turner 1969: 69). Prime Minister Billy Hughes introduced an Unlawful Associations Bill, which provided that the IWW or any other association that incited the taking of life or the destruction of property was unlawful. Hughes declared that many IWW members were foreigners, including Germans, and the organisation 'holds a dagger at the heart of society'. The Bill was passed within five days, creating a summary offence, punishable by six months' imprisonment, to belong to such an association (Turner 1969: 70).

A year later – after IWW members had continued their activities under different organisational names – the Unlawful Associations Act 1916 (Cth) was amended to authorise the government to declare any organisation illegal whose purposes were proscribed by the Act. Six-month sentences were added for distributing an association's propaganda or raising or contributing funds (Turner 1969: 86). Within weeks, some 80 people had been jailed, substantially destroying the IWW. According to newspaper reports, the trials were conducted with 'indecent haste', with no opportunity for the accused to deny the allegations against them. In some cases, disdaining to conceal their membership, IWW members demanded the full six months' penalty (Turner 1969: 86–9).

In 1925, following a lengthy seamen's strike, the Bruce-Page government vowed to take vigorous action against Bolshevism and threats to law and order in general. The result was the current Part IIA of the Crimes Act. It was used to ban the postal transmission of allegedly communist-affiliated publications, and discourage the renting of meeting halls to communists. In 1928, Prime Minister Bruce boasted that, although no prosecutions had been conducted, the legislation had succeeded in its purpose because it had encouraged large numbers of people to leave unlawful associations (Douglas 2001: 270).

The sole judicial test of Part IIA of the Crimes Act came in *R v. Hush; Ex parte Devanny* ([1932] HCA 64, (1932) 48 CLR 487), which was, in effect, a bid to outlaw the Communist Party of Australia (CPA). Devanny, the publisher of the party's newspaper *Workers' Weekly*, was charged with soliciting contributions of money for an unlawful association. He was deemed to have solicited because the newspaper appealed for funds for the CPA. Only two members of the High Court addressed the substance of Part IIA, with the other four judges overturning Devanny's conviction by a magistrate on essentially technical grounds. The majority ruled that the prosecution's 61 paragraph-long averments, which judges described as 'an amazing document', were insufficient, by themselves, to sustain the conviction. (The averments were an apparent attempt to satisfy the requirements of a since-repealed section.)

Of the two judges who went further, Justice Starke insisted that the party's general references to Marxist concepts demonstrated that its objects were to overthrow the Constitution and existing structure of government. Dissenting from the majority decision, he emphatically rejected the defence that the party's literature merely peaceably prophesised the profound changes to be wrought by the adoption of the communist ideal. Justice Starke held that phrases such as 'transform the imperialist war of the capitalist class into civil war' and 'defend the colonial revolutions in India, China and all other colonies' and the adoption of the statutes of the Third International that called on workers to 'follow the same road as the great proletarian revolution in Russia' left no doubt that the magistrate was correct to convict Devanny. He was equally dismissive of constitutional objections, saying 'the survival of the Constitution' was clearly incidental to the federal legislative and executive powers.

Justice Evatt, who joined the majority, was the only judge to suggest that a distinction had to be drawn between advocacy of complete and radical social, economic and political change, and advocacy of the use of actual violence to secure that change. He doubted that Part IIA applied to 'far distant' threats of force and opined that its provisions were 'largely invalid' if they proposed to prevent 'all advocacy of Communism as against Capitalism'.

Douglas argues that the subsequent lack of enforcement of the legislation pointed to numbers of political and evidentiary problems involved in securing convictions (Douglas 2001: 283–97). Nevertheless, World War II wartime powers were invoked to ban communist organisations. The party was banned under the National Security (Subversive Associations) Regulations 1940, relying on the defence power in the Australian Constitution (see Chapters 4 and 9). Moreover, Communist Party leaders were put on trial for sedition in the early years of the Cold War (see Chapter 6), and a further move to ban the Communist Party was made in 1950–1.

In the Communist Party Case of 1951, the High Court ruled constitutionally invalid the Menzies government's attempt to self-define the federal defence power to justify its domestic peacetime use to ban the CPA (*Australian Communist Party v. The Commonwealth* [1951] HCA 51; (1951) 83 CLR 1). After winning the 1949 election in the wake of a major coal miners' strike, Prime Minister Menzies claimed a 'political mandate' to place Australia on a 'semi-war footing' against communism. Against a backdrop of Cold War anti-communism, the Communist Party Dissolution Act 1950 (Cth) was the incoming government's first piece of legislation. The Act's recitals claimed that its measures were required for the 'security and defence of Australia' in the face of a dire threat of violence, insurrection, treason, subversion, espionage and sabotage.

The 1950 Act's recitals summarised the case against the Communist Party by reference to its objectives and activities: it was said to engage in activities designed, in accordance with 'the basic theory of communism, as expounded by Marx and Lenin', to create a 'revolutionary situation' enabling it 'to seize power and establish a dictatorship of the proletariat'. To this end, it engaged in 'activities ... designed to ... overthrow ... the established system of government in Australia and the attainment of economic, industrial or political ends by force, ... intimidation or [fraud]...'

The Communist Party Dissolution Act went on to (1) declare the party unlawful, confiscating without compensation its property; (2) deal with 'affiliated organizations' by empowering the executive to declare them unlawful if satisfied that their existence was prejudicial to security and defence; (3) create an offence for a person knowingly to be an officer or member of an unlawful association and liable to 5 years imprisonment; and (4) prohibit persons declared to be a party member from being employed by a federal authority or holding office in a trade union declared by the executive to be 'vital to the security and defence of Australia'.

The High Court rejected the use of these recitals to validate the government's claim to be exercising the defence, incidental and executive power of the Commonwealth. Some judges warned of the corrosive dangers of unfettered executive power. Justice Dixon stated:

> History and not only ancient history, shows that in countries where democratic institutions have been unconstitutionally superseded, it has been done not seldom by those holding the executive power. Forms of government may need protection from dangers likely to arise from within the institutions to be protected. (83 CLR 1 at 187)

Menzies called a referendum to override the decision and was defeated, despite his efforts to whip up a red-baiting campaign in the context of the Cold War (Winterton 2003: 108–44). However, the principle in the Communist Party case, reinforced by the referendum defeat, was undermined in 2007. The High Court, in *Thomas v. Mowbray* ([2007] HCA 33), permitted the federal government to, in effect, self-define the defence power in order to impose a control order – a form of detention without trial – on a terrorist suspect. In dissent, Justice Kirby commented: 'I did not expect, during my service, I would see the *Communist Party Case* sidelined, minimised, doubted and even criticised and denigrated in this Court' ([2007] HCA 33, [386]). The extraordinary reasoning of the majority in *Thomas v. Mowbray*, and its implications for the 'war on terror' are discussed in Chapter 7.

In its 2006 report, one of the reasons the Australian Law Reform Commission gave for proposing the repeal of Part IIA of the Crimes Act was that it was unnecessary because of the powers to proscribe terrorist organisations under the same post-2001 counter-terrorism legislation. The report described those new powers as 'a more modern and appropriate way to deal with organisations that advocate politically motivated violence, rather than the outdated definitions found under Part IIA' (ALRC 2006: 98). That recommendation was acted upon four years later. In effect, measures continue to exist to outlaw organisations regarded as a threat to the political order (see Chapter 7 for an examination of the terrorism laws).

Canada

The politically repressive potential of unlawful associations laws was seen in Canada. In the aftermath of the 1917 Russian Revolution and the 1919 Winnipeg general strike, the Criminal Code was amended to provide that organisations that advocated the use of unlawful means to achieve political change became illegal organisations (Penner 1988: 118). The Canadian legislation, first adopted in 1919, resembled closely the 1926 Australian provisions, discussed above, except that their penalties were more draconian. Section 98 of the Criminal Code stated:

> Any association, organization, society or corporation whose professed purpose or one of whose professed purposes is to bring about any governmental, industrial, or economic change within Canada by use of force, violence or physical injury, or which teaches, advocates, advises or defends the use of force, violence, terrorism or physical injury to person or property, or threats of such injury, in order to accomplish such change, or for any other purpose, or which shall by any means prosecute or pursue such purpose or professed purpose, or shall so teach, advocate, advise or defend shall be an unlawful organization. Anyone convicted of being a member of, or defending such an organization or having its literature in his possession may suffer a penalty of twenty years imprisonment.

The law was used throughout the 1920s and early half of the 1930s to harass communists, other left parties and organisations, and labour unions generally (Berger 1981: 135). Police frequently broke up meetings, raided offices and confiscated literature. In 1931, the Canadian and Ontario police arrested eight leaders of the Communist Party, who were subsequently convicted and sentenced to up to five years in prison. The crux of the Crown's case was that the whole program and strategy of the party were based on the advocacy and defence of force and violence. The judge instructed the jury that no imminent likelihood of violence was necessary:

> I must instruct you that if you think force and violence a logical, natural result of their teachings, it is a matter of law that they are advocating, advising and defending force and violence for the overthrow of governmental and industrial Institutions. It is not a question of time, but a question of the intent and meaning of their teachings and documents. (Spector 1931)

All the party's property in Ontario was declared confiscated and prosecutors said up to 5,000 party members could be arrested. However, the severe sentences imposed on the party leaders assisted them to make political capital out of their trials (Penner 1988: 120–2). In the years after the conviction, public opinion turned against the law. As a result of public opposition, the communists were released early from jail and the law was repealed in 1936 (Penner 1988: 120). Nevertheless, the law of sedition was simultaneously reinforced. The unlawful associations also served as the model for the Defence of Canada Regulations under the War Measures Act, used to suppress aliens and dissenters during World War II and during the Quebec October Crisis of 1970 (Berger 1981: 135). (For a discussion of the emergency regulations see Chapter 8.)

Chapter 4
Treason and Mutiny

The offences examined in this chapter are often regarded as outdated, anachronistic and rarely-used. They are largely associated with the former days of the absolute monarchy in Britain or thought to be confined to war-time situations. These crimes are usually seen as punishing activities in support of a foreign enemy.

However, the historical record points to an opposed conclusion: these offences, the most serious of all in the common law and on the statute books, have generally been prosecuted when those in ruling circles have felt threatened by domestic political opponents in periods of intense social and political unrest. Notably, these episodes have included the struggles for democracy in response to the French Revolution, for voting rights during the Chartist movement, and for socialism during the massive killing and other horrors of World Wars I and II.

Much of the material in this chapter relates to these historical experiences. It would be short-sighted to conclude that such cases could not arise again. Rather, the pattern of resort to these prosecutions, and the arbitrary manner in which many cases were pursued, and often decided with scant regard for the niceties of the law, suggest that these offences, even if lying dormant for decades, are likely to feature in future times of economic and political upheaval. In at least one case, the 'war on terrorism' has already provided the context for a revival of the law of treason. In 2006, a United States federal grand jury issued the first indictment for treason against the US since 1952, charging American-born Adam Yahiye Gadahn, previously named Adam Pearlman, for aiding an enemy of the US by appearing in videos in which he spoke supportively of al-Qaeda. Gadahn, however, remained at large in an unknown location.

Relatively recent treason-related cases internationally include those of Mordechai Vanunu, imprisoned for revealing details of Israel's nuclear weapons program to the British press in 1986; George Speight, who was sentenced to life imprisonment as the principal instigator of the Fijian coup of 2000, in which 36 government ministers and officials were kidnapped and detained; and Abdullah Öcalan, the leader of the separatist Kurdistan Workers Party, who was imprisoned by the Turkish state in 1999.

Treason is regarded as one of the oldest political crimes, dating back to the English absolute monarchy. It is the offence that covers some of the more serious acts of betrayal of one's own sovereign or state. Historically, treason also covered the murder of specific social superiors, such as the murder of a husband by his wife (treason against the king was known as high treason and treason against a lesser superior was petit treason). The scope of the law of treason has varied throughout history, at times covering almost the entire criminal law (ALRC 2006: 49).

High treason has been regarded as the most serious offence of all. In 'early common law it was considered "high treason" to kill the king or promote a revolt in the kingdom' (Schmalleger 2002: 454). Those deemed traitors to the throne were likely to be publicly beheaded, and their head paraded through the streets of London. An estimated 1,500 people lost their lives that way (Ackroyd 2001).

Treason is regarded of such significance, and capable of such misuse, that it is the only crime specifically defined in the US Constitution (Article III). It is also defined by several federal statutes, while the law concerning sabotage and espionage has been declared in a variety of statutes, including the Espionage Act (1917), Smith Act (1940), McCarran Act (1950), Internal Security Act (1952) and Communist Control Act (1954), as well as state and local laws.

During wartime, the offences of treason, mutiny, espionage and sabotage often have been broadened and augmented by the adoption of extraordinary executive powers. During World War I, for instance, the British parliament passed the Defence of the Realm Acts (DORA) and in World War II, the Emergency Powers (Defence Act) (Ingraham 1979: 292–5). These statutes provided for the arbitrary detention of aliens, and citizens considered a threat to the war effort (see Chapter 9).

Treason

Britain

The British law of treason is statutory and has been so since the Treason Act 1351 (25 Edw. 3 St. 5 c. 2). The Act is written in Norman French, but is more commonly cited in its English translation. The legislation has been amended several times, and currently provides for four categories of treasonable offences, namely:

- 'when a man doth compass or imagine the death of our lord the King, or of our lady his Queen or of their eldest son and heir';
- 'if a man do violate the King's companion, or the King's eldest daughter unmarried, or the wife of the King's eldest son and heir';
- 'if a man do levy war against our lord the King in his realm, or be adherent to the King's enemies in his realm, giving to them aid and comfort in the realm, or elsewhere'; and
- 'if a man slea the chancellor, treasurer, or the King's justices of the one bench or the other, justices in eyre, or justices of assise, and all other justices assigned to hear and determine, being in their places, doing their offices'.

Another Act, the Treason Act 1702 (1 Anne stat. 2 c. 21), provides for a fifth category of treason, namely:

- 'if any person or persons ... shall endeavour to deprive or hinder any person who shall be the next in succession to the crown ... from succeeding after the decease of her Majesty (whom God long preserve) to the imperial crown of this realm and the dominions and territories thereunto belonging'.

The maximum penalty for treason was changed from death to life imprisonment in 1998 under the Crime and Disorder Act. Before 1998, the death penalty was mandatory, subject to the royal prerogative of mercy, despite the abolition of the death penalty for murder in 1965.

A revealing saga involving the law of high treason occurred in Britain in 1794. Amid the tumult produced by the French Revolution, the leaders of the reform societies in Britain were unsuccessfully placed on trial. Although the three charged with high treason were acquitted by juries in three separate trials, the verdicts cannot be seen as any guarantee of political liberty. Rather, the trials and the sedition trials that preceded them in 1792 and 1793 substantially served the government's purposes. Most of the men charged withdrew from active radical politics, as did many others fearful of government retribution (Thompson 1966: 137–8).

The treason trials were an extension of the sedition trials of 1792 and 1793 against parliamentary reformers in both England and Scotland (see Chapter 6). Over 30 radicals were initially arrested; three were tried for high treason: Thomas Hardy, John Horne Tooke and John Thelwall. Others included Samuel Adams, Jeremiah Joyce and Daniel Adams. There was jubilation when Hardy, Tooke and Thelwall were acquitted (Young 1976: 10). Young observes that the political agenda behind the trials was bound up with suppressing democratic dissent at home; not fear of a foreign invasion:

> Increasing social unrest, now taking the form of massive demonstrations and riots in the streets of London, did not help the English ruling class feel at ease. The immediate threat was not merely the possibility of armed invasion from revolutionary France, it was that the obnoxious democratic ideas of revolutionary France might penetrate from across the Channel. (Young 1976: 10)

Despite the jailing of Thomas Paine and other leading radical reformers for sedition for publishing anti-monarchy material, or perhaps because of the public outcry caused by their imprisonment, the radical societies enjoyed a surge in membership in 1793–4. Several societies decided to convene in Edinburgh to decide how to summon 'a great body of the people' to convince parliament to reform itself along democratic lines, since it did not seem willing to reform itself. William Pitt's government viewed this as an attempt to establish an anti-parliament. Three leaders of the convention were tried for sedition in Scotland and sentenced to 14 years' service at Botany Bay.

The harsh sentences caused such a political shock that some leaders of the societies spoke of an insurrection being necessary to resist the government (Barrell and Mee 2006: xxiv–xxv). The threat of an actual rebellion did not eventuate, but the government arrested more than 30 members of the societies on suspicion of 'treasonable practices' involving a conspiracy to convene a 'pretended general convention of the people, in contempt and defiance of the authority of parliament, and on principles subversive of the existing laws and constitution, and directly tending to the introduction of that system of anarchy and confusion which has fatally prevailed in France' (Barrell and Mee 2006: xxvii).

After the arrests, the government introduced a bill to suspend habeas corpus, allowing those arrested to be held without bail or charge. A parliamentary committee asserted that the radical societies had been planning to 'over-awe' the sovereign and parliament by the show of 'a great body of the people', if not to overthrow the government and install a French-style republic. The prisoners were eventually charged with an assortment of crimes, but seditious libel and treason were the most severe.

The government insisted that the radicals had committed a new kind of treason, a 'modern' or 'French' treason. While previous defendants had tried to replace one king with another from another dynasty, these democrats wanted to overthrow the entire monarchical system and remove the king entirely. 'Modern French treason, it seemed, was different from, was worse than, old-fashioned English treason' (Barrell and Mee 2006: xxxi). Unfortunately for the prosecution, the treason statute, which dated back to 1351, was ill-suited to this alleged new kind of treason. Two defendants, Hardy and Horne Took, were charged with engaging in a conspiracy to 'levy war against the king ... to subvert the constitution, to depose the King, and put him to death; and for that purpose, and *with Force and Arms* ... to excite insurrection and rebellion' (emphasis in original) (Barrell and Mee 2006: xxxi).

Those charged with treason faced hanging, drawing and quartering if convicted: each would have been 'hanged by the neck, cut down while still alive, disembowelled (and his entrails burned before his face) and then beheaded and quartered' (Thompson 1966: 19). In effect, the entire radical movement was on trial; there were supposedly 800 warrants ready to be executed if the government won its case (Thompson 1966: 137). At Hardy's trial, his counsel Thomas Erskine argued that the radicals had proposed reforms and a convention of delegates that had earlier been proposed by Pitt himself (Barrell and Mee 2006: xxxi–xxxii). After a nine-day trial, which was exceptionally long for the time, the jury acquitted Hardy, and a crowd enthusiastically carried him through the streets of London (Thompson 1966: 19).

Although all the three treason trial defendants were acquitted, the administration and the loyalists declared they were 'morally guilty' (Barrell and Mee 2006: xxxv). When, in October 1795, crowds threw refuse at the king and insulted him, demanding a cessation of the war with France and lower bread prices, parliament immediately passed the Seditious Meetings Act and the Treasonable Practices Act, known as the 'gagging acts'. Under these laws, it was almost impossible to have a public meeting and speech at such meetings was severely curtailed (Thompson 1966: 19). Despite their formal failure, the trials intimidated the radicals, nearly all of whom retreated from active politics (Thompson 1966: 19).

Moreover, to remedy the perceived gap that the failed treason trials revealed in its legal armoury, the Pitt government introduced an Incitement to Mutiny Bill to provide severe punishments, including the death penalty, for this crime, which

Pitt asserted 'exceeded the bounds of ordinary treason' (Young 1976: 11). The resulting Incitement to Mutiny Act is discussed below (in the section on mutiny).

During the twentieth century, treason laws were used against Irish insurgents in 1916. Roger Casement was hanged for negotiating with Germany to provide arms to Irish revolutionaries for use in the Irish Easter 1916 uprising. Participants in that revolt were shot by firing squad: Patrick Pearse, Thomas J. Clarke, Thomas MacDonagh, Joseph Mary Plunkett, Edward (Ned) Daly, William Pearse, Michael O'Hanrahan, John MacBride, Éamonn Ceannt, Michael Mallin, Cornelius Colbert, Seán Heuston, Seán Mac Diarmada, James Connolly and Thomas Kent.

However, Irish Republican Army (IRA) and other republican guerrillas were not prosecuted or executed for treason for levying war against the British government during the final decades of the twentieth century. Instead, they were jailed for murder, violent crimes or terrorist offences. The disparity between the treatment of Irish rebels in the two periods is not easy to explain in purely legal or evidentiary terms; it seems related to the political calculations involved in launching treason prosecutions.

In 1946, William Joyce, nicknamed Lord Haw-Haw, a pro-fascist politician and Nazi propaganda broadcaster to the United Kingdom during World War II, became the last person to be put to death for treason in the UK. He was convicted of 'being a person owing allegiance to our Lord the King, and while a war was being carried on by the German Realm against our King, did traitorously adhere to the King's enemies in Germany, by broadcasting propaganda'.

Before the trial, Joyce's American nationality came to light, and it seemed that he could not be convicted of betraying a country that was not his own. On that basis, he was acquitted of two charges. However, the Attorney General, Sir Hartley Shawcross, successfully argued that Joyce's possession of a British passport, even though he had mis-stated his nationality to get it, entitled him (until it expired) to British diplomatic protection in Germany and therefore he owed allegiance to the King at the time he commenced working for the Germans. As a result, Joyce was convicted of the third charge against him.

His conviction was upheld by the Court of Appeal, and by the House of Lords (on a 4–1 vote). In the appeal, Joyce argued that possession of a passport did not entitle him to the protection of the Crown, and therefore did not perpetuate his duty of allegiance once he left the country, but the House unanimously rejected this argument. Joyce also argued that jurisdiction had been wrongly assumed by the court in electing to try an alien for offences committed in a foreign country. This argument was rejected, on the basis that a state must exercise such jurisdiction in the interests of a 'proper regard for its own security' (*Joyce v. DPP* [1946] AC 347, 372).

As Joyce's case illustrated, treason convictions depend on the ancient notion of allegiance. To overcome that requirement, and other perceived difficulties with treason trials, the Treachery Act 1940 (3 & 4 Geo. VI c. 40) was adopted during World War II to facilitate the prosecution and execution of enemy spies. The offence of treachery was designed to make securing convictions easier as it could be proved under the same rules of evidence as ordinary offences. It was also deemed necessary because there was doubt whether the treason laws were applicable to German spies and saboteurs. Breach of a duty of allegiance was not an element of treachery.

The day after Joyce's execution, a former British soldier, Theodore Schurch, was executed for treachery under that legislation, making him the last man to be executed for a crime other than murder in the UK. After working for both Italian and German intelligence, he was arrested in Rome in 1945 and tried in a court martial. He was found guilty of all charges against him, nine counts of treachery and one of desertion. Schurch was the only British soldier executed for treachery in World War II, but 16 people were shot by firing squad or hanged for the offence of treachery (Hansard, 1 February 1965).

The Treachery Act 1940 was introduced for the duration of the 'war emergency' (section 6), and was suspended in February 1946. It was only finally repealed, however, in 1968 for England and Wales and in 1973 for the rest of the United Kingdom.

Another treason-related Act, the Treason Felony Act 1848 (11 & 12 Vict. c. 12) remains in force. The offences in that Act were originally high treason under the Treason Act, and consequently the penalty was death. However, it was found that juries were often reluctant to convict people of capital crimes, and it was thought that the conviction rate might increase if the sentence were reduced to exile to the penal colonies in Australia (the penalty today is life imprisonment). Consequently in 1848 three categories of treason were reduced to felonies. It is treason felony to 'compass, imagine, invent, devise, or intend':

- to deprive the Queen of her crown,
- to levy war against the Queen, or
- to 'move or stir' any foreigner to invade the United Kingdom or any other country belonging to the Queen.

Delivering a House of Lords judgement on the Treason Felony Act in 2003, Lord Steyne pointed to some of the political estimations involved in the adoption of the legislation:

> 1848 was the year of revolutions on continental Europe, but there was only one Chartist demonstration on 10 April 1848 in a relatively tranquil Britain. But there was a fear that the contagion of revolution, with its associations with the Terror after 1789, might spread to Britain. This was probably one of the reasons why Parliament passed the Treason Felony Act 1848. (*R v. Attorney General ex parte Rusbridger* [2003] UKHL 38, [2]).

The Act was last used in *R v. Gallagher* ((1883) 15 Cox 291), a case involving the Fenian Brotherhood, which sought to use acts of sabotage to pressure the British government into granting independence to Ireland. Nevertheless, the Act is still on the statute books.

In 2001, *The Guardian* newspaper mounted an unsuccessful legal challenge to the Act, alleging that it 'makes it a criminal offence, punishable by life imprisonment, to advocate abolition of the monarchy in print, even by peaceful means'. The newspaper had notified the Attorney General of its intention to publish a series of articles urging the abolition of the monarchy, and asked the Attorney General to announce an intention not to apply the 1848 Act. However, the Attorney General declined to give any such assurance.

The Guardian then sought a legal declaration that the Human Rights Act 1998 meant that the 1848 Act would be interpreted as meaning that only violent conduct was criminal. The House of Lords held that this was a hypothetical question that did not deserve an answer, since the newspaper was not being prosecuted. Most of the judges agreed with Lord Steyn's view that 'the part of section 3 of the 1848 Act which appears to criminalise the advocacy of republicanism is a relic of a bygone age and does not fit into the fabric of our modern legal system. The idea that section 3 could survive scrutiny under the Human Rights Act is unreal' (*R v. Attorney General ex parte Rusbridger* [2003] UKHL 38, [28]).

Nonetheless, the 1848 Act has not been repealed. Although the last reported case under the Act in the United Kingdom was in 1883, its equivalent was used in Australia during World War I in 1916 to prosecute the 'Sydney Twelve' (see below).

United States

To avoid the abuses of the English law (including executions by Henry VIII of those who criticised his repeated marriages), treason was specifically defined in the United States Constitution, the only crime so mentioned. Article III Section 3 delineates treason as follows:

> Treason against the United States, shall consist only in levying War against them, or in adhering to their Enemies, giving them Aid and Comfort. No Person shall be convicted of Treason unless on the Testimony of two Witnesses to the same overt Act, or on Confession in open Court.

> The Congress shall have Power to declare the Punishment of Treason, but no Attainder of Treason shall work Corruption of Blood, or Forfeiture except during the Life of the Person attainted.

Congress has, at times, passed statutes creating related offenses which undermine the government or the national security, such as sedition in the 1798 Alien and Sedition Acts, or espionage and sedition in the 1917 Espionage Act, which do not require the testimony of two witnesses and have a much broader definition than Article III treason.

The Constitution does not itself create the offence of treason; it only restricts the definition (the first paragraph), permits Congress to create the offence, and restricts any punishment for treason to the convicted person only (the second paragraph). The crime is specified by the United States Code at 18 USC, which sets the death penalty for the offence. Section 2381 states:

> Whoever, owing allegiance to the United States, levies war against them or adheres to their enemies, giving them aid and comfort within the United States or elsewhere, is guilty of treason and shall suffer death, or shall be imprisoned not less than five years and fined under this title but not less than $10,000; and shall be incapable of holding any office under the United States.

The requirement of testimony of two witnesses was inherited from the British Treason Act. (Since 1945, this has been abolished in British law and treason cases are now subject to the same rules of evidence and procedure as a murder trial, but the US requirement still stands.)

There is a further offence of misprision of treason, which places a positive burden on citizens to report acts of treason. Section 2382 of the Code states:

> Whoever, owing allegiance to the United States and having knowledge of the commission of any treason against them, conceals and does not, as soon as may be, disclose and make known the same to the President or to some judge of the United States, or to the governor or to some judge or justice of a particular State, is guilty of misprision of treason and shall be fined under this title or imprisoned not more than seven years, or both.

In the history of the United States there have been almost 40 federal prosecutions for treason. Several men were convicted of treason in connection with the 1794 Whiskey Rebellion but were pardoned by President George Washington. One famous treason trial, that of former Vice President Aaron Burr in 1807, resulted in acquittal, since no two witnesses came forward to testify to his alleged secessionist plans (25 F Cas 55 August 31, 1807).

Most states have provisions in their constitutions or statutes similar to those in the US Constitution. There appears to have been two successful prosecutions for treason at the state level, that of Thomas Dorr in Rhode Island and that of John Brown in Virginia. Both were instructive cases. In 1843, Dorr was sentenced to solitary confinement at hard labour for life for agitating for universal male suffrage in his state. Public opinion finally forced his release after 12 months (King 1859).

Brown was hanged after being convicted of treason against the Commonwealth of Virginia in 1859 for attempting to organise armed resistance to slavery. He had led a raid on a federal armoury, in which seven people were killed. His execution presaged the American Civil War, which followed 16 months later. When Brown was hanged, church bells rang in protest, minute guns were fired, large memorial meetings took place throughout the North, and famous writers such as Emerson and Thoreau joined many Northerners in praising Brown (Collier and Collier 2000).

After the Civil War, no person involved with the Confederate States of America was tried for treason, though a number of leading Confederates (including Jefferson

Davis and Robert E. Lee) were indicted. Those who had been indicted received a blanket amnesty issued by President Andrew Johnson as he left office in 1869.

World War II produced several cases, including that of 'Tokyo Rose' (*Iva Ikuko Toguri D'Aquino v. US* 192 F.2d 338 (1951), rehearing denied 345 US 931 (1953)). She was an American citizen who participated in English-language propaganda broadcast transmitted by Radio Tokyo to Allied soldiers in the South Pacific. After the Japanese defeat, Toguri was detained for a year by the US military before being released for lack of evidence. But when she returned to the US, she was charged with eight counts of treason. Her 1949 trial resulted in a conviction on one count, which stated, 'That on a day during October, 1944, the exact date being to the Grand Jurors unknown, said defendant, at Tokyo, Japan, in a broadcasting studio of The Broadcasting Corporation of Japan, did speak into a microphone concerning the loss of ships.' She was fined $10,000 and given a 10-year prison sentence. She was paroled after serving six years and two months, and released in 1956. In 1974, investigative journalists found that key witnesses had lied during testimony. Toguri was pardoned by President Gerald Ford in 1977 (Goldstein 2006).

Another controversial case was *Kawakita v. United States* (343 US 717 (1952)), in which the Supreme Court reviewed a treason accusation against Tomoya Kawakita, a dual US/Japanese citizen. Kawakita was found guilty of torturing American prisoners of war while living in Japan as a civilian during World War II. He asserted that during his time in Japan, he had effectively renounced his US citizenship, and thus could not be tried for treason. He further argued that a person who has a dual nationality can be guilty of treason only to the country where he resides, not to the other country which claims him as a national. However, the US Constitution places no territorial limitations on treason. The court found that Kawakita owed allegiance to the US during his time in Japan. He was found guilty of eight overt acts, his US citizenship was revoked, and he was sentenced to death. President Dwight D. Eisenhower commuted the sentence to life imprisonment in 1953. Ten years later President John F. Kennedy ordered him released on the condition that he be deported and barred from re-entering the United States.

The Cold War saw frequent associations between treason and support for (or insufficient hostility toward) Communist-backed causes. Indeed, Senator Joseph McCarthy characterised the Franklin Delano Roosevelt and Harry Truman administrations as 'twenty years of treason'. Nevertheless, the Cold War period produced no prosecutions for treason.

During the Vietnam War, President Nixon, confronted by widespread anti-war protests, charged that criticism of the war efforts gave 'aid and comfort to the enemy' within the meaning of the US Constitution (ALRC 2006: 232). Again, no prosecutions ensued. However, a new precedent was set during the 'war on terrorism'. In 2006, a federal grand jury issued the first indictment for treason against the United States since 1952, charging US citizen Adam Yahiye Gadahn, in absentia, for videos in which he spoke supportively of al-Qaeda and threatened attacks within the US.

Australia

In Australia, opponents of war or the political establishment can also face prosecution under two sets of laws: federal and state. In some Australian states, the criminal law has been codified; in others, the common law, including old English statutes, applies. One would expect that in the twenty-first century, more than a century after Australian federation, treason would be prosecuted as a federal matter. However, the relevant federal provision, the Criminal Code, specifically saves the operation of State and Territory laws. The case of the 'Sydney Twelve', discussed below, illustrates the potential for state law to be applied.

In federal law, section 80.1 of the Criminal Code, contained in the schedule of the Criminal Code Act 1995, makes treason punishable by life imprisonment and defines the offence as follows:

> 80.1 Treason
> (1) A person commits an offence if the person:
>   (a) causes the death of the Sovereign, the heir apparent of the Sovereign, the consort of the Sovereign, the Governor-General or the Prime Minister; or
>   (b) causes harm to the Sovereign, the Governor-General or the Prime Minister resulting in the death of the Sovereign, the Governor-General or the Prime Minister; or
>   (c) causes harm to the Sovereign, the Governor-General or the Prime Minister, or imprisons or restrains the Sovereign, the Governor-General or the Prime Minister; or
>   (d) levies war, or does any act preparatory to levying war, against the Commonwealth; or
>   (g) instigates a person who is not an Australian citizen to make an armed invasion of the Commonwealth or a Territory of the Commonwealth.

By subsection (2), life imprisonment also applies if a person (a) receives or assists another person who, to his or her knowledge, has committed an offence against this Subdivision (other than this subsection) with the intention of allowing him or her to escape punishment or apprehension; or (b) knowing that another person intends to commit an offence against this Subdivision (other than this subsection), does not inform a police constable of it within a reasonable time or use other reasonable endeavours to prevent the commission of the offence.

Life imprisonment further applies to a second category of treason, covered by section 80.1AA, entitled 'Treason – materially assisting enemies etc'. Under subsection (1):

> A person commits an offence if:
>   (a) the Commonwealth is at war with an enemy (whether or not the existence of a state of war has been declared); and

(b)   the enemy is specified, by Proclamation made for the purpose of this paragraph, to be an enemy at war with the Commonwealth; and

(c)   the person engages in conduct; and

(d)   the person intends that the conduct will materially assist the enemy to engage in war with the Commonwealth; and

(e)   the conduct assists the enemy to engage in war with the Commonwealth; and

(f)   when the person engages in the conduct, the person:

   (i)   is an Australian citizen; or

   (ii)   is a resident of Australia; or

   (iii) has voluntarily put himself or herself under the protection of the Commonwealth; or

   (iv) is a body corporate incorporated by or under a law of the Commonwealth or of a State or Territory.

Subsection (4) has similar provisions for where (a) a country or organisation is engaged in armed hostilities against the Australian Defence Force and (b) a person engages in conduct; and (c) the person intends that the conduct will materially assist the country or organisation to engage in armed hostilities against the Australian Defence Force; and (d) the conduct assists the country or organisation to engage in armed hostilities against the Australian Defence Force.

Subsections (1) and (4) do not apply to conduct by way of, or for the purposes of, the provision of aid of a humanitarian nature, but a defendant bears an evidential burden in relation to that defence. The same burden of proof applies to a defence in section 80.3 for acts done in 'good faith', for example to show that the sovereign or a government is mistaken in any policies or actions, or point out errors or defects with a view to reform, or urge lawful change, or seek to ameliorate feelings of ill-will or hostility between different groups, or publish a report or commentary about a matter of public interest. In applying the 'good faith' defence, a court may also consider, among other things, whether there was an intention to cause violence or create public disorder or a public disturbance, and whether there was an artistic, academic, scientific, news or other public interest purpose.

Some of these defences, as well as formulations such as 'materially assists', may offer limited protection against political victimisation. The Australian Law Reform Commission in 2006 recommended the replacement of the previous term 'assist' because it created 'valid concerns that the offences could be interpreted or applied to proscribe legitimate political protest, and punish merely rhetorical encouragement or support for those who disagree with Australian government policy' (ALRC 2006: 230). Even with the modified language, doubts remain that the treason offence could still extend to urging conscientious objection or calling on soldiers to lay down their arms (ALRC 2006: 233).

Moreover, section 24AA of the Crimes Act 1914 retains the related offence of treachery, also punishable by life imprisonment. It forbids any act intended to overthrow the Constitution by revolution or sabotage; or overthrow by force or violence the established government of the Commonwealth, of a State or of a proclaimed country; or to levy war, or do any act preparatory to levying war, against a proclaimed country. It also prohibits assistance 'by any means whatever' to anyone against whom the Australian Defence Force is or is likely to be opposed.

One twentieth century case in which treason, or more exactly treason felony, charges were initially laid, and then subsequently dropped, was that of the Sydney Twelve. A dozen members of the Industrial Workers of the World (IWW) were arrested on 23 September 1916 in Sydney after a series of fires, allegedly lit by arsonists, in factories, warehouses and stores. The 12 men were: John Hamilton, Peter Larkin, Joseph Fagin, William Teen, Donald Grant, Benjamin King, Thomas Glynn, Donald McPherson, Thomas Moore, Charles Reeve, William Beattie and Bob Besant.

They were originally charged with treason under section 12 of the Crimes Act 1900 (NSW), which was based on the British Treason Felony Act 1848. The 12 were charged that they, among other things, 'did feloniously and wickedly compass, imagine, invent, devise or intend to levy war against His Majesty' in order to force him to change his measures, 'did conspire to raise, make, and levy insurrection and rebellion against the King', 'did feloniously and wickedly conspire to burn down and destroy buildings' and 'did endeavour to intimidate or overawe' parliament (Turner 1969: 36). It was widely believed, based on media reports, that the men had been charged with treason, for which the penalty was death. Actually, the maximum penalty for treason felony was life imprisonment (Rushton 1973: 56).

At the committal hearing, the prosecution alleged that the accused had set fire to business premises with the intention of coercing the federal government over several questions, including conscription. Representing the Crown, Ernest Lamb, KC, declared: 'The facts of the case will show that there was a gigantic conspiracy to cause havoc and destruction in Sydney, and to endanger the lives of the people' (Turner 1969: 37). On this basis, the 12 were committed for trial, and denied bail (Turner 1969: 40). Before their trial began, however, the felony treason charge was replaced by three counts of conspiracy: to commit arson, to defeat the ends of justice and seditious conspiracy (Rushton 1973: 53–4).

Exactly why the treason felony charge was abandoned is not clear (Rushton 1973: 53–4). It was widely believed in the labour movement that the men were framed or railroaded for their anti-war views and opposition to conscription. That belief was reinforced by the fact that the charges were laid in the lead-up to a referendum on conscription called by Prime Minister Billy Hughes, the former Labor and future Nationalist party leader. Moreover, the case against the 12 was accompanied by government and media hysteria against the IWW. This was typified in the Tottenham murder case involving three members of the IWW and the murder of a policeman at Tottenham, New South Wales, on 26 September 1916. The prosecution in this case made every effort to connect this murder with the charges against the Sydney IWW men, which provided propaganda in the prosecution of the Sydney Twelve. Two of the Tottenham IWW members were found guilty and hastily executed on 20 December 1916, the first executions in New South Wales for ten years (Turner 1969: 41–59). After the Sydney Twelve were convicted, Hughes pushed the Unlawful Associations Act 1916 through federal parliament in five days during December 1916, then had the IWW declared an unlawful association.

In his comprehensive examination of the Sydney Twelve affair, Turner suggested that a jury would have hesitated to convict on the more serious charge, and that the treason charge had served its propaganda purpose during the conscription campaign. The historian also pointed out that conspiracy was an easier charge to sustain than treason, which required proof of some overt act (Turner 1969: 48–9). While all the circumstances point to a political decision made by the federal government, many of the official records are missing, making it difficult to determine who decided to alter the charges and why (Ruston 1973: 54).

For the subsequent conspiracy trial, the conviction and jailing of the men and their ultimate release, substantially exonerated, after intensive public campaigns and two judicial inquiries (see Chapter 5).

Canada

Section 46 of the Criminal Code of Canada has two degrees of treason, called 'high treason' and 'treason'. However, both of these belong to the historical category of high treason, as opposed to petty treason which does not exist in Canadian law. Section 46 reads as follows:

High treason
(1) Every one commits high treason who, in Canada,
  (a) kills or attempts to kill Her Majesty, or does her any bodily harm tending to death or destruction, maims or wounds her, or imprisons or restrains her;
  (b) levies war against Canada or does any act preparatory thereto; or
  (c) assists an enemy at war with Canada, or any armed forces against whom Canadian Forces are engaged in hostilities, whether or not a state of war exists between Canada and the country whose forces they are.
Treason
(2) Every one commits treason who, in Canada,
  (a) uses force or violence for the purpose of overthrowing the government of Canada or a province;
  (b) without lawful authority, communicates or makes available to an agent of a state other than Canada, military or scientific information or any sketch, plan, model, article, note or document of a military or scientific character that he knows or ought to know may be used by that state for a purpose prejudicial to the safety or defence of Canada;
  (c) conspires with any person to commit high treason or to do anything mentioned in paragraph (a);

(d) forms an intention to do anything that is high treason or that is mentioned in paragraph (a) and manifests that intention by an overt act; or

(e) conspires with any person to do anything mentioned in paragraph (b) or forms an intention to do anything mentioned in paragraph (b) and manifests that intention by an overt act.

It is also illegal for a Canadian citizen to do any of the above outside Canada. The penalty for high treason is life imprisonment. The penalty for treason is imprisonment up to a maximum of life, or up to 14 years for conduct under subsection (2)(b) or (e) in peacetime.

Mutiny

Mutiny is often regarded as an offence confined to the armed forces, but the historical record demonstrates that it has wider application to civilian expressions of opposition to the deployment of the military, including domestically. In particular, incitement to mutiny provisions have been used to outlaw and punish appeals to working class-based resistance to war and military repression. This section focuses on the application of mutiny law to civilians; the application of military law is generally beyond the scope of this book.

In Britain, the Incitement to Mutiny Act 1797 made it a felony to maliciously and advisedly endeavour to seduce any member of the armed forces from his duty and allegiance to the Crown or to incite mutiny. The Act was introduced after the failure of the 1794 treason trials (see above), followed by the 1797 Spithead and Nore mutinies in the British fleets at Portsmouth and the Thames estuary.

At Nore, the mutiny took on aspects of an embryonic social revolution. Among other things, the sailors demanded an end to impressments, unequal pay and poor quality rations. In the midst of a war with revolutionary France, they also wanted better leave entitlements, and to remove cruel or unpopular officers from ships and have them banned from serving on them again. Under the leadership of radical delegates to an unofficial Fleet Parliament, the demands expanded to the dissolution of parliament and an immediate peace with France. For a time, the fleet blockaded London and stopped trade in and out of the port. Cut off from food and racked by internal dissent, the mutiny eventually dissolved, with ships slipping their cables and deserting the cause.

The elected mutiny leader, former naval officer and French Revolution supporter Richard Parker, faced swift vengeance from the Admiralty. After a brief trial he was hanged from a ship's yardarm for treason and piracy. In the reprisals that followed, a total of 29 leaders were hanged, others sentenced to be flogged, imprisoned or transported to Australia (Gill 1913).

Prime Minister William Pitt originally proposed that the crime of incitement to mutiny be an aggravated misdemeanour, leaving to the discretion of the court the imposition of penalties, which could range up to banishment and transportation.

However, in its final form the Act created yet another capital felony, adding to the 350 or so already existing (Young 1976: 11). Strictly speaking, the Act created four distinct offences. Section 1 stated:

> Any person who shall maliciously and advisedly endeavour to seduce any person or persons serving in his Majesty's forces by sea or land from his or their duty and allegiance to his Majesty, or to incite or stir up any such person or persons to commit any act of mutiny, or to make or endeavour to make any mutinous assembly, or to commit any traitorous or mutinous practice whatsoever, shall, on being legally convicted of such an offence be adjudged guilt of felony ...

Thus, the offences were (1) endeavouring to seduce any member of the armed forces from their duty and allegiance, (2) endeavouring to incite an armed forces member to an act of mutiny, (3) endeavouring to incite an armed forces member to make any mutinous assembly, and (4) endeavouring to incite an armed forces member to commit any traitorous or mutinous practices.

Despite the alleged danger of mutinies, there are only two reported cases relating to the Act before the twentieth century. In *R v. Fuller* ([1797] 2 Leach 790), Fuller was convicted and hanged for giving a soldier in the Coldstream Guards 'several inflammatory and seditious handbills'. In *R v. Tierney* ([1804] Russell and Ryan 74), Tierney was convicted, and presumably hanged, for trying to seduce a hospitalised sailor from his duty and allegiance (Young 1976: 12-13).

After lying dormant between 1804 and 1912, the Act was revived to deal with the rise of militant socialist-led working class struggles (Young 1976: 14–20, Ewing and Gearty 2000: 119ff). In 1912, the first such prosecution in the twentieth century concerned the publication in *The Syndicalist* of an 'Open Letter to British Soldiers' (later reprinted as a leaflet, *Don't Shoot*) that appealed to soldiers not to shoot striking workers. Tom Mann, a prominent socialist and union leader, and four other men were imprisoned for six to nine months with hard labour for urging soldiers to 'refuse to murder your kindred' and 'help us win ... the world for workers' (Babington 1990: 142).

Before examining this case and subsequent use of the Act, it must be recalled that the issue of military violence against strikers was hardly an academic one. During the so-called Featherstone Colliery Riots of September 1893, four people, including two bystanders, were killed when an infantry Captain ordered soldiers to fire on striking coal miners and their supporters after a local magistrate had read the proclamation from the Riot Act 1714 (see Chapter 1).

The 1912 imprisonment of Tom Mann and others took place in the context of the biggest strike Britain had ever seen: the 1912 miners' strike, when more than a million coal miners struck for a national minimum wage. Reflecting emerging working class discontent with the compromising record of the Labour Party, the syndicalist movement was urging workers to cease relying on parliament and advocating militant trade unionism and other forms of 'direct action' (Young 1976: 14). The 1912 prosecutions became widely controversial because Mann was an internationally known socialist who had led the 1911 Liverpool transport general strike (Torr 1944).

The first to be charged was a railwayman who had distributed *The Syndicalist's* open letter to soldiers in and around London, at Aldershot, Hyde Park Corner and Hounslow barracks (Young 1976: 15). Then, in *R v. Bowman* ((1912) 22 Cox CC 729; 76 JP 271), the editor and printers of *The Syndicalist* were charged, according to the language of the Incitement to Mutiny Act, with 'seduc[ing] divers persons serving in His Majesty's Forces by land from their duty and allegiance to our said Lord the King and ... incit[ing] them to mutiny and disobedience'. They were also charged with the common law misdemeanour of 'endeavouring to incite and stir up persons serving in His Majesty's land forces to commit acts of disobedience to the lawful orders of their superior officers'. It seemed to have been accepted that incitement to commit mere acts of disobedience was not actionable under the Act itself (Young 1976: 15). *The Syndicalist's* open letter to British soldiers said the following:

> YOU are called upon by your officers to MURDER US. Don't do it ... Don't you know that when you are out of the colours, and become a 'Civy' again, that you, like us, may be on strike, and you, like us, be liable to be murdered by other soldiers? Boys, don't do it! MURDER is MURDER! ... Boys, don't do it! Act the Man! Act the Brother! Act the Human Being! Property can be replaced. Human life, never ... Instead of fighting against each other we should be fighting with each other ... Comrades, have we called in vain? Think things out and refuse any longer to murder your kindred (22 Cox CC at 729–30).

It is unclear from the record of the case whether the publication was actually distributed to soldiers or merely passed out in an area where soldiers were likely to receive it. The defence argued that because no specific member of the army was approached, there was no specific contravention of the statute (22 Cox CC at 731). The prosecution countered that the soldiers were addressed as a class: 'If to incite a single soldier is an offence punishable by penal servitude for life, it should be an absurdity to hold that it is no offence to incite the whole British army' (22 Cox CC at 731). The judge, Justice Horridge, sided with the prosecution, saying there was no need to prove that soldiers were actually seduced. In effect, his instruction to the jury made it irrelevant whether the article was intended, or its publication designed, to incite any concrete act of mutiny. It was sufficient if the article made a general suggestion that soldiers should rebel when ordered to open fire against strikers. The judge instructed the jury:

> Ask yourselves this question: Why was this article printed and published? Was it ... to induce soldiers to disobey their officers in the event of being ordered to quell a strike? Or was it ... merely a comment upon the issue of armed military force by the State for the suppression of industrial riots? ... There is a distinction: to criticise the use of military force, or to suggest that soldiers are to rebel when that force is used (22 Cox CC at 732–3)

As one scholar points out, this test does not require any 'clear and present danger' of mutiny, by contrast to the American approach, which is examined below (Boasberg 1990: 114–21). Instead, the focus is on the intent of the defendants, regardless of the circumstances. Despite Justice Horridge's purported distinction between political comment and suggestion of rebellion, the ruling allows any call for disobedience, however hypothetical, to be classified as incitement to mutiny.

After *The Syndicalist's* editor and printers were arrested, Mann publicly denounced the prosecution and challenged the government to arrest him as well, because he was the chairman of the Industrial Syndicalist League, which was responsible for *The Syndicalist*. At his trial, Mann accused the government of prosecuting him because of his connection to the syndicalist movement, noting that others had written and spoken as he did without being charged. Nonetheless, he was convicted and sentenced to six months' imprisonment (Young 1976: 16–17). By contrast, the railway worker who was first arrested was sentenced to two months in jail, and offered by the judge the option of avoiding punishment by giving an undertaking not to repeat the offence. The worker rejected the offer, saying his conscience would not permit him to accept (Young 1976: 17).

The jailing of the syndicalists stood in sharp contrast to the lack of any prosecution in 1914 of Tory politicians who urged army officers to mutiny, and army officers who did so, in order to defeat the Home Rule Bill for Ireland. Bonar Law, a future prime minister, for example, declared in parliament 'any officer who refuses is only doing his duty'. F.E. Smith, a future Solicitor General and, as Lord Birkenhead, a Lord Chancellor, openly incited illegal Ulster loyalist militia, stating: 'Home rule will be dead for ever on the day when 100,000 men armed with rifles assemble at Balmoral' (Young 1976: 18–20).

The contrast highlighted the political and class character of the law, which was invariably directed against socialist and working class opponents of the ruling establishment, while members of that establishment were protected, even when involved in explicitly mutinous activities.

After a public outcry and a parliamentary debate, the sentences for Mann and Guy Bowman, the editor, were later commuted to two months (Hansard 1912). Even so, their jailing set a precedent that was to be invoked in the 1920s against the young Communist Party, which had been formed in response to the 1917 Russian Soviet revolution.

In 1922, during the four-month engineer's lockout, the editor of *Out of Work*, a newspaper published by the Communist Party-backed National Unemployed Workers Movement (NUWM) was convicted and jailed for three weeks for inciting disaffection among the Metropolitan Police. *Out of Work* had published an article appealing to the police not to use their batons against the unemployed. Although she was charged under the Police Act 1919, her prosecution was symptomatic of a wider assault on the NUWM, which saw many members arrested for sedition, obstruction or acting in a manner likely to breach the peace (Young 1976: 35).

The first major use of the 1797 Act against the Communist Party was the controversial Campbell case. As a prelude to the tenth anniversary of the Great

War (now known as World War I), in July 1924 the Communist Party's *Workers'*
Weekly carried an open letter calling upon soldiers, sailors and airmen to

> begin the task of not only organising passive resistance when war is declared,
> or when an industrial dispute involves you, but to definitely and categorically
> let it be known that, neither in a class war nor a military war, will you turn your
> guns on your fellow workers, but instead will line up with our fellow workers
> in our attack upon the exploiters and capitalists, and will use your arms on the
> side of your own class ... [and form] committees in every barracks, aerodrome,
> and ship [to be] the nucleus of an organisation that will prepare the whole of the
> soldiers, sailors and airmen not only to refuse to go to war, or to refuse to shoot
> strikers during industrial conflicts, but will make it possible for the workers,
> peasants and soldiers, sailors and airmen, to go forward in a common attack
> upon the capitalists, and smash capitalism forever, and institute the reign of the
> whole working class. (Ewing and Gearty 2000: 120)

Campbell, the acting editor of *Workers' Weekly* was arrested and charged under
the 1797 Act with 'attempting to seduce from loyalty to the King members of
the Navy, Army and Air Force'. Without a search warrant, police occupied the
party's headquarters for more than two hours and seized piles of party documents,
including 'all the branch files' (Ewing and Gearty 2000: 121). When some
backbenchers of the then Labour government sought to object in parliament to
the government's decision to prosecute, the Speaker of the House of Commons
ruled that the matter was sub judice and could not be debated. According to the
Cabinet records, various ministers strongly condemned the offending article, but
ultimately sought a 'possible way out' from the political uproar, with the Attorney
General dropping the prosecution in return for Campbell writing a letter saying he
was only acting temporarily as editor (Ewing and Gearty 2000: 123).

The Cabinet discussion exposed the myth of non-political interference in the
criminal law system. Prime Minister Ramsay MacDonald said he 'must be informed
before action is taken, and that political cases should come to him in advance in
accordance with a well established convention' (Ewing and Gearty 2000: 123). In
line with the Attorney General's 'way out', the prosecution told the magistrate that
since Campbell's arrest it had been represented that the article was only meant to
be a comment on the use of the armed forces. Therefore, it was covered by the
defence outlined by Justice Horridge in *Bowman*. The magistrate duly agreed,
whereupon the Communist Party claimed a 'victory for the workers' as a result of
'severe pressure' on the government from the labour movement. In a subsequent
parliamentary censure debate, the Prime Minister and Attorney General cited
precedents for an established practice that Cabinet sanction be obtained before
commencing prosecutions of a political nature. Nevertheless, the Tory opposition
insisted that the *dropping* of a prosecution was another matter. The affair became
the subject of a successful censure motion that brought down the government within
two months (Young 1976: 38–40, Ewing and Gearty 2000: 123–5).

It was not long before the incoming Tory government invoked the incitement to mutiny law against the Communist Party in the sedition trial of 1925. Government ministers played a key part in proceedings, and the Home Secretary told parliament that his Cabinet colleagues were unanimous in their support for the prosecution (Ewing and Gearty 2000: 137). Twelve Communist Party leaders were arrested and charged with three conspiracies: to publish and utter seditious libels and words; to incite persons to commit breaches of the Incitement to Mutiny Act 1797; and to endeavour to seduce from their duty persons serving in His Majesty's Forces. On the evening of the arrests, the Home Secretary publicly celebrated them, directly prejudicing the prospects of a fair trial. He told a public meeting that the audience would be pleased to know that a 'certain number of notorious Communists' had been arrested (Ewing and Gearty 2000: 139).

In the lead-up to the trial, the Home Office and MI5, the intelligence service, had expressed concern about 'Bolshevist propaganda' at military centres. The posters considered objectionable carried messages about pay and conditions, such as: 'A General lifts 75/9d a day. A private gets 2/9d. What about a bit of the top? Immediate increase for the rank and file.' Also of concern were the democratic demands issued by the Communist Party in its 14-point program for the armed forces. The demands included the formation of soldiers' and sailors' committees, the right to join trade unions and political parties, no troops to be used against strikers, no compulsory church parades, and boys not be sent on active service (Young 1976: 42–3).

But the prosecution was not based on any specific statement made by the accused. Instead, opening the case, the Attorney General asserted that the party was 'illegal' because it had as its objects 'the forcible overthrow by arms of the present existing state of society, and, as a means to that end, the seduction from their allegiance of the armed forces of the Crown'. He referred at great length to documents of the Communist International that stated that its purpose was 'to organise an armed struggle for the overthrow of the international bourgeoisie'. He argued that the charges did not deny the right to free speech. 'Every man was entitled to try to persuade his fellow-citizens that the government ought to be overthrown or that this constitution ought to be changed' but it was essential to do so within the law rather than by seeking 'forcibly to overthrow the rule of the majority and government as by law established' (Ewing and Gearty 2000: 140). This proposition made a mockery of free speech – the charges amounted to seeking to outlaw a political party that was campaigning for support for socialist ideas among members of the public.

On both the sedition and mutiny charges, the defence submitted that literature reproducing the ultimate aims of the international communist movement did not prove that the accused had incited anyone to disorder or crime. (For the implications of this case for the law of sedition see Chapter 6.) The incitement to mutiny charges were also based on general appeals to soldiers not to shoot strikers that had been published in *Workers' Weekly*. Defence counsel argued that this aspect of the case was equally flawed because when the articles appeared no industrial dispute had actually arisen. Therefore, soldiers were being asked not to shoot people whom there was no reason to believe they would shoot anyway. So even if Justice Horridge had been correct in the *Bowman* case to rule that a general appeal to the troops, not addressed to a particular person, was enough to constitute an offence – a ruling that the defence did not accept – here the incitement was too remote (Ewing and Gearty 2000: 142).

Justice Swift, however, instructed the jury that it would be laughable, if it were not so serious, to imagine that anyone would be allowed to persuade soldiers and sailors to disobey orders. He stated that the 1797 Act was a 'musty old Act' but remained essential to the maintenance of the armed forces. It would be a 'bad day for the country' if the government 'was not strong enough to bring those suspected of [treason, insurrection, tumult and sedition] before a Court of law' or if there was 'the slightest faltering either on the part of the jury or the Judge in putting down the offence'. It took the jury just 10 minutes to return guilty verdicts on all charges (Ewing and Gearty 2000: 143–4).

The Communist Party leaders were sentenced to periods of 6 to 12 months' imprisonment. The longer sentences went to those with prior convictions for seditious speeches, most probably in breach of Defence of the Realm or Emergency regulations (see Chapter 9). Remarkably, the judge gave the seven who had no previous convictions the option of avoiding prison by renouncing communism – an option that was defiantly rejected (Ewing and Gearty 2000: 145). The judge's ploy only underscored the political character of the trial. The connection to the government's political agenda was further reinforced when, in an attempt to deflect popular criticism of the prosecution, the government published a command paper of selected documents that police had seized during the arrests and related raids on Communist Party offices (Ewing and Gearty 2000: 148–51).

In summary, these cases set precedents for the use of incitement to mutiny charges to outlaw any appeal for members of the armed forces, police or other officers of the state to disobey orders or act in solidarity with government opponents. Arrests can be made, charges laid and convictions obtained, regardless of how general the appeal is, how remote the potential circumstances and how unlikely a mutinous outcome.

Further prosecutions followed from 1928 in response to a campaign by the Communist Party to win support among soldiers. In that year, four Scottish miners were jailed for a month for sedition for having circulated to four soldiers a pamphlet that advocated trade unionism in the armed forces. According to the charge, this call was 'calculated to excite disaffection, commotion, and resistance to lawful authority among His Majesty's lieges, and particularly among His Majesty's Forces (Ewing and Gearty 2000: 235).

During 1930, at least four Communist Party members were jailed under the 1797 Act for distributing anti-war leaflets to soldiers, and another received an 18-month sentence (Young 1976: 51–2, Ewing and Gearty 2000: 236). After the *Daily Worker*, the Communist Party newspaper, denounced the latter's sentence, four members responsible for the publication were convicted for contempt of court. Although the content of the leaflets is not known, leaflets circulated by party members at that time included calls for soldiers to protest against compulsory church parades, defend the Soviet Union and refuse to serve in the British colony of India (Ewing and Gearty 2000: 235). A number of arrests followed a mutiny aboard a naval ship at Plymouth. A communist was later convicted, and bound over to keep the peace for 12 months, for making an allegedly inflammatory speech to an audience that apparently did not include any servicemen (Ewing and Gearty 2000: 236).

In 1931, 19-year-old John Gollan, a future Communist Party leader, was acquitted of incitement to mutiny, but jailed for six months on a common law charge of 'inciting soldiers to disaffection' for participating in an anti-recruitment campaign in Edinburgh (Young 1976: 51–2).

Later that year, after the coalition national government headed by Labour Party leader Ramsay Macdonald cut public servants' wages by about 10 per cent, and sailors' by up to 25 per cent, 12,000 sailors refused to obey orders to fall in for work. When the *Daily Worker* celebrated the 'Invergordon Mutiny', two men involved in printing the newspaper were charged under the 1797 Act. One received a nine-month sentence; the other two years with hard labour (Young 1976: 53–5, Ewing and Gearty 2000: 237–9).

During 1932, confronted by hunger marches that brought to London a million-signature petition against benefit cuts, a cabinet committee orchestrated the arrests of two NUWM leaders for attempting to cause disaffection in the police force. Both were jailed, one for two years and the other for three months. The latter, NUWM leader Wal Hannington, was charged for simply reminding police officers that they came from the working class and appealing for them to show solidarity with the unemployed. In court, he unsuccessfully argued that he could not cause disaffection among the police if it were already there. While probably true, his defence failed because the wording of the Police Act, like the incitement to mutiny legislation, prohibited 'attempting' or 'endeavouring' to cause, not 'causing' disaffection (Young 1976: 58–9).

Probably the last charge under the 1797 Act occurred in 1933, when four South Wales miners, all members of the Communist Party district committee, were charged with various offences under the Act, including conspiring to endeavour to seduce soldiers from their duty and allegiance. Their offence, reported by a police informer, was to ask him to distribute copies of the party's *Soldiers' Voice* among the troops (Young 1976: 61–2).

In 1934, the national government introduced the Incitement to Disaffection Act, which substantially reproduced the language of the 1797 Act but was designed to be easier to use, both legally and politically. It provided for summary prosecutions, in order to overcome the cumbersome machinery of indictment. In moving the bill, the Attorney General cited passages from Communist Party publications, notably one that urged servicemen that if war did come 'then it must be turned into a civil war against the capitalist war-mongers and their bankrupt system' (Ewing and Gearty 2000: 242). Such anti-war statements are clearly declarations of political program, not an immediate call for mutiny.

The new Act changed the words 'duty and allegiance' to 'duty or allegiance'. Thus, it became a crime to invite a soldier not to do his duty in a way that did not challenge his allegiance. Despite this, the Act was rarely used for a number of years (Ewing and Gearty 2000: 251, Young 1976: 76 ff). The first prosecution, in 1937, partially backfired. An 18-year-old economics student was initially jailed for 12 months for suggesting to an air force corporal that if he felt 'revolutionary', he could fly to Madrid to support the Republicans in the Spanish Civil War. Justice Singleton declared: 'You have pleaded guilty to an offence which strikes at the very safety of the Realm.' The severity of the sentence aroused such strong protest throughout the United Kingdom that the Home Secretary subsequently reduced it to a few months (Young 1976: 77).

During World War II, the Emergency Powers (Defence) Act 1939 effectively supplanted the 1934 Act, outlawing wider anti-war activities, including endeavouring to incite people not to obey conscription notices or to enlist voluntarily (despite the latter being a legal right). Numbers of pacifists and anarchists were prosecuted (Young 1976: 77–80).

There was no further prosecution under the 1934 Act until 1972. An anarchist, Michael Tobin, was given the maximum penalty of two years' imprisonment for circulating leaflets that explicitly appealed to soldiers to desert and join the Irish Republican Army. Conducting his defence, Tobin explained that his activities had a political purpose, saying 'a useful job would have been done if their distribution led to a questioning of the real aims and actions of the British government in Northern Ireland'. Tobin was refused leave to appeal and later complained to the European Commission on Human Rights that the British government had prevented him from exercising his rights to freedom of expression. By contrast, another defendant who admitted drafting the leaflets was acquitted after insisting that he was not trying to cause disruption or unrest, just gain publicity (Young 1976: 81).

The 1934 'duty or allegiance' amendment was cited in 1975 to help convict a pacifist anti-war activist for distributing leaflets to soldiers urging refusal to serve in Northern Ireland. In *R v. Arrowsmith* ([1975] QB 678, [1975] 2 WLR 484), the court held that although the act of seducing a soldier from his allegiance was more serious than seducing a soldier from his duty, an accused could be convicted of having either or both intents. The judges ruled that the relevant criminal intent 'may be to seduce from duty or from allegiance or both' ([1975] 2 WLR 484, 491).

The Labour government's dispatch of troops to the British-ruled enclave of Northern Ireland in 1969 had understandably provoked considerable public opposition. Three turning points had poisoned relations between the army and the local Catholic minority, and provoked armed resistance, primarily led by the Irish Republican Army. The first came in July 1970, when the army imposed a three-day curfew in the Catholic area of the Falls Road in Belfast, and conducted house-to-house searches (Hamill 1986: 34–40). The second event was the introduction of internment without trial in August 1971, with the initial detention of 346 Catholics (Hamill 1986: 56–70). The third was 'Bloody Sunday' in January 1972, when soldiers of the Parachute Regiment killed 13 unarmed civilians during a demonstration in Derry against internment (Bell 1993: 256–75).

The army quickly lost whatever early support it had among residents, yet the British government poured more troops into the province. From an initial deployment of 3,000 troops, the numbers peaked at 21,688 in July 1972, and were still at 12,000 when finally withdrawn in 1998 (Dewar 1997: 105, Ministry of Defence 1999). The mobilisation worsened the situation, at great cost to the population, with the number of civilians killed by the security forces growing from 10 in 1969 to 83 in 1972, before falling back to 10 in 1992 (Sutton 1994: 206).

Arrowsmith had circulated leaflets published by the British Withdrawal from Northern Ireland Campaign (BWNIC) that advised soldiers of various methods of quitting the armed forces, ranging from going absent without leave to conscientious objection and open refusal to be posted to Northern Ireland. The circular urged soldiers who believed it was wrong for British troops to be in Ireland to 'consider whether it is better to be killed for a cause you do not believe in or to be imprisoned for refusing to take part in the conflict'.

When Arrowsmith appealed against her 18-month sentence, the Court of Appeal damned the leaflet in vitriolic terms. While claiming to be politically neutral, Lord Justice Lawton, speaking for the judges, revealed definite political concerns that soldiers might well be minded to desert:

> This leaflet is the clearest incitement to mutiny and to desertion. As such, it is a most mischievous document. It is not only mischievous but it is wicked. This court is not concerned in any way with the political background against which this leaflet was distributed. What it is concerned with is the likely effects on young soldiers aged 18, 19 or 20, some of whom may be immature emotionally and of limited political understanding. It is particularly concerned about young soldiers who either come from Ireland or who have family connections with Ireland: there are probably a large number of them in the British Army. ([1975] 2 WLR 484, 488)

Lord Justice Lawton added that Arrowsmith's argument that she was merely giving information to those in the services who were already disaffected was 'an insult to the intelligence of the jury who were trying her' ([1975] 2 WLR 484, 494).

The court declared that it was no defence for Arrowsmith to argue that a previous incident had led her to believe that the Director of Public Prosecutions did not regard the leaflet as subversive. The judges further ruled that the word 'maliciously' in the Incitement to Disaffection Act simply meant intentional or deliberate; it did not require the prosecution to prove ill-will, spite or seditious intention. They also rejected the defence submission that 'lawful excuse' should be considered a defence under the Act. However, they accepted that Arrowsmith's false belief that she would not be prosecuted meant that, for the sake of making it appear that justice had been done, her otherwise warranted sentence of 18 months should be quashed. Arrowsmith was then released, after serving about seven months.

In the following year, a trial of 14 BWNIC activists for conspiracy to breach the Act provoked a vigorous public defence campaign, which generated considerable media coverage and popular support. Several defendants also conducted their own defences, making explicitly political statements against the military occupation of Northern Ireland. After a 51-day trial, the jury speedily delivered not guilty verdicts (Young 1976: 85–90, Harlow 1992, 165-6). Hosts of other prosecutions under the 1934 Act, involving protesting supporters of the BWNIC 14, were subsequently withdrawn (Young 1976: 90–4).

Given the legal precedent established in *Arrowsmith*, however, this outcome was hardly reassuring. Rather, it again pointed to the political character of such cases. Given the draconian nature of the law, and its judicial interpretation, prosecutions depend on the political climate, and successful defences hinge on political challenges rather than purely legal arguments. While many commentators hailed the verdicts as a victory for civil liberties, Young concluded that it was at best a limited victory, observing that 'the Act itself still exists, and no point of law was established in the 1975 trials which even mitigates its sweeping applicability' (Young 1976: 100).

United States

For the most part, US authorities, unlike those in Britain, have sought to respond to alleged incitements to mutiny under espionage law and sedition provisions. According to one scholar, 'Britain's policy of dividing seditious libel and incitement to mutiny into two separate offences makes more sense than the United States' effort to clump them both, along with myriad other crimes, into one overbroad Espionage Act (Boasberg 1990: 107).

As reviewed in Chapter 2, the most prominent of the Espionage Act sedition cases were *Schenck* and *Debs*, both decided by the Supreme Court in 1919. Eugene Debs was arrested in 1916 for making a speech in Ohio advocating socialism and supporting other Socialist Party supporters who had been jailed for violating the Espionage Act by urging resistance to the military draft. Debs's speeches against World War I and the Wilson administration and the war had earned the undying enmity of President Woodrow Wilson, who later called Debs a 'traitor to his country' (Salvatore 1984). At his trial, Debs called no witnesses, instead asking to address the court, which he did for two hours. After being convicted, he addressed the court again at his sentencing hearing, emphatically defending his socialist views. Debs declared:

> Your honor, I ask no mercy, I plead for no immunity. I realize that finally the
> right must prevail. I never more fully comprehended than now the great struggle
> between the powers of greed on the one hand and upon the other the rising
> hosts of freedom. I can see the dawn of a better day of humanity. The people
> are awakening. In due course of time they will come into their own. (Pietrusza
> 2007: 269–70)

Debs was sentenced to 10 years in prison. He was also disenfranchised for life. Debs appealed his conviction to the Supreme Court. In its ruling on *Debs v. United States*, the court examined several statements Debs had made regarding World War I and socialism. While Debs had carefully worded his speeches in an attempt to comply with the Espionage Act, the court found he still had the intention and effect of obstructing the draft and military recruitment. Among other things, the court cited Debs's praise for those imprisoned for obstructing the draft. Justice Oliver Wendell Holmes stated that little attention was needed since Debs's case was essentially the same as that of *Schenck v. United States*, in which the court had just upheld a similar conviction.

There were two counts. One alleged that in his speech Debs intentionally caused and incited and attempted to cause and incite insubordination, disloyalty, mutiny and refusal of duty in the military and naval forces of the United States. The second alleged that by the same speech he intentionally obstructed and attempted to obstruct the recruiting and enlistment service of the United States. In a dismissive judgement, that consisted of fewer than 1,800 words, delivered by Justice Holmes, the court declared that the statute and the charges were consistent with the First Amendment.

> The main theme of the speech was socialism, its growth, and a prophecy of its ultimate success. With that we have nothing to do, but if a part or the manifest intent of the more general utterances was to encourage those present to obstruct the recruiting service and if in passages such encouragement was directly given, the immunity of the general theme may not be enough to protect the speech. (249 US 211, 212–3)

Despite objections as to its admissibility, the court also relied on an anti-war proclamation to which Debs had subscribed:

> This document contained the usual suggestion that capitalism was the cause of the war and that our entrance into it 'was instigated by the predatory capitalists in the United States.' It alleged that the war of the United States against Germany could not 'be justified even on the plea that it is a war in defence of American rights or American 'honor.' It said: 'We brand the declaration of war by our Governments as a crime against the people of the United States and against the nations of the world. In all modern history there has been no war more unjustifiable than the war in which we are about to engage.'
>
> Its first recommendation was, 'continuous, active, and public opposition to the war, through demonstrations, mass petitions, and all other means within our power.' Evidence that the defendant accepted this view and this declaration of his duties at the time that he made his speech is evidence that if in that speech he used words tending to obstruct the recruiting service he meant that they should

have that effect. The principle is too well established and too manifestly good sense to need citation of the books. (249 US 211, 215–6)

Debs ran for president in the 1920 election while in prison at the Atlanta Federal Penitentiary. He received 913,664 write-in votes, slightly fewer than he had won in 1912, when he received 6 per cent, the highest number of votes for a Socialist Party presidential candidate in the US (Salvatore 1984).

Since World War II, specific provisions for incitement to mutiny or insubordination have existed in the United States Code 18. They are contained in Chapter 115, which covers 'Treason, sedition and subversive activities'. The two relevant sections, formerly enshrined in the Smith Act (see Chapter 2), treat these activities more seriously when the US is at war. 18 USC § 2387 states:

Activities affecting armed forces generally

(a) Whoever, with intent to interfere with, impair, or influence the loyalty, morale, or discipline of the military or naval forces of the United States:

(1) advises, counsels, urges, or in any manner causes or attempts to cause insubordination, disloyalty, mutiny, or refusal of duty by any member of the military or naval forces of the United States; or

(2) distributes or attempts to distribute any written or printed matter which advises, counsels, or urges insubordination, disloyalty, mutiny, or refusal of duty by any member of the military or naval forces of the United States—

Shall be fined under this title or imprisoned not more than ten years, or both, and shall be ineligible for employment by the United States or any department or agency thereof, for the five years next following his conviction.

(b) For the purposes of this section, the term 'military or naval forces of the United States' includes the Army of the United States, the Navy, Air Force, Marine Corps, Coast Guard, Navy Reserve, Marine Corps Reserve, and Coast Guard Reserve of the United States; and, when any merchant vessel is commissioned in the Navy or is in the service of the Army or the Navy, includes the master, officers, and crew of such vessel.

18 USC § 2388 states:

Activities affecting armed forces during war

(a) Whoever, when the United States is at war, willfully makes or conveys false reports or false statements with intent to interfere with the operation or success of the military or naval forces of the United States or to promote the success of its enemies; or

Whoever, when the United States is at war, willfully causes or attempts to cause insubordination, disloyalty, mutiny, or refusal of duty, in the military or naval forces of the United States, or willfully obstructs the recruiting or enlistment service of the United States, to the injury of the service or the United States, or attempts to do so—

Shall be fined under this title or imprisoned not more than twenty years, or both.

(b) If two or more persons conspire to violate subsection (a) of this section and one or more such persons do any act to effect the object of the conspiracy, each of the parties to such conspiracy shall be punished as provided in said subsection (a).

(c) Whoever harbors or conceals any person who he knows, or has reasonable grounds to believe or suspect, has committed, or is about to commit, an offense under this section, shall be fined under this title or imprisoned not more than ten years, or both.

(d) This section shall apply within the admiralty and maritime jurisdiction of the United States, and on the high seas, as well as within the United States.

For members of the US armed forces, military law also applies. The Uniform Code of Military Justice (UCMJ) defines mutiny thus:

Art. 94. (§ 894) 2004 Mutiny or Sedition

(a) Any person subject to this code (chapter) who—

(1) with intent to usurp or override lawful military authority, refuses, in concert with any other person, to obey orders or otherwise do his duty or creates any violence or disturbance is guilty of mutiny;

(2) with intent to cause the overthrow or destruction of lawful civil authority, creates, in concert with any other person, revolt, violence, or other disturbance against that authority is guilty of sedition;

(3) fails to do his utmost to prevent and suppress a mutiny or sedition being committed in his presence, or fails to take all reasonable means to inform his superior commissioned officer or commanding officer of a mutiny or sedition which he knows or has reason to believe is taking place, is guilty of a failure to suppress or report a mutiny or sedition.

(b) A person who is found guilty of attempted mutiny, mutiny, sedition, or failure to suppress or report a mutiny or sedition shall be punished by death or such other punishment as a court-martial may direct.

During the Vietnam War, anti-mutiny and anti-insubordination provisions in the US Code and the UCMJ were invoked against numbers of members of the armed forces to try to suppress widespread opposition to the war (Wulf 1972). Partly because of conscription, the deepening public opposition to the war had a major impact in the ranks, producing resistance, refusals to embark to Vietnam, and soldiers talking 'Marx all night' (Wulf 1972: 665). Those prosecuted included the 'Fort Jackson Eight', whose leaders were members of the Socialist Workers Party, which at that time still purported to be a Trotskyist party. The eight had circulated a petition on their base demanding that the post's commanding general provide them with facilities to hold an open meeting to discuss the Vietnam War, the civil rights of Americans, including those within the armed forces, and the civil liberties of soldiers at Fort Jackson (Wulf 1972: 671). In another instance, a black Marine was prosecuted under both 18 USC § 2387 and the UCMJ on multiple counts of urging and attempting to cause insubordination, disloyalty and refusal of duty for saying in private conversations such things as there was no 'sense in going overseas and fighting the white man's war' (Wulf 1972: 674). After the marine was sentenced to ten years' imprisonment, the Court of Military Appeals set aside the section 2387 convictions, but the soldier still served more than two years in confinement (Wulf 1972: 674).

Formally, military law requires obedience only to lawful orders. Disobedience to unlawful orders is the obligation of every member of the US armed forces, a principle established by the Nuremberg trials and reaffirmed in the aftermath of the My Lai Massacre. However, a US soldier who disobeys an order after deeming it unlawful will almost certainly be court-martialled to determine whether the disobedience was proper. A review of some of the Vietnam War cases concluded that 'by insisting on the suppression of dissent in order to avert the possibility of the slightest departure from its disciplinary code', the army 'demands more than it should be entitled to expect, both constitutionally and practically' (Wulf 1972: 680).

As noted in Chapter 2, during the Vietnam War, both the Congress and the Supreme Court were prepared to dispense with First Amendment free speech. In 1965, both chambers of Congress overwhelmingly voted for a law to make the wilful destruction or mutilation of a military draft card a criminal offence. In *United States v. O'Brien* (391 US 367 (1968)), the Supreme Court upheld a conviction under this legislation, ruling that such a law could override First Amendment rights so long as it furthered a 'substantial governmental interest'. The judges declined to examine the actual congressional purpose, despite evidence that it was indeed to suppress anti-war opinion (Stone 2004: 474–7). That ruling paved the way for a prosecution for conspiracy to advocate draft resistance. Four men, including the famous paediatrician Dr Benjamin Spock, were sentenced to two years' jail in the Boston Five conspiracy trial, although their convictions were later overturned by a federal appeals court on technical grounds (*United States v. Spock* 416 F2d 165 (1st Cir 1969), Stone 2004: 477–82).

Australia

In Australia, during both world wars, similar incitement of disaffection provisions were adopted, via executive regulations, and employed to suppress socialist and anti-war opinion.

During World War I, Tom Barker, a leader of the International Workers of the World and editor of its newspaper *Direct Action*, was twice convicted of publishing material likely to prejudice recruiting. The first was in 1915 for writing and printing 'perhaps the most famous Australian poster of World War I' (Turner 1969: 15). The poster was a parody of the official recruitment propaganda. It urged 'capitalists, parsons, politicians, landlords, newspaper editors, and other stay-at-home patriots' to head the call 'to arms' because 'your country needs you in the trenches'. As for workers, the poster advised them to 'follow your masters'. A Labor Party parliamentarian called on the authorities to not waste a moment in apprehending the 'disloyal ruffians who printed that cowardly and lying document'. He was incensed that the poster impugned the character of the 'well-to-do classes' who were 'doing their duty' most 'nobly and wholeheartedly'. The New South Wales Chief Secretary George Black, a former radical socialist, instructed the police to find the culprit. Barker was charged under the NSW War Precautions Regulations with publishing a poster prejudicial to recruiting. He was convicted, but won on appeal because the NSW state regulations intruded in a field where federal law prevailed (Turner 1969: 15–17).

Although Barker's first conviction was quashed on appeal, in 1916 he was convicted again, this time under federal regulations. His jailing provided a trigger for the 'Sydney Twelve' prosecution, discussed earlier in this chapter. (In the Sydney Twelve trial, the prosecution alleged that IWW members burned down buildings to seek to pressure the government to release Barker.) By the time that the Sydney Twelve trial was conducted, Barker had been released, after the Governor-General cut his sentence from a year to three months (Turner 1969: 23, 37–8).

Throughout World War II, the National Security Act 1939–40 conferred almost unlimited powers upon the executive, including that of creating criminal offences. Section 5 of the Act authorised the Governor-General to make regulations for securing the public safety and the defence of the Commonwealth and for prescribing all matters necessary or convenient for the more effectual prosecution of the war.

Three members of the Trotskyist movement – Jack Wishart, Gil Roper and Allan Thistlewayte – were imprisoned for up to eight months for possessing or circulating material that argued that the war was being fought in the interests of the business elites and urged soldiers to elect committees to watch their officers (Greenland 1998: 96–104). Wishart was jailed for merely possessing copies of a document, without any evidence that he or anyone else actually circulated them to members of the armed forces. He was convicted of the offence that with intent to endeavour to cause disaffection among members of the Second Australian Imperial Forces, engaged in the service of the King, he had in his possession a document, the dissemination of which among soldiers would constitute an endeavour to cause disaffection.

In *Wishart v. Fraser* ([1941] HCA 8; (1941) 64 CLR 470), the Australian High Court unanimously upheld the constitutional validity of the National Security Act and Regulations. The judges also dismissed Wishart's argument that there was no evidence that he intended to cause disaffection among members of the armed forces because the document, copies of which were seized from his office and bedroom in a police raid, was outdated and copies had been retained by him only by accident. The documents were discovered during police raids that accompanied the proscription of the Trotskyist Communist League of Australia on 25 June 1940 (Greenland 1998: 101). Wishart said he had intended to burn the documents before the police raids.

Justice Dixon ruled that it was 'hardly open to doubt' that the document was written to cause disaffection among soldiers, and that it was fairly open to the trial magistrate to infer that Wishart 'had never completely given up his intention of using the document he retained if the opportunity arose or offered'. The underlying anti-communist viewpoint that animated both the prosecution and the High Court ruling was exemplified by Justice Williams, who noted that when the police searched the appellant's office and home, they found about 14 copies of the document 'together with copies of another document entitled "This Imperialist War" and a mass of communist literature'. The judge noted that Wishart was a member of the executive of the Communist League of Australia and

> [H]e admitted that in the middle of 1940 it was still a principle of the doctrines of the Fourth International that communist *nuclei* should be formed in every military unit and he considered that this principle should be acted upon. He said that he looked upon the army as an instrument of capitalist oppression, that he considered that soldiers' committees should be organized which would take over control of the army in due course, and that he would have liked the general situation to have advanced to such a stage on 25th June that the right time for doing this would have arrived, although it had not in fact done so.

> All this is evidence to show that the clear intention he had at the end of February to endeavour to disaffect the troops still persisted on 25th June, although, on that date, the fear of punishment was causing him to bide his time until the situation became more propitious for the resumption of that persistent and systematic propaganda which Lenin had advised his disciples must be carried on to final victory.

The inference was that anyone who was a disciple of Lenin must have the requisite subversive intent, regardless of any proof. Presumably, the judge took judicial notice of Lenin's writings, but it is not known if he actually read any of them. On that basis, Wishart's conviction and sentence of 12 months' imprisonment were upheld. The ruling illustrates how far incitement to mutiny or disaffection measures can be extended to criminalise political opinion, well beyond any 'clear and present danger' of actual incitement.

Chapter 5
Espionage, Official Secrets and Sabotage

These offences too raise a host of political, as well as legal, issues. First and foremost, both espionage and sabotage are generally broadly and vaguely defined offences that are open to political exploitation. In particular, 'whistleblowing', and other forms of the leaking of secret or classified official information in order to expose government abuses, can be prosecuted under espionage and official secrets legislation. Sabotage, although more rarely invoked, has the potential to cover acts of resistance and opposition to government policies, especially in the context of anti-war protests, such as occupations of military facilities.

Secondly, the definitions of these offences often hinge upon conceptions of what is prejudicial or harmful to 'the interests of the state' or 'national defence' or 'security'. Those accused of divulging government secrets or obstructing military activities may do so with the belief that their actions are indeed beneficial or even essential for the wellbeing of society. Courts, however, have ruled that 'the interests of the state' and other notions of national security can be interpreted, for the purposes of the criminal law, only by the legally constituted government of the day. Moreover, numbers of espionage and sabotage offences stipulate that an intention to harm 'the interests of the state' can be deduced from an accused person's known character – in effect, from his or her political beliefs.

Thirdly, both espionage and sabotage have been extended to cover threats to economic interests that are judged to be of critical importance to the state. This can pave the way for the protection of major or powerful business and financial interests, at the expense of the interests of working people.

Espionage and Official Secrets

Offences in this field are many, and there is a considerable scope for overlap. Broadly speaking, there are two types of offences: those covering espionage in the sense of spying for a foreign power or agency, and those dealing with leaking official information. These kinds of offences provide scope for governments to use them for various political purposes. In particular, official secrets provisions, adopted in the name of combating espionage or protecting national security, can be used to lend political legitimacy to operations to reduce or prevent scrutiny of the political, intelligence and military establishment. Governments are wont to argue that they are merely protecting the nation from external threat.

Of course, most national states also conduct espionage against other national states, through a vast array of intelligence and military agencies, the largest of which is possibly the Central Intelligence Agency (CIA). Indeed, espionage is normally part of an institutional effort (governmental or corporate), and the term is most readily associated with state spying on potential or actual enemies. Many nation states routinely spy on their formal allies as well, although they never comment on this. Governments may also employ private companies to collect information on their behalf.

Documentary evidence of these practices came to light in 2010, as the result of more than 250,000 US diplomatic cables being posted on WikiLeaks, a website specialising in publishing information supplied by government whistleblowers. Among other things, the documents showed that US Secretary of State Hillary Clinton signed a secret order directing American diplomats to act as spies around the world against friends and enemies alike. In the memo, US diplomats were instructed to gather personal details about UN Secretary-General Ban Ki-moon as well as UN Security Council permanent representatives from Britain, China, Russia and France.

The leaked cable from Clinton, dated July 2009, included requests to find out personal passwords and encryption keys used by diplomats and officials in private and commercial computer networks. The cable demanded biometric information on 'undersecretaries, heads of specialised agencies and their chief advisers, top SYG (Secretary-General) aides, heads of peace operations and political field missions, including force commanders'. Clinton also wanted credit card numbers, email addresses, phone, fax and pager numbers and frequent-flyer account numbers.

The secret 'national human intelligence collection directive' was sent to US missions in New York, Vienna and Rome, as well as 33 embassies and consulates, including those in London, Paris and Moscow. It was also sent to the CIA, the US Secret Service and the FBI, indicating an intelligence-gathering operation involving thousands of US officials.

According to the report of the leaks in *The Australian*, 'International treaties ban spying at the UN, but it is no secret many countries attempt to seek information clandestinely from within the walls of the UN building. Britain was accused of bugging other UN member states ahead of the key vote on Iraq in 2003 ... The recipients would have had to resort to hacking and other intrusive methods to meet requests' (*The Australian* 2010).

A spy breaking the host country's laws may be deported, imprisoned, or even executed. An alleged spy breaking his or her own country's laws can be imprisoned for espionage or treason, or executed, as were the Rosenbergs (see below). For example, when Aldrich Ames handed dossiers of CIA agents in the Eastern Bloc to the CIA's Russian counterpart, the KGB, he was sentenced to life in prison in 1994. His contact, who had diplomatic immunity, was declared *persona non grata* and taken to the airport. Ames's wife was threatened with life imprisonment if her husband did not cooperate; he did, and she was given a five-year sentence. Hugh Francis Redmond, a CIA officer in China, spent 19 years in a Chinese prison for espionage (from 1951 to 1970) – and died there – as he was operating without diplomatic cover and immunity.

A series of WikiLeaks exposures during 2010 led to calls for the espionage laws to be toughened to crack down on embarrassing leaks of secret documents. A US Republican senator proposed rewriting the Espionage Act to target WikiLeaks. Senator John Ensign of Nevada announced a bill that would make it illegal to identify informants working with the US military, which WikiLeaks allegedly did earlier in 2010 when releasing files about the killing of civilians by US and allied forces during the war in Afghanistan. In a later release of politically damaging Iraq war files, WikiLeaks removed names, but the US Defense Department argued that the information could still identify dozens of people.

Existing law (18 USC 798) made it illegal to disclose classified information about a 'code, cipher, or cryptographic system of the United States' or 'the communication intelligence activities of the United States' (see below). Any violation was a federal felony punishable by prison terms of up to 10 years. Ensign's proposal would have added the names of informants and other people secretly aiding the US government to the list of types of information that could not legally be disclosed.

An earlier, well-documented example of governments using official secrets provisions to suppress politically damaging or embarrassing material was the enactment of the UK Official Secrets Act of 1911 which, because of the alleged threat of German espionage in the period leading up to World War I, went through all its parliamentary processes in one afternoon. Although the professed primary objective was to tackle espionage, section 2 of this statute had a significantly wider application. 'Over subsequent years it was used with draconian effect, not only on those who might be engaged in activities which threatened national security, but also on anyone who revealed government information for whatever reason, there being no defences provided under the Act' (Rowland 2004). Adverse criticism of section 2's use in a line of cases led to it eventually being replaced by the Official Secrets Act 1989 (Birkinshaw 2001: 115–21, Robertson 1993: 158–67). Whether this 1989 statute actually overcame the repressive processes bound up with section 2, however, is open to question.

Courts have generally allowed governments great leeway to invoke sweeping powers under the banner of fighting espionage. In 1979, in a judgment subsequently relied upon by British courts, the European Court of Human Rights held that legislation permitting monitoring of mail, etc. clearly interfered with an individual's rights under article 8 (1) of the European Convention on Human Rights. Powers of secret surveillance of citizens, being features of a police state, could only be tolerated under the Convention if they were strictly necessary to safeguard the institutions of the state. The court ruled, however, that since democratic societies found themselves threatened by 'highly sophisticated' forms of espionage and by terrorism, legislation granting powers of secret surveillance over the mail, etc. of 'subversive elements' within their jurisdiction was, under exceptional conditions, necessary in a democratic society in the interests of 'national security' and/or for the prevention of disorder or crime. Failure to inform an individual beforehand that he had been subject to surveillance was not in principle incompatible with article 8 (2).

This decision in *Klass and others v. Federal Republic of Germany* ((1979–80) 2 EHRR 214, ECtHR) considered legislation in Germany which permitted the state authorities to open and inspect mail and to listen to telephone conversations in order to protect against, inter alia, 'imminent dangers' threatening the 'free democratic constitutional order' and 'the existence or the security' of the state.

Espionage and its punishment are largely unregulated by international law, except for the laws of war. Because states have traditionally denied involvement in such activities, international law has denied the existence of espionage as a legal concept to be regulated by law (Kish 1995).

The extension of espionage law to cover economic espionage was signalled in 1996, when US President Bill Clinton signed the Economic Espionage Act (EEA) into law.

Before this legislation, there was no specific US federal law against stealing trade secrets. The EEA covers a range of trade secret theft, including the robbery of private technical, business, and financial information that is vital to an entity's economic stability. The act contains two separate provisions. The first provision, under Section 1831, is directed toward foreign economic espionage and requires that the theft of a trade secret be done to benefit a foreign government, any instrument of a foreign government, or foreign agent. By contrast, the second provision, under Section 1832, makes the commercial theft of trade secrets a criminal act, regardless of who benefits.

Reflecting the allegedly more serious nature of economic espionage, a defendant convicted for violating Section 1831 can be imprisoned for up to 15 years and fined $500,000 or both. Corporations and other organisations can be fined up to $10 million. A defendant convicted for theft of trade secrets under Section 1832 can be imprisoned for up to 10 years and fined $500,000 or both. Corporations and other entities can be fined no more than $5 million.

Many government secrecy provisions extend beyond what can be regarded as crimes against the state. Secrecy measures cover numerous circumstances, ranging from protection of individual privacy to suppression of information about law enforcement operations. The breadth of these laws was highlighted by a report by the Australian Law Reform Commission in 2010 on Secrecy Laws and Open Government in Australia. The commission undertook a mapping exercise to identify and analyse provisions in federal legislation that imposed secrecy or confidentiality obligations on individuals or bodies regarding official information. It identified 506 secrecy provisions in 176 pieces of primary and subordinate legislation. Approximately 70 per cent of the statutory secrecy provisions created criminal offences. Around 75 per cent of these offences were indictable offences – punishable by imprisonment for a period exceeding 12 months (ALRC 2010).

Britain

In the UK, espionage that takes the form of spying is still covered by the Official Secrets Acts of 1911 and 1920. Official information is further protected by the Official Secrets Act 1989.

Under section 1 of the 1911 Act, a person commits an offence, referred to in a note to the act as 'spying', if he or she, for any purpose prejudicial to the safety or interests of the state:

(a) approaches, inspects, passes over or is in the neighbourhood of, or enters any prohibited place,

(b) makes any sketch, plan, model, or note which is calculated to be or might be or is intended to be directly or indirectly useful to an enemy; or

(c) obtains, collects, records, or publishes, or communicates to any other person any secret official code word, or pass word, or any sketch, plan, model, article, or note, or other document which is calculated to be or might be or is intended to be directly or indirectly useful to an enemy.

For the prosecution to obtain a conviction under this section, it need not show that the accused person was guilty of any particular act tending to show a purpose prejudicial to the safety or interests of the state. He or she may be convicted if, from the 'circumstances of the case', or his conduct, or his 'known character as proved', it appears that his or her purpose was a purpose prejudicial to the safety or interests of the state.

This offence covers all such acts committed by any person within the UK's jurisdiction, and such acts committed elsewhere by British officers or subjects. It is not necessary for the person concerned to have been warned beforehand that they were subject to the Official Secrets Act. The 1920 Act creates further offences of doing any 'act preparatory' to spying, or of soliciting, inciting, seeking to persuade, or aiding and abetting any other person to commit spying.

The maximum sentence for spying is 14 years' imprisonment; however, longer sentences may be passed as consecutive sentences for a series of offences. George Blake, who spied for the Soviet Union in the 1950s, was sentenced to 42 years' imprisonment – three consecutive 14-year terms.

Foreign intelligence officers acting in the UK under diplomatic cover may enjoy immunity from prosecution. Such persons can only be tried for spying (or any criminal offence) if diplomatic immunity is waived beforehand. Those officers operating without diplomatic cover have no such immunity from prosecution.

In 1989, a Czechoslovak intelligence officer known only as 'Erwin van Haarlem' was convicted of an offence under section 7 of the Official Secrets Act 1920 and sentenced to 10 years' imprisonment, with a recommendation that he should be deported on his release. Vaclav Jelinek did not disclose his real name during the investigations or at the trial and was sometimes referred to as '*the spy with no name'*. He was released and deported to Prague in 1994, under section 46 of the Criminal Justice Act 1991, which permits the early release of prisoners who are subject to deportation orders.

The Official Secrets Act 1989 largely, but not exclusively, applies only to members of the security and intelligence services, and to other public servants or contractors who work with security and intelligence information. Section 1 creates an offence relating to the disclosure of security and intelligence information. The other main sections are section 2, which relates to the disclosure of defence information; section 3 on information concerning international relations; and section 4 on law enforcement information that would assist a criminal or the commission of a crime.

Section 5 outlaws further disclosure or publication of information obtained in contravention of other sections of the act. This section applies to everyone, regardless of whether they are a government employee, or whether they have signed the act. It allows, for example, the prosecution of newspapers or journalists who publish secret information leaked to them. Other sections cover secret information belonging to foreign governments or international organisations, and retention of information beyond the official need for it. Penalties under all these various sections range up to two years' imprisonment and a fine.

In section 2 (since repealed) of the Official Secrets Act 1911 there was an exception regarding a duty to communicate information 'in the interest of the state'. That exemption was considered in *R v. Ponting (*[1985] Crim LR 318). Clive Ponting, a senior civil servant in the Ministry of Defence, was charged under the Act. In preparing a briefing for the minister, Ponting saw documents which showed that the government had provided incorrect information to parliament about the sinking of the Argentinian ship *Belgrano* during the Falklands War. When the minister did not correct the information, Ponting provided copies of the documents to an opposition member of parliament. In his defence, Ponting argued that he had disclosed the documents 'in the interests of the state'. The trial judge, however, directed the jury that the 'interests of the state' were the interests according to the recognised organs of government and the policies as expounded by the government of the day. Nevertheless, the jury found Ponting not guilty.

In 2000, David Shayler, a former member of the UK Security Service, was indicted on three counts of unlawful disclosure of documents and information contrary to sections 1 and 4 of the Official Secrets Act 1989. On Appeal the House of Lords rejected his argument that he had leaked the documents for a good purpose, and to expose a series of crimes. The court noted that when the act was debated in parliament, an amendment designed to introduce a public interest defence was rejected (*Shayler, R v.* [2002] UKHL 11).

Shayler was prosecuted in August 1997 for passing secret documents to the *Mail on Sunday* that alleged that MI5 was paranoid about socialists, and that it had previously investigated Labour Party ministers. Shayler also stated that MI6 had been involved in a failed assassination attack on Libyan leader Muammar al-

Gaddafi in 1996. He said the intelligence services were planting misleading stories in the mainstream media, such as a 1996 article linking Colonel Gaddafi's son with a currency counterfeiting operation. This was later confirmed when Gaddafi's son served a newspaper with a libel writ. According to Shayler too, the 1994 bombing of the Israeli embassy in London was known to the intelligence services before it happened, and could have been prevented.

Shayler was convicted on one charge of passing on information acquired from a telephone tap (a breach of section 4 of the act), and two others of passing on information and documents obtained by virtue of his membership of the service (a breach of section 1). He was sentenced to 6 months in prison (Hollingsworth and Fielding 1999).

United States

US law defines espionage toward itself as 'the act of obtaining, delivering, transmitting, communicating, or receiving information about the national defense with an intent, or reason to believe, that the information may be used to the injury of the United States or to the advantage of any foreign nation'. Espionage is covered by a series of offences, contained in sections 792 to 798 of Chapter 37, entitled Espionage and Censorship, of the United States Code title 18, as well as by Article 106 of the Uniform Code of Military Justice.

The primary US Code offences are harbouring or concealing persons, gathering, transmitting or losing defence information, gathering or delivering defence information to aid foreign government, photographing and sketching defence installations, use of aircraft for photographing defence installations, publication and sale of photographs of defence installations, and disclosure of classified information. Penalties range up to death or life imprisonment for gathering or delivering defence information to aid a foreign government, or seeking to do so during wartime.

Julius and Ethel Rosenberg were tried and convicted in 1951 for conspiracy to commit espionage, accused of passing information about the atomic bomb to the Soviet Union. They were executed in 1953 at the height of the post-World War II Red Scare, orphaning two young children. Theirs was the first execution of civilians for espionage in US history (Roberts 2001).

Since the execution, decoded Soviet cables, codenamed VENONA, have supported courtroom testimony that Julius acted as a courier and recruiter for the Soviets, but doubts remain about the level of Ethel's involvement. The decision to execute the Rosenbergs was highly political and remains controversial. Other atomic spies who were caught by the FBI offered confessions and were not executed. Ethel's brother, David Greenglass, who supplied documents to Julius, served 10 years of his 15-year sentence. Harry Gold, who identified Greenglass, served 15 years in prison as the courier for him and the British scientist, Klaus Fuchs. Morton Sobell, who was tried with the Rosenbergs, served 17 years and 9 months.

Julius Rosenberg and others began providing information to the Soviets in the context of World War II, when the US and the Soviet Union were officially allied in war against Nazi Germany. The US, beginning after the Nazi invasion, extended significant material support to the Soviet Union through the Lend Lease Act, which made available US tanks, planes and munitions to the Soviet Union as it suffered the brunt of the Wehrmacht's military might. Despite being allies during the war, the US government did not share information with the Soviet Union for the nuclear warfare Manhattan Project. However, the Soviets were aware of the project and made a number of attempts to infiltrate its operations at the University of California, Berkeley. A number of project members voluntarily gave secret information to Soviet agents, many because they were sympathetic to communism, or the Soviet Union's role in the war, and did not believe that the US should have a monopoly on atomic weapons. After the war, the US continued to protect its nuclear secrets. Nevertheless, the Soviet Union was able to produce its own atomic weapons by 1949.

Ethel Rosenberg was indicted along with her husband so that the prosecution could use her to pressure him into giving up the names of others who were involved. However, neither Julius nor Ethel Rosenberg named anyone else and during testimony each asserted their right under the US Constitution's Fifth Amendment to not incriminate themselves whenever asked about involvement in the Communist Party of the USA (CPUSA) or with its members.

What the state wanted of Julius Rosenberg – as with the artists of the 'Hollywood Ten' – was a confession and a denunciation of communism. Most historians now agree that Ethel was not involved in providing information to the Soviet Union, although she may have been aware of her husband's activities. The grand jury testimony, released more than 50 years after the trial, points in this direction and suggests that the prosecution had determined to gain a conviction against Ethel regardless of the evidence. In any case, the Rosenbergs were charged and convicted of 'conspiracy', a crime based solely on intent (Roberts 2001).

The Rosenbergs were sentenced to death by Judge Irving Kaufman under Section 2 of the Espionage Act of 1917 (now 18 US Code 794), which prohibits transmitting or attempting to transmit to a foreign government information 'relating to the national defense'. In imposing the death penalty, Kaufman noted that he held them responsible not only for espionage but also for the deaths of the Korean War:

> Citizens of this country who betray their fellow-countrymen can be under none of the delusions about the benignity of Soviet power that they might have been prior to World War II. The nature of Russian terrorism is now self-evident ... I consider your crime worse than murder ... I believe your conduct in putting into the hands of the Russians the A-Bomb years before our best scientists predicted Russia would perfect the bomb has already caused, in my opinion, the Communist aggression in Korea, with the resultant casualties exceeding 50,000 and who knows but that millions more of innocent people may pay the price of

your treason. Indeed, by your betrayal you undoubtedly have altered the course of history to the disadvantage of our country. No one can say that we do not live in a constant state of tension. We have evidence of your treachery all around us every day for the civilian defense activities throughout the nation are aimed at preparing us for an atom bomb attack. (Kaufman 1951)

Nobel Prize winner Jean-Paul Sartre called the case 'a legal lynching which smears with blood a whole nation. By killing the Rosenbergs, you have quite simply tried to halt the progress of science by human sacrifice ... your country is sick with fear ... you are afraid of the shadow of your own bomb' (Schneir and Schneir 1973: 254). Many other prominent people, including Albert Einstein, Pablo Picasso and Nobel-Prize-winning physical chemist Harold Urey, protested. The International Longshoremen's Association Local 968 stopped working for a day in protest. Pope Pius XII appealed to President Dwight D. Eisenhower to spare the couple, but Eisenhower refused, and all other appeals were also unsuccessful. Some likened the affair to the witch-hunts that marred Salem and early modern Europe, a comparison that provided the inspiration for Arthur Miller's critically acclaimed play, *The Crucible* (Schrecker 1998).

In 2008, the release of previously secret grand jury transcripts confirmed that crucial testimony was perjured in the trial. The transcripts, which had been sealed for 55 years, only became available through the National Archives and Records Administration after a lawsuit by historians and an independent archive. A New York court ordered that the testimony of all but four of 45 grand jury witnesses be released. This included both the testimony of Ethel Rosenberg herself and that of Ruth Greenglass, the wife of David Greenglass, Ethel's brother.

The testimony of Ruth Greenglass strongly suggested that at least Ethel Rosenberg was convicted based on perjured testimony. During the Rosenberg trial, Ruth Greenglass claimed that Ethel Rosenberg typed up secrets stolen by David Greenglass, who was a machinist at Los Alamos in New Mexico, the centre of the US atomic bomb project. The Greenglasses testified that Ethel then passed the typed sheets via Julius Rosenberg to Soviet intelligence. The grand jury testimony completely contradicts that version of events. After stating to the grand jury that she had assisted Julius Rosenberg with espionage, prosecutors asked Greenglass, 'Didn't you write [the atomic bomb information] down on a piece of paper?' 'Yes,' she answered, 'I wrote [the atomic bomb information] down on a piece of paper and [Julius Rosenberg] took it with him.' This grand jury testimony confirmed the account given by former Soviet intelligence officials, who said that the information they received was written in longhand.

In 2001, David Greenglass, who spent 10 years in prison for espionage, disavowed his own testimony about his sister's typed notes. He said the government blackmailed him by threatening to execute his wife. He stated in an interview in 2001: 'I don't know who typed it, frankly, and to this day I can't remember that the typing took place. I had no memory of that at all—none whatsoever.' He said he gave false testimony to protect himself and his wife, Ruth, and that he was encouraged by the prosecution to do so. He refused to express any remorse for his decision to sacrifice his sister, saying only that he did not realise that the death penalty would be invoked (Roberts 2001).

The execution of the Rosenbergs contrasts with the treatment of Robert Philip Hanssen, a former American FBI agent who spied for Soviet and Russian intelligence services against the United States for more than 20 years. Despite the fact that he revealed highly sensitive security information to the Soviet Union, federal prosecutors agreed not to seek the death penalty in exchange for his guilty pleas to 15 espionage and conspiracy charges. Hanssen, who was arrested in 2001, was charged with selling American secrets to Moscow for more than $US1.4 million in cash and diamonds over a 22-year period (Wise 2003).

Australia

As noted by the Australian Law Reform Commission in 2010, secrecy provisions contained in Australian legislation are many and varied (ALRC 2010). These include particular provisions in the legislation covering the intelligence agencies, such as the Australian Security Intelligence Organisation Act 1979. When it comes to espionage-related offences and the disclosure of government information, Australia, like Britain, has two main overlapping sets of law: one relating to espionage and the other to official secrets. The first set is found in Part 5.2 of the Criminal Code Act 1995, covering espionage and similar activities. Section 91.1 states:

> (1)   A person commits an offence if:
>   (a)   the person communicates, or makes available:
>   (i)   information concerning the Commonwealth's security or defence; or
>   (ii)   information concerning the security or defence of another country, being information that the person acquired (whether directly or indirectly) from the Commonwealth; and
>   (b)   the person does so intending to prejudice the Commonwealth's security or defence; and
>   (c)   the person's act results in, or is likely to result in, the information being communicated or made available to another country or a foreign organisation, or to a person acting on behalf of such a country or organisation.
> Penalty: Imprisonment for 25 years.

The official secrets provisions are found in the Crimes Act 1914, primarily in sections 70 and 79. Section 70 forbids a Commonwealth officer or former officer to 'publish or communicate' without authorisation, 'any fact or document' that 'it is his or her duty not to disclose'. The penalty is imprisonment for two years.

Section 70(1) includes an exception to the offence where a person discloses the information 'to some person to whom he or she is authorised to publish or communicate it'. Section 70(2) contains a different exception by requiring that the publication or communication be 'without lawful authority or excuse', proof of which lies with the defendant. The scope of each exception, and the extent of any difference between them, is unclear. Courts have held that section 70 does not create an exception or defence relating to disclosure in the public interest. However, this issue might be a factor in sentencing in a particular case (ALRC 2010: 3.112–14)

Since 2000, a number of prosecutions for the breach of secrecy provisions have been brought under section 70, even where specific secrecy offences would have been available. Successful prosecutions for breaches of section 70, include:

- an officer of the Australian Taxation Office – for providing documents containing summaries of taxpayers and tax agents to a private business associate;
- an officer of the Australian Customs Service – for providing reports about security at Sydney Airport to journalists;
- an officer of the Office of Indigenous Policy Coordination – for disclosing information relating to the then draft *Declaration on the Rights of Indigenous Peoples* to her daughter, and information relating to federal indigenous policy to a member of the Mutitjulu community in the Northern Territory; and
- an officer of the Centrelink welfare agency – for disclosing personal details of Centrelink customers to a firm which offered to pay for information leading to the whereabouts of various people. (ALRC 2010: 3.94)

A distinction has been drawn between the communication of a fact or a document in one case. A former officer of the Australian Customs Service, Allan Kessing, was convicted of providing reports about airport security arrangements to two journalists (*Kessing v. R* [2008] NSWCCA 310). On appeal, the New South Wales Court of Criminal Appeal held that the trial judge had misdirected the jury in saying that it was sufficient if the prosecution could establish that Kessing had confirmed the accuracy of material that journalists had obtained from another source. The judges stated that:

> The offence under s 70 may be committed by publishing or communicating a fact which came to the knowledge of the accused by virtue of having been a Commonwealth officer or by publishing or communicating a document which came into his or her possession by virtue of having been a Commonwealth officer or by both. This was a case in which the offence charged was the communication of the documents. To confirm the accuracy of a document leaked by another to a journalist may be to communicate a fact, but in my opinion it is not to communicate the document. (*Kessing v. R* [2008] NSWCCA 310, [61])

However, the *Crimes Act* provides no guidance as to the meaning of the term 'publishes or communicates'. In *Kessing v. R*, the judges adopted a very broad approach:

> To 'communicate' is to transmit or to impart knowledge or make known (*Macquarie Concise Dictionary*, 3rd ed). One may 'communicate' a document by communicating the contents of the document. This is how the Crown particularised this case. Generally, 'to publish' connotes to make publicly known, however, in the law of defamation publication applies to making the matter complained of known to any person other than the person defamed. (*Kessing v. R* [2008] NSWCCA 310, [31])

Further, Justice Bell confirmed that communication can be direct or indirect:

> Communication of the contents of a document requires no more than that the contents be conveyed or transmitted to another. This may be done directly by handing the document to another or by reading the document to another. It may be done indirectly by leaving the document on a park bench for another to collect or in any of a variety of ways. The essential feature of communicating a fact or document for the purposes of s 70 is that the communication is intentional. (*Kessing v. R* [2008] NSWCCA 310, [36])

In the end, despite the misdirection of the jury, the court dismissed Kessing's appeal, concluding that no substantial miscarriage of justice actually occurred. Kessing had been sentenced to nine months' imprisonment, but with the sentence suspended on the condition of good behaviour.

The other main Crimes Act provision, section 79, establishes a range of offences that extend beyond government officers to anyone who takes unauthorised possession of official information. Different subsections deal with information that has been obtained in contravention of section 91.1 of the Criminal Code; that relates to a prohibited place; and that 'by reason of its nature or the circumstances under which it was entrusted' to a government official made it a duty for that official to 'treat it as secret'. A version of section 79 formed part of the Crimes Act when it was first enacted in 1914 and was based on provisions of the UK Official Secrets Act 1911.

The secrecy offence most similar to the Criminal Code espionage offences is section 79(2), which concerns the disclosure or other handling of information with the intention of prejudicing the Commonwealth's security or defence. However, subsection (2) has application to a broader category of information than the espionage offences, and does not require that the information was communicated, or was likely to be communicated, to a foreign country or organisation.

Penalties can be as severe as seven years of imprisonment if the person has (under subsection (2)) 'the intention of prejudicing the security or defence of the Commonwealth or a part of the Queen's dominions', or if the person 'knowing or having reasonable ground to believe, at the time when he or she receives' the information, that it was communicated to him or her in contravention of subsection (2) or section 91.1 of the Criminal Code.

On a prosecution under subsection (2), as in Britain, it is not necessary to show that the accused person was guilty of a particular act tending to show the requisite intention. Instead, he or she may be convicted if, from the circumstances of the case, from his or her conduct or from his or her known character as proved, it appears that his or her intention fell within subsection (2).

Despite the breadth of that provision, there have been few prosecutions. This may be for a number of reasons, including the acceptance of espionage as part of international activity, the existence of diplomatic immunity in many instances, and concerns about tit-for-tat retaliation by the relevant governments. By their very nature, both espionage and official secrets prosecutions have the potential to politically backfire or lead to unwanted public scrutiny of the operations of the intelligence and security agencies.

A 1995 prosecution of George Sadil, a former Australian Security Intelligence Organisation (ASIO) officer accused of taking documents in order to hand them to a Russian spy, never proceeded to a jury trial. The Director of Public Prosecutions dropped the more serious espionage-related charges, which required a jury trial, even though Sadil had been committed for trial following the expulsion of seven Russian diplomats. Sadil had been a Russian interpreter with ASIO for some 25 years and classified documents were discovered in his place of residence. Federal Police arrested and charged him under the Crimes Act 1914 with several espionage and official secrets related offences. Ultimately, Sadil pleaded guilty to 13 charges of removing ASIO documents contrary to his duty, and was sentenced to three months' imprisonment. He was subsequently released on a 12-month good behaviour bond (Four Corners 2004).

Of the few prosecutions under section 79, another example is the conviction in 2003 of Simon Lappas for offences under sections 79(3) and 78 of the *Crimes Act* (which was subsequently repealed and replaced by section 91.1 of the *Criminal Code*). Lappas, an employee of the Defence Intelligence Organisation, had given several classified documents to an unauthorised person, Sherryll Dowling, so she could sell the documents to a foreign country (*R v. Lappas* (2003) 152 ACTR 7). Lappas was found guilty and, on appeal, sentenced to two years' imprisonment. Dowling pleaded guilty to two charges of receiving the classified documents and was placed on a five- year good behaviour bond (Transcript of Proceedings, *R v. Dowling*, Supreme Court of the Australian Capital Territory, Gray J, 9 May 2003).

ASIO secrecy provisions were invoked in 2009. A former ASIO officer, James Seivers, was convicted of leaking classified documents relating to the October 2002 terrorist bomb blasts on the Indonesian resort island of Bali. He was charged under section 18(2) of the Australian Security Intelligence Organisation Act 1979 with having 'made a communication of information or matter that had come into (his) possession by reason of being an officer of' ASIO. Seivers's co-tenant,

Francis O'Ryan, was convicted of aiding and abetting him (*James Paul Seivers v. R* [2010] ACTCA 9).

Thousands of holiday-makers from Australia and other countries had been in Bali's Kuta nightclub district when the bombings killed 200 innocent people, including 88 Australians and 40 Indonesians, mostly nightclub workers and taxi drivers. Travel advisories issued by the Australian government had assured the Australian public that Bali was 'calm' and tourist services 'normal', despite a heightened terrorist risk produced by Australia's participation in the US-led invasion of Afghanistan.

Seivers and O'Ryan were convicted for sending to the newspaper *The Australian* in 2004 three ASIO documents showing that Australian authorities were warned by their US intelligence partners two weeks before the Bali bombings that an al-Qaeda-linked group was planning attacks on 'sin spots' and 'nightclubs'. Prosecutors alleged that Seivers, who had access to the documents during a 2004 Senate inquiry into the bombings, passed them to O'Ryan, who posted them to *The Australian's* Sydney offices. O'Ryan was said to have written on two of the documents, 'please see details of prior intelligence through which a tragedy might have been prevented' and 'sin spots-nightclubs'.

According to the documents, US intelligence agencies told their Australian counterparts that Jemaah Islamiah (JI) spiritual leader Abu Bakar Bashir headed a group called Majeklis Mujahedden Indonesia that was preparing large-scale bombings. The leaked documents suggested that the Australian government and its intelligence advisers may have deliberately chosen to ignore the warnings in order to politically exploit the outcome. Prime Minister John Howard certainly seized upon the Bali events, which he dubbed Australia's own 'September 11', to intensify the 'war on terror' both at home and abroad.

Seivers was sentenced to 12 months' imprisonment, including six months of periodic detention. However, he was acquitted on appeal, on evidentiary grounds, because of the jury's lack of access to the testimony of O'Ryan, who pleaded guilty, and objectionable comments by the Crown Prosecutor, who invited the jury to conclude that O'Ryan had been motivated by an interest in securing Seivers's acquittal. The ACT Supreme Court concluded not only that the fairness of the trial was compromised but also that the verdict in the trial was unsafe and unsatisfactory (*James Paul Sievers v. R* [2010] ACTCA 9). O'Ryan's conviction was subsequently overturned as well (ABC News 2011).

Sabotage

Sabotage is another offence that is subject to political interpretation. How the physical activity involved is characterised may depend on the political or commercial purpose motivating it. Thus, a saboteur could alternatively be treated as a hero or martyr if their cause is officially approved or backed by strong public opinion. One of the most prominent sabotage cases of the twentieth century was that of Nelson Mandela.

Mandela served as President of South Africa from 1994 to 1999. Before his presidency, he was the leader of Umkhonto we Sizwe, the armed wing of the African National Congress (ANC). In 1962 he was arrested and convicted of sabotage and other charges, and sentenced to life in prison. Mandela served 27 years in prison. Following his release in 1990, he led the ANC in negotiations that led to a multi-racial power-sharing political system that ensured the continuation of South African capitalism. Mandela has since received more than 250 awards by governments, universities and other institutions, including the 1993 Nobel Peace Prize (Mandela 1995).

At his trial in 1964, Mandela was charged with the capital crimes of sabotage (which he admitted) and offences that were equivalent to treason but easier for the government to prove. He was also accused of plotting a foreign invasion of South Africa, which Mandela denied. In his statement from the dock at the opening of the defence case, Mandela defended the ANC's choice to use violence as a tactic. His statement described how the ANC had used peaceful means to resist apartheid for years until the 1961 Sharpeville Massacre. He said that event, together with the referendum establishing the Republic of South Africa, the declaration of a state of emergency and the banning of the ANC, made it clear to him and his compatriots that their only choice was to resist through acts of sabotage. Doing otherwise would have been tantamount to unconditional surrender, he stated. Mandela also explained that the 1961 manifesto of Umkhonto we Sizwe was motivated by concerns that the National Party's apartheid-based economic policies would make foreigners unwilling to risk investing in the country. He was convicted of planning armed action, in particular four charges of sabotage, and sentenced to life imprisonment (Mandela 1995).

Sabotage can take many different forms, including industrial, economic, intelligence and military operations designed to damage or disrupt a political, governmental or commercial rival. Generally speaking, sabotage is a deliberate action aimed at weakening another entity through subversion, obstruction, disruption or destruction. It can be aimed against a government or a private body, such as a company or other employer. Even the latter, however, may be viewed so seriously that it also can be regarded as a threat to the state.

In a workplace setting, sabotage is the conscious withdrawal of efficiency generally directed at causing some change in employment conditions. Workplace sabotage occurs when disgruntled workers damage or destroy equipment or interfere with the smooth running of a workplace. This can be as part of an organised group activity, or the action of one or a few workers in response to personal grievances. In the past, Luddites and radical syndicalist organisations such as the Industrial Workers of the World (IWW) have advocated sabotage as a means of self-defence and direct action against unfair working conditions.

During the nineteenth century, measures taken by the British government against the Luddites included a mass trial at York in 1812 that resulted in many executions and penal transportations. 'Machine breaking' was subsequently made a capital crime by the Frame Breaking Act, and 17 men were executed after an 1813 trial in York. Many others were transported as prisoners to Australia (Hobsbawm 1964: 6). For the IWW, sabotage came to mean any withdrawal of efficiency, including slowdowns, strikes and the creative bungling of job assignments (Carlson 1983: 196–7).

In wartime, the word is used to describe the activity of an individual or group not associated with the military of the parties at war (such as a foreign agent or an indigenous supporter), in particular when actions result in the destruction or damaging of a productive or vital facility, such as equipment, factories, dams, public services, storage plants or logistic routes. Acts of sabotage do not always have a primary objective of inflicting casualties. Saboteurs are usually classified as enemies, and like spies may be liable to prosecution and criminal penalties instead of detention as a prisoner of war. It is common for a government in power during war or supporters of the war policy to use the term loosely against opponents of the war.

Britain

No separate sabotage offence exists under British legislation. However, sabotage can be covered by other criminal provisions. In the 1962 decision of the House of Lords in *Chandler (Terence Norman) v. DPP (No 1)* ([1962] UKHL 2, [1964] AC 763), the judges ruled that the Official Secrets Act 1911 extended to sabotage. Members or supporters of an organisation known as the Committee of 100 had attempted to hold an anti-nuclear war demonstration at an Air Force base, during which they planned to occupy the base and block its entrance. They were charged with conspiracy to commit and to incite others to commit a breach of section 1 of the Official Secrets Act, which provided that 'if any person for any purpose prejudicial to the safety or interests of the State approaches or is in the neighbourhood of, or enters any prohibited place within the meaning of this Act, he shall be guilty of felony'.

The main point of law related to the interpretation of the words 'purpose prejudicial to the safety or interests of the State'. Earl Russell, the founder of the Committee of 100,explained in evidence that their ultimate purpose was to prevent a nuclear war and that their more immediate purpose was to get the facts about nuclear warfare known to the public by any means they could and in particular by pursuing a campaign of non-violent civil disobedience. Counsel for the defence argued that the trial judge had wrongly barred evidence that the accused believed, and reasonably believed, that it was not prejudicial but beneficial to the interests of the State to immobilise the nuclear-armed aircraft. Therefore the jury were entitled to hold that no offence had been committed because the accused did not have a purpose prejudicial to the State, and it was for the jury to determine their purpose. The law lords, however, unanimously ruled that the judge was correct to deny the jury the right to hear the relevant evidence and decide the issue. They agreed that, as a matter of law, the 'interests of the State' are determined exclusively by the government of the day, at least where the issues at stake concern the operations of the armed forces.

Members of the courts made some interesting comments on the nature of the state. Lord Reid, for example, observed:

> 'State' is not an easy word. It does not mean the Government or the Executive. 'L'Etat c'est moi' was a shrewd remark, but can hardly have been intended as a definition even in the France of the time. And I do not think that it means, as [defence] Counsel argued, the individuals who inhabit these islands. The statute cannot be referring to the interests of all those individuals because they may differ and the interests of the majority are not necessarily the same as the interests of the State. Again we have seen only too clearly in some other countries what can happen if you personify and almost deify the State. Perhaps the country or the realm are as good synonyms as one can find, and I would be prepared to accept the organised community as coming as near to a definition as one can get.
>
> Who, then, is to determine what is and what is not prejudicial to the safety and interests of the State? The question more frequently arises as to what is or is not in the public interest. I do not subscribe to the view that the Government or a Minister must always or even as a general rule have the last word about that.
>
> But here we are dealing with a very special matter—interfering with a prohibited place ... It is, in my opinion, clear that the disposition and armament of the armed forces are and for centuries have been within the exclusive discretion of the Crown and that no one can seek a legal remedy on the ground that such discretion has been wrongly exercised. (*Chandler (Terence Norman) v. DPP (No 1)* ([1962] UKHL 2, [3])

The judges also ruled that a side note to Section 1, which stated, 'Penalties for spying', did not protect the defendants, who argued that they were not seeking to spy on the base. Lord Reid said it was 'impossible to suppose that the section does not apply to sabotage, and what was intended to be done in this case was a kind of temporary sabotage' ([1962] UKHL 2, [2]). Other law lords made similar statements, equating a planned peaceful occupation of a military facility with sabotage.

United States

American sabotage law is predominantly focused on attack on military-related infrastructure. However, the scope of what the US Code terms 'national-defense utilities' is so broad that the provisions can extend far beyond the protection of wartime and military operations. This is particularly so when the concepts of 'national defense' and 'security' have been given extended interpretations since the declaration of the 'war on terrorism' in 2001. In the US, as in Britain, the sabotage offence has been invoked against anti-war protesters breaking into military bases.

During World War I, American government concern about sabotage was triggered in 1916 when operatives supported by the German government blew up a munitions supply terminal at Black Tom Pier on the New Jersey side of New York Harbour. Germany was seeking to prevent the materials from being used by the Allies in the war, a campaign that also involved the torpedoing of the *Lusitania*. The bombing at Black Tom and a second explosion at a nearby shell manufacturing plant helped justify the passage of the federal Espionage Act in 1917 (Witcover 1989: 339).

Wartime, military and 'national defense' sabotage is now covered by Chapter 105, entitled sabotage, of the US Code. The most serious offences deal with when the US is at war, or in times of national emergency. Section 2153, on 'Destruction of war material, war premises, or war utilities' states:

> (a) Whoever, when the United States is at war, or in times of national emergency as declared by the President or by the Congress, with intent to injure, interfere with, or obstruct the United States or any associate nation in preparing for or carrying on the war or defense activities, or, with reason to believe that his act may injure, interfere with, or obstruct the United States or any associate nation in preparing for or carrying on the war or defense activities, willfully injures, destroys, contaminates or infects, or attempts to so injure, destroy, contaminate or infect any war material, war premises, or war utilities, shall be fined under this title or imprisoned not more than thirty years, or both.

> (b) If two or more persons conspire to violate this section, and one or more of such persons do any act to effect the object of the conspiracy, each of the parties to such conspiracy shall be punished as provided in subsection (a) of this section.

Section 2155, however, extends the range of the sabotage provisions far into peacetime activities. It provides that:

> Whoever, with intent to injure, interfere with, or obstruct the national defense of the United States, willfully injures, destroys, contaminates or infects, or attempts to so injure, destroy, contaminate or infect any national-defense material, national-defense premises, or national-defense utilities, shall be fined under this title or imprisoned not more than 20 years, or both, and, if death results to any person, shall be imprisoned for any term of years or for life.

Section 2151 contains wide definitions, including of 'national-defense utilities':

> The words 'national-defense utilities' include all railroads, railways, electric lines, roads of whatever description, railroad or railway fixture, canal, lock, dam, wharf, pier, dock, bridge, building, structure, engine, machine, mechanical contrivance, car, vehicle, boat, aircraft, airfields, air lanes, and fixtures or appurtenances thereof, or any other means of transportation whatsoever, whereon or whereby such national-defense material, or any troops of the United

States, are being or may be transported either within the limits of the United States or upon the high seas or elsewhere; and all air-conditioning systems, dams, reservoirs, aqueducts, water and gas mains and pipes, structures, and buildings, whereby or in connection with which air, water, or gas may be furnished to any national-defense premises or to the Armed Forces of the United States, and all electric light and power, steam or pneumatic power, telephone and telegraph plants, poles, wires, and fixtures and wireless stations, and the buildings connected with the maintenance and operation thereof used to supply air, water, light, heat, power, or facilities of communication to any national-defense premises or to the Armed Forces of the United States.

These measures require a specific intent or purpose to damage the national defense of the United States. Nevertheless, pacifists and other anti-war activists have been convicted under these provisions for seeking to expose and oppose military operations, particularly those involving nuclear warfare. Courts have firmly rejected defences based on good faith, belief in the lawfulness of the protest and the illegality of the war preparations.

An illustrative case occurred in 2002–5, during the protests against the US-led invasions of Afghanistan and Iraq. Three nuns, Carol Gilbert, Jackie Hudson and Ardeth Platte, were jailed for between 30 and 41 months for attempting in 2002 a 'citizen weapons inspection', public exposure and symbolic disarmament of a Minuteman III nuclear missile silo near New Raymer, Colorado. The rocket silo reportedly housed 49 rockets, which the defence department had recently outfitted with W-87 nuclear warheads, each with 25 times the explosive force of the Hiroshima bomb. The nuns also declared that the billions of dollars spent on the missiles could go to programs for the poor and needy.

The nuns were convicted of charges under section 2155 for 'injury, interference and obstruction of national defense materials and national defense premises and property' and under 18 USC section 1361, 'depredation against government property'. Armed with bolt cutters, a hammer and baby bottles filled with their own blood, they had broken into the missile site and painted bloody crosses on the silo. It was the day before the one-year anniversary of the war in Afghanistan. Their 'primary motive was to expose the existence of this deadly weapon – and their good faith belief in its criminality – to public scrutiny' and their stated purpose was to 'expose the site and to stop the threatened use of weapons of mass destruction, which they alleged was in violation of various domestic and international laws and treaties', including the Nuremberg principles against aggressive war. At their trial in 2003, however, US District Judge Robert Blackburn barred the jury from hearing international law and Nuremberg defences. Blackburn also granted an *in limine* motion by the prosecutor, prohibiting the sisters from speaking about the moral and legal justification for their actions (*United States v. Ardeth Platte* 401 F.3d 1176 (10th Cir. 2005)).

In 2005, the nuns' appeal was dismissed by the 10th US Circuit Court of Appeals. A three-judge panel noted the potential benefit of civil disobedience, but declared that the nuns knew, or should have known, their protest was not a 'trivial intrusion on some obscure military facility'. The court adopted a sweeping definition of national defence as 'a generic concept of broad connotations referring to military establishments and the related activities of national preparedness'. This definition was taken from the US Supreme Court decision in *Gorin v. United States* (312 US 19, 28 (1941)), a World War II prosecution under the Espionage Act, and had been adopted in an earlier prosecution under section 2155, *United States v. Kabat* (797 F.2d 580, 586 (8th Cir. 1986)).

The appellate court rejected the nuns' argument that they knew none of their actions could prevent the launch of a missile, insisting that the nuns' desire for publicity itself indicated an intention to cause a 'major disruption'. The judges further declared: 'Civil disobedience can be an act of great religious and more courage and society may ultimately benefit. But if the law being violated is constitutional, the worthiness of one's motives cannot excuse the violation in the eyes of the law' (*United States v. Ardeth Platte* 2005). The court also ruled that surreptitiousness was not a requisite for violation of section 2155, that international law defences did not apply, and that 'sabotage' is not an element of the offence, despite sabotage being the title of the relevant chapter, Chapter 105, of the US Code. The judges further dismissed an argument that the statute's definition of national defence covered facilities that the nuns contended were illegal: 'Even assuming that some facilities violate the law, we are unaware of any constitutional privilege of private citizens to injure or interfere with such facilities' (*United States v. Ardeth Platte* 2005).

Australia

In Australia, sabotage is an offence under both federal and state and territory criminal codes. The federal Crimes Act 1914 lists sabotage as one of the 'offences against the government'. Section 24AB of the Act defines the crime and provides as follows:

Sabotage

(1) In this section:
'act of sabotage' means the destruction, damage or impairment, with the intention of prejudicing the safety or defence of the Commonwealth, of any article:

    (a) that is used, or intended to be used, by the Defence Force or a part of the Defence Force or is used, or intended to be used, in the Commonwealth or a Territory not forming part of the Commonwealth, by the armed forces of a country that is a proclaimed country for the purposes of section 24AA;

    (b) that is used, or intended to be used, in or in connexion with the manufacture, investigation or testing of weapons or apparatus of war;

    (c) that is used, or intended to be used, for any purpose that relates directly to the defence of the Commonwealth; or

(d) that is in or forms part of a place that is a prohibited place within the meaning of section 8.

'article' includes any thing, substance or material.

(2) A person who:

(a) carries out an act of sabotage; or

(b) has in his or her possession any article that is capable of use, and which he or she intends for use, in carrying out an act of sabotage; shall be guilty of an indictable offence.

Penalty: Imprisonment for 15 years.

(3) On a prosecution under this section it is not necessary to show that the accused person was guilty of a particular act tending to show an intention to prejudice the safety or defence of the Commonwealth and, notwithstanding that such an act is not proved against him or her, he or she may be convicted if, from the circumstances of the case, from his or her conduct or from his or her known character as proved, it appears that his or her intention was to prejudice the safety or defence of the Commonwealth.

(4) On a prosecution under this section, evidence is not admissible by virtue of subsection (3) if the magistrate exercising jurisdiction with respect to the examination and commitment for trial of the defendant, or the judge presiding at the trial, as the case may be, is of the opinion that that evidence:

(a) would not tend to show that the defendant intended to prejudice the safety or defence of the Commonwealth; or

(b) would, having regard to all the circumstances of the case and notwithstanding subsection (5), prejudice the fair trial of the defendant.

(5) If evidence referred to in subsection (4) is admitted at the trial, the judge shall direct the jury that the evidence may be taken into account by the jury only on the question whether the defendant intended to prejudice the safety or defence of the Commonwealth and must be disregarded by the jury in relation to any other question.

Despite the extraordinary width of the definition, and the broad scope opened up by subsection (3) to rely upon bad character evidence rather than direct proof of an intention to prejudice the safety or defence of the Commonwealth, there is no record of any prosecution under this section.

During World War I, however, as discussed in Chapter 1, 12 members of the syndicalist International Workers of the World (IWW) were accused of setting Sydney factories, warehouses and stores alight to force the federal Labor government to drop its plans to introduce conscription. They were originally charged with 'treason felony' for endeavouring, among other things, to 'intimidate or overawe' parliament (Turner 1969: 36). That charge was later replaced by three counts of conspiracy: to commit arson, to defeat the ends of justice and seditious conspiracy (Rushton 1973: 53–4). In 1916, while the 12 were still awaiting trial, Prime Minister Billy Hughes declared: 'The IWW not only preach but they practise sabotage'

(Turner 1969: 47–8). A jury found each of the 12 guilty of at least one arson-related conspiracy. Eventually, after an unsuccessful legal appeal and two contradictory judicial inquiries, the convictions unravelled. All the men were released by late 1921, although they were never compensated (Turner 1969: 247–50).

Chapter 6
Sedition and Politically Motivated Violence

Sedition is an inherently political offence, specifically targeting advocacy regarded as threatening to the government or socio-economic order. Of course, any acts directed at overthrowing the established order are regarded as serious criminal offences. The law of sedition, however, is aimed specifically at suppressing the expression of supposedly dangerous ideas, rather than any overt acts. Invariably also, the law is defined in terms that leave wide discretion in the hands of governments, prosecutors and courts. Sometimes, sedition offences have remained unused for decades, prompting predictions of their demise. However, in times of war or political crisis, charges of sedition have commonly been used to punish and silence critics for uttering remarks that in other periods might have been treated as acceptable. Principles of free speech have proven to be of little or no protection to those accused.

This variable and unpredictable usage of sedition law means that its application may have little relationship to the actual wording of the legislation or common law offences. The historical record shows that political and strategic calculations by governments and prosecuting authorities can play a larger part in decisions to arrest and charge government opponents than concerns about the legal niceties of the law. One prominent American scholar observed:

> It is an outstanding feature of every sedition act that the way it is enforced differs from the way it looks in print as much as a gypsy moth differs from the worm from which it has grown. (Chafee 1945: 459)

Since the 1970s, law reform commissions and others in a number of jurisdictions, including Britain, Australia and Canada, have called for the abolition of sedition offences, or their replacement by others, such as inciting political violence or terrorism-related offences (ALRC 2006: 59 ff). In Australia the federal sedition law was initially extended in 2005, as part of a package of anti-terrorism legislation, to cover the urging of resistance to Australian military operations. After considerable public opposition to this move, in 2010, the Australian government adopted the 2006 recommendation of the Australian Law Reform Commission, which suggested re-badging sedition as 'urging violence'. Essentially, this proposal was made in order to avoid the popular opprobrium attached to the term sedition. The substance of the law was changed only slightly (see below), but the switch may make it politically easier to launch prosecutions. Indeed, American cases have revealed a tendency to revive sedition and seditious conspiracy provisions, notably in the political atmosphere generated by the 'war on terrorism' (see below).

A 2006 prosecution in New Zealand illustrated the potential for sedition offences that were previously thought to be redundant to be brought back into prominence during the twenty-first century. It seems that sedition had not been prosecuted in New Zealand since 1942 (ALRC 2006: 133). However, the Auckland District Court found Timothy Selwyn guilty of sedition for issuing a statement calling for acts of civil disobedience to protest against the government's foreshore and seabed legislation, which was being pushed through parliament at the time. The controversial legislation sought to annul traditional Maori land claims to coastal waters. Selwyn admitted to conspiring to commit wilful damage when an axe was embedded in the prime minister's electorate office window. He also admitted to being involved in two statements, one claiming responsibility for the axe incident, and the other calling for 'like minded New Zealanders to take similar action of their own'. Selwyn was sentenced to two months' imprisonment for sedition and wilful damage (ALRC 2006: 133–4).

While the jury found Selwyn guilty of publishing a statement with seditious intent, it acquitted him of a separate charge of being party to a seditious conspiracy (Braddock 2006). Sedition was defined broadly by Part 1 of the Police Offences Act 1927 to include the making or publishing of any statement 'that incites, encourages, advises, or advocates violence, lawlessness, or disorder'. It appears that the protest was intended to be symbolic. Selwyn argued that putting the axe through the window had been an act of civil disobedience 'at the extreme end'. The axe symbolised 'determination' and the broken glass 'the shattered justice of the Foreshore and Seabed Act' (Braddock 2006).

In New Zealand, the charge of sedition had previously been used only under conditions of war or industrial upheaval. In 1913–14, three leaders of a national general strike were jailed for sedition and inciting violence. During World War I, the sedition laws were used on three occasions to prosecute prominent anti-conscription campaigners, while in 1942 the editor of a pacifist newsletter was convicted of publishing a subversive document and sentenced to two years in prison (Braddock 2006).

There is a long history, dating back to the days of the English Star Chamber, of sedition laws being exploited to persecute political dissenters, particularly in periods where those in office fear unrest developing from below (Head 1979). A classic eighteenth-century case that illustrated the capacity of governments and the courts to use sedition offences against critics was *R v. Tutchin* ((1704) 14 State Trials (OS) 1096). According to Lord Chief Justice Holt:

> If people should not be called to account for possessing the people with an ill opinion of the government no government can subsist. For it is very necessary for all governments that the people should have a good opinion of it. And nothing can be worse to any government than to endeavour to produce animosities as to the management of it: this has always been looked upon as a crime, and no government can be safe without it is punished. ((1704) 14 State Trials (OS) 1096, 1128)

Tutchin was later sentenced to seven years' imprisonment with a whipping every fortnight for the duration of the sentence. He had committed the supposedly heinous offence of alleging corruption in the ministry and ill-management in the navy during a period when the political authority of the new form of constitutional monarchy was still insecure.

Chief Justice Holt's view of sedition – which prohibits any provoking of serious criticism, censure or rebuke of a government, the military or the security forces – cannot be simply dismissed as an 'antiquated' view of the relationship between the state and its members, as some commentators and authorities have done (for example, ALRC 2006: 49). It represents a thread that has reappeared in every period of economic and political tumult.

Another notorious example was the 1792 prosecution of Tom Paine for publishing *Rights of Man*, in defence of the French Revolution. As discussed in Chapter 1, his now famous treatise was found to vilify the 1688 English Revolution, represent that the King, Lords and Commons tyrannised over the people and bring them into hatred and contempt ((1792) 22 State Trials (OS) 357).

This anti-democratic tradition continued in the British colonies. In Australia, for example, those subjected to sedition prosecutions have included: John Macarthur, founder of the Australian merino wool industry, for challenging the authority of Governor Bligh in 1807–8; Henry Seekamp, the editor and owner of the *Ballarat Times* during the Eureka Stockade in 1854; anti-conscriptionists who opposed Australia's involvement in World War I; and Fred Paterson, who later became Australia's first communist MP, for expressing support for workers' struggles against capitalism at a public meeting in 1930 (ALRC 2006: 53). Other prosecutions included action against radical Henry Holland (1868–1933), jailed for sedition in NSW during 1909 over advocacy of violent revolution during the Broken Hill miners' strike.

The law of sedition developed specific traits during the nineteenth century that related directly to the rise of the working class. The common law identified two new strands of the definition of sedition, which were generally accepted by the middle of that century and then codified in many instances into statutes. These strands were, as enunciated by *Halsbury's Laws of England*, to 'raise discontent or disaffection amongst the Sovereign's subjects' and to 'promote feelings of ill-will and hostility between different classes of those subjects' (Halsbury 1976: para 827). References to 'discontent' and 'different classes' point to official concerns about the emergence of socialist and Marxist organisations seeking to develop a class-based political consciousness that gave articulate expression to rising disaffection among working people. One scholar commented that these categories are 'extremely broad and arbitrary and the reason for their appearance in the middle of the century probably stems from the emergence of a working-class consciousness and the bourgeoisie's realisation that the gulf between itself and the worker had to remain as wide as possible' (Boasberg 1990: 108).

As explored in this chapter, although other political crimes – such as unlawful assembly – became more frequently prosecuted as means of dealing with unrest in the twentieth century, repressive uses of sedition law continued, including during the Cold War anti-communist campaigns in Australia between 1949 and 1961, and there have been signs of a return to the 'gypsy moth' of sedition law enforcement since the end of the twentieth century.

Historical Evolution

Sedition as a distinct offence or group of offences arose from the earliest days of the emerging capitalist class in Britain, during the seventeenth century, first in its struggles against the absolutist monarchy and then in its strivings to consolidate its ascendancy, particularly against the emerging industrial working class.

The law of sedition is said to have its origins in the feudal doctrine of treason, which punished acts deemed to constitute a violation of a subject's allegiance to a monarch or lord (Kyer 1979: 266–7). Sedition and treason are also regarded as conceptually related, because seditious words or conduct can arguably incite opposition to established authority. In the words of a nineteenth century British judge, sedition 'frequently precedes treason by a short interval' (*R v. Sullivan* (1868) 11 Cox CC 44, 45).

Before the early 1600s, behaviour that could now be classified as sedition was prosecuted as treason or other felony (such as scandalum magnatum), or punished via martial law (Hamburger 1985, Manning 1980). Stephen's *History of the Criminal Law of England* reveals that the seditious offences at common law have their origins in the infamous Court of Star Chamber:

> There is no reason to doubt that practically libels attracted comparatively little attention till the Court of Star Chamber was at the height of its power, by which time the invention of printing, and the great intellectual movement of which it was one symptom, had given an importance to political writings which they did not possess before. (Stephen 1883: Vol. II, 302)

Stephen cited from Hudson's treatise on the Star Chamber where Hudson concluded that 'in all ages libels have been severely punished in this court, but most especially they began to be frequent about 42 and 43 Elizabeth (1600) when Sir Edward Coke was her attorney-general'.

Before 1600 dissenting behaviour was likely to be dealt with under one of the many specific and often ad hoc statutes passed creating new forms of treason or particular felonies. For example Stephen cites the case of *Udall* ((1589) 1 State Trials 1271) in which the accused was charged under 23 Eliz. C2 (1581) for felony to 'devise, write, print or set forth any book etc. to the defamation of the queen or the stirring or moving of any rebellion'. Stephen says of the two Star Chamber cases *De Libellis Famosis* ((1606) Coke 254; 77 ER 250) and *John Lamb's Case* ((1611) 5 Coke 108; 77 ER 822): 'These are the earliest authorities upon the law of libel of any importance, and even in Coke it would be difficult to find anything less satisfactory' (Stephen 1883: Vol. II, 304).

Coke's report of *De Libellis Famosis* establishes it as authority for the proposition that libellers can be punished by confession in the Star Chamber with punishment to include pillory and loss of ears. The case concerned the composition and publication of an infamous libel in verse against the Archbishop of Canterbury. The ratio of the case was stated thus: 'If it be against a magistrate, or other public person, it is a greater offence; for it concerns not only the breach of the peace, but also the scandal of government' (77 ER 251).

This new open-ended weapon was devised for use by the Crown against the rising parliamentarians. Significantly, the ordinary courts, sympathetic to the parliamentary interests, resisted it in this period. Stephen gives two examples. First, the 1629 case against Sir John Elliot and others for seditious speeches in Parliament ((1629) 3 State Trials 293). The defendants were convicted in the Star Chamber but the conviction was quashed in 1668 by a writ of error. By comparison 14 common law judges in *Pine's Case* refused to convict one who had spoken disrespectfully of Charles I despite the strength of his language. Pine had said Charles I was 'as unwise a king as ever was, and so governed as never a king was, for he is carried as a man would carry a child with an apple ... before God he is no more fit to be king than Hickwright [Pine's shepherd]'. In accordance with the common law of the time, the judges resolved that 'unless it were by some particular statute no words will be treason' ((1629) 3 State Trials 359).

However, the victorious parliamentarians and their judicial representatives were to find sedition an irresistible tool once they had consolidated their power after the civil war of the 1640s and the 'glorious revolution' of 1688. The common law courts began to adopt the Star Chamber's precedents with relish. By the 1680s there were frequent prosecutions for political libels and seditious words. Stephen describes them as containing 'extravagant cruelty' (Stephen 1883: Vol II, 313).

Convictions were based on mere criticism of government. As quoted at the outset, *Tutchin* was decided on the basis that it was seditious to 'produce animosities as to the management of' government. Similarly in *Francklin* ((1704) 14 State Trials (OS) 1096) the charge was 'to bring his present Majesty and his administration of the government into suspicion and ill-opinion of his liege subjects'.

This state of affairs lasted for a whole century. Any criticism of public men, laws or institutions was liable to be treated as sedition. This is how Stephen summed up the situation prior to 1792:

> The first question to be considered is, What, in the latter part of the eighteenth century, was the proper definition of a seditious libel? Omitting technicalities, I think it might at that time have been correctly defined as written censure upon public men for their conduct as such, or upon the laws, or upon the institutions of the country. This is the substance of Coke's case, 'De libellis famosis', which is the nearest approach to a definition of the crime with which I am acquainted.

It was a definition on which the Star Chamber acted invariably, and which was adopted after the Restoration by the Court of King's Bench. It is in harmony with the whole spirit of the period in which it originated, and in particular with the law as to the licensing of books and other publications which then and afterwards prevailed. It was in substance recognised and repeated far into the eighteenth century, and was never altered by any decision of the Courts or any Act of Parliament. That the practical enforcement of this doctrine was wholly inconsistent with any serious public discussion of political affairs is obvious, and so long as it was recognised as the law of the land all such discussion existed only on sufferance. This, however, by no means shows that it was not the law. (Stephen 1883: Vol II, 348)

In early 1792, a step was taken to reform this situation with the passage of Fox's Libel Act. The Act ended the practice of juries being precluded from the decision on whether a statement was seditious. However, the period immediately after the passing of the Act saw a new profusion of sedition prosecutions against English supporters of the French Revolution. These included the trial of Paine for publishing *Rights of Man*. Other cases included that of *Frost* ((1792) 22 State Trials (OS) 471), who was imprisoned for six months and pilloried for drunkenly declaring himself for equality, for no king and that the constitution was bad. In *Winterbotham* ((1793) 22 State Trials 875), a minister was sentenced to four years' imprisonment for a sermon in favour of the French Revolution, against taxes and against the strength of the monarchy.

Despite these prosecutions, or perhaps because of the public outcry they caused, the radical societies enjoyed a surge in membership in 1793–4. Several societies decided to convene in Edinburgh to decide how to summon 'a great body of the people' to convince parliament to reform itself along democratic lines. William Pitt's government viewed this as an attempt to establish an anti-parliament. Three leaders of the convention were tried for sedition in Scotland and sentenced to 14 years' service at Botany Bay (Barrell and Mee 2006: xxiv–xxv).

In 1804 Lord Ellensborough expressly relied on the wide language of Lord Chief Justice Holt in *Tutchin* to convict the defendant in *Cobbett* ((1804) 29 State Trials (OS) 1). He told the jury:

The question for your consideration is, whether this paper is such as would be injurious to the individuals, and whether it is calculated to be injurious to the particular interest of the country. It is no new doctrine, that if a publication be calculated to alienate the affections of the people, by bringing the government into disesteem, whether the expedient be by ridicule or obloquy, the person so conducting himself is exposed to the inflictions of the law. It is a crime. It has ever been considered as a crime; whether it be wrapped in one form or in another. The case of the *King v. Tutchin*, decided in the time of Lord Chief Justice Holt, has removed all ambiguity from this question; and, although at the period when that case was decided, great political contentions existed, the matter was not again brought before the judges of the Court by any application for a new trial.

After this period the courts began to confine the crime of seditious libel to cases where the words invited illegal acts. The history of this issue was considered at length by the Canadian Supreme Court in *Boucher v. The Queen* ([1951] 2 DLR 369) (a prosecution against the Jehovah's Witness sect). The majority held that seditious intention must involve an intention to incite to violence or to create public disturbance or disorder against the Crown or the institutions of government for the purpose of disturbing that constituted authority. The Canadian judges relied on cases such as *Burdett* ((1820) 4 B. and Ald. 95), where the court upheld a jury direction of this character: 'I told the jury that they were to consider whether the paper contained a sober address to the reason of mankind, or whether it was an appeal to their passions calculated to incite them to acts of violence and outrage'.

Also in *Lovett* ((1839) 9 Car. and P. 462, 466; 173 ER 912) Justice Littledale told the jury: 'if this paper has a direct tendency to cause unlawful meetings and disturbances, and to lead to a violation of the laws, that is sufficient to bring it within the terms of this indictment, and it is a seditious libel'.

Later cases such as *Sullivan* ((1868) 11 Cox CC 44) and *Burns* ((1886) 16 Cox CC 355) confirmed this distinction between legal and illegal suggestions, although it became tinged with assertions about morality. In *Burns*, for example, Justice Cave instructed the jury:

> If you think that these defendants, if you trace from the whole matter laid before you that they had a seditious intention to incite the people to violence, to create public disturbances and disorder, then undoubtedly you ought to find them guilty. If from any sinister motive, as, for instance, notoriety, or for the purpose of personal gain, they desired to bring the people into conflict with the authorities, or to incite them tumultuously and disorderly to damage the property of any unoffending citizens, you ought undoubtedly to find them guilty. On the other hand, if you come to the conclusion that they were actuated by an honest desire to alleviate the misery of the unemployed – if they had a real *bona fide* desire to bring that misery before the public by constitutional and legal means, you should not be too swift to mark any hasty or ill-considered expression which they might utter in the excitement of the moment. ((1886) 16 Cox CC 355, 363)

At the same time, scope for the old absolutism was retained in the development of the crime of seditious conspiracy, especially in Ireland. The first case of seditious conspiracy noticed by Stephen was that of *Bedhead Yorke* ((1795) 25 State Trials (OS) 1003). This branch of the law flourished during the great working class struggles of the first half of the last century. Some notable cases include the trial of Hunt and others for holding the meeting at St Peter's Field, Manchester, that was the subject of the infamous 'Peterloo' massacre by troops in 1819, the trial of Vincent and others in connection with the Chartist disturbances of 1839, the trial of O'Connell and others in 1844 for agitating for the repeal of the Union and the trial of Parnell and others for similar behaviour in 1880.

As Stephen stated, *O'Connell* ((1844) 11 Cl. and F. 155) is a clear indication of the breadth of the seditious conspiracy net. When all the judges were consulted by the House of Lords they found nine of the eleven counts in the indictment to be good and only two to be bad. The nine good counts charged, with different modifications: a conspiracy with intent to raise discontent and disaffection amongst the liege subjects of the Queen; to stir up jealousies, hatred, and ill-will between different classes of Her Majesty's subjects; and especially to promote amongst Her Majesty's subjects in Ireland feelings of ill-will and hostility towards Her Majesty's subjects in the other parts of the United Kingdom, and especially in England; to diminish the confidence of Her Majesty's subjects in Ireland in the general administration of the law therein; and to bring into hatred and disrepute the tribunals established by law in Ireland for the administration of justice; to bring about changes in the law by meetings held to hear seditious speeches and by seditious writings. The other counts, which were held bad, charged in substance a conspiracy to cause meetings to be held for the purpose of obtaining changes in the government and constitution of the realm 'by means of the exhibition and demonstration of the great physical force at such meetings'. This language was held to be too vague but presumably the counts would have been good if more exactly drawn. In Stephen's words:

> The remarkable part of this decision is that it shows how wide the legal notion of a seditious conspiracy is. It includes every sort of attempt, by violent language either spoken or written, or by a show of force calculated to produce fear, to effect any public object of an evil character, and no precise or complete definition has ever been given of objects which are to be regarded as evil. All those which are mentioned in O'Connell's case are included in the list, but there may be others. (Stephen 1883: Vol. II, 380)

Despite this breadth, the sedition-related offences were used somewhat less during the twentieth century in Britain. The most recent reported case seems to be *Aldred* ((1909) 22 Cox CC 1). There is apparently no report of the case of John Maclean, the Russian (Bolshevik) Consul in Glasgow, who was convicted of sedition in 1918 for calling for the end of World War I to be hastened by strikes and mutinies. Under wartime regulations, he was sentenced to five years' imprisonment but after a long hunger strike, he was released six months later (see Chapter 9).

Nor is there any law report of another major, and instructive, sedition case that led to the arrest and jailing of 12 leading members of the young Communist Party of Great Britain (CPGB) in 1925. This case reflected the concerns aroused within the political and legal establishment by the 1917 Russian Soviet revolution, and the support for it among British workers. The prosecution had been preceded a year earlier by the so-called Zinoviev letter affair, in which a forged document was used to claim that the Communist International had instructed the party to prepare for 'armed warfare' against the government (Ewing and Gearty 2000: 136).

From the outset, senior government ministers played key roles in the decision to arrest and charge the CPGB leaders, and the prosecution was launched on the basis of definite political calculations in the lead-up to the 1926 General Strike. It seems that the Attorney General Sir Douglas Hogg (later Lord Hailsham) personally recommended the arrests to Cabinet, whose members were asked whether there were 'any factors in the national or industrial situation which rendered a prosecution undesirable'. No objections were expressed. In parliament, the Home Secretary subsequently denied that Cabinet had made the decision, but declared that if there had been a Cabinet decision, it 'would not have disavowed the action taken' (Ewing and Gearty 2000: 137). This instance made a mockery of the supposed English constitutional principle that Cabinets did not direct the instigation of proceedings by the Director of Public Prosecutions.

Arrest warrants were issued the day after the Cabinet approval, and their execution was accompanied by police ransacking of the offices of the CPGB, the Red International of Labour Unions, the Young Communist League and the National Minority Movement. On the same evening, the Home Secretary told a meeting that the audience would be 'pleased to hear' that 'notorious Communists' were being arrested. The following week, he read to the Cabinet a number of documents that had been seized during the raids (Ewing and Gearty 2000: 138–9).

The 12 accused faced three charges, to which they all pleaded not guilty: conspiracy to publish seditious libels and words; conspiracy to incite persons to commit breaches of the 125-year-old Incitement to Mutiny Act 1797; and conspiracy to endeavour to seduce from their duty persons serving in His Majesty's Forces. The charges related to the publication of books, pamphlets and newspapers, including the party's *Workers' Weekly*.

Opening the case, Attorney General Hogg claimed that the CPGB was 'illegal' because it sought 'the forcible overthrow by arms of the present existing state of society, and, as a means to that end, the seduction from their existing allegiance of the armed forces of the Crown'. Hogg did not argue that the accused intended to incite an immediate uprising. Instead, he asserted that one of the themes of the literature was 'armed struggle for the overthrow' of the international bourgeoisie (Ewing and Gearty 2000: 140–1).

The defence argued that 'nothing short of a direct incitement to disorder and violence was a seditious libel' which must 'obviously tend to provoke people to commit a definite crime'. This test was not satisfied by literature reproducing the ultimate objects of the international communist movement, nor were things seditious simply because they were published by the Communist Party (Ewing and Gearty 2000: 141–2). Justice Swift asked the jury to apply three tests: Was the object of the documents to lead to civil war? Did the language used imply that it was lawful and commendable to employ physical force in any manner or form against the government? Did the language tend to subvert the government and the laws of the Empire? The judge instructed the jury that it would be 'a bad day for the country' if the government 'was not strong enough to bring those suspected of [treason, insurrection, tumult and sedition] before a Court of law' or if there were 'the slightest faltering either on the part of the jury or the Judge in putting down the verdict'.

Within 10 minutes, the jury returned guilty verdicts against all defendants on each count. The 12 were sentenced to periods of 6 to 12 months' imprisonment, with the heaviest sentences reserved for the five who had previous convictions, mainly for seditious speeches, most probably in breach of emergency regulations. The seven other defendants were given the option of imprisonment or renouncing communism, a choice they defiantly repudiated. *The Times* declared, nonetheless, that the trial had been conducted 'with the perfect fairness which is happily associated with the administration of justice in this country' (Ewing and Gearty 2000: 143–5).

By the first half of the twentieth century, the focal point for the development of the law of sedition had shifted to the politically volatile climate of the Empire. Thus came Indian cases such as *Amba Prasad* ([1897] ILR 20 All. 55) and *King-Emperor v. Sadashiv Narayan Bhalerao* ((1947) 74 Ind. App. 89), African cases such as *Wallace-Johnson* ([1940] AC 231 (PC)) and Caribbean cases such as *Joshua* ([1955] 1 All ER 22 (PC)). In the opening years of the twenty-first century, colonial-era sedition laws were invoked in Uganda and Nigeria against journalists who revealed politically embarrassing information (ALRC 2006: 138).

The former British colonies in Australia and New Zealand also came to the fore during the twentieth century. Industrial struggles and World War I produced cases in New Zealand that illustrate that the pursuit of basic working class interests in the teeth of State repression is open to be regarded as sedition. In both *Holland* ((1914) 33 NZLR 931) and *Young* ((1914) 33 NZLR 1191) the defendants were convicted of sedition for advising waterside workers on strike to violently resist the police and troops who had been sent with Gatling guns to break their strike. In *Holland*, Chief Justice Stout concluded that 'the jury certainly would be justified in regarding counsels of that kind as intended to promote feelings of ill-will and hostility between waterside workers and employers' ((1914) 33 NZLR 931, 936).

Working class opposition to the horrors of World War I provoked a notorious use of sedition conspiracy charges in Australia as well, directed against the syndicalist International Workers of the World (IWW), a trend that re-emerged in the Great Depression of the 1930s and after World War II, directed against members of the Communist Party of Australia (see the Australian case study below).

Britain

The United Kingdom currently has no statutory sedition offences. Instead, there are common law sedition offences, whose history has been discussed above. These offences are generally regarded as requiring an incitement to cause violence or disorder (Boasberg 1990: 107). However, the conclusions drawn by Stephen, and the instructions given to the jury in the 1925 sedition case, both cited above, suggest otherwise.

In 1977, the Law Commission of England and Wales recommended against codifying a sedition offence because seditious conduct would be caught by offences of incitement or conspiracy to commit other relevant offences. The commission also advised against codifying an offence that would have 'the implication that the conduct in question is "political"' (ALRC 2006: 120).

A private bid to require a prosecution for sedition failed in the 1991 case of *R v. Chief Metropolitan Stipendiary Magistrate; Ex parts Choudhury* ([1991] 1 QB 429). The applicant sought summonses against the author and publisher of the novel, *The Satanic Verses*, for the common law offence of seditious libel. The applicant argued that the book caused widespread discontent and disaffection among citizens, provoking acts of violence between Muslim and non-Muslim people. The Divisional Court rejected the application for judicial review of the magistrate's decision not to issue the summonses, holding that sedition must involve incitement of hostility toward a person or body in public office, that is a representative of the state itself. Lord Justice Watkins stated:

> Proof of an intention to promote feelings of ill will and hostility between different classes of subjects does not alone establish a seditious intention. Not only must there be proof of an incitement to violence in this connection, but it must be violence or resistance or defiance for the purpose of disturbing ... some person or body holding office or discharging some public function of the state. ([1991] 1 QB 429, 453)

One scholar has argued that sedition offences have been 'superseded by public-order legislation, including the statutory crime of inciting racial hatred' (Feldman 2002: 899). This assertion, however, ignores the distinction drawn in *Choudhury*. Sedition is an offence reserved for conduct regarded as a threat to the authority or stability of the state. Past experience, examined above, and developments in the United States, reviewed below, indicates that this law could be reactivated.

United States

Three sections of the US Code deal with sedition. Two, which explicitly outlaw advocacy of revolution, rebellion or insurrection, were examined in Chapter 3. Both derived from the Smith Act, now codified as 'advocating overthrow of government' in 18 USC 2385, and the accompanying 18 USC 2383, headed 'rebellion or insurrection'. In addition, there is 18 USC 2384, which states:
Seditious conspiracy

> If two or more persons in any State or Territory, or in any place subject to the jurisdiction of the United States, conspire to overthrow, put down, or to destroy by force the Government of the United States, or to levy war against them, or to oppose by force the authority thereof, or by force to prevent, hinder, or delay the execution of any law of the United States, or by force to seize, take, or possess

any property of the United States contrary to the authority thereof, they shall
each be fined under this title or imprisoned not more than twenty years, or both.

This offence is said to have three principal elements. There must be a 'conspiracy'
involving two or more people within US jurisdiction; the conspiracy must oppose
the US government or threaten its laws or property; and the use of 'force' must be
part of the conspiracy (ALRC 2006: 128). The offence requires only that a crime
be planned, however, not that it necessarily be attempted.

All three provisions in Chapter 18 of the US Code potentially run afoul of the
First Amendment of the US Constitution. As discussed in Chapter 3, from the
1960s, the US Supreme Court, particularly Justice Douglas, sought to reconcile
these laws with the right to espouse revolution, drawing a difficult and uncertain
line between theoretical advocacy and incitement of insurrection. There remains
a fundamental contradiction between the revolutionary origins of the United
States and laws such as these which seek to protect the present polity from being
overturned itself. In a 1967 judgement, Douglas posed the dichotomy thus:

> The word 'revolution' has of course acquired a subversive connotation in
> modern times. But it has roots that are eminently respectable in American
> history. This country is the product of revolution. Our very being emphasizes
> that when grievances pile high and there are no political remedies, the exercise
> of sovereign powers reverts to the people. Teaching and espousing revolution –
> as distinguished from indulging in overt acts – are therefore obviously within
> the range of the First Amendment. (*WEB Du Bois Clubs v. Clark* 389 US 309
> (1967), 315–16)

In another 1967 decision, the Supreme Court held that an offence of uttering
seditious words was so broad that 'the possible scope of "seditious utterances" or
acts has virtually no limit'. Justice Brennan spoke of a 'pall of orthodoxy' enabling
selective prosecutions of people who articulated views critical of the government
(*Keyishian v. Board of Regents* 385 US 589 (1967), 598–9, 603). Therefore, the
measure infringed the First Amendment.

Two years later came the decision in *Brandenburg v. Ohio* (395 US 444 (1969),
which is generally cited as the current authority. Caution should be exercised in
interpreting the content of this ruling, however, because it involved the prosecution
of a Ku Klux Klansman for threatening racial violence, not an indictment of a
government opponent. The relevant Ohio statute made it unlawful to advocate
sabotage, violence or terrorism to achieve industrial or political change. In
acquitting the Klansman, the court revisited all its prior decisions about subversive
advocacy and belatedly adopted the version of the 'clear and present danger' test
earlier advocated by Justices Holmes and Brandeis (see Chapters 2 and 3).

As a result, the Supreme Court's approach seemed to permit the punishment
of subversive advocacy if three conditions were met: there must be express
advocacy of law violation, a call for immediate law violation, and the immediate

law violation must be likely to occur (ALRC 2006: 128). These three provisos do not offer any guarantee against use of the sedition offences to harass and persecute selected political opponents. As previously noted, the historical record demonstrates that 'just about every time the country has felt seriously threatened the First Amendment has retreated' (Lee Bollinger cited in Stone 2004: 523). This warning has been underlined by the revival of the seditious conspiracy offence in the context of the 'war on terrorism'.

In 1995, a blind Egyptian Islamic cleric, Sheik Omar Abdel Rahman, and nine other defendants were convicted of various offences, including seditious conspiracy under section 2384 of the US Code. Rahman and one of his co-accused were sentenced to life imprisonment, and the other received sentences ranging upward from 25 years' imprisonment. Rahman was accused of inciting members of his congregation during his sermons to undertake subversive activities, such as plotting to bomb the UN headquarters and other buildings in New York City. In his sermons, Rahman urged his followers to, among other things, 'do jihad with the sword, with the cannon, with grenades, with the missile ... against God's enemies'. He stated that 'being called terrorists was fine, so long as they were terrorising the enemies of Islam, the foremost of which was the United States and its allies' (*United States v. Rahman* 189 F 3d 88 (1999), 104, 107.

Rahman's sentence and the constitutionality of section 2384 were affirmed on appeal. Among the arguments rejected by the appellate court was that the section was illegal because it failed to satisfy the requirements of the Treason Clause of the US Constitution, Art. III, § 3, which specifies that no one shall be convicted of treason unless on the testimony of two witnesses to the same overt act. The defendants contended that because the seditious conspiracy statute punishes conspiracy to 'levy war' against the United States without a conforming two-witness requirement, the statute was unconstitutional. According to the court, 'the plain answer is that the Treason Clause does not apply to the prosecution ... seditious conspiracy under Section 2384, differs from treason not only in name and associated stigma, but also in its essential elements and punishment (*United States v. Rahman* 189 F 3d 88 (1999), 104, 115).

The court held that the fact that Rahman's speech or conduct was religious did not immunise him from prosecution. It also rejected arguments based on the line of Supreme Court First Amendment cases from *Dennis* to *Yates* and *Brandenburg v. Ohio*. The judges said:

> The prohibitions of the seditious conspiracy statute are much further removed from the realm of constitutionally protected speech than those at issue in *Dennis* and its progeny. To be convicted under Section 2384, one must conspire to use force, not just to advocate the use of force. We have no doubt that this passes the test of constitutionality. (*United States v. Rahman* 189 F 3d 88 (1999), 104, 117)

One study of US sedition law concluded that 'prosecutions of seditious conspiracy are more likely to occur in a climate of society's heightened apprehension about terrorist plots against the nation' (Cohan 2003: 203). It need only be added that this 'climate' has been substantially orchestrated by a number of governments, as discussed in the next chapter.

Australia

Unlike Britain, Australia has long had a codified federal sedition law, alongside a variety of statutory and common law offences in the states and territories. In 2010, the federal offence of sedition was abolished, along with the unlawful associations provisions (see Chapter 3), and replaced by offences that were couched in terms such as 'urging force or violence'. On closer examination, however, little of substance has changed. In order to understand this, it is necessary to place the amendments in their historical legislative context.

For many years, numbers of federal offences were established in considerable detail in sections 24A–24F of the Crimes Act 1914 (Cth). In 2005, under the banner of combating terrorism, the offences were modified and extended, with particular implications for anti-war political activity. The new sedition offences were enacted by Schedule 7 of the Anti-Terrorism Act (No 2) 2005 (Cth), which repealed the Crimes Act offences and replaced them with offences located in Part 5.1 of the Criminal Code. The stated purposes of the new sedition provisions were to modernise the language of the offences and to 'address problems with those who incite directly against other groups within the community' (ALRC 2006: 70).

However, most of the old law of sedition was retained in the form of section 30A(3) of the Crimes Act, which defines 'seditious intention' in relation to the 'unlawful association' offences as 'an intention to use force or violence to effect any of the following purposes: (a) to bring the Sovereign into hatred or contempt; (b) to urge disaffection against the following: (i) the Constitution; (ii) the Government of the Commonwealth; (iii) either House of the Parliament; (c) to urge another person to attempt to procure a change, otherwise than by lawful means, to any matter established by law of the Commonwealth; (d) to promote feelings of ill-will or hostility between different groups so as to threaten the peace, order and good government of the Commonwealth.

Five new offences were created in section 80.2 of the Criminal Code under the heading 'Sedition'. The first three largely covered the same fields as the previous Crimes Act provisions, with the exception that 'recklessness' was added as a mental element for some aspects of the offences. The first offence, under the sub-heading 'Urging the overthrow of the Constitution or Government', provided:

(1) A person commits an offence if the person urges another person to overthrow
        by force or violence:
   (a)   the Constitution; or
   (b)   the Government of the Commonwealth, a State or a Territory; or
   (c)   the lawful authority of the Government of the Commonwealth.

(2) Recklessness applies to the elements of the offence under subsection (1) that it is:

(a) the Constitution; or

(b) the Government of the Commonwealth, a State or a Territory; or

(c) the lawful authority of the Government of the Commonwealth that the first-mentioned person urges the other person to overthrow.

The second offence, 'Urging interference in Parliamentary elections', in section 80.2(3)–(4), stated:

(3) A person commits an offence if the person urges another person to interfere by force or violence with lawful processes for an election of a member or members of a House of the Parliament.

(4) Recklessness applies to the element of the offence under subsection (3) that it is the lawful processes for an election of a member or members of a House of Parliament that the first-mentioned person urges the other person to interfere with.

The third offence, 'Urging violence within the community', in section 80.2(5)–(6), stated:

(5) A person commits an offence if:

(a) the person urges a group or groups (whether distinguished by race, religion, nationality or political opinion) to use force or violence against another group or other groups (as so distinguished); and

(b) the use of the force or violence would threaten the peace, order and good government of the Commonwealth.

(6) Recklessness applies to the element of the offence under subsection (5) that it is a group or groups that are distinguished by race, religion, nationality or political opinion that the first-mentioned person urges the other person to use force or violence against.

The fourth and fifth offences went beyond the previous Crimes Act provisions. The fourth offence, 'Urging a person to assist the enemy,' in section 80.2(7), stated:

(7) A person commits an offence if:

(a) the person urges another person to engage in conduct; and

(b) the first-mentioned person intends the conduct to assist an organisation or country; and

(c) the organisation or country is:

(i) at war with the Commonwealth, whether or not the existence of a state of war has been declared; and

(ii) specified by Proclamation made for the purpose of paragraph 80.1(1)(e) to be an enemy at war with the Commonwealth.

The fifth offence, 'Urging a person to assist those engaged in armed hostilities', in section 80.2(8), stated:

(8) A person commits an offence if:
   (a)   the person urges another person to engage in conduct; and
   (b)   the first-mentioned person intends the conduct to assist an organisation or country; and
   (c)   the organisation or country is engaged in armed hostilities against the Australian Defence Force.

Each of the five offences carried a maximum penalty of imprisonment for seven years, an increase from the maximum penalty of three years specified for the previous sedition offences. The fault element for the act of 'urging' another person to engage in the relevant conduct was intention, but three of the offences included recklessness as a fault element in relation to the circumstances or results arising from the person's 'urging'.

There was a further change. Under section 80.5 of the Criminal Code, proceedings for a sedition offence could not be commenced without the written consent of the Attorney-General. According to the Explanatory Memorandum to the Anti-Terrorism Bill (No 2) 2005 (Cth), this proviso was designed to provide an additional safeguard to a person charged with a sedition offence. However, by placing the prosecutorial discretion firmly in the hands of a leading member of the government, this measure only highlighted the sensitive political character of such decisions.

Section 80.3 of the Criminal Code provided for narrowly-defined 'good faith' defences to the treason and sedition offences in Division 80. The provisions in section 80.3 substantially replicated those in the old s 24F of the Crimes Act. Under section 80.3, comments made in good faith must have, for example, pointed out mistakes in government policy, urged people lawfully to change laws or policies, or commented on matters that produce feelings of hostility between groups with a view to bringing about removal of those matters. Section 80.3(1) (f) also allowed the publication in good faith of a report or commentary about a matter of public interest. In deciding whether an act was done in good faith, the court could look to matters such as whether the act was done: with a purpose intended to be prejudicial to the safety or defence of the Commonwealth; to assist an enemy of Australia; or with the intention of causing violence or creating public disorder or a public disturbance.

Under the 2010 amendments, the first three offences remained, with some modifications, under the new heading of 'Urging violence against the Constitution etc.'. The offences, relating to 'urging another person to overthrow by force or violence' (section 80.2(1)), 'urging interference in Parliamentary elections' (section 80.2(3)) and 'urging violence against groups or members of groups' (sections 80.2A and 80.2B), were arguably tightened in two ways. First, the word 'intentionally' was added before the word 'urges' and second, new provisos were added that the accused person must intend that 'force or violence will occur'. Given that intent was already required for 'urging' (section 5.2 of the Criminal Code), the first modification is probably meaningless. The provisos about intending violence or force to occur may limit prosecutions, although that likelihood needs to be assessed in the light of the historical usage and interpretation of the law of sedition and seditious conspiracy in Australia (see below).

In assessing the two provisos, account must also be taken of the fact that the 'urging violence' provisions overlap with existing federal offences, and may be also covered by other offences, such as conspiracy and inciting, attempting or aiding and abetting another offence. Furthermore, section 11.4 of the Criminal Code makes it an offence to urge the commission of another offence. Such other offences could include treason, treachery, sabotage, inciting mutiny, electoral offences and terrorism offences (ALRC 2006: 74–80). In an important respect, the urging violence offences extend the scope of incitement. Proving that a person who urges the commission of a terrorism offence is guilty of incitement under the Criminal Code requires evidence that the person intended that the offence incited be committed. The urging violence offences require an intention to urge the conduct, and an intention that 'force or violence will occur', but not an intention that a specific crime be committed.

Further, the amendments extended the second offence to include urging interference by force or violence with lawful processes for referenda (as well as parliamentary elections). The urging community violence offence was extended to cover circumstances in which a person urges a group to use force or violence against a group, or a member of a group, distinguished by national origin or ethnic origin (in addition to race, religion, nationality or political opinion). New subsections, 80.2A(2) and 80.2B(2) replicated these offences, contained in subsections 80.2A(1) and 80.2B(1), but did not require that the force or violence would threaten 'the peace, order and good government of the Commonwealth'. These alternative offences carried lower penalties of five years' imprisonment, compared to the penalty of seven years for the other offences. The implications of these extensions are not yet clear, but they potentially widen the scope of the provisions, particularly in the event of social tensions that assume an ethnic character.

The 2010 amendments abolished the fourth and fifth offences, formerly in section 80.2(7)–(8) of the Criminal Code, concerning assisting the enemy or those engaged in armed hostilities against Australia. There was an overlap between those provisions and the treason offence in section 80.1. Under section 80.2(7), it was an offence for a person to 'urge another to assist' an organisation or country at war with the Commonwealth, and under section 80.1(1)(e) it was treason to 'engage in conduct that assists', by any means whatever, an enemy at war with the Commonwealth. The explanatory memorandum to the 2010 Bill explained: 'these sections will be repealed because the treason offences in proposed sections 80.1 and 80.1AA will adequately criminalise action taken by a person to assist an enemy engaged in hostilities against Australia and the ADF'.

Despite the 2010 amendments, further overlaps exist with the hodge-podge of state and territory sedition laws (ALRC 2006: 81–4). Section 80.6 of the Criminal Code expressly states that its Division 80 – now titled, 'Treason and urging violence' – is not intended to exclude the operation of state and territory laws, to the extent that they are capable of operating concurrently with the federal provisions.

The 2005 extensions to the law of sedition had serious implications for political dissent, particularly anti-war dissent. Sedition or 'seditious intention' then included 'urging disaffection' against the government, promoting 'feelings of ill-will or hostility between different groups' or urging conduct to assist an organisation or country engaged in armed hostilities' against the Australian military, whether or not a state of war has been declared. Anyone could be guilty of sedition if they urged such conduct, even without intending their remarks to actually create disaffection, ill-will or armed resistance (ALRC 2006: 76, 87). Under sections 30A–30F of the Crimes Act, organisations that supported such sentiments could be declared 'unlawful associations', also exposing their property to seizure and their members, supporters and donors to imprisonment for up to one year (ALRC 2006: 86–8).

Most notably, these laws could have allowed for the criminalisation of any sympathy or support for resistance to the growing range of Australian military interventions, including the occupations of Afghanistan and Iraq or operations in the Asia-Pacific region, such as the dispatch of troops to the Solomon Islands, Papua New Guinea, Indonesia or the Philippines. The Australian Law Reform Commission (ALRC) pointed out: '[I]t may be said colloquially that strong criticism of Australia's recent military interventions in Afghanistan or Iraq "gives aid and comfort" to – and thus "assists" – the enemy' (ALRC 2006: 15). The commission concluded:

> The breadth of the term 'assists' creates valid concerns that the offences could be interpreted or applied to proscribe legitimate political protest, and punish merely rhetorical encouragement or support for those who disagree with Australian government policy. (ALRC 2006: 230)

The ALRC wrote: 'It is essential that a clear distinction be drawn between legitimate dissent and speech that constitutes a criminal offence' (ALRC 2006: 176). Its *Fighting Words* report argued that requiring proof of violent purpose would help protect 'rhetorical statements that the person does not intend anyone to act upon, as well as expressions in artistic, academic, scientific and media contexts' (ALRC 2006: 176).

The 'good faith' defences in section 80.3 offer limited protection. The ALRC pointed out that these 'have been criticised for lacking clarity and failing to protect media reporting and artistic expression' (ALRC 2006: 243). In general, the defences cover only actions or words assessed by a court (subjectively) as being 'constructive', 'law-abiding' or 'reforming' in their intent, rather than as advocating civil disobedience or revolutionary forms of politics (ALRC 2006: 243–62). The defences also specify that in considering them, courts should have regard to whether an accused intended to assist a country or organisation that is engaged in armed hostilities with the Australian Defence Force (section 80.3(2) (c)). Thus, support for resistance to an Australian military intervention could fall outside the defences.

There is no reason to believe that a contemporary federal government would not be willing to orchestrate prosecutions for political purposes. The collapse of the justifications for the United States-led invasion of Iraq – 'weapons of mass destruction', and Saddam Hussein's supposed links to al-Qaeda-backed terrorism – suggest that lies were told to divert attention away from the real motives of the 'war on terror', both domestically and internationally.

The 2005 amendments aroused deep public concerns. By adopting the vague words 'urging' and 'assist', the government had potentially outlawed a range of basic expressions of political opposition. The ALRC recommended abolition of these sections because of

> valid concerns that the offences could be interpreted or applied to proscribe legitimate political protest, and punish merely rhetorical encouragement or support for those who disagree with Australian government policy. Importantly, these provisions make it an offence to urge conduct by others that is itself lawful. For example, urging people not to enlist for service in the ADF [Australian Defence Force] might constitute the offence if this 'assists' an enemy. (ALRC 2006: 230)

After receiving hundreds of concerned submissions and conducting weeks of consultations, the ALRC suggested that the government drop the 'red rag' term 'sedition' and re-badge the laws under the heading of 'urging political or inter-group violence'. The ALRC report expressed no disagreement with the government's underlying objectives in the 'war on terror'. Essentially, the recommendations offered tactical advice on how to achieve those objectives without inflaming public opinion:

> It would be unfortunate if continued use of the term 'sedition' were to cast a shadow over the new pattern of offences. The term 'sedition' is too closely associated in the public mind with its origins and history as a crime rooted in criticising – or 'exciting disaffection' against – the established authority. (ALRC 2006: 66-67)

While re-badged accordingly, the provisions have little to do with protecting ordinary people from politically-motivated violence. Acts of terrorism, political force and violence were serious crimes long before the 2005 or 2010 amendments. The narrowing of the offences in 2010 to require an intention that force or violence will occur is no guarantee against wider or selective use for various political purposes.

The historical record shows that these concerns are not far-fetched. Moreover, while sedition law largely fell into disuse in Britain during the twentieth century, Australia, as discussed below, was 'distinguished above all in the English common law world since World War II for its contribution to the law of sedition' (Head 1979: 99).

Australia: A Case Study in Sedition Law

During the twentieth century – right up until the 1960s – Australia had a record of major sedition trials against government opponents. In each instance there is documented evidence that the prosecutions were instigated by leading figures in the government of the day, directed against political activists who were regarded as subversive.

One of the most controversial Australian sedition cases was the 1916 prosecution of the 'Sydney Twelve' for seditious conspiracy following the withdrawal of the treason felony charges against them, as discussed in earlier chapters. The 12 members of the syndicalist International Workers of the World (IWW) were accused of lighting fires in Sydney business premises to force the government to drop its plans to introduce conscription. They were arrested against a backdrop of growing discontent over the horrors of World War I, wide opposition to an ultimately defeated federal government-sponsored referendum on conscription, and increasing working class militancy, which was to lead to a virtual general strike in New South Wales (Turner 1969: 3, 20, 90–1). The 1917 strike, which initially erupted against work 'speed-up' by the railways management, became 'the biggest industrial upheaval ever experienced in Australia' (Turner 1969: 91).

There was a particularly close relationship between the trial and the conscription referendum, in which the 'yes' campaign was led aggressively by Prime Minister Billy Hughes and New South Wales Premier William Holman. The arrests occurred on 23 September 1916 and the committal hearing opened on 10 October, just two weeks before the referendum on 28 October. During the arrests, police raided the Sydney headquarters of the IWW, detained all those present and seized all the documents and literature they found, including copies of the IWW newspaper *Direct Action* (Turner 1969: 30). Backed by a ferocious mass media, Hughes and Holman sought to demonise the IWW, which actively agitated against conscription, and hence discredit the 'no' campaign. While the 12 were still awaiting trial, Prime Minister Hughes declared: 'The IWW not only preach but they practise sabotage ... They are to a man anti-conscriptionist' (Turner 1969: 47–8). It is difficult to imagine more prejudicial and *sub judice* comments on the eve of a major political trial.

On the other side of the country, in Western Australia, seditious conspiracy charges were laid against another 12 IWW members, with the federal government apparently instigating and footing the bill for the prosecution (Turner 1969: 44). In that case, there was no allegation of arson, or other specific unlawful acts (except that one defendant was charged with threatening to destroy the property of a Senator). Instead, the indictment accused these 12 syndicalists of conspiring to 'carry into execution an enterprise having for its object to raise discontent and disaffection amongst the subjects of our Lord the King' and to 'promote feelings of ill-will and enmity between different classes of the subjects of our said Lord the King' (Turner 1969: 45). In essence, the Crown case alleged that the IWW itself was a seditious conspiracy. The prosecution contended that the IWW advocated sedition, sabotage and other 'lawless acts'. Even more than in the Sydney case, it was the organisation rather than the individuals that was on trial.

The Sydney indictment was somewhat more specific. It alleged a conspiracy involving various acts of arson, agitation to procure the release of Tom Barker, an IWW leader jailed for prejudicing war recruitment (see Chapter 3), and efforts to coerce the government into changing legislation. Thus, there were three counts: conspiracy to commit arson, conspiracy to defeat the ends of justice and seditious conspiracy. For sedition, there were the requisite charges of seeking to foment 'discontent and dissatisfaction', 'contempt of the government', 'ill-will between classes' and 'bring into disrepute' lawful tribunals (Turner 1969: 50). The allegations hinged on the testimony of three police informers, who were accomplices in what they claimed were acts of sabotage.

Summing up for the Crown, Ernest Lamb, KC, said the case was 'of supreme importance to the people of Australia and ... the whole of the people of the Empire'. Justice Robert Pring instructed the jury that the law of sedition, which forbade the promotion of 'ill-will or hostility' between different classes of subjects, covered the propagation of class war between employees and employers. This conception could even make advocacy of industrial action seditious. Justice Pring added that the British people were justly proud of their liberty of speech, but they were only entitled to discuss matters 'in a fair and temperate way' and the IWW went far beyond this limit (Turner 1969: 54–5). After five hours of deliberation, the jury found seven men guilty of all three counts, four guilty of conspiracy to commit arson and seditious conspiracy, and one guilty of seditious conspiracy. In other words, all 12 syndicalists were convicted of seditious conspiracy – the only charge that led to guilty verdicts in each instance.

Sentencing the men, Justice Pring declared: 'You are members of an association which I do not hesitate to state, after the revelations in this case, is an association of criminals of the very worst type, and a hotbed of crime' (Turner 1969: 58). The sentences ranged from 15 to 5 years of hard labour. One of the men remarked after his sentence was passed: 'Fifteen years for fifteen words'. He had been accused of saying: 'For every day that Tom Barker is in gaol it will cost the capitalist class £10,000.'

In February 1917, the state's highest court, the Court of Criminal Appeal, upheld Justice Pring's rulings and the verdicts. It found two errors only, and reduced the sentences of two of the men from 15 to 10 years (Turner 1969: 80). However, there was an active campaign for the release of the Sydney Twelve, with the leading figures including Henry Boote, editor of the *Australian Workers*

Union's weekly paper, *The Worker*. The peak trade union body, the Labor Council of New South Wales, commissioned a report into the case in 1918, and demanded a Royal Commission. In a bid to head off the defence campaign, a government inquiry was commissioned, headed by Justice Phillip Street, in 1918. Both the Labor Council and Street reports found problems with the case, including that the chief witness, an informer, had concocted evidence. Nevertheless, Justice Street insisted that there was no evidence of police misconduct and reported that 'no fresh facts' had been elicited that raised any doubt about the guilt of the 12 men (Turner 1969: 140).

Ultimately, in a further move to quell the discontent, and to meet an election pledge, in 1920, Justice Norman Ewing was appointed to conduct a Royal Commission. His report described two key prosecution witnesses as 'liars and perjurers' who 'would not hesitate to take any steps in the way of making evidence to incriminate others'. He also thought it probable that incriminating evidence had been planted on some of the accused. Justice Ewing concluded that six of the men were not 'justly or rightly' convicted of any offence. Four may have been involved in seditious conspiracy, but he recommended their release. Another was considered rightly convicted of sedition, but also recommended for immediate release because his sentence had been 'greatly in excess of the offence'. One was found to have been rightly convicted of arson, but based on evidence not admitted at the trial – a letter the accused had written before the alleged conspiracy. Justice Ewing, like Justice Street, rejected any suggestion of a police frame-up (Turner 1969: 237–9). Ten men were released in August 1920 – after four years in custody – and two late in 1921. The state's Labor government dismissed calls from the trade union movement for those wrongly convicted to be compensated (Turner 1969: 247–50).

After reviewing the evidence in detail, Turner concluded that three, perhaps four, of the twelve were involved in arson or preparations for arson, although the Crown case against them was largely faked. The other defendants had certainly not been involved, and probably had no knowledge of what their co-accused were doing (Turner 1969: 211). Turner drew the following conclusions about the law of sedition:

> Sedition is essentially a political offence. The aim is to prevent or limit advocacy of the overthrow of the existing government or social order. Since overt acts which threaten the government or social order constitute offences in their own right, the charge of sedition is characteristically used against propagandists – speakers, writers, publishers. The definition of sedition is so wide as to offer a considerable margin of discretion to the Crown authorities who decide on prosecution and the judges and juries who determine the cases. What is considered seditious at one time will be accepted as tolerable criticism at another. It is in times of crisis – whether arising from domestic turmoil or involvement in war – that governments are most likely to accuse their opponents of sedition. It is in these times that juries, reflecting the panic which sweeps the community, are most likely to convict. (Turner 1969: 143)

The 1929 Wall Street crash and the onset of the 1930s Great Depression produced another controversial use of the sedition law. Fred Paterson, a prominent member of the Communist Party of Australia (CPA), and later to become that party's only Member of Parliament, was arrested in January 1930 on sedition charges. It was a period of 'acute economic failure, widespread social dislocation and dire personal suffering' and the CPA was portrayed in the mass media as 'poised to strike, viper-like, at the bosom of Australia's political well-being' (Fitzgerald 2002: 49). Paterson was arrested for having addressed a lunchtime gathering in Brisbane's Domain on the subject of 'the law and the working class'. He was charged under Queensland's sedition law, which was similar to the federal Crimes Act. The allegation was that he advisedly spoke and published seditious words, namely:

> If the workers shed a little blood in their own interests as they did for the capitalists in the war they will be emancipated. They should take the law into their own hands. Although I hope that I will not have to shed any of my blood, if the necessity arises I am willing to do in conjunction with the workers as a whole. But before I do so the workers will have to be thoroughly organised to have a successful issue. There was no harm in the spilling of blood in the late war in the capitalists' interests, so why could it not be spilt in the worker's interests, who could not be much worse off than they are now? (Fitzgerald 2002: 50)

The two policemen who allegedly witnessed Paterson's speech both recounted over 200 consecutive words without a word of difference and without the aid of notes. Paterson, who represented himself in court, neither confirmed nor denied that he had uttered the words. His defence rested on the proposition that no individual, let alone a pair of constables who had allegedly not attended the meeting with the deliberate intention of charging him, could listen to an hour-long speech and recall a select 'seditious' passage word for word, yet at the same time not be able to repeat accurately any other statements made before or after the offending remarks. Paterson told the jury:

> Sedition is a serious crime, next on the criminal code to treason, yet the crown comes along here with the most unreliable evidence ... Would any of you, the jury, go to a political meeting and on returning home remember the exact words used without the aid of notes? ... The original Siamese twins were born together, lived together, ate together, slept together, but the police variety think together. (Fitzgerald 2002: 50–1)

After a retirement of less than 15 minutes the jury returned a verdict of not guilty. Paterson later revealed that the crown prosecutor, Fred O'Rourke, had told him in his chambers on the day of the trial that it was purely a political prosecution, aimed at getting a conviction to prevent Paterson, who was about to sit his final bar exam, from becoming a barrister (Fitzgerald 2002: 52).

The political use and abuse of sedition laws in Australia was revived during the opening years of the so-called Cold War, from the late 1940s to the early 1950s. Successive governments, both Labor and Coalition, exploited sedition prosecutions to harass, disrupt, vilify and, in some instances, jail, political dissenters.

The next most prominent twentieth-century cases in Australia occurred in 1948 and 1949. The High Court upheld the jailing of two leaders of the Communist Party of Australia (CPA), Gilbert Burns and Lance Sharkey, who both made statements refusing to support Australia militarily in response to hypothetical questions about a war against the Soviet Union (*Burns v. Ransley* (1949) 79 CLR 101; *R v. Sharkey* (1949) 79 CLR 121).

On each occasion, the majority of High Court judges ruled that the prosecution need not prove that the accused subjectively intended to 'excite disaffection' (Head 1979: 99–105). The majority decisions rejected the distinction made by the US Supreme Court between exhortations that create a 'clear and present danger' of violence or disorder, and 'mere doctrinal justification or prediction of the use of force under hypothetical conditions' (Head 1979: 101).

As legal scholar Laurence Maher has demonstrated in some detail, these prosecutions, and other threatened prosecutions, became vehicles for wider political, surveillance and prosecutorial campaigns against the CPA, and for permitting extensive operations by the intelligence and police services, including frequent search and seizure raids on party members (Maher 1992, Maher 1994). These efforts reached crescendos during Prime Minister Robert Menzies' 1950–1 bid to ban the CPA and in the lead-up to the mid-1950s Petrov Royal Commission.

Drawing on the official archives, Maher showed that decisions were taken to launch the sedition prosecutions, which required the approval of the Attorney-General, for purely political purposes. Under pressure from the United States government to 'get tough with' the Communist Party, Chifley sent the head of the Defence Department to Washington, where he 'made as much as he could of the prosecutions of Burns, Sharkey and Healy as one important indication of the Chifley Government's anti-communist resolve' (Maher 1992: 305). The Labor government also had its own domestic reasons to harass the CPA. As Maher explained, citing another archive document:

> [T]hese three cases were part of the overall political struggle of the time which, for example, saw the Chifley Government crush the CPA-inspired coal strike in June–August 1949 and take a variety of other measures in 1948–9 to strengthen Australia's internal security apparatus in the face of increasing anxiety about communist disruption of Australia's industry and defence preparedness. (Maher 1992: 304–5)

In the case of Burns, Maher noted that the Acting Attorney-General Nicholas McKenna 'discussed the case with [Prime Minister Ben] Chifley before making his decision' (Maher 1992: 300). Chifley's Labor government claimed it was doing no more than enforcing the criminal law, and dishonestly denied that the proceedings were directed against the CPA. In court, prosecution counsel echoed these claims, making statements that were 'all false, and hypocritical in the extreme' (Maher 1992: 303). These practices, which involve clear and deliberate deception and abuses of the legal system, are a reminder of the extent to which the extraordinary powers given to governments and the intelligence and security agencies can be used to violate legal and political rights.

In *Burns v. Ransley*, the High Court was evenly divided about whether the words uttered by Burns were expressive of a seditious intention and so, under the Judiciary Act, the opinion of Chief Justice Latham prevailed and the conviction of Burns stood. He went to jail for six months.

In common parlance, Burns, a member of the CPA for 25 years, had been 'set up'. The occasion was a crowded public debate in the Brisbane Temperance Hall between the Australian Communist Party (as it was then known) and the Queensland People's Party. Someone in the body of the hall put the following question to Burns: 'We all know that we could become embroiled in a third world war in the immediate future between Soviet Russia and the Western Powers. In the event of such a war what would be the attitude and actions of the Communist Party in Australia?' Burns answered: 'If Australia was involved in such a war, it would be between Soviet Russia and American and British Imperialism. It would be a counter-revolutionary war. We would oppose that war. It would be a reactionary war.' At that stage, the questioner interjected: 'Mr. Chairman, I want a direct answer.' Burns responded: 'We would oppose that war. We would fight on the side of Soviet Russia. That is a direct answer.' At the time of the interjection Burns had his hands behind his coat on his hips and leaned forward towards the moveable rostrum which was the stand the speakers used for their notes, and he gripped both sides of the rostrum before he spoke. The reply was in a loud tone of voice and was emphatic. After that reply there was silence for a few seconds, then there was general consternation throughout the hall and a buzz of conversation. A number of persons called to the chairman. The next question put to Burns was: 'If you made a seditious statement in Russia such as you have made here tonight, would you walk out of here a free man, as you most probably will do, or would you be gaoled?' Burns replied: 'I think I will be a very lucky man if I do not see the inside of a capitalist gaol within the next ten years.' Someone in the audience said: 'You should be behind bars.' Burns replied: 'You might think my right place is behind bars.'

Burns was charged with having a seditious intention within the meaning of the Crimes Act section 24A(1) (b) and (d). Section 24A defined seven categories of seditious intention:

    (a) to bring the Sovereign into hatred or contempt;
    (b) to excite disaffection against the Sovereign or the Government or Constitution of the United Kingdom or against either House of the Parliament of the United Kingdom;

(c) to excite disaffection against the Government or Constitution of any of the Queen's dominions;

(d) to excite disaffection against the Government or Constitution of the Commonwealth or against either House of the Parliament of the Commonwealth;

(e) to excite disaffection against the connexion of the Queen's dominions under the Crown;

(f) to excite Her Majesty's subjects to attempt to procure the alteration, otherwise than by lawful means, of any matter in the Commonwealth established by law of the Commonwealth; or

(g) to promote feelings of ill-will and hostility between different classes of Her Majesty's subjects so as to endanger the peace, order or good government of the Commonwealth.

The whole Court agreed that the relevant sections of the Crimes Act were constitutionally valid, coming within the executive power or the incidentals power of section 51 of the Australian Constitution. However, there was little agreement on whether and why Burns' words were seditious. All the judges agreed that encouragement of people to fight against their own state in a time of war is seditious but Justices Dixon and McTiernan decided that no such encouragement had been intended by Burns. Dixon emphasised that Burns was not on trial for being a disaffected person but for intentionally exciting disaffection in others. He concluded that: 'His answer is a disclosure of his own views actuated by the persistence of his questioner; not an active attempt to effect a purpose of causing his listeners to adopt an attitude of mind'. Dixon further concluded that the statement was devoted to a contingency 'spoken of as an hypothesis, an hypothesis involving a dilemma' (*Burns v. Ransley* (1949) 79 CLR 101, 117–18).

Similarly, McTiernan stressed the need to prove a criminal intention. He asserted that the words in themselves were evidence of such an intention but concluded that when all the circumstances were considered there was a reasonable doubt that Burns had no intention other than to give the information sought by the person who asked the question.

However Chief Justice Latham and Justice Rich had no time for such subtleties. Latham determined that the hypothetical element in the statement did not in itself exclude the words used from the category of seditious words because:

> Almost any statement referring to the future and applying to human action can be shown to involve a hypothetical element. The future is unknown, and any statement as to action in any future circumstances must necessarily depend upon the happening of particular circumstances. A statement that the view of the Communist Party is that Russia should be supported as against Australia and the British Sovereign in any war in which Australia, the Sovereign, and Russia may be involved is a statement which is presented as a policy to be approved and to be put into effect. Such a statement shows a present intention to

excite disaffection against the Sovereign and the Government. (*Burns v. Ransley* (1949) 79 CLR 101, 108–9)

The chief justice opined that stimulation of thoughts was enough to 'excite disaffection':

> In other contexts the word might have a different significance, but in the context of the Act there can be in my opinion no real question but that 'exciting disaffection'refers to the implanting or arousing or stimulating in the minds of people a feeling or view or opinion that the Sovereign and the Government should not be supported as Sovereign and as Government, but that they should be opposed, and when the statement in question is made in relation to a war it means that they should, if possible, be destroyed. (*Burns v. Ransley* (1949) 79 CLR 101, 109)

Rich went further in denying any exculpatory role for hypothesis:

> I do not think that the fact that the words complained of were uttered in answer to questions or were based on contingencies or were hypothetical statements alters or affects the intention expressed by them. They were part of the debate and were made on the platform before the audience. The appellant was explaining the policy of the Communist Party and its attitude to the Sovereign and the Commonwealth Government if either stood in its way. In debating the subject his object was to make a favourable impression on the audience and convert them to the acceptance of the policy of which he was the exponent (*Burns v. Ransley* (1949) 79 CLR 101, 111–12).

Justice argued that Burns' remark about expecting to be jailed within ten years had some bearing on his intention. A more shabby result is difficult to imagine. A man 'set up' to declare his organisation's stance on a fundamental issue of socialist politics was imprisoned for six months. To achieve that, the artificial majority of the High Court dismissed the distinction between exhortation to arms and mere hypothetical pronouncement that had been adopted by the US Supreme Court in 1942 in *Schneiderman v. United States*:

> There is a material difference between agitation and exhortation calling for present violent action which creates a clear and present danger of public disorder or other substantive evil, and mere doctrinal justification or prediction of the use of force under hypothetical conditions at some indefinite future time-prediction that is not calculated or intended to be presently acted upon, thus leaving opportunity for general discussion and the calm processes of thought and reasons. ((1942) 320 US 156)

If there were some qualms over convicting a rank and file communist for provoked remarks, only Justice Dixon was in dissent in the next case, when it came to convicting the CPA general secretary for a statement that was carefully worded to avoid prosecution. Some six months after the Burns' statement, Laurence Sharkey was rung in his office by a reporter from the *Daily Telegraph* who had been instructed by his editor to get a statement from Sharkey on Communist Party policy toward an invasion of Australia by 'communist forces'. After some opposition, Sharkey agreed to do so on the basis that the reporter would take down the statement on the telephone but read it back to him as many times as Sharkey wished in order that he might make corrections. In the event the whole process took four telephone calls, a considerable length of time, and ten or eleven re-readings. The final form read as follows:

> Australian Communists would welcome invading Communist forces if those forces were resisting aggression. If Soviet forces in pursuit of aggressors entered Australia, Australian workers would welcome them. Australian workers would welcome Soviet forces pursuing aggressors as the workers welcomed them throughout Europe when Red troops liberated the people from the power of the Nazis. I support the statements made by the French Communist leader Maurice Thorez. Invasion of Australia by forces of the Soviet Union seems very remote and hypothetical to me. I believe the Soviet Union will go to war only if she is attacked and if she is attacked I cannot see Australia being invaded by Soviet troops. The job of Communists is to struggle to prevent war and to educate the mass of the people against the idea of war. The Communist Party also wants to bring the working class to power but if Fascists in Australia use force to prevent the workers gaining that power, Communists will advise the workers to meet force with force. (*R v. Sharkey* (1949) 79 CLR 121, 125)

Sharkey also told the reporter that he, Sharkey, was the CPA general secretary and spoke for other communists in Australia. Sharkey was charged with having a seditious intention covered by four paragraphs of the Crimes Act section 24A(1) – paras (b), (c), (d) and (g). Justice Dixon dissented from the majority (Chief Justice Latham and Justices Rich, McTiernan, Williams and Webb) but he agreed that the words were capable of being expressive of the intentions to effect the purpose of exciting disaffection against the Sovereign or against the Commonwealth or Constitution of the Commonwealth (s24A (1) (b) (in part) and (d) (in part)). He dissented only to the extent of ordering a new trial on the grounds that the jury's verdict had been based on other seditious intentions under section 24A (1) (c) and (d) that the words were not capable of expressing and on other seditious intentions under section 24A (1) (b) and (g) that were invalid. Apart from these technicalities, which the other judges preferred to ignore, Dixon was then in essential agreement that Sharkey's words were seditious in at least three ways.

Even so, Justice Dixon was correct in his technicality (leaving aside the constitutional points, which are beyond the scope of this book). It is impossible to regard Sharkey's statement as expressive of an intention to cause disaffection against the Government, Constitution or Parliament of the United Kingdom or any of the Queen's dominions (paras (b) and (c)) and there is also nothing in it which adverts to the Houses of Parliament of the Commonwealth (para (d)). Apart from some constitutional discussion, the reasoning in the majority judgements can only be described as presumptuous.

The chief justice took the lead by refusing to examine in any detail how Sharkey's statement infringed paras (b), (c), (d) or (g) of section 24A (1). In addition he again bluntly rejected any defence that the defendant's only intention was to express a hypothetical view in reply to a question: 'It was not the statement of an abstract theoretical question. It was a statement made by the accused "officially" recommending what he described as the policy of the Communist Party' (*R v. Sharkey* (1949) 79 CLR 121, 140). Furthermore, Latham used Sharkey's own careful language as evidence of a seditious intention:

> Sharkey's statement was, as the evidence clearly showed, very carefully prepared. It was not made casually and without purpose. The jury could reasonably take the view upon the evidence that he intended and desired to present and recommend a policy involving disloyalty to Australia and so to excite disaffection, but to make his statement in such words as to create also a certain amount of confusion which could provide grounds for argument which might enable him to escape legal liability for what he was really doing. (*R v. Sharkey* (1949) 79 CLR 121, 141)

The other judgements were in similar vein. Neither Justices Rich nor McTiernan in fact gave any reasoning whatsoever for their conclusions that the jury could reasonably find Sharkey's words to be spoken with a seditious intention. Williams expressed concern over the points made by Dixon but he overcame the objections by appealing to the old notion of the Empire at war:

> The question is whether the words uttered were reasonably capable of being evidence of an intention to effect the purposes in (b), (c) and (d). On consideration I am of opinion that the words were so capable. They were not uttered with respect to a possible war between Soviet Russia and the Commonwealth alone, but with respect to a possible world war between Soviet Russia and the British Commonwealth and its allies. It is for the Sovereign to declare such a war but His Majesty or his representative would only do so in conformity with the wishes of the Governments and Parliaments of the United Kingdom and Dominions. (*R v. Sharkey* (1949) 79 CLR 121, 160)

Similarly, Webb relied on the fact that 'the House of Lords and the House of Commons are essential parts of the political and legal organization of Australia' to conclude that 'although the reply does not mention the Sovereign, or any House of Parliament, or Constitution, or Government, I think the jury could also find that a welcome to Soviet troops invading any part of the British Commonwealth in any contingency would be calculated to excite disaffection to the full extent set out in pars (b), (c) and (d) and was so intended' (*R v. Sharkey* (1949) 79 CLR 121, 164–5).

Justice Webb also took Sharkey's reference to Fascists in Australia as evidence of a seditious intention and took judicial notice of 'happenings in Europe' – including the Berlin blockade – to reinforce his conclusion.

One final point should be made about *R v. Sharkey*. The main provision relied upon by the court below had been para (g) of section 24A(1), which rendered it seditious to promote feelings of ill-will and hostility between the classes so as to endanger the peace, order or good government of the Commonwealth. The High Court judges too were perturbed by Sharkey's concentration on the behaviour of the working class. For example, Justice McTiernan summed it up in this way:

> It is open to the jury taking the words with the circumstances to infer that the supposition with which they begin was used as an occasion to make an appeal based upon class feeling to the workers of Australia calculated and meant to excite them to enmity and disaffection from the Sovereign and the Government of Australia and to promote feelings of ill-will and hostility between them and the rest of the Australian people so as to endanger the peace, order and good government of the Commonwealth. (*R v. Sharkey* (1949) 79 CLR 121, 159)

Such emphasis took the 1914 New Zealand cases to their logical conclusion – any appeal to the working class as a class can be interpreted as sedition. The result of this grand exercise in jurisprudence was that Sharkey was sent off to 18 months' imprisonment. Thus, the High Court left the law in an unsatisfactory state which makes it vulnerable to abuse.

Another Cold War prosecution of a CPA leader, that of William Fardon Burns in 1950, arose from articles published in the party newspaper, *Tribune*, urging 'resistance' to Australia's involvement in the Korean War. After examining the archive record, Roger Douglas established that although Burns was ultimately convicted, and jailed for six months, on one of three counts of publishing seditious words, it was a 'classical political trial' conducted by the Menzies government that coincided with the passage of the Communist Party Dissolution Act 1950 (Douglas 2005).

Douglas concluded that while 'sedition laws are weapons which are used sparingly', such prosecutions, whether legally successful or not, serve a wider purpose. Douglas referred to the 'more subtle, more ubiquitous, and more effective forms of repression which typically accompany prosecutions for political crimes' (Douglas 2005: 248). Douglas suggested that in the light of the problematic prosecution of Burns, and the subsequent experiences of the Vietnam War, federal governments subsequently pursued the war against communists by less legally perilous means, including surveillance (Douglas 2001; Douglas 2002).

Yet, as Maher's 1994 article noted, one further 'particularly ill-conceived' sedition prosecution was conducted in 1953, arising out of a *Communist Review* article criticising the royal family (Maher 1994; Douglas 2005: 247). Moreover, the High Court upheld yet another anti-communist sedition conviction in 1961 and as Maher recorded in his 1992 article, calls were made for sedition prosecutions against anti-war groups during the 1990–1 Gulf War (see also ALRC 2006: 59).

Australia's most recent federal sedition case was in 1960–1. It was described at the time as 'one of Australia's most significant trials', in which, with the help of the media, 'a virtual blackout has descended on an affair that has some of the undertones of the famous framed political trials of modern history' (Murray-Smith 1961: 32).

Regrettably, the case has remained largely unknown since. Brian Cooper, a 24-year-old former junior officer in the Australian colonial administration of Papua New Guinea, was charged with 'exciting disaffection against the government' for remarks he made during a series of informal lunchtime meetings in Madang – where he had been working in September 1960 – encouraging local people to demand independence. On 30 November 1960, he was dramatically arrested in Sydney amid blazing newspaper headlines and flown back to the colony to stand trial for sedition. 'EXTRADITED' declared the Sydney *Sun* the next day on its front page, in six-centimetre capitals (Stent 1980: 60).

Cooper's prosecution was a politically-driven travesty, which tragically helped cause his suicide four years later. Historical records show that the Australian Security Intelligence Organisation (ASIO) framed him up, and Prime Minister Robert Menzies personally ordered the prosecution. Cooper was convicted, without a jury, by a trial judge who admitted irrelevant and prejudicial evidence of his alleged 'communist' and 'atheist' views, and the High Court swiftly dismissed his appeal, arguing incongruously that the inadmissible evidence worked in Cooper's favour.

The victimisation of Brian Cooper was mostly buried for decades. Cooper himself wrote an article on the case for *Overland* in 1961 (Cooper 1961), as did William Stent in 1980 (Stent 1980), but little else has been published. The present author briefly examined Cooper's case in a 1979 article on the historical roots (in the English Star Chamber) of sedition law, and the High Court's shameful record on it (Head 1979). *Cooper v. The Queen* ((1961) 105 CLR 177) became the third in a trilogy of cases in which the High Court approved the jailing of members or alleged sympathisers of the CPA for making political comments that were clearly presentations of hypothetical or theoretical alternatives, not intended to 'excite' any immediate action.

The Australian Law Reform Commission's 2006 *Fighting Words* report on the sedition laws gave the Cooper case only the barest mentions in two footnotes (ALRC 2006: 59, fn 79, and 82, fn 55). The notes provided no indication of the basis of the High Court's ruling or its implications for the potential abuse of the amended sedition provisions in the Anti-Terrorism Act (No 2) 2005. The report merely cited the case as authority for the proposition that Australian state and territory sedition laws 'do not require an intention to cause violence or disorder to be proved in order for a person to be convicted of sedition' (ALRC 2006: 82).

However, research by Anthony Yeates revealed previously unknown aspects of Cooper's prosecution, that demonstrate the need for a more serious and careful review of the case. In particular, de-classified ASIO records document the close involvement of Menzies and his key ministers, as well as the ASIO director-general (Yeates 2007).

One of the documents cited by Yeates – a letter dated 28 November 1960 from ASIO's regional director in Port Moresby to ASIO headquarters – noted that 'His Honour [the Administrator of Papua and New Guinea] further told me that the action in this case has been taken on the directions of the Prime Minister' (Yeates 2007).

According to the secret letter sent by ASIO's regional director, some of the Menzies government's most senior officials were involved or consulted in the decision, including the Administrator of the Territory of Papua and New Guinea, and the Commonwealth Solicitor-General, Sir Kenneth Bailey. Menzies directed that the prosecution be launched after 'the investigation by Mr K. Edmunds, Attorney-General's Department and Mr J. Davis, Commonwealth Investigation Service, had revealed that a prima facie case had been established' (Stent 1980: 61–2).

It is entirely possible that the Menzies government may not have survived without the highly-publicised witch-hunt against Cooper and 'communism'. The 'red scare' served to divert attention from the soaring joblessness and social deprivation. At the December 1961 election, the government lost its majority of 32 seats and survived by a handful of preference votes in one Queensland electorate. The *Sydney Morning Herald* described the election result as a 'massive national vote of no-confidence in the government's policies and an outright rejection of the record on which Mr Menzies took his stand' (Head 2007: 69).

In January 1961, when Cooper landed in Port Moresby for his trial, a large police contingent awaited his arrival at the airport. Media publicity ensured that the courtroom was full of spectators. The Crown prosecutor opened by telling the territorial Chief Justice, Alan Mann, that Cooper had demonstrated 'prior motivation' to commit a criminal act. A former co-worker testified that Cooper had been 'addicted to listening to Radio Peking' and often expressed communist views. ASIO's regional director said Cooper had a history as a communist sympathiser. Despite strong objections, Justice Mann permitted the Crown prosecutor to question Cooper about his political and religious beliefs.

Ten local men were called to testify that Cooper had made the most fantastic suggestions to small lunchtime gatherings, exhorting them to tie up police officers, grab rifles, steal beer and rum, 'expel all the white people' and seek help from 'the Russians and the Chinese'. In his evidence, Cooper said his words had been taken out of context. He had opposed violence and instead advocated the formation of mass organisations, including trade unions and political parties, to convince the government that local people were ready for self-government.

The judge conceded that the words attributed to Cooper were highly improbable. 'I cannot believe that the accused really expected to see an immediate armed uprising of natives in the Madang area.' Yet, the judge concluded that this only made Cooper's utterances all the more sinister, because his real purpose had been to encourage a political movement. '[H]is intention was to start a movement which would be likely to extend along the Northern coast of New Guinea, and which would cause the utmost embarrassment to the Administration at a time when international attention was critically focused on the situation of primitive people in this and other areas.'

When Cooper appealed, the High Court unanimously ruled that much of the evidence was not only 'obviously irrelevant and clearly inadmissible'; it should never have been tendered or entertained. Its only purpose was to 'create prejudice in the mind of the tribunal' and there were 'few things more objectionable in a criminal case' (*Cooper v. The Queen* ((1961) 105 CLR 177, 183). Nevertheless, the court rejected the appeal because 'the offence was clearly proved by admissible evidence' and the trial had been conducted before a judge alone, without a jury.

The wording of the applicable law, section 52 of the Criminal Code of Queensland (which applied to the Territory of New Guinea), required the prosecution to prove that Cooper 'advisedly spoke and published seditious words'. The only relevant meaning of sedition under section 46 of the Code was to 'excite disaffection against the government … as by law established'. Without citing any judicial authority or offering any explanation, the court ruled that, while the word 'advisedly' was 'used somewhat curiously in s 52 of the Code', it went with the word 'publishes'. Therefore it required only an intention to publish, and nothing more (*Cooper v. The Queen* ((1961) 105 CLR 177, 183). In other words, despite the word 'advisedly', the judges did not canvass the possibility that the charge of sedition required an actual or subjective intention to 'excite disaffection'.

Instead, the High Court accepted the trial judge's conclusion that Cooper had been 'only playing with words' when he advised his audience not to resort to illegal violence. In effect, the court sanctioned an interpretation of sedition so wide that it covers advocacy of mass political action. This reasoning was not an aberration, nor is its logic confined to the particular words of the Queensland law, or to state and territory laws more generally as suggested by the ALRC (ALRC 2006: 82). The judgement in *Cooper* was entirely in line with the High Court's rulings against Burns and Sharkey, in which the court ruled that the prosecution need not prove intention to 'excite disaffection'. At the very least, the *Cooper* ruling highlights the ongoing potential for the use of state and territory sedition provisions to criminalise political advocacy, whatever the impact of the 2010 changes to Australian federal law.

Chapter 7
Terrorism

During the first decade of the twenty-first century, a sprawling legal phenomenon arose with long tentacles, as yet full unexplored. Counter-terrorism laws and prosecutions became the most prominent measures directed against crimes that were regarded as threatening the interests of the state itself. Long-standing legal principles, including habeas corpus, the presumption of innocence and freedom of thought and association, were overridden or eroded. Novel concepts, such as 'preventative' punishment, offences of 'praising' or 'glorifying' terrorism (itself defined in broad terms) and detention without trial were introduced.

The full scope and potential use of these provisions cannot be covered here. But is necessary to review the contours and main features of the legislation, and to examine some important terrorist trials. These trials provide indications of the how far the anti-terrorism laws can be utilised to suppress traditional forms of political dissent.

Anti-terrorism legislation has been officially justified as being aimed at protecting members of society against violent acts. However, it is almost invariably targeted at conduct that is motivated by a political, ideological or religious purpose in a manner that either challenges, disturbs or seeks to change the established order. Nearly all legal definitions of terrorism refer to such motives, even if the inherently political character of such classifications has prevented any commonly agreed definition.

Anti-terrorism measures suddenly rose to centre stage this century, following the fatal attacks in the US on 11 September 2001, yet terrorism was hardly a new trend. It had been a feature of conflicts, both civil and military, for centuries. The recorded history of terrorism goes back at least to Sicarii Zealots – a Jewish extremist group fighting Roman rule in Judaea Province at the first century AD. The term 'terrorism' itself was originally used to describe the actions of the Jacobin Club during the 1790s in its period of rule by terror following the French Revolution. One of the first reported usages of the term in its modern context was by Sergey Nechayev, who founded the anti-Tsarist Russian People's Retribution in 1869, describing himself as a 'terrorist' (Hoffman 1998: 83–167, Chaliand 2007: 56–68).

The classification of 'terrorist', like that of 'saboteur' or 'traitor' is notoriously susceptible to abuse for political purposes. African National Congress leader Nelson Mandela, for example, was sentenced to life imprisonment and was imprisoned for 27 years for conduct that would probably today fall under anti-terrorism law. As discussed in Chapter 5, he was convicted on four charges of sabotage for planning armed actions against the apartheid regime, before being released in 1990 to enter negotiations with the regime, leading to a power-sharing political and economic system. Mandela was later awarded a Nobel Peace Prize. Other groups, when involved in an armed struggle, have been labelled 'terrorists' by Western governments or media, only to be later called, as national leaders, 'statesmen', 'heroes' or even 'peace-makers'. Another example, and Nobel Peace Prize laureate, was Menachem Begin, a Zionist anti-British terrorist who later became an Israeli prime minister (Coady and O'Keefe 2002).

Today's primary 'terrorist' targets – al-Qaeda-linked groups – were yesterday's 'freedom fighters' in the eyes of the Western powers and mass media during the guerrilla war against the Soviet-backed regime in Afghanistan. Billions of dollars were siphoned into Osama bin Laden's Islamic fundamentalist movement by the Carter, Reagan, and George Bush senior administrations until the early 1990s (Blum 2002: 155). Likewise, ousted Iraqi president, Saddam Hussein, was also once a close ally of Washington, particularly during the fratricidal Iran-Iraq war of the 1980s (Blum 2002: 133–4, 145–6).

All legal definitions of terrorism also exclude what has been termed state terrorism – acts of violence or intimidation organised, supported or sanctioned by governments or government agencies. These may include wars of aggression, military interventions, coups, assassinations, renditions and torture. Considerable evidence has been produced of such crimes being committed since 2001. In some instances, law suits seeking to prosecute or obtain redress for such actions have been dismissed by courts on various grounds, including 'state secret' doctrines invoked by the government allegedly responsible (see Chapter 9 under the heading of lawlessness).

One difficulty in surveying the law in the counter-terrorism field is that the legislation has been continually amended since 2001. Again reflecting the highly political character of terrorism law, governments in the US, Britain and Australia have repeatedly extended or bolstered the measures in response to alleged new terrorist threats, often accompanied by scare campaigns, such as the Australian government's 2005 declaration of an alert, which was used to recall the Senate to pass sweeping new provisions within 36 hours (see below). On numerous other occasions, amendments have been introduced in efforts to overcome perceived gaps or loopholes, sometimes exposed by court decisions. Numbers of official reviews and reviewers have been appointed to examine and possibly recommend further changes to the legislation. This ongoing process means that some of the details examined in this chapter may alter, even before this book goes to print. Nevertheless, the underlying tendency toward an extraordinary strengthening of the power of the state apparatus, and unprecedented peacetime erosions of basic legal and democratic rights is unlikely to change.

Another problem is that the terminology of the terrorism provisions is generally so broad that it is difficult to predict the precise circumstances in which police, intelligence and prosecuting authorities will decide to proceed against political or religious groups or individuals. The extent of the discretions entailed in making these law enforcement decisions is so great that there is considerable scope for selective and discriminatory interventions and prosecutions. It is particularly necessary to examine this area of law from the standpoint of the political circumstances and context in which it has been activated in numbers of criminal cases.

Legally defining terrorism has proved controversial, precisely because the term has become so politically, as well as emotionally, charged. Various legal systems and government agencies use different definitions. International agencies such as the UN have been slow to formulate a universally agreed upon, legally binding definition. A 1988 study counted 109 definitions of terrorism that covered a total of 22 different definitional elements (Schmid et al. 1988: 5–6). Another, in 1999, listed over 100 definitions and concluded that the 'only general characteristic generally agreed upon is that terrorism involves violence and the threat of violence' (Laqueur 1999: 6). Yet, this fails to distinguish terrorism from many other crimes, and indeed from such activities as global diplomacy, not to speak of war and military interventions to topple governments.

Some of the definitional difficulties relate to distinguishing between what is seen as legitimate resistance to oppression, including national oppression, and what is classified as criminally reprehensible behaviour. A briefing paper for the Australian Parliament noted: 'During the 1970s and 1980s, the United Nations attempts to define the term foundered mainly due to differences of opinion between various members about the use of violence in the context of conflicts over national liberation and self-determination' (Martyn 2002). Sami Zeidan, a Lebanese diplomat and scholar, explained some of the political reasons underlying the definitional difficulties as follows:

> The difficulty of defining terrorism lies in the risk it entails of taking positions. The political value of the term currently prevails over its legal one. Left to its political meaning, terrorism easily falls prey to change that suits the interests of particular states at particular times. The Taliban and Osama bin Laden were once called freedom fighters (mujahideen) and backed by the CIA when they were resisting the Soviet occupation of Afghanistan. Now they are on top of the international terrorist lists. Today, the United Nations views Palestinians as freedom fighters, struggling against the unlawful occupation of their land by Israel, and engaged in a long-established legitimate resistance, yet Israel regards them as terrorists. Israel also brands the Hizbollah of Lebanon as a terrorist group, whereas most of the international community regards it as a legitimate resistance group, fighting Israel's occupation of Southern Lebanon. In fact, the successful ousting of Israeli forces from most of the South by the Hizbollah in 2000 made Lebanon the only Arab country to actually defeat the Israeli army. (Zeidan 2006: 491–2)

A further study noted:

> [T]errorism is a pejorative term. It is a word with intrinsically negative connotations that is generally applied to one's enemies and opponents, or to

those with whom one disagrees and would otherwise prefer to ignore ... Hence the decision to call someone or label some organization 'terrorist' becomes almost unavoidably subjective, depending largely on whether one sympathizes with or opposes the person/group/cause concerned. If one identifies with the victim of the violence, for example, then the act is terrorism. If, however, one identifies with the perpetrator, the violent act is regarded in a more sympathetic, if not positive (or, at the worst, an ambivalent) light; and it is not terrorism. (Hoffman 1998: 32)

Another scholar drew attention to the difficulties that the political and emotional connotations of the term 'terrorism' create in making its legal use susceptible to being used for other political purposes.

Despite the shifting and contested meaning of 'terrorism' over time, the peculiar semantic power of the term, beyond its literal signification, is its capacity to stigmatize, delegitimize, denigrate, and dehumanize those at whom it is directed, including political opponents. The term is ideologically and politically loaded; pejorative; implies moral, social, and value judgment; and is 'slippery and much-abused.' In the absence of a definition of terrorism, the struggle over the representation of a violent act is a struggle over its legitimacy. The more confused a concept, the more it lends itself to opportunistic appropriation. (Saul 2006: 3)

Even states that are allies can disagree, for reasons of history, culture and politics, over whether or not members of a certain organisation are terrorists. For many years, some branches of the US government refused to label members of the Irish Republican Army (IRA) as terrorists, even though they were branded as terrorists by the British government. This was highlighted by *Quinn v. Robinson* (783 F.2d 776, 54 USLW 2449), where a US federal court determined that an IRA member could not be extradited to the UK to face charges of murder and conspiracy to cause explosions, because of the 'political offence' exception, an international law principle that had been incorporated in the relevant US–UK extradition treaty.

The greatest concern with the counter-terrorism legislation, however, is that all the various definitions adopted since 2001 are so broad and vague, and politically loaded, that they have given governments and their security agencies considerable scope to persecute and criminalise political dissenters and government opponents. Legitimate protests, acts of civil disobedience and industrial action could be targeted under these provisions. Although the measures were initially used against alleged Islamic fundamentalists, supporters of other causes not favoured by the Western powers have found themselves accused of terrorism, including Kurdish and Sri Lankan Tamil separatists. In 2010, some leading US politicians called for WikiLeaks founder Julian Assange to be treated as a 'terrorist' for disseminating leaked diplomatic cables that revealed US involvement in illegal spying, wars of aggression, coup plots, assassinations and other crimes. A wider range of groups could be subjected to prosecutions in the future, particularly in the event of intense unrest and protests over austerity measures imposed because of the global financial crisis that began in 2008.

In most Western States, notably the participants in the United States-led 'Coalition of the Willing' that invaded Iraq in 2003, the alleged threat of terrorism has been used, particularly since 11 September 2001, as a pretext to make far-reaching inroads into basic democratic rights, including free speech, freedom of political association protections against arbitrary detention, and the right to open and public trial for any serious offence. Despite criticisms by civil liberties groups, both the British and American governments introduced an array of measures, including detention without trial and proscription of organisations (Hancock 2002: 2–8). Amnesty International condemned the Bush administration for breaching the International Covenant on Civil and Political Rights and other international protocols against arbitrary detention and inhuman treatment of prisoners (Amnesty International 2002). In Australia, more than 40 pieces of legislation have been introduced to substantially increase the surveillance, detention and proscription powers of the government and its security and intelligence agencies. Like its US and UK counterparts, the Australian legislation has four fundamental features. It (1) defines terrorism in vague terms; (2) permits the banning of political groups; (3) allows for detention without trial; and (4) shrouds the operations of the intelligence and police agencies in secrecy and provides for semi-secret trials (Head 2002, Head 2004).

The 'War on Terrorism'

Under President George W. Bush's doctrine, the 'war on terror' is an endless state of war. 'Terrorism' is not a tangible enemy, nor even an ideological or political cause. It is, at most, a set of tactics, to which resort can be had by a multitude of disaffected political currents.

Moreover, the collapse of the reasons used to justify the United States-led invasion of Iraq – 'weapons of mass destruction', and Saddam Hussein's supposed links to al-Qaeda-backed terrorism – suggest that lies were told to divert attention away from the real motives of the 'war on terror', both domestically and internationally. The Middle East and Central Asia, it should not be forgotten, host the most substantial proven energy reserves worldwide. The outrages in New York and Washington provided the pretext for the implementation of plans prepared much earlier – during the 1990s – for the conquest of Afghanistan and Iraq (Bacevich 2002).

Whether or not the Bush administration knew in advance of plans for terrorist acts on 11 September remains an unanswered question. The report of the US national commission investigating the terrorist attacks of 11 September was filled with criticisms of the Bush and Clinton administrations and the performance of the government agencies responsible for intelligence, national security emergency response. But the commission attributed all of these failures to incompetence, mismanagement, or 'failure of imagination'. The fundamental premise of its investigation was that the CIA, the FBI, the US military and the Bush White House acted in good faith. The report thus excluded, *a priori,* the most important question raised by the events of 9/11: did US government agencies permit – or even assist – the carrying out of this terrorist atrocity, in order to provide the Bush administration with the necessary justification to carry out its program of war in Central Asia and the Middle East and a huge build-up of forces of state repression at home (The 9/11 Commission 2004).

Despite professing to be introducing democracy to the Middle East by removing governments in Afghanistan and Iraq, Washington and its allies have for decades diplomatically and militarily propped up dictatorships like the Saudi monarchy and Gulf kingdoms, in the interests of controlling access to the region's oil wealth (Shalom 1993: 63–88). Equally, the claims of exporting democracy are belied by the erosions of democratic rights at home.

In 2010, the *Washington Post* conducted an investigation into the scale of the US domestic intelligence apparatus built up since the 9/11 terrorist attacks. The project concluded that federal government was carrying out the collection and integration of personal information on hundreds of thousands, and potentially millions, of Americans, most of whom had committed no criminal offence and were not engaged in anything that could reasonably be considered 'terrorism'. A total of 4,058 federal, state and local organisations had 'counter-terrorism' functions, with one quarter of these either newly created since 9/11 or involved in counter-terrorist activities for the first time since then. US police agencies were deploying technologies tested on the battlefields of Iraq and Afghanistan and using them to monitor and target American citizens. State and local police agencies were monitoring legal political activities, including protests over environmental, immigration and other issues, and filing reports with counter-terrorism 'fusion centers' in the 50 states. The *Washington Post* report drew attention to an aspect of the connection between the foreign and domestic features of the 'war on terrorism'. It noted: 'The special operations units deployed overseas to kill the al-Qaeda leadership drove technological advances that are now expanding in use across the United States' (Priest and Arkin 2010).

In Australia, a number of prominent legal and political commentators have warned that the anti-terrorism legislation passed in late 2005 by the federal and state parliaments contained police-state features. The president of the Human Rights and Equal Opportunity Commission, John Von Doussa, said:

> It might sound over-dramatic to say that the proposed laws are of the kind that may identify a police state, but let us reflect for a moment on that proposition. The defining characteristic of a police State is that the police exercise power on behalf of the executive, and the conduct of the police cannot be effectively challenged through the justice system. Regrettably, that is exactly what the laws which are currently under debate will achieve. (Von Doussa 2005)

A former Australian prime minister, Malcolm Fraser, made a similar judgement in a lecture delivered in 2005:

> These are powers whose breadth and arbitrary nature, with lack of judicial oversight, should not exist in any democratic country. If one says, but they will not be abused, I do not agree. If arbitrary power exists, it will be abused. (Fraser 2005)

Fraser observed that the government was really saying, 'trust us'. His answer was as follows: '[N]o part of the coalition's invasion and occupation of Iraq gives any member of that coalition the right to say on these issues: "Trust us".' The former prime minister referred to the lies about 'weapons of mass destruction' that could be dropped on London within 45 minutes. He also referred to the Australian government's false 'children overboard' allegations against a boatload of asylum seekers in 2001, and the government's abandonment of David Hicks, an Australian citizen detained by the Bush administration in Guantánamo Bay, Cuba.

Britain

As a result of the political processes referred to above, the main UK legislation is spread over several acts, including the Terrorism Act 2000, Anti-terrorism, Crime and Security Act 2001, Prevention of Terrorism Act 2005, Terrorism Act 2006 and the Counter-Terrorism Act 2008.

This legislation has significantly altered the criminal law as it relates to police investigations, police powers and prosecutions in terrorist offences. Many new offences have been created, police powers have been expanded, and the relationship between the state and the individual has been in many cases fundamentally altered. The legislation raises many significant issues relating to freedom of speech, freedom of association and the right to a fair trial.

The concerns about how these provisions and powers can be used for political purposes are all the greater because of the string of 'miscarriage of justice' cases of the 1970s to 1990s, including the *Birmingham Six, Guildford Four and Maguire Seven*. The Birmingham Six were sentenced to life imprisonment in 1975 for the Birmingham pub bombings. Their convictions were declared unsafe and overturned by the Court of Appeal in 1991. After spending 16 years behind bars, the six men were later awarded compensation ranging from £840,000 to £1.2 million. The Guildford Four and the Maguire Seven were two sets of people whose wrongful convictions for the Guildford pub bombings were also eventually quashed. In 1975 and 1976, the Guildford Four were convicted of bombings, apparently carried out by the IRA, and the Maguire Seven were convicted of handling explosives found during the investigation into the bombings. Both groups' convictions were declared 'unsafe and unsatisfactory' and reversed after they had served 15 years in prison. When the convictions of the Maguire Seven were quashed in 1991, the court held that members of the London Metropolitan Police had beaten some of the defendants into confessing to the crimes and withheld information that would have cleared them (Blom-Cooper 1997).

The Guildford bombings were most likely the work of the 'Balcombe gang', members of which publicly claimed responsibility at their own trial for other IRA-related murders and bombings. They were sentenced to life imprisonment, but were released under the terms of the 1998 Good Friday Agreement, which essentially established a power-sharing arrangement between the IRA, the Northern Ireland loyalists and the British government (Moysey 2008). That settlement provided another example of the transformation of officially-designated 'terrorists' into politically-acceptable figures in the eyes of the government, the establishment and mainstream media.

The British terrorism legislation contains numerous features of note, including a wide definition of terrorism, sweeping provisions directed against 'encouraging' or signifying support for terrorism, and broad executive powers to proscribe organisations. Other key provisions expand the scope of the measures, include those relating to possession of terrorist-linked materials, failure to disclose information to the authorities, fund-raising and preventative detention. The Terrorism Act 2000 defined terrorism as follows:

> (1)   In this Act 'terrorism' means the use or threat of action where:
>   (a)   the action falls within subsection (2),
>   (b)   the use or threat is designed to influence the government or to intimidate the public or a section of the public and
>   (c)   the use or threat is made for the purpose of advancing a political, religious or ideological cause.
> (2)   Action falls within this subsection if it:
>   (a)   involves serious violence against a person,
>   (b)   involves serious damage to property,
>   (c)   endangers a person's life, other than that of the person committing the action,
>   (d)   creates a serious risk to the health or safety of the public or a section of the public or
>   (e)   is designed seriously to interfere with or seriously to disrupt an electronic system.

For these purposes, 'action' includes action outside the UK (Terrorism Act section 1(4)(a)); a 'person' or 'property' refers to any person, or to any property, wherever situated (section 1(4)(b)); and 'the public' includes the public of a country other than the UK (section 1(4)(c)). The use or threat of action falling within head (1) that involves the use of firearms or explosives is terrorism, whether or not head (2) is satisfied (section 1(3)). This latter sub-section was applied in *R (on the application of the Islamic Human Rights Commission) v. Civil Aviation Authority* ([2006] EWHC 2465 (Admin), [2007] ACD 5 at [43], [44]).

'The government' means the government of the UK, of a part of the UK, or of a country other than the UK (section 1(4)(d)). 'The government' is not limited to countries governed by democratic or representative principles, and can include a tyranny, dictatorship, military junta or usurping or invading power: *R v. F* ([2007] EWCA Crim 243, [2007] QB 960, [2007] 2 All ER 193, [2007] 2 Cr App Rep 20). The Court of Appeal dismissed the appeal of F, a Libyan dissident who was being prosecuted for possession of a document or record 'likely to be useful' to a terrorist, namely a blueprint for setting up an underground organisation in Libya to oppose the government of Colonel Gaddafi. Thus, dissidents fighting any regime that is currently favoured by the UK government can be subjected to terrorism charges.

Moreover, the Terrorism Act 2006 amended the definition to include 'international governmental organisations' in addition to 'the government'. This extended the offence to cover acts directed against the UN and other international institutions. The Secretary of State can also make orders and regulations, and give directions, under the Terrorism Act 2000 (sections 123, 124).

> Many offences are 'Convention offences' for the purposes of those terrorism offences which refer to the term. They range from preparation of explosions to development of biological or nuclear weapons, threats to protected persons, hostage-taking and hijacking of ships or aircraft. Other offences on the list include terrorist fund-raising, conspiracy to commit a Convention offence, attempting, encouraging or assisting the commission of a Convention offence, and aiding, abetting, counselling or procuring the commission of a Convention offence. The Secretary of State may by order modify this list of offences (Terrorism Act 2006 section 20(9)).

Organisations can be outlawed by executive order. Schedule 2 to Part II of the Terrorism Act 2000 listed certain proscribed organisations. The list has been added to by the Home Secretary, and now includes al-Qaeda and the Egyptian Islamic Jihad among several others, and the Home Secretary retains the power to remove or amend names on the schedule. Organisations that unlawfully 'glorify' acts of terrorism can now be proscribed (Section 21, Terrorism Act 2006). The procedure for appealing against proscription is set out in Sections 5–6.

Membership (or professing membership) of a proscribed organisation is an offence carrying a maximum penalty of 10 years' imprisonment. It is a defence for a person to show that the organisation was not proscribed when he last joined, and that he has not taken part in any of its activities while it has been proscribed. It is an offence for a person to invite support for a proscribed organisation (section 12(1)); to arrange a meeting which he knows is to support a proscribed organisation (or to further its activities or to be addressed by a member of a proscribed organisation) (section 12(2)); and to address a meeting with the purpose of encouraging support for a proscribed organisation (section 12(3)). There are statutory defences. The maximum penalty for these offences is also 10 years' imprisonment.

It is even an offence for a person to wear, in a public place, an item of clothing (or wear or display an article) in such a way as to arouse reasonable suspicion that he is a member or supporter of a proscribed organisation (section 13). The maximum sentence for this offence is 6 months' imprisonment. Under section 56 of the Terrorism Act, it is an offence, punishable by life imprisonment, for a person to direct, at any level, the activities of an organisation that is concerned in the commission of terrorist acts.

The possession provisions are highly problematic. Section 57 of the Terrorism Act created an offence for a person to possess an article in circumstances that give rise to a reasonable suspicion that the possession is for a purpose connected with the commission, preparation or instigation of terrorist acts. This offence partly reverses the onus of proof. It is a defence to prove that the possession was not for such a purpose. However, the effect of section 118 of the 2000 Act is that, if a defendant adduces evidence that raises an issue as to whether his possession of the article in question was for such a purpose, the burden shifts back to the prosecution of proving beyond reasonable doubt that the possession of the article was held for such purpose.

A court may assume possession if the article is found at premises at the same time as the person is present, or on premises that he controls (unless he proves he did not know of its presence or that he had no control over it). The maximum sentence for this offence is 15 years' imprisonment. Under section 58, it is an offence to collect or make a record of information of a kind likely to be useful to a person committing or preparing an act of terrorism, or to possess a document or record containing information of that kind.

A five-judge constitution of the Court of Appeal in *R v. Rowe* ([2007] EWCA Crim 635; [2007] QB 975), upheld a conviction on two counts of possessing an article for terrorist purposes contrary to section 57. Rowe had possessed a notebook which contained mortar instructions and a substitution code which listed components of explosives and places of a type susceptible to terrorist bombing. The court ruled that documents and records can be 'articles' for the purposes of section 57.

Some judicial decisions have sought to limit the scope of these possession offences. In *R v. Zafar* ([2008]EWCA Crim 184), the appellants had been convicted of offences under section 57. Four 20-year-old Bradford University students and a 19-year-old school student were found with material on their computers said to be inciting Islamic terrorism. Aitzaz Zafar, Usman Malik and Awaab Iqbaal had been sentenced to be jailed for three years each, Akbar Butt for 27 months, and the school student, Mohammed Irfan Raja had been given two years' youth detention.

In an atmosphere of fear generated by politicians and the media after the attempted terror bombings in London and Glasgow in 2007, the young men were convicted merely for downloading material readily available on the Internet. The prosecution alleged that they had been in possession of computer discs and hard drives that contained extremist jihadist propaganda and literature, and that the purpose was to incite one or more of them to travel to Pakistan to take part in 'jihad'. The Court of appeal quashed the convictions, holding that there must be a direct connection between the article possessed and the act of terrorism alleged. In this case, the prosecution alleged that the terrorist act was to travel to Pakistan to fight the pro-Western government in Afghanistan, but there was no evidence of use or intent to use the material on the discs specifically to incite this. The court stated:

> We have concluded that, if section 57 is to have the certainty of meaning that the law requires, it must be interpreted in a way that requires a direct connection between the object possessed and the act of terrorism. The section should be interpreted as if it reads:

A person commits an offence if he possesses an article in circumstances which give rise to a reasonable suspicion that he intends it to be used for the purpose of the commission, preparation or instigation of an act of terrorism. (*R v. Zafar* ([2008] EWCA Crim 184, [29])

Nevertheless, the court left open considerable room for section 57 to be applied to anyone accused of possessing documents that merely incite possible terrorist acts:

> Not without hesitation we have concluded that possessing a document for the purpose of inciting a person to commit an act of terrorism falls within the ambit of section 57. We have considered the definition of 'instigate' in a number of dictionaries and, in each case, have found the word 'incite' as a synonym. Black's Law Dictionary, 7th Ed, defines 'instigate' as 'to goad or incite (someone) to take some action or course.' We have concluded that section 57 must be construed having regard to the normal meaning of instigate. (*R v. Zafar* ([2008] EWCA Crim 184, [31])

In *R v. K* ([2008] EWCA Crim 185), the appellant faced three counts under section 58. It was alleged that he had been in possession of a copy of the 'al-Qaeda Training Manual', a publication relating to the formation and organisation of 'jihadist' movements, and a publication that argued that Muslims should work toward the establishment of an Islamic state. The Appellant had argued, at a preparatory hearing, that the prosecution was an abuse of process, as section 58 was incompatible with the European Convention on Human Rights because of lack of certainty, and that the provision was not intended to cover the kind of publications that formed the subject of two of the charges. The trial judge had rejected these arguments and held that whether possession amounted to an offence depended on the circumstances and context of the possession. The Court of Appeal held that section 58 applied only to documents that provide 'practical assistance' to a person preparing or committing an act of terrorism, and not those that might merely encourage. A document had to contain information of such a nature as to raise a reasonable suspicion that it was intended to be used to assist in the preparation or commission of a terrorist act. Extrinsic evidence might be called to explain the nature of the information, or establish a defence of reasonable excuse for possession, but not to establish that an apparently innocent document was intended to be used for a terrorist purpose. To show 'reasonable excuse' for possession, a defendant would need to show that the document or record was possessed for another purpose than to assist in the preparation or commission of an act of terrorism, even if that purpose infringed another provision of civil or criminal law.

In *R v. Samina Malik* ([2008] EWCA Crim 1450), the appellant had been convicted under section 58 (although acquitted of offences under section 57). Her computer had been seized by police and found to contain 'jihadist' material and publications relating to terrorism. The prosecution also relied on other documents, including notes written by the appellant whilst in police custody, to demonstrate her support for violent jihad. On appeal, the prosecution conceded that the convictions were unsafe. The Court of Appeal did not accept all the grounds of appeal, nor all of the prosecution's concessions, but quashed the convictions. It held that there was a wide overlap between sections 57 and 58, and that by proceeding against the appellant on alternative counts relating to the same material, the jury may have been left confused. The trial judge had not had the benefit of the Court of Appeal's judgement in *R v. K*, and his directions given to the jury had not differentiated between material that could fall within section 58 and that which could not. Those directions had not included the 'practical utility' test as set out in *R v. K*.

These efforts by the Court of Appeal to limit the scope of sections 57 and 58 were, however, thrown into doubt by the House of Lords in *R v. G; R v. J* ([2009] 2 WLR 724, [2009] 2 All ER 409, [2009] 2 Cr App R 4, [2009] UKHL 13) in which both sections were re-examined. In the first place, the court insisted that an intention to help commit, prepare or instigate a terrorist act was not needed to be convicted under section 57. Delivering the judgement, Lord Rodger stated:

> [T]he Crown does not need to prove what the accused's purpose connected with the commission, preparation or instigation of an act of terrorism actually was – something which might well be impossible to prove. It is enough if the Crown satisfies the Court or jury, beyond reasonable doubt, that the circumstances give rise to a reasonable suspicion that the defendant's possession was for the relevant purpose. The defendant is then given a defence under subsection (2) (*R v. G; R v. J* [2009] UKHL 13, [55]).

Secondly, the House of Lords disapproved of the interpretation placed upon section 57(2) in *R v. Zafar.* Lord Rodger stated:

> On its face, it is indeed open to the interpretation that, if a defendant adduces evidence sufficient to raise a defence under section 57(2), then, in order to obtain a conviction, the Crown must prove beyond reasonable doubt that the defendant's possession of the article was for a purpose connected with the commission etc of an act of terrorism. That would, however, be to misapply

section 118(2) and to mix up what the Crown has to prove in order to establish
the offence and what the Crown has to prove in order to rebut the defence. (*R v.
G; R v. J* [2009] UKHL 13, [67])

Lord Rodger said the prosecution was only obliged to rebut the defence
beyond a reasonable doubt, not prove beyond a reasonable doubt that the accused's
possession was for a purpose in connection with an act of terrorism.

Thirdly, the House of Lords said the Court of Appeal's decision in *R v. K* had
imposed on the defence in section 58(3) a construction that was 'utterly different'
from a correct one. The Court of Appeal had robbed the adjective 'reasonable' in
section 58(3) of all substance by saying that it excused a defendant who proved
only that his purpose was not connected with an act of terrorism (*R v. G; R v. J*
[2009] UKHL 13, [76-77]).

The House of Lords upheld the conviction of G, who had been in prison at
the time of the alleged offence, even though he had collected the incriminating
information precisely because he knew how 'this terrorism stuff' had 'really
got on the nerves of the prison officers'. Lord Rodger said: 'On no view could a
desire to wind up prison officers in this way be a reasonable excuse for collecting
and recording the information' (*R v. G; R v. J* [2009] UKHL 13, [89]). By this
interpretation, an accused could be convicted for possessing material linked to
terrorism even if his or her purpose had nothing whatever to do with instigating an
act of terrorism, but, for example, related to annoying law enforcement personnel.

Despite the ruling in *R v. G; R v. J,* a Scottish student won an appeal in 2010
against his conviction under section 57 in *Siddique v. Her Majesty's Advocate*
([2010] ScotHC HCJAC_7). Siddique was originally sentenced to eight years'
imprisonment for downloading from the Internet materials relating to the Islamic
fighters resisting the US-led occupation of Iraq. His counsel argued that this
material 'could all simply have been the product of genuine research of someone
with a reasonable inquiring, presumably, mind about the fate of his fellow
Muslims in and around the Middle East'. The court held that there had been a
miscarriage of justice because the judge's directions to jury failed to properly refer
to 'circumstances which give rise to a reasonable suspicion' when addressing this
defence.

There are extensive anti-fundraising measures. Section 15 of the Terrorism
Act makes it an offence to invite a person to provide money or other property,
intending that it should be used (or having reasonable cause to suspect it may
be used) for the purposes of terrorism. Receiving money or property intending
it should be used (or having reasonable cause to suspect it may be used) for
terrorist purposes is also an offence, as is providing money or property knowing
(or having reasonable cause to suspect) that it will or may be used for the purposes
of terrorism. 'Providing' money or property means giving, lending or otherwise
making available whether or not this is in return for something else.

If a person uses money or property for the purposes of terrorism, this is also
an offence, and it is also an offence to possess money or property intending that

it should be used (or having reasonable cause to suspect it may be used) for the purposes of terrorism (section 16). There are further offences that relate to where a person becomes involved in an arrangement where money or property is made available for the purposes of terrorism (section 17); and where a person engages in money laundering connected with terrorism (section 18). Where a person believes or suspects that another person has committed an offence under sections 15 to 18, and that belief is based on information that comes to him in the course of his trade, profession, business or employment, it can be an offence not to disclose this information to the police soon as reasonably practicable (section 19). All the offences in sections 15 to 18 carry a maximum penalty of 10 years' imprisonment. In addition, a court has wide powers of forfeiture following any conviction.

Even wider disclosure of information offences have been created. As a result of sections 38–9 of the Terrorism Act and section 117 of the Anti-terrorism, Crime and Security Act 2001, where a person has information which he knows or believes might be of 'material assistance' in preventing the commission of an act of terrorism, or in securing the apprehension, prosecution or conviction of a person (in the UK) for an offence involving an act of terrorism, it is an offence not to disclose the information as soon as reasonably practicable. Disclosure should be made to a police officer. A person charged with this offence has a defence if he can show that he had a reasonable excuse for not disclosing the information. The offence is punishable by five years' imprisonment.

In 2010, a jury unanimously acquitted the wife of a convicted airline bomb plotter of a charge of failing to pass on information that would be useful in preventing an act of terrorism. Her husband, Abdulla Ahmed Ali, had been jailed for 40 years for planning to blow up transatlantic jets. The prosecution argued that Cossor Ali had known that her husband was planning to commit mass murder by targeting passenger jets but had failed to tell police. However, in a unanimous verdict, the jury accepted Mrs Ali's defence that she knew nothing about it. A key question centred on the meaning of the Arabic word '*shahada*', used by Ali in referring to her husband. While the prosecution claimed it meant 'martyrdom', the defence argued that it simply meant a 'good death' in the eyes of Allah (Times Online 2010).

The Terrorism Act 2006 created several new offences, some of which were controversial, and also significantly extended police powers in terrorist investigations. It further provided that certain offences can be prosecuted even if they are committed outside the UK (section 17). Several offences contradict the right to freedom of expression, by punishing the communication of ideas, rather than any actions.

'Encouragement of terrorism' is criminalised by section 1. The offence is committed if a person makes a statement that is likely to be understood by some or all members of the public to whom it is published as 'a direct or indirect encouragement or other inducement to them' to commit, prepare or instigate acts of terrorism. The person must publish the statement intending members of the public to be directly or indirectly induced by it to commit or prepare such acts.

Alternatively, the person making the statement must be reckless as to whether members of the public will be directly or indirectly encouraged, etc.

Statements 'likely to encourage' include a statement that 'glorifies' the commission or preparation of terrorist offences, where the public could reasonably be expected to infer that the conduct being glorified should be emulated by them. Where a person is charged with this offence, and it is not proved that he intended to encourage or induce acts of terrorism, it is a defence to show that it was clear that the statement did not express his views, and was not endorsed by him. Encouragement of terrorism carries a maximum sentence of 7 years' imprisonment.

Dissemination of 'terrorist publications' is outlawed by section 2. This offence is committed where a person distributes, circulates, gives, sells or lends a terrorist publication; offers a publication for sale or loan or provides a service enabling others to obtain or look at such a publication. The section provides a definition of a 'terrorist publication' as a publication likely to be understood as an encouragement or inducement to commit terrorist acts, or to be useful in the commission of such acts. The person who distributes, etc., the publication must intend to encourage the commission of acts of terrorism, intend his act to provide assistance in doing so, or be reckless as to either. A matter likely to be understood as indirectly encouraging acts of terrorism will include anything which 'glorifies the commission or preparation' of terrorist acts. There are separate provisions that deal specifically with publications on the internet. The offence carries a maximum sentence of 7 years' imprisonment.

The application of this dissemination section was examined in *R v. Abdul Rahman* ([2008] EWCA Crim 1465). The Court of Appeal gave sentencing guidance in relation to offences under section 2 of the 2006 Act. The first appellant, who pleaded guilty to disseminating a terrorist publication under section 2, and offences under sections 5 and 57 of the Terrorism Act 2000, was sentenced to six years' imprisonment. The second appellant pleaded guilty to an offence under section 2 and in mitigation argued that he had been unaware of the change in the law. He was sentenced to three years' imprisonment. The appellate court held that the quality and quantity of the material in question would not necessarily be the only factors affecting the gravity of the offence. Whether a defendant intended the dissemination of extremist material to encourage the commission etc. of terrorism, or was merely reckless as to the consequences, was likely to be significant. The first Appellant's sentence was reduced by six months because he had had a change of heart and no longer espoused terrorism. The second appellant's sentence was reduced by a year to reflect the lower starting point that should have been adopted given that the dissemination in his case was reckless. The court made a general political observation that where sentences were more severe than warranted, this was 'likely to inflame rather than deter extremism'.

Preparation and training offences take the terrorism measures well beyond the traditional criminal law concepts of attempt and complicity, and provide for severe penalties of up to life imprisonment. Section 5 of the 2006 Act makes it an offence for a person who intends to commit or assist an act of terrorism, to engage in any conduct in preparation in order to give effect to his intention. The maximum sentence is life imprisonment.

Section 6 outlaws training for terrorism. It is an offence to provide instruction or training in certain specified skills – these include making or handling 'noxious substances', and any 'method or technique' for doing anything else capable of being done for terrorist purposes. It is also an offence to receive instruction or training in these skills. The maximum sentence is 10 years' imprisonment and a court may order forfeiture of anything it considers to have been in a person's possession and connected with an offence under this section. Attendance at a place used for terrorist training is covered by section 8. It is an offence for a person to attend any place (in or outside the UK) where training is provided while he is there which is wholly or partly for purposes connected with terrorist acts. The person must know or believe that instruction or training is being provided there for such purposes, or a person attending could not reasonably have failed to understand that such training was being provided. It is irrelevant whether the person charged actually receives instruction or training himself. The offence carries a maximum sentence of 10 years' imprisonment.

Police powers have been increased. Under section 43 of the Terrorism Act 2000, a police officer may stop and search a person whom he reasonably suspects to be a terrorist to discover whether he has in his possession anything which may constitute evidence that he is a terrorist. Any person arrested under suspicion of being a terrorist may also be searched. Items that the officer reasonably suspects may constitute evidence that the person is a terrorist may be seized.

Even more fundamentally, the principle of habeas corpus – no detention without trial – is overturned to allow a terrorist suspect to be held in police custody prior to charge for a maximum of 28 days. This power is also reminiscent of the measures used in relation to Ireland, where internment without trial was introduced during the 1970s. A person arrested under section 41 of the Terrorism Act 2000 (i.e. on suspicion of being a terrorist) may be held initially by the police without charge for 48 hours. Since the passage of the Terrorism Act 2006, detention beyond 48 hours can be extended by a High Court Judge, at intervals of 7 days, to a maximum of 28 days.

The British courts have held this power to be potentially consistent with the European Convention on Human Rights, despite Article 5, which provides the right to liberty, subject only to lawful arrest or detention. In order to justify the detention of terrorist suspects, the British government derogated from that article by invoking Article 15 of the Convention, which permits justified, necessary and proportionate responses 'in time of war or other public emergency threatening the life of the nation'. In 2004, the House of Lords accepted that indefinite detention without trial of foreign national terrorist suspects, unable to be prosecuted or deported, could be permissible under the 'public emergency' clause, in the context of the 9/11 attacks in the United States (*A and others v. Secretary of State for the Home Department* [2004] UKHL 56). However, the majority ultimately declared the particular circumstances to be discriminatory and disproportionate to the exigencies of the public emergency. In a dissent on the threshold issue of whether the threat of terrorism constituted a 'public emergency threatening the life of the nation', Lord Hoffman stated that the gravest threat to Britain arose not from potential terrorist attacks, but from legislation such as that resorted to by the government:

> This is one of the most important cases which the House has had to decide in recent years. It calls into question the very existence of an ancient liberty of which this country has until now been very proud: freedom from arbitrary arrest and detention. The power which the Home Secretary seeks to uphold is a power to detain people indefinitely without charge or trial. Nothing could be more antithetical to the instincts and traditions of the people of the United Kingdom ... Whether we should survive Hitler hung in the balance, but there is no doubt we shall survive Al Qaeda. The Spanish people have not said that what happened in Madrid, hideous crime as it was, threatened the life of the nation. Their legendary pride would not allow it. Terrorist crime, serious as it is, does not threaten our institutions of government or our existence as a civil community ... The real threat to the life of the nation, in the sense of a people living in accordance with its traditional laws and political values, comes not from terrorism but from laws such as these. ([2004] UKHL 56, [86–97])

Nonetheless, the eight-to-one majority view was that the courts had to defer heavily to the executive government's assessment of national security. In the words of Baroness Hale:

> Assessing the strength of a general threat to the life of the nation is, or should be, within the expertise of the Government and its advisers ... If a Government were to declare a public emergency where patently there was no such thing, it would be the duty of the court to say so. But here we are considering the immediate aftermath of the unforgettable events of 11 September 2001. The attacks launched on the United States on that date were clearly intended to threaten the life of the nation. (([2004] UKHL 56, [226])

The potential for the terrorism legislation to be used against anti-war protestors was demonstrated by the 2008 trial of Juliet McBride, a member of the Aldermaston Women's Peace Camp, who was charged with a terrorist offence for conducting a peaceful 'no Trident replacement' protest at the Atomic Weapons Establishment (AWE) at Aldermaston in March 2007. It was the first trial pursuant to the controversial provisions of section 128 of the Serious Organised Crime and Police Act 2005 (SOCPA) as amended by section 12 of the Terrorism Act 2006. The amendment created a 'strict liability' offence of trespass on a 'nuclear licensed site'. A prosecution could be brought only with the Attorney General's consent.

For more than 20 years, the Aldermaston peace camp group had held a monthly protest at the site against British-manufactured nuclear weapons. When section 128 was amended in 2006 the relevant minister assured parliament that the Aldermaston women were not its target, and that peaceful protestors who had not gone substantially beyond the fence would not be prosecuted. On the day of her arrest, McBride had crossed the outer perimeter fence and was sitting on the inner fence holding a peace flag. Although she was peaceful at all times, had not entered the site, and her protest related to a political matter, the Attorney General agreed that she should be prosecuted.

Following a visit to the site itself and consideration of a series of conflicting maps detailing the site boundary, District Judge Sanders agreed that the Ministry of Defence and AWE Aldermaston had mistakenly assumed that the boundary of the nuclear licensed site was marked by the outer perimeter fence. In fact, the correct boundary is the inner fence, and so McBride had not entered the licensed area when arrested and there was no trespass. The court awarded the defendant her costs (Doughty Street Chambers 2008).

A 2009 trial, that of Baluchistan human rights activist Faiz Baluch and Hyrbyair Marri, a former Baluchistan MP and government minister, illustrated how the terrorism provisions could be used to criminalise support for selected anti-government groups overseas. The men were charged with being key supporters of the banned Baluchistan Liberation Army (BLA). Baluch was acquitted of all charges and Marri was acquitted of three charges, with the jury unable to come to a verdict on the other two. Human rights campaigners alleged that the men had been set up by agents of the Pakistani government of former military dictator General Musharraf because they had exposed war crimes and crimes against humanity by the Pakistani military (Doughty Street Chambers 2009).

For a case study of how various measures can be used to deprive an individual of liberty without trial for protracted periods, see *Secretary of State for the Home Department v. Saadi* ([2009] EWHC 3390 (Admin)). Libyan national Faraj Faraj Hassan Al-Saadi, who had been under restriction for six years in the United Kingdom on terrorism charges, won a long court battle to have his control order revoked.

Faraj Hassan came to the UK in 2002, fleeing persecution in Libya. He was arrested shortly thereafter and spent 15 months detained without trial before being eventually charged under the Terrorism Act in 2003 and served with an Italian extradition warrant. Although the extradition order was ultimately suspended he continued to be detained for another four years on the basis of secret evidence, with the government seeking to deport him to Libya. Whilst his deportation was ruled unlawful, he was then made the subject of a control order in addition to a UN financial sanction which prevented him from obtaining any income.

Faraj Hassan's main contention was that almost eight years had passed since the last form of terrorism alleged, during the bulk of which he had been detained, or under bail restrictions or a control order, and in those circumstances there was no necessity for a control order. Justice Wilkie agreed, ruling that:

Accordingly, whilst, in my judgment, AS remains a person whose attitudes of disaffection may, from the mainstream point of view, be unattractive, that falls some way short of being sufficient evidence of a risk of his engagement in terrorist related activity so as to necessitate the onerous intrusion into his life represented by a control order.

United States

Both federal and state anti-terrorism provisions exist in the US. Many of the federal measures are derived from the USA PATRIOT Act of 2001. They are primarily codified in Chapter 113B, entitled Terrorism, of Title 18 of the United States Code, which provides for criminal penalties ranging from 10 years' imprisonment to the death penalty. Section 2331(1) defines 'international terrorism' as:

activities that ... involve violent acts or acts dangerous to human life that are a violation of the criminal laws of the United States or of any State, or that would be a criminal violation if committed within the jurisdiction of the United States or of any State; [and] appear to be intended ... to intimidate or coerce a civilian population; ... to influence the policy of a government by intimidation or coercion; or ... to affect the conduct of a government by mass destruction, assassination, or kidnapping; and [which] occur primarily outside the territorial jurisdiction of the United States, or transcend national boundaries in terms of the means by which they are accomplished, the persons they appear intended to intimidate or coerce, or the locale in which their perpetrators operate or seek asylum.

Section 2331(5) defines domestic terrorism as 'activities that (A) involve acts dangerous to human life that are a violation of the criminal laws of the US or of any state, that (B) appear to be intended (i) to intimidate or coerce a civilian population, (ii) to influence the policy of a government by intimidation or coercion, or (iii) to affect the conduct of a government by mass destruction, assassination, or kidnapping, and (C) occur primarily within the territorial jurisdiction of the US'. Terrorism is also included in the definition of racketeering, and terms relating to 'cyber-terrorism' are redefined, including 'protected computer', 'damage' and 'loss'.

The USA PATRIOT Act authorised a vast array of measures to boost the powers of the domestic security services (Title 1), enhance controversial surveillance procedures, including to gather 'foreign intelligence information' from both US and non-US citizens (Title II), to facilitate the prevention, detection and prosecution of 'international money laundering' and the 'financing of terrorism' (Title III), and to expand the enforcement and investigative powers of the Immigration and Naturalization Service (Title IV).

Title VIII, entitled 'Terrorism criminal law', had many other provisions. New penalties were created to convict those who attack mass transportation systems.

If the activity was undertaken while the mass transportation vehicle or ferry was carrying a passenger, or the offence resulted in the death of any person, then the punishment is life imprisonment. A number of measures penalised activities that are deemed to support terrorism. It was made a crime to harbour or conceal terrorists, and those who do are subject to imprisonment of up to 10 years.

The definition of terrorism was further expanded to include receiving military-type training from a foreign terrorist organisation and narco-terrorism. Other provisions merged the law outlawing train wrecking (18 USC § 992) and the law outlawing attacks on mass transportation systems (18 USC § 1993) into a new section of Title 18 of the US Code (18 USC § 1992) and also to criminalise the act of planning a terrorist attack against a mass transport system.

Some of the main provisions of Chapter 113B of Title 18 are as follows. Section 2332a creates an offence to use, threaten, or attempt or conspire to use, a weapon of mass destruction. Punishment is life imprisonment, or death, if any deaths resulted. 'Weapon of mass destruction' is defined to include 'any weapon that is designed or intended to cause death or serious bodily injury through the release, dissemination, or impact of toxic or poisonous chemicals, or their precursors'.

Section 2332f covers bombings of places of public use, government facilities, public transportation systems and infrastructure facilities. It makes it an offence to 'unlawfully deliver, place, discharge, or detonate an explosive or other lethal device in, into, or against' a place of public use, a state or government facility, a public transportation system, or an infrastructure facility **(A)** with the intent to cause death or serious bodily injury, or **(B)** with the intent to cause extensive destruction of such a place, facility, or system, where such destruction results in or is likely to result in major economic loss. Punishment is the same as for section 2332a. Attempts and conspiracies to commit the offence are equally punishable.

Section 2339 covers harbouring or concealing terrorists.

> Whoever harbors or conceals any person who he knows, or has reasonable grounds to believe, has committed, or is about to commit, an offense under section 32 (relating to destruction of aircraft or aircraft facilities), section 175 (relating to biological weapons), section 229 (relating to chemical weapons), section 831 (relating to nuclear materials), paragraph (2) or (3) of section 844 (f) (relating to arson and bombing of government property risking or causing injury or death), section 1366 (a) (relating to the destruction of an energy facility), section 2280 (relating to violence against maritime navigation), section 2332a (relating to weapons of mass destruction), or section 2332b (relating to acts of terrorism transcending national boundaries) of this title, section 236 (a) (relating to sabotage of nuclear facilities or fuel) of the Atomic Energy Act of 1954 (42 USC 2284 (a)), or section 46502 (relating to aircraft piracy) of title 49, shall be fined under this title or imprisoned not more than ten years, or both.

Section 2339C deals with the financing of terrorism, and concealing the financing of terrorism. It is an offence to 'by any means, directly or indirectly, unlawfully and willfully' to provide or collect funds with the intention that such funds be used, or with the knowledge that such funds are to be used, in full or in part, in order to carry out any act 'intended to cause death or serious bodily injury to a civilian, or to any other person not taking an active part in the hostilities in a situation of armed conflict, when the purpose of such act, by its nature or context, is to intimidate a population, or to compel a government or an international organization to do or to abstain from doing any act'. Attempts and conspiracies are equally punishable, by imprisonment for up to 20 years. The concealment offences carry penalties of up to 10 years.

Section 2339D covers 'receiving military-type training from a foreign terrorist organization'. It states: 'Whoever knowingly receives military-type training from or on behalf of any organization designated at the time of the training by the Secretary of State under section 219(a)(1) of the Immigration and Nationality Act as a foreign terrorist organization shall be fined under this title or imprisoned for ten years, or both.' To violate this subsection, a person must have knowledge that the organisation is a designated terrorist organisation, that the organisation has engaged or engages in terrorist activity or that the organisation has engaged or engages in terrorism.

A provision that prohibited 'material support' for terrorists, including 'expert advice or assistance' was struck down by a federal court, which found that it violated the First and Fifth Amendments to the US Constitution. The court said the provision was so vague it would cause a person of average intelligence to have to guess whether they were breaking the law. The court found that this could potentially have the effect of allowing arbitrary and discriminatory enforcement of the law, as well as possible chilling effects on First Amendment rights. The law was then amended to seek to overcome the ruling by defining 'material support or resources', 'training' and 'expert advice or resources'.

Section 2339A now provides: 'Whoever provides material support or resources or conceals or disguises the nature, location, source, or ownership of material support or resources, knowing or intending that they are to be used in preparation for, or in carrying out' an act associated with terrorism, or attempts or conspires to do such an act, shall be liable to 15 years' imprisonment, or life imprisonment if any death results. The term 'material support or resources' is defined extensively, to mean 'any property, tangible or intangible, or service, including currency or monetary instruments or financial securities, financial services, lodging, training, expert advice or assistance, safehouses, false documentation or identification, communications equipment, facilities, weapons, lethal substances, explosives, personnel (1 or more individuals who may be or include oneself), and transportation, except medicine or religious materials'. The term 'training' is defined as 'instruction or teaching designed to impart a specific skill, as opposed to general knowledge'. 'Expert advice or assistance' is defined as 'advice or assistance derived from scientific, technical or other specialized knowledge'. Section 2339B likewise covers 'providing material support or resources to designated foreign terrorist organizations'.

The potential for anti-terrorism laws to be used against organisations engaged in lawful advocacy, even those teaching about explicitly non-violent political lobbying, was underscored in 2010 when the US Supreme Court upheld 6–3 a provision of law making it a federal crime to 'knowingly provide material support or resources to a foreign terrorist organization', even if the 'support' consisted only of 'expert advice or assistance' for 'lawful, non-violent purposes'.

The challenged law was part of the Antiterrorism and Effective Death Penalty Act 1996 (AEDPA), signed into law on the first anniversary of the Oklahoma City bombing (18 US C Section 2339B(a)(1)). It provided that the US Secretary of State could designate any 'foreign organization' as 'terrorist' based on 'classified information' establishing that it 'engages in terrorist activity' which 'threatens the security of United States nationals or the national security of the United States'. As a result of the court's ruling, an individual can be sentenced to as much as 15 years' imprisonment if found to 'provide material support' for a designated organisation, even if only by means of engaging in discussions with it or speaking on its behalf. In effect, at the application of the Obama administration, the Supreme Court gave its imprimatur to the prosecution and imprisonment of US citizens for advocating support of organisations opposing the policies of the US government or its allies anywhere on the planet.

The plaintiffs in *Humanitarian Law Project v. Holder (*561 US ____ (2010) were a coalition of US-based human rights organisations, non-profit groups and citizens who obtained a lower court injunction to protect them from being criminally prosecuted for advising and assisting the separatist groups, the Partiya Karkeran Kurdistan (PKK) and Liberation Tigers of Tamil Eelam (LTTE). Both were designated as 'foreign terrorist organizations' by President Bill Clinton's Secretary of State Madeleine Albright in 1997. The Obama administration's Attorney General, Eric Holder, appealed the injunction to the Supreme Court, where he was represented by Solicitor General Elena Kagan.

The injunction allowed the plaintiffs to 'train members of the PKK on how to use humanitarian and international law to peacefully resolve disputes', to 'engage in political advocacy on behalf of Kurds who live in Turkey'; and to 'teach PKK members how to petition various representative bodies such as the United Nations for relief'. The plaintiffs also were allowed to 'train members of the LTTE to present claims for tsunami-related aid to mediators and international bodies', to 'offer their legal expertise in negotiating peace agreements between the LTTE and the Sri Lankan government', and to 'engage in political advocacy on behalf of Tamils who live in Sri Lanka'.

Rejecting plaintiffs' claims that the law unconstitutionally criminalised conduct protected by the First Amendment's guarantees of freedoms of speech and association, Chief Justice John Roberts, writing for the six-judge majority, stated that such actions

> meant to 'promot[e] peaceable, lawful conduct' ... can further terrorism ... Such
> support frees up other resources within the organization that may be put to

violent ends. It also importantly helps lend legitimacy to foreign terrorist groups – legitimacy that makes it easier for those groups to persist, to recruit members, and to raise funds – all of which facilitate more terrorist attacks. (at 25)

Comparing the struggles of these nationalist movements against US allies Turkey and Sri Lanka to an all-out world war, Roberts wrote:

> If only good can come from training our adversaries in international dispute resolution, presumably it would have been unconstitutional to prevent American citizens from training the Japanese Government on using international organizations and mechanisms to resolve disputes during World War II. (at 33-34)

The judgement accorded great deference to Congressional findings regarding the PKK and LTTE and noted that money is fungible, thus supporting the conclusion that 'humanitarian aid' could ultimately serve violent activities. The majority also gave deference to the executive branch, quoting a State Department affidavit (at 28). While the majority acknowledged the court had an important role to play – writing 'we are one with the dissent' that national security considerations do not 'automatically trump' judicial obligations – the majority quickly emphasised the judicial 'lack of competence' in such matters. The majority chastised the dissent for failing to address 'the real dangers at stake' (at 33).

Associate Justice Stephen Breyer wrote the dissent, stating:

> I cannot agree with the Court's conclusion that the Constitution permits the Government to prosecute the plaintiffs criminally for engaging in coordinated teaching and advocacy furthering the designated organizations' lawful political objectives. That this speech and association for political purposes is the kind of activity to which the First Amendment ordinarily offers its strongest protection is elementary. (Dissent at 1)

After reviewing precedents which make government enactments that interfere with First Amendment-protected conduct subject to 'strict scrutiny' – such measures can be upheld only if they are necessary to further a 'compelling state interest' – Breyer wrote:

> Speech, association, and related activities on behalf of a group will often, perhaps always, help to legitimate that group. Thus, were the law to accept a 'legitimating' effect, in and of itself and without qualification, as providing sufficient grounds for imposing such a ban, the First Amendment battle would be lost in untold instances where it should be won. Once one accepts this argument, there is no natural stopping place. (at 10)

Referring to the plaintiffs' proposal to 'train members of the PKK on how to use humanitarian and international law to peacefully resolve disputes', Breyer wrote:

> The majority justifies the criminalization of this activity in significant part on the ground that 'peaceful negotiations' might just 'buy time ..., lulling opponents into complacency.' And the PKK might use its new information about 'the structures of the international legal system ... to threaten, manipulate, and disrupt.' What is one to say about these arguments – arguments that would deny First Amendment protection to the peaceful teaching of international human rights law on the ground that a little knowledge about 'the international legal system' is too dangerous a thing; that an opponent's subsequent willingness to negotiate might be faked, so let's not teach him how to try? ... Moreover, the risk that those who are taught will put otherwise innocent speech or knowledge to bad use is omnipresent, at least where that risk rests on little more than (even informed) speculation. Hence to accept this kind of argument without more and to apply it to the teaching of a subject such as international human rights law is to adopt a rule of law that, contrary to the Constitution's text and First Amendment precedent, would automatically forbid the teaching of any subject in a case where national security interests conflict with the First Amendment. (at 13–14)

Breyer concluded that the court had failed to 'examine the Government's justifications with sufficient care' and failed to 'insist upon specific evidence, rather than general assertion' (at 23).

Australia

Between 2002 and 2004, the Australian government of Prime Minister John Howard and the Labor Party opposition combined to pass more than 30 pieces of so-called counter-terrorism legislation. The laws contained several almost unprecedented features:

- Secret interrogation and detention without trial: those detained or questioned by the Australian Secret Intelligence Organisation (ASIO) are prohibited from informing anyone, even family members, of their disappearance or the reasons for it.
- Lengthy jail terms for refusing to disclose information requested by the authorities.
- The outlawing of 'association' with a member or supporter of a proscribed terrorist organisation.
- People charged with a 'terrorist' offence can be tried semi-secretly, partly on the basis of evidence that they are forbidden to view or hear.

The legislation also

- defines terrorism in sweeping terms, capable of criminalising many traditional forms of protest and dissent;
- permits the banning of political groups by executive fiat, a power that the High Court rejected in the *Communist Party case (Australian Communist Party v. Commonwealth* (1951) 83 CLR 1);
- shrouds the operations of the intelligence and police agencies in secrecy (for full details, see Head 2002, Head 2004 and Head 2004b).

None of these measures were necessary to protect ordinary people from terrorism. The government and the police and security agencies had every power needed to detect, monitor, arrest and charge terrorists. Every conceivable terror act was already a serious crime – from murder to arson and hijacking. Furthermore, the criminal law amply covered all planning, preparing, conspiring, financing, supporting and attempting related to such activities. Moreover, ASIO and the state and federal police already possessed immense powers to infiltrate organisations, tap phones, bug premises, intercept mail, search homes and hack into computers (Head 2002).

Of particular concern is the exceptional range of the definition of 'terrorist act' given by section 100.1 of the Criminal Code Act 1995 (Cth). It specifies that:

terrorist act means an action or threat of action where:
  (a) the action falls within subsection (2) and does not fall within subsection (3); and
  (b) the action is done or the threat is made with the intention of advancing a political, religious or ideological cause; and
  (c) the action is done or the threat is made with the intention of:
    (i) coercing, or influencing by intimidation, the government of the Commonwealth or a State, Territory or foreign country, or of part of a State, Territory or foreign country; or
    (ii) intimidating the public or a section of the public.
  (2) Action falls within this subsection if it:
    (a) causes serious harm that is physical harm to a person; or
    (b) causes serious damage to property; or
    (c) causes a person's death; or
    (d) endangers a person's life, other than the life of the person taking the action; or
    (e) creates a serious risk to the health or safety of the public or a section of the public; or
    (f) seriously interferes with, seriously disrupts, or destroys, an electronic system including, but not limited to:
      (i) an information system; or
      (ii) a telecommunications system; or
      (iii) a financial system; or
      (iv) a system used for the delivery of essential government services; or

        (v) a system used for, or by, an essential public utility; or

        (vi) a system used for, or by, a transport system.

    (3) Action falls within this subsection if it:

        (a) is advocacy, protest, dissent or industrial action; and

        (b) is not intended:

            (i) to cause serious harm that *is* physical harm to a person; or

            (ii) to cause a person's death; or

            (iii) to endanger the life of a person, other than the person taking the action; or to create a serious risk to the health or safety of the public or a section of the public.

Thus, terrorism extends to acts or threats that advance 'a political, religious or ideological cause' for the purpose of 'coercing or influencing by intimidation' any government or section of the public. 'Advocacy, protest, dissent or industrial action' is exempted but not if it involves harm to a person, 'serious damage' to property, 'serious risk' to public health or safety, or 'serious interference' with an information, telecommunications, financial, essential services or transport system.

This definition could cover a demonstration or strike in which a person was injured or felt endangered, given that the purpose of many protests and strikes is to apply pressure to ('coerce' or 'intimidate') a government, employer or other authority. Nurses taking strike action that shuts down hospital wards in support of a political demand for greater health spending, for example, could be accused of endangering public health and thus be charged as terrorists.

In some instances, terrorist intent is not necessary. The legislation imposes jail terms ranging from life to 10 years for 'preparing, planning or training for terrorist acts' and for possessing documents or other objects used in the preparation of such acts. A person can be jailed for possessing such a 'thing' even if they did not know it would be used for terrorist purposes, but were merely 'reckless' as to that fact (Criminal Code sections 101.2, 101.4, 101.5, 101.6).

The various, related, terrorist offences could apply to a wide range of political activity, such as planning a protest outside government buildings or facilities where damage may occur. Demonstrators who prepared to block roads or entrances to financial institutions, such as the stock exchange, could be charged as terrorists, as could computer hackers. During questioning in a Senate committee hearing in 2002, the Attorney-General's representatives admitted that someone who cut through a fence at the Easter 2002 protest at the Woomera refugee detention centre or who marched into the parliament building in Canberra during a 1996 trade union rally could have been charged with terrorism (Senate Committee 2002: 27). The officials acknowledged that a picketing striker who caused property damage or a person who possessed a mobile phone used to discuss a violent act could be prosecuted (Senate Committee 2002: 17–24).

While citing the 11 September attacks in the United States as its justification, the government adopted a definition of terrorism that went beyond the USA PATRIOT Act, which covered activity that was dangerous to human life and violated existing criminal laws. The Australian version is based on the British Terrorism Act 2000, but went further in specifying disruption to various communications systems (Hancock 2002: 2–8).

Two types of detention without trial were introduced. First, the Australian Federal Police (AFP) could detain someone for investigation of a terrorist offence under section 23CA of the Crimes Act 1914 (Cth). Although a person could ordinarily be held for questioning for only four hours, the Act enabled police to apply to a 'judicial officer' (a magistrate, justice of the peace or bail justice), for an extension of the 'investigation period' of up to 24 hours. The police could also ask for a suspension of the questioning time limit for a non-exhaustive list of reasons, including to allow other 'authorities', inside or outside Australia, 'time to collect information', and 'to collate and analyse information' from other sources. There was no time limit on how long the questioning clock could be stopped and no limit on the number of times a 'judicial officer' could approve such AFP requests. As became clear when Dr Mohamed Haneef was detained in 2007 (see below), the provisions were broad enough to permit almost indefinite detention. In the wake of the public outcry over Haneef's mistreatment, amendments in 2010 set a 7-day limit on the amount of time that can be specified by a magistrate and disregarded from the investigation period, effectively capping the total detention time at 8 days.

Second, Division 3 of the Australian Security Intelligence Organisation Act 1979 (Cth) gave ASIO the power to detain and question people. ASIO and AFP officers could raid anyone's home or office, at any hour of the day or night, and forcibly take them away, interrogate and strip-search them and hold them incommunicado, effectively indefinitely through the issuing of repeated warrants. Detainees did not need to be suspected of a terrorist offence, or any other criminal offence. The Attorney-General could certify that their interrogation would 'substantially assist the collection of intelligence that is important in relation to a terrorism offence', even if no act of terrorism occurred. This power could be used to detain journalists and political activists, as well as the children, relatives or acquaintances of terrorism suspects. Any detainee who refused to answer ASIO's questions would be liable to five years' imprisonment. Initial detention could last for up to seven days, including three eight-hour blocks of questioning over three days, but the Attorney-General could approve further seven-day periods, on the basis that 'additional to or materially different' information had come to light.

In 2005, the Australian federal, state and territory governments introduced Anti-Terrorism Bills that were agreed upon by Prime Minister John Howard and the state and territory Labor leaders at a 'counter-terrorism' summit. In their impact on basic legal rights and civil liberties, the measures went beyond the 2002–4 laws. Firstly, they were self-evidently designed for use where the police and intelligence agencies can present no evidence of involvement in specific terrorist activity or planning. The Anti-Terrorism Bill (No. 1) changed the wording of many terrorist offences from 'the' terrorist act to 'a' terrorist act. In effect, it means that people can be convicted of planning or preparing for terrorism, and sentenced to life imprisonment, without evidence of a time, date, location or method of the supposed attack. The prosecution need only establish that the accused's conduct related to 'a' terrorist act – that is, any potential act. In addition, a person can be convicted even if 'a terrorist act does not occur'. These provisions give the police wide powers to arrest people on vague charges of, for example, 'assisting', 'preparing' or 'supporting' an unidentified terrorist act that never takes place.

Secondly, the laws grant powers to the federal and state police to intern 'suspects' without any charge. This can be done in two ways. First, anyone whom police allege may be involved in a future terrorist act, or may have information about such an act, can be subjected to 'preventative detention' for up to 48 hours by federal police or 14 days by state police. The grounds for obtaining a preventative detention order are broad and effectively remove the burden of proof on the Crown to prove its case beyond a reasonable doubt. The Criminal Code Act 1995 s105.4 provides for an 'issuing authority' – a judge, former judge or magistrate operating in a 'personal capacity' (i.e., not as a court, but as part of the executive) – to grant an order where:

(a) there are reasonable grounds to suspect that the subject:
    (i)   will engage in a terrorist act; or
    (ii) possesses a thing that is connected with the preparation for, or the engagement of a person in, a terrorist act; or
    (iii) has done an act in preparation for, or planning, a terrorist act; and
(b) making the order would substantially assist in preventing a terrorist act occurring; and
(c) detaining the subject for the period for which the person is to be detained under the order is reasonably necessary for the purpose referred to in paragraph (b).

Some pertinent questions can be asked. What are 'reasonable grounds'? How can the police predict that someone 'will engage in a terrorist act'? Does it mean reading their mind? How can the 'issuing authority' conclude that a thing – which could be anything from a mobile phone to a map – is connected to preparations for a terrorist act? If evidence exists of an act in preparation for, or planning a terrorist act, why not charge the person and put them on trial? How long is 'reasonably necessary'? (These questions are all the more pertinent because the power under section 189 of the Migration Act 1958 (Cth) to detain a person that an officer 'reasonably suspects' of being an unlawful non-citizen was used to wrongly detain more than 200 people in Australian immigration detention centres during the years from 2001 to 2005, including the well-publicised cases of Cornelia Rau and Vivian Solon (Crowley-Cyr 2005)).

An 'issuing authority' can approve the internment in an initial 'ex parte' hearing, that is without the 'suspect' being present. Suspects have limited rights to know why they are being detained. They may be held incommunicado and any conversations they hold with a lawyer can be monitored, violating lawyer-client privilege. Anyone – including family members, lawyers and the media –

who reveals that the person has been detained, can be jailed for five years. These provisions are designed to ensure that no one knows how many people have been rounded up, or why, or in what conditions they are being held. The Australian Press Council pointed out in its submission to the Australian Senate Legal and Constitutional Legislation Committee:

> Even in circumstances where a person has been detained illegally or inappropriately, the media are unable to investigate or report upon the detention. If detainees have suffered torture or abuse during their detention, they cannot inform the media of this, and the media are prohibited from reporting the abuse. (Australian Press Council 2005)

In the second form of detention, specially designated 'issuing courts' may grant 'control orders' – which can include house arrest, the fitting of personal tracking devices and bans on employment and all forms of communication – also without any initial notice or hearing. Like preventative detainees, those under house arrest can be barred from alerting anyone to their internment. The control orders can last 12 months and be renewed continuously. Detainees can only challenge them, possibly weeks or months later, in the same special courts. The grounds for granting a control order are equally as vague as for preventative detention, and lower the burden of proof to the 'balance of probabilities'. The Criminal Code section 104.4 states that a control order can be granted where:

(c) the court is satisfied on the balance of probabilities:
  (i) that making the order would substantially assist in preventing a terrorist act; or
  (ii) that the person has provided training to, or received training from, a listed terrorist organisation; and
(d) the court is satisfied on the balance of probabilities that each of the obligations, prohibitions and restrictions to be imposed on the person by the order is reasonably necessary, and reasonably appropriate and adapted, for the purpose of protecting the public from a terrorist act.

Again, this wording raises many crucial questions. The onus of proof falls far short of the criminal law standard of 'beyond a reasonable doubt'. Moreover, preventative detention and control orders can be imposed on top of each other. This is in addition to the earlier investigation, questioning and detention provisions introduced in 2003. The authorities could detain someone for a week of questioning, followed by 8 days of investigation, then 14 days of 'preventative detention' and a year or more of virtual house arrest.

These laws can allow governments and their security agencies to lock someone away based solely on what they allege the 'suspect' might be intending to do in the future. The legislation clears the way for practices commonly identified with totalitarian regimes. People can simply 'disappear' into police custody, without the media, or anyone else, being able to report it.

People placed under control orders can seek review by the court that made the order, but no time limit is set for the hearing of those applications, and they are only entitled to summaries of the grounds on which the orders have been made. Decisions by the Attorney-General to authorise an application for a control order are specifically protected from review under the Administrative Decisions Judicial Review Act 1977 (Cth) (ADJR Act). Preventative detention orders are also exempt from the ADJR Act, leaving a detainee only with the possibly expensive and lengthy option of seeking a writ or other common law form of review by a superior court.

Another aspect of the 2005 legislation is its capacity to chill political dissent, and to replace the 'unlawful associations' provisions as a means of proscribing political groups. Any organisation that 'advocates' a terrorist act can be outlawed by the Attorney-General, exposing its members, supporters and financial donors to imprisonment as well. Section 102.1(1A) of the Criminal Code defined 'advocates' as 'directly or indirectly counseling or urging' or 'directly or indirectly providing instruction' on the doing of 'a terrorist act', or 'directly praising' the doing of a terrorist act in circumstances where there is a risk that such praise might have the effect of leading a person to engage in a terrorist act.

'Praising' terrorism could extend to justifying or expressing sympathy for a hypothetical terrorist act, or even calling for an understanding of terrorism's social and economic roots. A 2010 amendment inserted the word 'substantial' before 'risk'. However, that leaves considerable discretion in the hands of the authorities and the courts as to the meaning of 'substantial'. The amendment also changed subsection 102.1(3) to extend the period of a regulation that proscribes a terrorist organisation from 2 to 3 years.

Under section102.1 of the Criminal Code, 'terrorist organisation' means: 'an organisation that is directly or indirectly engaged in, preparing, planning, assisting in or fostering the doing of a terrorist act (whether or not a terrorist act occurs)' or an organisation listed in regulations. To list an organisation, the Attorney-General 'must be satisfied on reasonable grounds' that the organisation meets the above definition or 'advocates the doing of a terrorist act (whether or not a terrorist act has occurred or will occur)'. Any person who directs or provides support to the activities of a terrorist organisation, knowing it to be terrorist, can be jailed for 25 years or, if they are 'reckless' as to whether the organisation is terrorist or not, for 15 years. A member of a group banned under a regulation faces up to 10 years imprisonment. Membership is defined to include 'informal membership' or taking 'steps to become a member'. It is a defence to have taken 'reasonable steps' to cease membership 'as soon as practicable' after knowing the organisation was terrorist, but the burden of proof lies on the defendant.

The legislation also retains a backdoor method for banning organisations by freezing their funds, even if they have not been formally declared terrorist. The Attorney-General can freeze assets or proscribe groups if a UN Security Council freezing order has been issued. Either the Minister can 'list' an organisation by Gazette notice or the Governor-General may make proscription regulations. Anyone collecting or providing donations for the organisation can be jailed for five years. If the funds are used for terrorist purposes, the penalty is life.

The potential for the anti-terrorism laws to be abused, in combination with migration legislation, was demonstrated in the 2007 case of a young Indian Muslim doctor, Mohamed Haneef. AFP officers arrested Haneef at Brisbane airport, as he was about to leave the country. Sensational media claims were made that Haneef was secretly fleeing Australia in the wake of failed bomb plots in London and Glasgow several days earlier. Yet Haneef had obtained emergency leave from the Gold Coast hospital where he worked to travel to India, where his newly-born daughter was ill.

He was initially held for nearly two weeks without charge under the AFP's expanded Crimes Act investigation power, discussed above. The doctor was eventually charged under section 102.7 of the Criminal Code (Cth) with 'intentionally' providing support or resources to a terrorist organisation that would help it engage in terrorist activity, while being 'reckless' as to whether the organisation was terrorist. That offence carries 15 years jail. Police alleged that before he left the United Kingdom in 2006 to work in the Gold Coast Hospital, Haneef gave a mobile phone SIM card to his cousin Sabeel Ahmed. The card was allegedly found in the jeep driven by Ahmed's brother Kafeel that was used in the attack on Glasgow airport. By this logic, anyone who sold petrol to the jeep driver, or provided any other resources, could also be charged. Ultimately, after media reports, police admitted that the SIM card was not in the jeep, and the Director of Prosecutions (DPP) dropped the charge.

In the meantime, Immigration Minister Kevin Andrews revoked Haneef's visa just after a magistrate had granted Haneef bail. The minister exercised a personal discretion vested in him by section 501 of the Migration Act 1958 (Cth) to cancel a visa if he considers a person fails the 'character test'. Attorney-General Philip Ruddock then issued a Criminal Justice Certificate under section 145 of the Migration Act. The stated intended effect of the twin decisions was that Haneef would be held in immigration detention pending trial, rather than being released on bail. Haneef commenced an action in the Federal Court challenging the visa decision. Two weeks later, the minister announced that after seeking advice from the Commonwealth Solicitor-General, David Bennett, he did not propose to change his decision, even though the DPP had withdrawn the charge against Haneef.

Section 501 empowers the minister to personally cancel a visa if he 'reasonably suspects that the person does not pass the character test' and he 'is satisfied that the refusal or cancellation is in the national interest'. To cancel Haneef's visa, Andrews relied upon a part of the character test which states that a person fails the test if 'the person has or has had an association with someone else, or with a group or organisation, whom the minister reasonably suspects has been or is involved in criminal conduct'.

Decisions made by the minister personally under section 501 of the Migration Act can be supported by secret 'protected information' under section 503A, which must not be divulged to the visa holder, and can even be withheld from the visa holder and his lawyers in court under section 503B. Furthermore, section 501 exempts ministerial decisions from the rules of natural justice, so no procedural fairness is required. Nor is there any right of review by the Administrative Appeals Tribunal (AAT).

The application for judicial review that Haneef lodged with the Federal Court argued that the decision was unlawful on several grounds, including that the minister had wrongly interpreted the word 'association' in section 501. The Migration Act did not define 'association'. Haneef alleged that the minister had unlawfully considered that any association, even a purely family one, was sufficient to fail the character test. In *Haneef v. Minister for Immigration and Citizenship* ([2007] FCA 1271), Federal Court Justice Spender agreed, saying that 'completely innocent' people could be stripped of visas simply because they had a relative, friend or even lawyer whom police suspected of criminal conduct. The Full Federal Court unanimously upheld Justice Spender's decision in *Minister for Immigration & Citizenship v. Haneef* ([2007] FCAFC 203).

By the time that his case went to the Federal Court, Haneef had been released and returned to India. Some media commentators observed that his release was secured more by the 'court of public opinion' than the judicial process. A crucial element had been a decision by Haneef's barrister, Stephen Keim, to leak to the media police interview transcripts, which showed that the police had no real evidence against Haneef.

The outcome of the case, and the subsequent government inquiry conducted in 2008 by former NSW Supreme Court justice John Clarke, left many unanswered questions about the Howard government's apparent role in orchestrating the witch-hunt against Haneef. There is considerable evidence that Prime Minister Howard and other senior ministers played a direct hand in instigating the legal proceedings against Haneef (Head 2009).

One review of the terrorist prosecutions in Australia since 2002 pointed out that none of the 37 men charged had been accused of actually engaging in a terrorist act contrary to section 101.1 of the Criminal Code Act 1995 (McGarrity 2010). Instead, many of the charges related to possessing a thing or engaging in an act in preparation for a terrorist attack (sections 101.4 to 101.6). The conduct alleged included making inquiries about explosives, investigating potential sites for a terrorist attack, possessing or contributing to jihadi material, and giving or receiving practical advice about how to carry out a terrorist attack.

A second category of charges related to involvement with a terrorist organisation. In most cases, these charges involved allegations that an accused received or made funds available to a terrorist organisation (section 102.6) and/ or provided physical assistance to a terrorist organisation, including training with a terrorist organisation (section 102.5) or providing support or resources to a terrorist organisation (section 102.7). Only one defendant, Jack Thomas, was charged with offences in relation to a proscribed organisation (al-Qaeda). In the other cases, the prosecution had to prove that the defendants were involved in a terrorist organisation as defined by section 102.1, i.e., that it was 'directly or indirectly engaged in, preparing, planning, assisting in or fostering the doing of a terrorist act'. In a third category of cases, three Tamil men had the charges against them downgraded from terrorist organisation offences to financing offences under section 21 of the Charter of the United Nations Act 1945 (Cth).

After reviewing the outcomes of the trials, which produced a number of mixed verdicts (for example only six of the 10 verdicts handed down in one major case were guilty verdicts), the author concluded:

> In this author's opinion, the courts have passed this test with flying colours – juries have demonstrated their competency in weighing the evidence, without reference to personal prejudices, and judges have rigorously protected the fundamental human rights of persons accused of terrorism offences. However, the laws themselves can, at best, be given a conceded pass. As this article demonstrates, the laws are in desperate need of reform – as are the processes adopted by investigatory and policing agencies. (McGarrity 2010: 127)

This assessment cannot be accepted. In most cases, not only the laws but the interpretations placed upon them by the judges were cause for serious concern. As the examples cited below illustrate, juries steadfastly refused to convict a number of defendants, or rejected serious charges against them. However, convictions were obtained in cases where defendants were enticed into making statements and taking actions by undercover police agents. Indeed, such police entrapments emerged as a modus operandi of ASIO and the state and federal police forces. In other disturbing cases, the evidence consisted primarily of the making of political or religious statements, particularly directed against Australian's engagement in the US-led military interventions in Afghanistan and Iraq.

In 2005, providing the first real test of the anti-terrorism laws, a Sydney jury threw out charges laid against a young unemployed worker, Zeky Mallah. After a 13-day trial, Mallah, 21, was found not guilty of preparing to storm government offices and shoot dead intelligence or foreign affairs officers in a supposed suicide mission. The New South Wales Supreme Court jury accepted the young man's testimony, and the argument of his lawyers, that he had made false threats of violence in a bid to gain media publicity. His aim, Mallah told the court, had been to highlight his harassment and denial of basic rights by the federal government and ASIO.

Together with ASIO, the state police had conducted a classic entrapment campaign. A detective posed as a journalist to lure Mallah into making violent threats by offering $3,000 for his story. The jury rejected the charge that Mallah had 'prepared to commit a terrorist act' by attempting to sell a videotape, a three-page statement and photographs to the police spy. In the material, Mallah denounced ASIO and the Foreign Affairs Department for seizing his passport in 2002 and vowed to seek revenge. The jury also dismissed a second charge of preparing a terrorist act, which was based simply on the grounds that Mallah had bought a .22 calibre rifle and 97 rounds of ammunition. Mallah testified that he bought the rifle for protection after his home was broken into.

Even though the jury concluded that Mallah's threats to maim officials were not serious, the presiding judge, Justice James Wood, sentenced Mallah to 30 months' imprisonment after Mallah pleaded guilty to a lesser charge of making a threat against a Commonwealth officer.

During the pre-trial proceedings, Justice Wood also rejected a defence application to disallow the evidence gathered illegally and improperly by the undercover detective. Australian criminal law does not prohibit the use of incriminating material gathered through entrapment. But the relevant evidence legislation gave judges a discretion to exclude it. Wood ruled that the 'public interest' in securing a conviction outweighed Mallah's unlawful and unfair treatment (*R v. Mallah* [2005] NSWSC 317; [2005] NSWSC 358).

One of the most publicised cases was that of Jack Thomas, who was dubbed by the media as 'Jihad Jack' and initially brought to court in shackles, prejudicing his chances of a fair trial by seeking to create the impression of a dangerous and violent fanatic. In 2006, after deliberating for more than two days, a jury acquitted Thomas of the only two charges that alleged that he was actually involved in, or intended to carry out, terrorist acts. The first was that he worked and trained with al-Qaeda in Pakistan between July 2002 and January 2003, providing himself as a resource to that organisation. The second was that he had agreed to become an al-Qaeda 'sleeper', awaiting terrorist instructions upon his return to Australia in mid-2003. However, Thomas was found guilty of two lesser offences – intentionally receiving funds from a terrorist organisation and travelling on a false passport. He had admitted receiving cash and an air ticket from someone in Pakistan and removing from his passport a visa granted by the Taliban, in an attempt to return home to Australia.

Later in 2006, a Full Bench of the Victorian Supreme Court quashed the sole remaining 'terrorist' conviction against Thomas. The ruling was based on the fact that the confession Thomas gave to police was illegally obtained in a Pakistani jail through torture and coercion by Pakistani, US and Australian authorities. Thomas had been found guilty on the basis of a taped interview that he had given to AFP in Pakistan in 2003, even though the interview was clearly inadmissible as a matter of law. The interview not only involved a forced confession, extracted after two months of physical and psychological duress, but also a deliberate flouting by the AFP of Australian law, which requires a prisoner to be given access to legal advice before being interrogated (*R v. Thomas* [2006] VSCA 165).

Even though the court had already directed a verdict of acquittal, it then accepted a re-trial submission from the Commonwealth Director of Public Prosecutions, based on entirely new evidence – a television interview Thomas had given to the Australian Broadcasting Corporation for broadcast after his trial (*R v. Thomas (No 4)* [2008] VSCA 107). Thomas was also placed under a control order

– the first such order made – the constitutional validity of which he unsuccessfully challenged in the High Court (*Thomas v. Mowbray* [2007] HCA 33). At the re-trial, however, a jury again acquitted him on the remaining terrorist-related charge. In a sentencing hearing, Justice Elizabeth Curtain ruled that while his passport offence was serious, he was unlikely to reoffend and ordered his immediate release. Thomas had already spent five months behind bars in Pakistan and nine months in Australia. His lawyers said their client, who suffered a breakdown in his high-security prison cell in 2006, would never recover from the ordeal of the previous six years (*R v. Thomas* [2008] VSC 620).

Another high-profile prosecution was that of Faheem Khalid Lodhi, a 36-year-old architect, in 2006. Members of the New South Wales Supreme Court jury clearly had doubts about convicting him, on circumstantial evidence, of preparing to commit an unspecified terrorist act. They announced their verdicts five days after telling the judge that they were deadlocked. Following an initial week of deliberations, they had reported that they were unlikely to reach a verdict, but they were ordered to continue.

Lodhi became the first person to be convicted of planning an unidentified terrorist act. He was found guilty of collecting two maps of the national electricity supply system, seeking a price list for potentially explosive chemicals, and possessing information on the manufacture of poisons and bombs. He was acquitted of downloading 38 aerial photographs of military sites in preparation of a terror act. The jury was told that his possible targets were the national electricity grid or three Sydney military bases – Victoria Barracks, HMAS Penguin or Holsworthy Barracks. He was acquitted, however, of any plan involving these defence facilities.

The prosecution case relied heavily on citing Lodhi's political and religious views – particularly his opposition to the invasion of Iraq – as proof that he was intent on terrorist retaliation. When Crown Prosecutor Richard Maidment SC asked Lodhi about the Iraq invasion, Lodhi said he believed it contravened international law and the United Nations charter. It was an 'illegal invasion ... because the basis on which Iraq was invaded was wrong and everybody knows that it was wrong'. Such views about the Iraq war were widely held in Australia. Lodhi denied suggestions that, in response, he had planned a terrorist attack on Australian soil (*R v. Lodhi* [2006] NSWSC 691). His appeal was dismissed, and a further appeal to the High Court was refused (*Lodhi v. The Queen* [2008] HCATrans 225).

In 2007, the Director of Public Prosecutions (DPP) dropped all charges against Izhar ul-Haque, a Sydney medical student, after a New South Wales Supreme Court judge, Michael Adams, ruled that 'misconduct' by AFP and ASIO officers made their interviews with the young man inadmissible. Justice Adams said ASIO officers had committed 'the crime of false imprisonment and kidnap at common law' against ul-Haque in a deliberate attempt to coerce answers from him. Adams detailed how ASIO officers had confronted the young man, forced him into a car and then taken him to a park where he was threatened with serious consequences if he did not co-operate fully. Ul-Haque was then taken to his home, where as many as 30 ASIO, AFP and NSW police conducted a search, while his family watched, and then interviewed again amid continuing threats against him until 4am, even though ASIO only had a search warrant.

Justice Adams ruled that this constituted a 'gross breach of the powers given to the officers given under the warrant'. One interrogation, in which officers insisted that ul-Haque confess to unstated crimes, was 'reminiscent of Kafka'. AFP officers had demanded ul-Haque become their informant against Faheem Lodhi, the Sydney architect who was later charged with terrorism offences. Because the student refused to wear a wire and spy for the authorities, he was charged three months later, in 2004, with 'training with a terrorist organisation'. The training allegedly occurred during a previous visit to Pakistan, the country of his birth, even though Lashkar-e-Toiba (LeT), an Islamic group fighting against Indian control of Kashmir, was not listed as a terrorist group at the time.

Court documents show that the AFP charged ul-Haque for two unlawful purposes. The first was to pressure him into becoming an undercover informer. One AFP agent wrote in a briefing note to ASIO: 'The AFP are hoping to use ul-Haque against Lodhi and although he is not co-operating with them at the present time, I believe when he is charged he may change his mind.' The other purpose was to satisfy political directives to charge as many people as possible under the terror laws. In previously suppressed evidence, a senior AFP officer testified that the police had been directed to 'lay as many charges under the new terrorist legislation against as many suspects as possible because we wanted to use the new legislation' (*R v. Ul-Haque* [2007] NSWSC 1251).

Even more troubling was the 2008 prosecution of Belal Khazaal. Essentially, he was tried in the New South Wales Supreme Court for advocating and writing about terrorism, not for being involved in terrorist acts, even in the most indirect manner. He was charged with 'knowingly collecting or making a document connected with terrorism' and 'inciting a person to commit a terrorist act'. The 'document' that Khazaal was accused of compiling had not been linked to any terrorist activity or planning. Nor was it published surreptitiously, an essential requirement of any terrorist plot. He posted on a publicly-available jihadist web site an Arab-language book composed of material gathered from other identified sources already in the public domain.

It appears that the manuscript, whose title has been translated as *Provisions on the Rules of Jihad – Short judicial rulings and organisational instructions for fighters and Mujahideen against infidels,* offered inflammatory support and advice for an Islamic fundamentalist 'holy war'. It praised the terrorist attacks of 11 September 2001, hailing al-Qaeda's 'impressive success of the conquest of New York'. The media played up the prosecution's assertions that the book listed 'targets that should be assassinated', including US President George Bush and members of his cabinet, such as Donald Rumsfeld and Colin Powell, US generals and intelligence officials, along with 'infidels' in Arab countries. Other texts apparently provided a checklist for assassins, from organising budgeting and transport to checking wiring before using a time-bomb.

However, no specific terrorist act was outlined, and no evidence was produced in court suggesting that any assassination or other terrorist activity was committed or attempted as a result of someone reading the material, which was posted online in 2003. Once ASIO and the police raised objections to the book with Khazaal in 2004, he removed it from the Internet. Two months later, however, he was arrested and charged.

There is no doubt that the perspective advanced by Khazaal was repugnant. The 11 September atrocities, which involved the indiscriminate killing of nearly 3,000 innocent people, embodied al-Qaeda's contempt for ordinary working people. Nevertheless, Khazaal was exercising a basic democratic right when he expressed his views. The struggle for freedom of expression and other democratic rights has spanned centuries, precisely to protect the voicing of political, ideological and religious opinions, no matter how unpopular, dissenting or abhorrent. Once a government is allowed to outlaw a particular point of view, the precedent can be used against any other.

Both sections of the Criminal Code under which Khazaal was charged are sweeping in their terms. Section 101.5 creates an offence, punishable by 15 years imprisonment, to 'collect or make a document' that is knowingly 'connected with preparation for, the engagement of a person in, or assistance in a terrorist act' even if 'the terrorist act does not occur'. There was a defence that he did not intend to facilitate a terrorist act, but he bore 'an evidential burden' in proving his lack of intention, effectively reversing the centuries-old principle of 'innocent until proven guilty'. Section 11.4, which covers incitement, defines incitement as 'urging' the commission of an offence. Although the accused must intend that the offence be committed, Khazaal could be found guilty 'even if committing the offence incited is impossible'. Ultimately, a jury was unable to reach a verdict on the incitement charge, while finding him guilty of compiling a document that could be used to assist a terrorist attack. He was sentenced to 12 years' imprisonment. Khazaal's conviction set a precedent that could be used against anyone making a statement that could be construed as advocating or supporting terrorism (*R v. Khazaal* [2009] NSWSC 1015).

Australia's two largest and most protracted terrorist trials to date ended with distinctly mixed results in 2008 to 2010 in Melbourne and Sydney. Both trials had their origins in large-scale and highly-publicised police raids in November 2005, just after the 2005 amendments were passed to alter the wording of most terrorism offences from 'the terrorist act' to 'a terrorist act'. That amendment directly facilitated the prosecutions. A Muslim cleric, Abdul Nacer Benbrika, was arrested along with 21 others, some in Victoria and some in New South Wales.

In Victoria in 2008, after a Supreme Court trial that ran for 115 days, the jury took nearly four weeks to find Benbrika and 6 others of the 12 defendants guilty of terrorist-related offences. They acquitted four defendants of all charges and were unable to reach a unanimous verdict on another, who faced a re-trial. Media outlets in Australia and internationally published misleading reports of the trial's outcome, claiming that the men had been convicted of planning mass killings at major sporting events. According to *The Australian*, they were 'guilty of a terror plot' that involved bombing football finals or a car racing Grand Prix. Reuters claimed: 'An Australian jury found a Muslim cleric and five of his followers guilty of planning to an attack on a sporting event in Melbourne during 2005 to force Australian troops out of Iraq.'

In reality, none of the men was charged with carrying out, or even preparing for, a specific terrorist act. Instead, Benbrika and his alleged followers were charged with being members of an unnamed terrorist organisation – apparently consisting only of themselves. Eight of the men were also charged with ancillary offences, such as providing resources or funds to the same group, or possessing items (Islamic fundamentalist CDs) connected with the preparation of a terrorist act.

During the trial, the prosecution was forced to abandon its reliance on star witness, Izzydeen Atik, a former member of the group who received a reduced sentence for turning police witness and testifying that Benbrika had told him of plans to attack sporting events. Justice Bernard Bongiorno warned jurors not to rely on Atik's evidence because he was a conman, liar and social security fraudster. What the jury was not told was that Atik had secretly pleaded guilty to membership of a terrorist organisation and about 40 previous fraud charges, and been jailed with a four-year non-parole period – with a discount of two years for assisting the police.

An undercover police infiltrator, referred to as Security Intelligence Officer 39 (SIO 39), provided the only allegation of any involvement with explosives. SIO 39 offered Benbrika cheap ammonium nitrate and, while being secretly filmed by police, took Benbrika to a remote hilltop to show him how to detonate an ice-cream container of the explosive. In other words, the only explosion presented as evidence in the trial was one conducted by a police officer for the purpose of entrapping the cleric.

The legislation gave the jury little scope to find the men not guilty. The defendants were not accused of membership of a specific terrorist group that had been listed by the United Nations or the government. They were charged under the Criminal Code definition of a terrorist organisation as one 'that is directly or indirectly engaged in, preparing, planning, assisting in or fostering the doing of a terrorist act (whether or not a terrorist act occurs)'. The words 'directly or indirectly' and 'fostering' are particularly open-ended. Moreover, 'membership' can include 'informal membership' and 'a terrorist act' can be a 'threat' of violence directed at 'coercing' a government or 'intimidating' a section of the public.

The case was based predominantly on covertly recorded conversations between the men that included various vague statements about wanting to do 'something big' or kill people to stop Australia's involvement in the US-led occupation of Iraq. Any talk of killing innocent people expresses the reactionary perspectives of Islamic fundamentalism and individual terror, but there is no evidence that Benbrika or anyone in the group took these words seriously enough to actually do anything. Jailing people for doing no more than voicing hostile sentiments toward the government and the wars in Iraq and Afghanistan sets a precedent for use against political dissent (*R v. Benbrika & Ors* [2009] VSC 21). Some convictions and sentences were overturned by the Victorian Court of Appeal (*Benbrika & Ors v. The Queen* [2010] VSCA 281).

Of the nine Islamic men arrested simultaneously in Sydney, four pleaded guilty to lesser charges, while five were found guilty of conspiracy and sentenced to maximum terms ranging from 23 to 28 years – the longest imprisonments imposed in an Australian terrorist trial. Again, there was no evidence that the men had planned any specific terrorist attack. Rather, they were convicted of 'conspiring to commit acts in preparation for a terrorist act'. Nevertheless, their sentences were more severe than for many murder cases.

The conspiracy charge effectively widened the scope of the terrorism laws. It allowed the men to be convicted on circumstantial evidence for doing things that are legal in themselves – such as expressing opposition to the invasions of Afghanistan and Iraq, viewing jihadist videos and buying various commonly-used chemicals.

Sentencing them in the New South Wales Supreme Court, Justice Anthony Whealy said: 'While I cannot be satisfied beyond reasonable doubt that any of the offenders intended directly to kill or take human life, it is clear beyond argument that the fanaticism and extremist position taken by each offender countenanced the possibility of the loss of life, if that were to occur'. The judge declared that 'an intolerant and inflexible fundamentalist religious conviction' was 'the most startling and intransigent feature of the crime. It sets it apart from other criminal enterprises, motivated by financial gain, by passion, by anger or revenge'.

Justice Whealy said some of the video material found in the men's homes showed the execution of hostages or prisoners by mujahideen. 'It is impossible to imagine that any civilised person could watch these videos,' he said. The judge also found it objectionable that the images 'appear designed to create anger and hatred against the United States and its allies'. The judge said the men had intended to carry out an action or issue a threat of action 'so as to coerce or influence by intimidation the Australian government to alter or abandon its policies of support for the United States and other western powers in Middle Eastern and other areas involving Muslims'.

By that standard, protestors against the US-led wars in Afghanistan, Pakistan and Iraq could be found guilty of conspiring to prepare terrorist-related activity. Moreover, one of the reasons that Justice Whealy gave for the severity of the sentences was that the men had refused to abandon their beliefs. He said none had shown remorse or stepped back from their 'extremist' views. None of the men had prior criminal records – the judge referred to some leading 'blameless lives'. However, he ruled that long jail terms were needed for 'punishment, deterrence, denunciation and incapacitation' (*Regina (C'Wealth) v. Elomar & Ors* [2010] NSWSC 10).

The federal Labor government voiced approval of the outcome. In a media statement, Attorney-General Robert McClelland 'acknowledged' the sentences, thanked all those involved in the trial and commended the security, intelligence and law enforcement agencies for 'their cooperation and dedicated work over a number of years'. He said the case demonstrated how these agencies were working 'effectively to enforce Australia's counter-terrorism laws' (McClelland 2010).

One further case highlighted the potential for the anti-terrorism laws to be used against supporters of overseas anti-government or separatist movements. In 2010, the federal Director of Public Prosecutions (DPP) abandoned nine terrorism charges against three prominent members of Australia's Tamil community. They had been accused of being members of the separatist Liberation Tigers of Tamil Eelam (LTTE) and providing funds to the LTTE, knowing it to be 'a terrorist organisation'.

However, the DPP said the three men – who all pleaded not guilty – would still be tried on five remaining charges of breaching the Charter of the United Nations Act 1945 by making money available to a 'proscribed organisation'. Aruran Vinayagamoorthy, Sivarajah Yathavan and Arumugam Rajeevan were arrested in 2007 as part of a series of police raids in Sydney and Melbourne, following a wave of similar arrests in the United States and France of alleged LTTE supporters, despite the LTTE not being listed as a terrorist organisation under the Australian anti-terrorism laws.

From the outset, the police admitted there was no evidence of any involvement in, or planning for, terrorist activity within Australia. Instead, they accused the three men of raising money for relief projects, including for victims of the 2004 Boxing Day tsunami, with the knowledge that some funds were going to the LTTE, which at that time controlled parts of the tsunami-affected north and east of Sri Lanka.

The Sri Lankan government immediately welcomed the arrests. While the Australian government insisted that the arrests and charges were purely a matter for the federal police and prosecution authorities, the case was part of an international operation against LTTE supporters. Similar police investigations were launched in Canada, Britain, the Netherlands, Germany and Italy.

The UN Charter Act provides a backdoor method for outlawing organisations via ministerial regulations, which mostly rely on an ever-expanding UN Security Council list. Anyone approached to support or donate to any overseas organisation must find and check the UN list, of which few people are even aware, and which runs to more than 800 pages of often obscure names of groups, businesses and individuals. If similar laws had existed in the past, people could have been jailed for giving money to the anti-apartheid movement in South Africa, Irish republican causes or East Timorese independence groups. The LTTE has been on the list since 2001, even though from 2002 until 2009 it was not outlawed in Sri Lanka itself because of a ceasefire agreement with the Sri Lankan government. Ultimately, the men were convicted, but given suspended sentences (*R v. Vinayagamoorthy & Ors* [2010] VSC 148).

Far from being entitled to a 'conceded pass', as suggested by the review mentioned above, the Australian counter-terrorism legislation has proven to be open to highly-political use, as well as to dubious enforcement practices by the police and intelligence agencies.

Chapter 8

Riot, Affray and Unlawful Assembly

Anti-riot laws have long been regarded by the powers-that-be as critical to the maintenance of the established order, and particularly the suppression of threatening political disturbances. The origins of riot law date back at least to the Norman conquest of England in 1066 and the development of the conception of the 'king's peace'. Any threat to the 'king's peace' was regarded as inimical to the power of the monarch, as well as to life and property.

Responding to the Peasants' Revolt of 1381, riot was made a treasonable offence, punishable by death. In 1550, some unlawful assemblies became acts of high treason. Execution could follow, under the Unlawful Assemblies Act, if 12 or more people gathered together to harm any of the king's officers, or to unlawfully change any laws. During the dying decades of the absolute monarchy, the notorious, inquisitorial Star Chamber became *the* court for cases of violence and riot, contributing to the major discontent that led to its abolition by parliament in 1641 as part of the English Civil War (Williams 1971: 241–56).

Lest it be thought that this is ancient, feudal, history, it was not long before the new rising ruling elite based on parliament sought to bolster and legitimise the riot law through the passage of the Riot Act of 1715. Apparently the public began to react unfavourably to the harsh sanctions of high treason being applied to riot. Before being hanged, those convicted could be tortured, physically degraded and disinherited. Juries simply refused to convict unless the riot was exceptionally violent and distasteful to the public. As a result, the 1715 Act reduced riot offences to the status of felonies, although the death penalty remained. One scholarly account of this early history concludes: 'Repressive approaches have not been limited to one era but have been frequently adopted in place of more moderate methods of control' (Williams 1971: 258).

Today, the death penalty no longer applies. Some might argue that riot, affray and unlawful assembly have become insufficiently serious offences to be regarded as crimes against the state. Alternatively, it could be argued that these crimes cover a wide range of behaviour that could not be deemed as threats to the existence of the state, or the established legal order. It is true that unlawful assembly and affray charges can be pursued for minor alleged acts of disorder, involving relatively small numbers of people. Anyone disobeying a police order to disperse, for example, could be charged. Even prosecutions for riot could relate to acts that could not be construed as presenting any challenge to the political order, but merely to local or police authorities.

The historical record, however, demonstrates that these offences are part of the criminal law arsenal used to suppress potentially serious political opposition.

Indeed, as will be seen, even more minor 'public order' offences, such as 'breaching the peace', have been utilised to target political opponents. This range of offences, when directed against public gatherings, rallies, demonstrations and street marches, has provided means for the de facto outlawing of types of political dissent. Disobedience or defiance of these measures can also trigger more serious charges, such as incitement of disaffection or sedition. Official resort to arrests and prosecutions for these offences should be understood as part of a continuum of options open to governments and policing agencies intent on protecting the state from threats from below.

Two contemporary cases, one from Australia and one from Canada, demonstrate the potential for serious riot-related charges to be prosecuted against people involved in political or social protests.

In 2008, an Australian Aboriginal community leader, Lex Wotton, was sentenced to seven years' imprisonment for allegedly leading a riot in protest at the police killing of an indigenous man on Australia's Palm Island. The sentence, handed down in the District Court in Townsville by Judge Michael Shanahan, followed the 2004 death of Mulrunji, or Cameron Doomadgee, on the floor of a police cell on the island, a former penal colony for Aboriginal people in northern Queensland.

In 2004, about 400 outraged Aboriginal residents of the island, 65 kilometres from Townsville, stormed the local police station, barracks and courthouse a week after Doomadgee was found dead, just an hour after he had been locked up for the offence of 'causing a public nuisance'. Arguably, the arrest was unlawful (Morreau 2007). The protest was triggered by the Queensland State Coroner's partial release of an autopsy report indicating that Doomadgee had died of internal bleeding after his liver was torn in half, his spleen ruptured and four ribs broken by a heavy blow. Despite the terrible injuries, which were consistent with a police bashing, the report claimed that his death was accidental. The killing was part of a familiar pattern. Since 1980, nearly 300 indigenous people had died in custody in Australian prison cells or police lockups. A coroner's report later ruled that Senior Sergeant Chris Hurley had caused Doomadgee's death (Clements 2006), although Hurley was later acquitted on manslaughter charges.

During the disturbance, police fled from the police station, courthouse and police residence, which were then set on fire. The Queensland authorities chose to charge Wotton with one of the most serious offences on the state's statute books. Under section 65 of the Criminal Code 1899 (Qld), 'Any persons who, being riotously assembled together, unlawfully pull down or destroy, or begin to pull down or destroy any building' are liable to life imprisonment. Otherwise, the maximum penalty, under section 63 of the Code, for participating in a riot is three years. That section defines riot as an 'unlawful assembly' of people who act 'in so tumultuous a manner as to disturb the peace'. By section 61 of the Code, an 'unlawful assembly' occurs when 'three or more persons conduct themselves so as to cause others within the neighbourhood reasonably to fear that they will tumultuously disturb the peace' (see *R v. Wotton* [2007] QDC 181).

In Canada during 2003, three members of the Ontario Coalition Against Poverty (OCAP), John Clarke, Gaetan Heroux and Stefan Pilipa, went on trial for 'participating in a riot' or 'counseling to participate in a riot' and 'counseling to assault police' – charges that could have led to jail terms of up to five years. The charges arose from a 2000 demonstration outside the provincial legislature in Toronto to protest against welfare and public housing cuts.

Ultimately, after four months of legal proceedings, the trial was declared by the presiding judge, Ontario Superior Court Justice Lee Ferrier, to be a mistrial due to a hung jury. The Crown then dropped the charges against Heroux and Pilipa but elected to proceed again against Clarke. All charges against Clarke were eventually dropped after a judge ruled that the Crown had failed to disclose evidence expeditiously.

In recent times nobody has been charged with riot in England and Wales. This is thought to be largely because if a riot offence is committed under the relevant provision, section 1 of the Public Order Act 1986, the local police service may be liable to pay compensation for any resulting damage. During the London poll tax demonstrations of 1990, some 500 people were arrested. They were mostly charged with the lesser offence of 'violent disorder' under section 2 of that Act. At least one, Tim Donaghy, was sentenced to three years' jail (Burns 1992: 105–116).

The origins of the modern law in the British-derived legal systems lie in the Riot Act 1715 (1 Geo.1 St.2 c.5), which authorised local authorities to declare any group of twelve or more people to be unlawfully assembled, and thus have to disperse or face punitive action. The Act, whose long title was 'An act for preventing tumults and riotous assemblies, and for the more speedy and effectual punishing the rioters', remained on the English statute books until 1973. The Act's preamble referred to 'many rebellious riots and tumults [that] have been [taking place of late] in divers parts of this kingdom, adding that those involved presum[e] so to do, for that the punishments provided by the laws now in being are not adequate to such heinous offences'.

The Act empowered local mayors, Justices of the Peace and sheriffs to make a proclamation ordering the dispersal of any group of more than twelve people who were 'unlawfully, riotously, and tumultuously assembled together'. If the group failed to disperse within one hour, anyone remaining gathered was guilty of a felony, punishable by death. The Act also authorised the authorities to use force to disperse them. Anyone assisting with the dispersal was indemnified against any legal consequences in the event of anyone in the crowd being injured or killed.

Riot and Affray

Britain

During the eighteenth and early nineteenth centuries, the emergence of protests, particularly those fuelled by the conditions of the Industrial Revolution and the growth of the working class, caused the British authorities to frequently resort to the military as riot controllers (Greer 1983: 581). Magistrates called for military assistance with increasing regularity, and in 1732 the Secretary at War informed the Attorney General that such requests were always granted. The author Henry Fielding, who was principal magistrate at London's Bow Street from 1748 to 1754, described the Riot Act as 'the most necessary of all our laws for the preservation and protection of the people' because the English 'mob' had established itself as the Fourth Estate of the realm. The magistrate 'alone with the soldier barred the way of the riotous mob' (Babington 1990: 7, 11).

During the second half of the eighteenth century, soldiers killed hundreds of rioters as industrial disputes, anti-machinery protests and food riots spread. As a result, 'mistrust of the military when employed in assisting the civil authorities was endemic throughout the country' (Babington 1990: 12–18, 36). By the late eighteenth century, the use of military force had caused such popular discontent that the Secretary at War warned magistrates against too readily calling out troops:

> Frequent use of soldiers to suppress civil commotions has an evident tendency to introduce military government, than which there cannot be a more horrible Evil in a State. (Greer 1983, 592)

Nonetheless, in effect, successive governments, with the eventual acquiescence of parliament, relaxed the principle that the Secretary at War should approve any troop callout by a magistrate. As a result of the rising civil unrest, the courts elaborated a common law right and duty of magistrates to opt for military intervention. In a series of statements in his dual role as a judge and parliamentarian toward the end of the eighteenth century, Lord Mansfield resurrected the feudal posse comitatus doctrine, which had been effectively extinguished in the seventeenth century. Posse comitatus arose in the Middle Ages, when both law enforcement, including the suppression of riots, and the waging of war was conducted by the king or his local representative, the sheriff, conscripting able-bodied free-men into a posse (Greer 1983: 578–81). Lord Mansfield insisted that this disused power could be resumed by local magistrates and justices of the peace. The principle, however, was effectively transformed from one of mobilisation of civilian volunteers to one of military deployment – the original posse comitatus doctrine was premised upon civilian posses, not militia or regular armed forces.

In 1781, the chief London magistrate, Brackley Kennett, was charged with criminal breach of duty for refusing to read the Riot Act and order military intervention to put down the Gordon Riots. For several days, anti-Catholic protesters, after being turned away from parliament, had confronted authorities, burning down buildings (including Mansfield's house). Eventually, the King convened the Privy Council, which issued an order for the armed forces to act without waiting for magistrates. Some 15,000 troops moved into London and, as a result, an estimated 285 rioters were killed (Babington 1990: 21–31). For his reluctance to call in the troops, Kennett was convicted and fined £1,000. Lord Mansfield instructed the jury:

> The common law and several statutes have invested justices of the peace with great powers to quell riots, because, if not suppressed, they tend to endanger the constitution of the country; and as they may assemble all the King's subjects, it is clear they may call in the soldiers, who are subjects and may act as such; but this should be done with great caution. (Greer 1983: 582)

Responding to those who denounced this doctrine as reminiscent of the 'martial law' prerogative claimed by the Tudors and Stuarts, Mansfield sought to distinguish between the use of troops in a military capacity and their roles as citizens, in the nature of the posse comitatus:

> The persons who assisted in the suppression of these tumults are to be considered mere private individuals acting as duty required ... The King's extraordinary prerogative to proclaim martial law (whatever that may be) is clearly out of the question ... The military have been called in – and very wisely called in – not as soldiers, but as civilians. (Engdahl 1985: 11, citing Cobbett (ed.))

Despite this distinction, which insisted that called-out soldiers were not above the law of the land, the Mansfield doctrine, as it became known, provided little protection for ordinary people against military violence, as the 281 deaths in London indicate. As noted in Chapter 1, one of the most bloody military mobilisations against an allegedly riotous assembly was the Peterloo Massacre of 1819. During the Chartist period, social tensions were so acute that it was eventually recognised in official circles that summoning military personnel could inflame rather than subdue disturbances.

> Commentators were aware that the appearance of uniforms could provoke the crowd to further violence, especially since certain military units, for example the yeomanry, were identified with the propertied classes against whom the riots in this era were generally directed. The opposite could also, ironically, be the case. Other army units often identified with, and on occasion even joined, the rioters. (Greer 1983: 585)

These considerations, which were also bound up with the development of industrialised society and the emergence of a large working class, fed into the creation of a modern police force, dating from Sir Robert Peel's Metropolitan Police Act 1829. The establishment of police forces, first in London and then other centres, was initially met with great public hostility as well (Babington 1990: 59–84). Although the primacy of the police for enforcing public order gradually became established, the army continued to play a significant role, particularly in putting down protests demanding the right to vote. The rise of the Chartist movement led to the creation of police forces across the country, but armed militia were still called out frequently between 1834 and 1848 (Babington 1990: 100). In 1839, for instance, troops opened fire in Newport, Wales, killing at least 22 people (Babington 1990: 104–5).

After World War I, armed military units were called out when half the Liverpool police force went on strike in 1919. Four battalions and a troop of tanks were deployed. After a magistrate read the Riot Act, two alleged rioters were shot, one fatally. At the height of the confrontation, the HMS Valiant steamed up the Mersey, carrying 8 x 15 inch guns (Bramall 1985: 79–80). At the subsequent inquest into the death, the coroner's jury returned a verdict of 'justifiable homicide' (Babington 1990: 146). According to Babington, the operation was a landmark because

> [T]his was the last occasion on which the Riot Act was ever read, before its repeal in 1967. It was also the last occasion to date on the British mainland on which soldiers either shot a rioter or charged a mob with fixed bayonets. (Babington 1990; 144)

The Riot Act drifted into disuse, and was repealed in 1973, by which time riot was no longer punishable by death. There remained the common law offence of riot. Its definition was summarised in the English decision *Field v. Receiver of Metropolitan Police* ([1907] 2 KB 859) as follows:

> There are five necessary elements of a riot (i) number of persons, three at least; (ii) common purpose; (iii) execution or inception of the common purpose; (iv) an intent to help one another by force if necessary against any person who may oppose them in the execution of their common purpose; (v) force or violence not merely used in demolishing, but displayed in such a manner as to alarm at least one person of reasonable firmness and courage.

The Public Order Act 1986 abolished the common law offences of riot, rout and affray and introduced statutory offences of riot, affray and violent disorder.

Section 1 of that Act defines a riot as 12 or more persons who 'together use or threaten unlawful violence for a common purpose and the conduct of them (taken together) is such as would cause a person of reasonable firmness present at the scene to fear for his personal safety'. Each of the 12 persons who uses violence is guilty of riot. It is immaterial whether or not the 12 or more use or threaten unlawful violence simultaneously. Furthermore, the 'common purpose' may be 'inferred from conduct'. Moreover, 'no person of reasonable firmness need actually be, or be likely to be, present at the scene' and 'riot may be committed in private as well as in public places'. And the 'violence' can be against the person or against property. The penalty is up to 10 years' imprisonment.

If there are fewer than 12 people present, section 2 of the Act provides for the lesser offence of 'violent disorder'. It requires at least three persons to use or threaten unlawful violence together. This is defined similarly to riot, but no common purpose is required. The sentence can be up to 5 years.

Section 3 of the Act creates the less serious offence of affray, stating that: 'A person is guilty of affray if he uses or threatens unlawful violence towards another and his conduct is such as would cause a person of reasonable firmness present at the scene to fear for his personal safety.' It further provides that 'where 2 or more persons use or threaten the unlawful violence, it is the conduct of them taken together that must be considered'. On the other hand, 'for the purposes of this section a threat cannot be made by the use of words alone'. The maximum punishment is 3 years' jail, or 6 months on summary conviction.

On the required mental element, section 6 of the Act specifies that a person is guilty of riot only if he intends to use violence or is aware that his conduct may be violent, and of violent disorder or affray only if he intends to use or threaten violence or is aware that his conduct may be violent or threaten violence. It adds a person whose awareness is impaired by intoxication or drug use shall be taken to be aware of that of which he would be aware if not intoxicated, unless he shows either that his intoxication was not self-induced or that it was caused solely by the taking or administration of a substance in the course of medical treatment.

Another offence exists under section 13 of the Act, which also gives police chiefs the power to apply to the Secretary of State for an order prohibiting public processions in a district for up to three months, if they reasonably believe that processions could 'result in serious disorder'. Anyone who organises, participates or incites participation in a banned procession, knowing it to be prohibited, can be jailed for up to three months.

In addition to abolishing the common law offences, the Act repealed sections of the Tumultuous Petitioning Act 1661 (presentation of petition to monarch or parliament accompanied by excessive number of persons), the Shipping Offences Act 1793 (interference with operation of vessel by persons riotously assembled), the Seditious Meetings Act 1817 (prohibition of certain meetings within one mile of Westminster Hall when parliament sitting), and the Public Order Act 1936 (conduct conducive to breach of the peace).

In *I v. Director of Public Prosecutions* ((2002) 1 AC 285), the House of Lords considered the interpretation of section 3(1) of the Public Order Act. In the leading judgement, Lord Hutton observed at paragraph 11 that the 1983 Report of the Law Commission on Offences Relating To Public Order stated, in paragraph 3.1, that it considered that the new statutory offence of 'affray should be similar to the common law offence with some clarification and narrowing of its elements'. For that reason, Lord Hutton accepted that reference to common law principles with respect to affray was permissible in construing the statutory offence contained in section 3. On this basis, Lord Hutton ruled that affray applied only where unlawful violence was used or threatened against someone actually at the scene of the alleged offence. He stated:

The offence of affray, both at common law and now under statute, was primarily intended to punish a person or persons who engaged in a face to face confrontation where violence was used or threatened and where reasonably firm-minded members of the public would be put in fear ... The present case demonstrates that a person should not be charged with the offence unless he uses or threatens unlawful violence towards another person actually present at the scene and his conduct is such as would cause fear to a notional bystander of reasonable firmness. (at paragraphs 17 and 28)

However, affray, unlike riot, does not require a common purpose, either by the wording of section 3, or the common law. Thus, affray is not necessarily a joint offence(*Taylor v. Director of Public Prosecutions* ([1973] 2 All ER 1108 at 1110, 1114, 1116)). This aspect of the law opens the way for the police and prosecutors to pursue charges of affray where they may lack the evidence for an assault conviction. Despite the serious nature of an affray charge, the English House of Lords recognised that a conviction for that offence may be easier to obtain than for assault. In *Button v. Director of Public Prosecutions* ([1966] AC 591), Lord Gardiner LC, in delivering the judgement of the court, said:

It was further argued that no practical purpose is served by re-establishing the law relating to affray, since it could only lead to the multiplication and overlapping of charges. Where a charge of affray could lie, it is said, so too would a charge of assault, and thus the latter charge suffices to protect the public. The respondent, however, contended that evidence is difficult to obtain in the mêlée of disturbance and fighting and that there are situations in which it would be possible to convict of affray on evidence that would not justify a conviction of assault. The Court of Criminal Appeal took the view that the offence of affray was a useful part of the criminal law in modern times. I agree with that view. (at 627–8)

In other words, affray has the potential be used by the law enforcement authorities even where the individual charged is not proven to have actually assaulted or threatened to assault anyone. This interpretation could facilitate a political or police frame-up, where a person has been accused of simply being involved in a disturbance. Circumstances such as self-defence or provocation could be disregarded if no act or threat of assault needs to be proven.

United States

The principle of the English 1715 Riot Act was incorporated into the first Militia Act of 1792. The act's long title was, 'An act to provide for calling forth the Militia to execute the laws of the Union, suppress insurrections and repel invasions'.

Section 3 of the Militia Act empowered the President to issue a proclamation to 'command the insurgents to disperse, and retire peaceably to their respective abodes, within a limited time', and authorised him to use the militia if they failed to do so. Substantively identical language is presently codified at chapter 15 of title 10, United States Code. Riot is defined by another section (2102) of title 18 of the Code as:

A public disturbance involving (1) an act or acts of violence by one or more persons part of an assemblage of three or more persons, which act or acts shall constitute a clear and present danger of, or shall result in, damage or injury to the property of any other person or to the person of any other individual or (2) a threat or threats of the commission of an act or acts of violence by one or more persons part of an assemblage of three or more persons having, individually or collectively, the ability of immediate execution of such threat or threats, where the performance of the threatened act or acts of violence would constitute a clear and present danger of, or would result in, damage or injury to the property of any other person or to the person of any other individual.

In the US, the states are primarily responsible for dealing with protests. In an emergency, and in the absence of constitutional restrictions, a governor can order the intervention of the militia to suppress a riot without complying with statutory formalities. When troops are ordered to quell a riot, they are not subject to local authorities but are in the service of the state. If the militia reports to civil authorities to help quash a riot, it has the same powers as civil officers and must render only such assistance as is required by civil authorities. During the 1999 anti-World Trade Organisation (WTO) protests in Seattle, 600 state troopers and 200 members of the National Guard were called in to bolster the Seattle police force.

Under US federal and state law private persons generally can, on their own authority, lawfully try to suppress a riot, and courts have ruled that they can arm themselves for such a purpose if they comply with appropriate statutory provisions concerning the possession of firearms or other weapons. Generally every citizen capable of bearing arms must help to suppress a riot if called upon to do so by an authorised peace officer.

Each state in the United States has its own interpretation of riot. In New York State, for example, the term 'riot' is not defined explicitly, but under § 240.08 of the NewYork Penal Law, 'A person is guilty of inciting to riot when he urges ten or more persons to engage in tumultuous and violent conduct of a kind likely to create public alarm.' It is left for the courts to decide whether conduct is violent or tumultuous, thus giving the law a vague character. Apparently, it does not matter if the disturbance was brief. One purpose of the New York definition, originally formulated in 1965, is to overcome the effect of a 1938 ruling (*People v. Edelson* 169 Misc. 386, 7 NYS 2nd 323) that riot required more than a brief disturbance (Note 1969: 474).

Most of the state statutes that define riot require three or more persons to be involved. Some statutes fix the minimum number at two. The jurisdictions differ on whether the original assembly must be an unlawful one. Some require premeditation by the rioters, but others prescribe that riots can arise from assemblies that were originally lawful or as a result of groups of persons who had inadvertently assembled. A previous agreement or conspiracy to riot is not usually an element of a riot. A common intent, however, to engage in an act of violence, combined with a concert of action, is sometimes necessary.

The elements that comprise the offence are determined either by the common law, originally inherited from Britain, or by the statute defining it. In some jurisdictions, the necessary elements are an unlawful assembly, the intent to provide mutual assistance against lawful authority, and acts of violence. Under some statutes, the elements are the use of force or violence, or threats to use force and violence, along with the immediate power of execution.

Other statutes provide that the essential elements are an assembly of persons for any unlawful purpose; the use of force or violence against persons or property; an attempt or threat to use force or violence or to do any unlawful act, coupled with the power of immediate execution; and a resulting disturbance of the peace. The force or violence contemplated by the statutes is the united force of the participants acting in concert.

Riot, rout, and unlawful assembly are usually related offences. In some jurisdictions, a rout differs from a riot in that the persons involved do not actually execute their purpose but merely move toward it. Of course, the degree of execution that converts a rout into a riot may be difficult to determine. An unlawful assembly occurs when people convene for a purpose that, if executed, would make them rioters.

Inciting to riot is another distinct crime, the gist of which is that it instigates a breach of the peace, even though the parties might have initially assembled for an innocent purpose. It means using language, signs, or conduct to lead or cause others to engage in conduct that, if completed, becomes a riot. The federal code (18 USC section 2102) states that the terms 'to incite a riot' and 'to organize, promote, encourage, participate in, or carry on a riot' include, but are not limited to, 'urging or instigating other persons to riot' but shall not cover 'the mere oral or written advocacy of ideas or expression of belief', not involving advocacy of any act of violence.

Conspiracy to riot is a further, separate offence, with potentially far-reaching application, as illustrated by a prosecution that arose from the Harlem riots of 1964. In *People v. Epton* (19 NY 2d 496 (1967), the defendant was convicted of conspiracy to riot and sentenced to a year in jail, even though the prosecution did not contend that he caused the disorders. Instead, he was accused of making political speeches that were regarded as inflammatory (Note 1969: 474).

The Harlem rioting had begun two days after a 15-year old black boy was shot and killed by an off-duty white New York policeman. For some months previously, Epton, as leader of the Harlem branch of the Progressive Labor Movement (PLM), had been making an issue of what he characterised as the policy of brutality by the police against the black residents of Harlem. However, there was no evidence that Epton had any hand in the riots that broke out, and the trial court dismissed a charge of riot. Nevertheless, he was convicted on the conspiracy charge because in speeches given on street corners and in the Harlem office of the PLM, in conversations with other members of PLM and the public, and in leaflets and posters, he spoke out about the need of Harlem residents to organise for self-defence against the police.

In the Supreme Court, Epton's appeal was dismissed for want of a substantial federal question (390 US 29). A New York appellate court rejected his argument that the overt acts alleged in the indictment were all constitutionally protected speech and, even if some were unprotected, the trial judge did not instruct the jury that they could only convict as to those. The court reasoned that in the context of the 1964 Harlem riots 'talk of terror, killing and warfare was "advocacy of the use of force or of law violation ... directed to inciting or producing imminent lawless action ... and likely to incite or produce such action"' (318 F. Supp. at 909, quoting *Brandenburg v. Ohio*, 395 US 444, 447).

A 1969 scholarly comment on the New York law observed that the sections of the Penal Law that pertained to riot were found in article 240, entitled 'Offences Against Public Order'. However, many of the acts proscribed by this article were also prohibited by other parts of the Penal Law. The authors attributed the apparent duplication to the difficulty of prosecuting individuals for isolated incidents such as arson or larceny. They suggested: 'It is easier to establish that a person is guilty of "violent and tumultuous" conduct, or that he urged others to engage in such conduct'. Later, they noted that during the 1965 Los Angeles riots, some 3,927 people were arrested but only 732 were eventually imprisoned (Note 1969: 476, 480). These observations illustrate the potential for riot law to be used for mass roundups, arbitrary arrests and dubious trials.

The politically-charged character of riot law was displayed after the urban riots that followed the 1968 assassination of Martin Luther King. The US Congress passed a new anti-riot act, making it unlawful for anyone to cross state lines 'with the intent to incite, organize, promote, encourage, participate in or carry on a riot' (Federal Riot Act, 18 USC, section 2101). This law was tested following the Chicago riots at the 1968 Democratic National Convention.

After a year of assassinations and unrest, tens of thousands of protestors from various groups went to Chicago to object to the Johnson administration's intensification of the Vietnam War and the growing inequality in society. In the biggest conflict, protestors and police began fighting. Law enforcement officers used tear gas and mace to subdue countless civilians. The Johnson administration declined to prosecute the demonstrators under the federal legislation, but in 1969, after Richard Nixon assumed the presidency, Attorney General John Mitchell directed a federal grand jury to proceed. Initially, eight demonstrators and two anti-war professors were indicted on charges of conspiracy to cross state lines with the intent to incite a riot and with crossing state lines to incite a riot (Stone 2004: 483–4).

On trial, the defendants accused the police witnesses, mainly undercover agents, of lying in their claims to have heard the defendants discuss violent plans.

They insisted that the events had turned violent because of the actions of the Chicago mayor and police. Ultimately, after a tumultuous four and a half month trial – which provided the somewhat politically disparate defendants with a public platform for their views – a jury found the remaining seven defendants not guilty on the conspiracy charge, but five guilty of crossing state lines with intent to incite a riot. Federal judge Julius Hoffman sentenced each to the maximum term of five years in prison and added on 175 contempt of court sentences of up to four years, including some against the defence lawyers. President Nixon invited the judge to breakfast with him at the White House (Stone 2004: 484–7).

On appeal, however, all the convictions were overturned because, among other things, the defendants had been denied a fair trial by the 'deprecatory and often antagonistic attitude' of the judge. The government subsequently abandoned the riot charges but retried the defendants and their lawyers on 38 of the contempt charges. Some were found guilty, but no sentences were imposed because of the trial judge's improper and provocative conduct (Stone 2004: 487).

Two of the most prominent riots in US history produced serious arrests, but no charges of riot per se. Both also highlighted the potential for the police and other authorities to provoke disturbances that then provide the pretext for arrests.

The Haymarket riot of 1886 arose out of the fight by workers for the eight-hour day. During the closing speech of a May Day street rally in Chicago, several companies of policemen, numbering 180 men, marched into the crowd and ordered the meeting to disperse. As soon as the order was given, someone threw among the policemen a dynamite bomb, which killed one officer. In an ensuing gun battle, another six policemen were killed, and 60 were wounded. Seven rally speakers and organisers were tried and found guilty of aiding and abetting or encouraging murder, and sentenced to death, although it was conceded that none of the defendants threw the bomb.

The Illinois Supreme Court upheld the verdicts (*Spies v. People*, 122 Ill. 1, 12 NE 865) although, after a petition campaign, the state governor pardoned two men. Six years later, after five had been hanged or committed suicide, another state governor pardoned the remaining defendants, issuing a report condemning the trial as unfair. He noted that the presiding judge was clearly biased against the defendants, that the defendants were not proved to be guilty of the crime with which they were charged, and that the jury was 'packed' by state prosecutors with members who were prejudiced against the defendants. Legal scholars have supported those conclusions (Avrich 1984).

In 1999, some 50,000 people protested against the World Trade Organisation (WTO) meeting in Seattle, objecting to corporate power, environmental damage and violation of human rights. A federal judge dismissed an application by the American Civil Liberties Union to nullify a 25-block 'no protest zone', asserting the city had sufficient justification for 'reasonable restrictions on public freedoms'. Police efforts to enforce the zone were eventually overwhelmed by the mass of protesters, some of whom chained themselves together and blocked intersections. In order to clear a path for the WTO delegates, the police began using tear gas, pepper spray, rubber bullets and batons. Over 600 people were arrested over the next few days, and detained but generally without charges being filed. Many misdemeanour charges, mostly for 'failure to disperse', were dropped. In 2003, a federal judge ruled that the police lacked probable cause to arrest protesters outside the 'no protest zone'. The following year, the City of Seattle settled with 157 individuals arrested outside the zone, agreeing to pay them a total of $250,000. In 2007, a federal jury found that the city had violated protesters' Fourth Amendment constitutional rights by arresting them without probable cause or hard evidence (Solnit and Solnit 2008).

Australia

Acts similar to the Riot Act have been enacted in some Australian states. For example, in Victoria the Unlawful Assemblies and Processions Act 1958 allowed a magistrate to disperse a crowd with the words (or words to the effect of):

> Our Sovereign Lady the Queen doth strictly charge and command all manner of persons here assembled immediately to disperse themselves and peaceably depart to their own homes. God save the Queen.

These provisions have been repealed, but the Act still allows a magistrate to appoint citizens as special police constables to disperse a 'riotous meeting'. It further provides, in section 5, indemnity for the hurting or killing of people 'so unlawfully riotously and tumultuously assembled' in an attempt to disperse them.

In New South Wales during the 1980s, a number of incidents occurred that saw persons charged with the common law offences of riot and affray. These incidents included the Viking Tavern, Milperra, shooting in September 1984 (affray: *R v. Annakin* (1988) 17 NSWLR 202) and the Mount Panorama disturbances in April 1985 (riot: *Anderson v. Attorney-General for NSW* (1987) 10 NSWLR 198). In *Annakin*, the court affirmed that an unlawful affray was an indictable common law misdemeanour; likewise, riot was a common law misdemeanour. In *Anderson*, Justice McHugh noted that, despite the antiquity of the offence of riot, the precise elements of the offence were not settled. Justice Kirby observed that riot was 'an area of the law where the courts do well to leave adaptation of the law to suit suggested modern conditions to Parliament'.

Against this background, legislation was enacted in 1988 in New South Wales which provided for statutory offences in the area of riot and affray. Part 3A (ss93A–93E) of the Crimes Act 1900 (NSW) was enacted. The common law offences of riot and affray were abolished (s93E). Statutory offences of riot (s93B) and affray (s93C) were created. The provisions follow closely the equivalent provisions in the Public Order Act 1986 (UK) (see above). Thus, section 93B states:

> (1) Where 12 or more persons who are present together use or threaten unlawful violence for a common purpose and the conduct of them (taken together) is

such as would cause a person of reasonable firmness present at the scene to fear for his or her personal safety, each of the persons using unlawful violence for the common purpose is guilty of riot and liable to imprisonment for 15 years.

(2) It is immaterial whether or not the 12 or more persons use or threaten unlawful violence simultaneously.

(3) The common purpose may be inferred from conduct.

(4) No person of reasonable firmness need actually be, or be likely to be, present at the scene.

(5) Riot may be committed in private as well as in public places.

Section 93D defines the mental element needed for a riot conviction. It states that a person is guilty of riot only if the person intends to use violence or is aware that his or her conduct may be violent. However, 'violence' is defined broadly by section 93A of the Act as any violent conduct, including violent conduct towards property, and 'it is not restricted to conduct causing or intended to cause injury or damage but includes any other violent conduct (for example, throwing at or towards a person a missile of a kind capable of causing injury which does not hit or falls short)'. This definition is far-reaching: it extends to property damage and to minor actions against persons, such as throwing an object toward them.

The NSW Summary Offences Act also contains a further, related, offence, of violent disorder. This offence seems to sit in between affray and unlawful assembly in terms of seriousness and penalty. Section 11A of that Act states that if 3 or more persons who are present together use or threaten unlawful violence and the conduct of them (taken together) is such as would cause a person of reasonable firmness present at the scene to fear for his or her personal safety, each of the persons using or threatening unlawful violence can be imprisoned for up to 6 months. It is immaterial whether or not the 3 or more persons use or threaten unlawful violence simultaneously. No person of reasonable firmness need actually be, or be likely to be, present at the scene.

A person is guilty of violent disorder only if he or she intends to use or threaten violence or is aware that his or her conduct may be violent or threaten violence. But violence is defined in the same broad manner as for riot under the Crimes Act.

In applying the riot and affray law, Australian courts have emphasised the need for general deterrence. That is, cases are decided and sentences imposed in a manner designed to set an example, and deter others from becoming involved in such conduct. For example, the Chief Justice of the Court of Appeal of the Supreme Court of Queensland in *Regina v. Norman and Parker* ([2006] QCA 517) cited remarks made by the Full Court of the Supreme Court of Victoria in *Regina v. McCormack & Ors* ([1981] VR 104):

A riot, like an affray, involves both violence and public alarm. They involve public alarm because they are currently or potentially dangerous. The level of violence used and the scale of the affray or riot are factors relevant to sentence ...

A riot usually carries with it an inherent danger of injury to persons or property or both. There is a danger that members of the crowd will respond to what has been called, 'the psychology of the crowd' ... [t]he danger is great when the crowd can be described as a mob threatening violence ... In our opinion the present or potential danger of injury inherent in a particular riot is a consideration relevant to the sentence of any rioter.

The Chief Justice of Queensland himself added at [34]:

Involvement in a riot is an intrinsically dangerous enterprise. Riots by nature endanger personal safety and the security of property. They may also, if of a certain scale, jeopardise the long term health of communities.

The severity of the sentences handed down by Australian courts is illustrated by *Regina v. Amir Ibrahim El Mostafa* ([2007] NSWDC 220), where the defendant was jailed for more than five years for a riot arising out of conflicts over elections in US-occupied Iraq. Initially, he was sentenced to eight years' imprisonment, but the judge erred in stating that the maximum penalty was 15 years, when in fact it was 10 years (the maximum penalty was increased to 15 years after the riot). El Mostafa, a Sunni Muslim who had participated in a demonstration against the Iraq elections, was subsequently involved in an incident in which about 30 to 35 men attacked a smaller group, firearms were discharged, at least one person was wounded by a bullet, and shots were fired into cars and shops. The judge did not find that El Mostafa was the principal or the organiser of the riot, but regarded him as 'being firmly towards the upper end of the middle of the [sentencing] range' because he played an organisational role.

Canada

In Canada, the Riot Act has been incorporated in a modified form into sections 32–3 and 64–9 of the Criminal Code of Canada. The proclamation is worded as follows:

Her Majesty the Queen charges and commands all persons being assembled immediately to disperse and peaceably to depart to their habitations or their lawful business, on pain of being guilty of an offence for which, on conviction, they may be sentenced to an imprisonment for life. God Save the Queen!

Unlike the original Riot Act, the Criminal Code requires the assembled people to disperse within 30 minutes. Paragraph 68 provides for life imprisonment should the proclamation be ignored. In the absence of a proclamation, paragraph 65 stipulates imprisonment for not more than 2 years as punishment for rioting.

Even before the Criminal Code of 1985 the Riot Act was seldom read in Canada, with 1958 events in Prince Rupert constituting only the second time that this had happened in Canadian history.

Unlawful Assembly

Unlawful assembly is also generally regarded as a threat to the established order, and therefore classified as a crime against the state. For example, Canada's *Criminal Code,* at section 63, defines an unlawful assembly as:

> An unlawful assembly is an assembly of three or more persons who, with intent to carry out any common purpose, assemble in such a manner or so conduct themselves when they are assembled as to cause persons in the neighbourhood of the assembly to fear, on reasonable grounds, that they will disturb the peace tumultuously; or will by that assembly needlessly and without reasonable cause provoke other persons to disturb the peace tumultuously. Persons who are lawfully assembled may become an unlawful assembly if they conduct themselves with a common purpose in a manner that would have made the assembly unlawful if they had assembled in that manner for that purpose.

In *R v. Patterson* ([1931] 3 DLR 267), the Ontario Court of Appeal Court stated:

> The statute was passed to secure orderly and peaceable conduct upon the streets, and to avoid tumultuous conduct of assembled crowds which might cause actual rioting, or which, in the opinion of persons of reasonable firmness and courage, might result in public disturbance. The object of those who assemble may be perfectly innocent, even highly commendable, yet, if the circumstances, in the mind of the ideal, calm, courageous, and reasonable man, are such as to lead him to fear that the public peace is in danger, it is the duty of those assembled to disperse ... No matter how worthy the cause, or how clear the right to be asserted may be, our law requires the worthy cause to be advocated and the right to be asserted in a peaceable way, and not by riot and tumult. The provision of the Code prohibiting unlawful assemblies is for the purpose of drawing the line between a lawful meeting and an assembly, either unlawful in its inception, or which is deemed to have become unlawful either by reason of the action of those assembled, or by reason of the improper action of others having no sympathy with the objects of the meeting.

Thus, perversely, a lawful gathering or protest can become unlawful as a result of the actions of others who oppose the gathering, even if those opposing actions are 'improper'. This proviso opens the door for political opponents, or provocateurs, to transform an otherwise peaceful demonstration or meeting into an unlawful assembly.

Britain

In Britain, unlawful assembly and related provisions were widely used during the Great Depression of the 1930s. Amid mass unemployment and mounting social discontent, national hunger marches and protests organised by the National Unemployed Workers Movement (NUWM) were particularly targeted. Prosecutions of NUWM leaders and supporters invoked some of the most serious crimes against the state, such as sedition and incitement to mutiny (see Chapters 3 and 4), as well as seemingly minor offences, including unlawful assembly, obstruction of police and breaching the peace. Even the most trivial offence could lead to jail, as illustrated by the arrest of NUWM leader Wal Hannington for inciting breaches of the peace. After magistrates found him guilty and made a binding over order, with two sureties required of £100 each, Hannington refused to produce the sureties, whereupon he was imprisoned for a month. The pattern was often repeated during NUWM campaigns (Ewing and Gearty 2000: 219).

Between October 1931 and February 1933, according to the Communist Party, a total of 1,432 people were prosecuted for crimes allegedly committed in the course of their political activities, of whom 480 were jailed, 734 fined and 130 bound over to 'keep the peace' (Ewing and Gearty 2000: 252–3). In late 1931, following the reduction of unemployment benefits, the Home Office appealed to the Metropolitan Police Commissioner to keep employment exchanges clear of political meetings whose 'natural result' was to 'excite the temper of the crowd' (Ewing and Gearty 2000: 254). As a result, the police chief Lord Trenchard secretly decreed what later became known as the Trenchard ban: a blanket ban on meetings near labour exchanges, on the ground that such meetings were 'liable to lead to breaches of the peace' (Ewing and Gearty 2000: 255). Despite doubts about the legality of such measures, there is evidence that similar bans were in operation in other parts of the United Kingdom (Ewing and Gearty 2000: 257). It soon became apparent that the ban, and campaigns against it, caused more disorder than the public meetings themselves.

One challenge to the ban led to the High Court case of *Duncan v. Jones* ([1936] 1 KB 216). Mrs Duncan's lawyers argued that her prosecution for obstruction of a police officer for refusing to comply with an order to stop addressing a meeting was an affront to the common law commitment to freedom of assembly, reputedly upheld in the nineteenth century case of *Beatty v. Gillbanks* ((1882) 9 QBD 308). Without bothering to reserve judgement, the judges unanimously dismissed Duncan's appeal. Hewart CJ declared: 'English law does not recognise any special right of public meeting for political or other purposes' ([1936] 1 KB 216, 221). Humphreys J claimed that the decision had 'nothing to with the law of unlawful assembly' but rather 'the duty of a police officer to prevent apprehended breaches of the peace' ([1936] 1 KB 216, 223). As Council for Civil Liberties general secretary Ronald Kidd observed, the ruling 'establishes the precedent that the police have the power to ban any political meeting in streets or public places at will' (Ewing and Gearty 2000: 269). Ewing and Gearty concluded that, in the hands of the High Court, the common law gave the executive just as much arbitrary power as it had held, via emergency legislation and regulations, during wartime (see Chapter 9). In their words, emergency law was transformed into 'the mainstream of the common law' with courts according 'judicial legitimacy to executive acts previously considered of, at the very least, doubtful legality' (Ewing and Gearty 2000: 272).

In 2005, the British government moved to effectively ban demonstrations from being held in Parliament Square or other politically sensitive locations without police authorisation. Under section 132 of the Serious Organised Crime and Police Act 2005, it became an offence to organise, take part in or carry on a demonstration in a 'public place' in a 'designated area' unless, when that demonstration starts, authorisation has been given under section 134 (2). It is a defence for the demonstrator to show that he reasonably believed that authorisation had been given.

An application for authorisation must be in the form of a written notice to the Metropolitan Police Commissioner, and the Act sets out the way in which applications must be made and the timescale for doing so. If the notice is given in the correct way, authorisation must be given for the demonstration, but the police may attach conditions. It is an offence, when taking part or organising, to fail to comply with a condition, or to do so knowing that the demonstration is being carried on otherwise than in accordance with the terms of the notice.

Organising a demonstration without notice carries a maximum sentence of 51 weeks' imprisonment and/or a fine. Taking part or carrying on a demonstration carries a fine. Failing to comply with conditions in the capacity of an organiser also carries a 51- week prison sentence and/or a fine. Failing to comply with conditions as a participant is punishable by a fine. These provisions effectively give police the power to arrest anyone who violates a condition that the police have imposed.

In 2010, hundreds of students and others were arrested during demonstrations against the trebling of tuition fees. Those who had managed to get into Parliament Square were subject to "kettling" operations, penned in by heavily-armed riot police for up to 10 hours (Stevens 2010).

United States

The First Amendment to the US Constitution guarantees individuals the right of freedom of assembly. Nevertheless, under the common law and state legislation a meeting of three or more persons may constitute an unlawful assembly if they have an illegal purpose or if their meeting will breach the public peace.

Claims of 'unlawful assembly' were often used against workers' picket lines until the 1940s, peaceful civil rights marches in the 1950s and 1960s, and anti-Vietnam War demonstrators in the late 1960s and early 1970s. Police actions to disperse such assemblies may hinge on subjective decisions on the spot about the dangers of a breach of the peace.

Under the common law, when three or more individuals assembled for an illegal purpose, the offence of unlawful assembly was complete without the commission of any additional overt act. Some modern state statutes require both assembly and the commission of one of the acts proscribed by the statutes, even if the purpose of the assembly is not completed. Generally, an unlawful assembly is a misdemeanour under both common law and statutes.

The basis of the offence of unlawful assembly is the intent with which the individuals assemble. The members of the assembled group must have in mind a fixed purpose to perform an illegal act. The time when the intent is formed is immaterial, and it does not matter whether the purpose of the group is lawful or unlawful if they intend to carry out that purpose in a way that is likely to precipitate a breach of the peace. In California (under Penal Code §407) an unlawful assembly occurs 'whenever two or more persons assemble together to do an unlawful act, or do a lawful act in a violent, boisterous, or tumultuous manner'.

An assembly of individuals to carry on their ordinary business is not unlawful. Conversely, when three or more persons assemble and act jointly in committing a criminal offence, such as assault, the assembly is unlawful. All those who participate in unlawful assemblies incur criminal responsibility for the acts of their associates performed in pursuit of their common objective. The mere presence of an individual in an unlawful assembly is enough to charge that person with participation in the illegal gathering.

Political gatherings and demonstrations raise the most troubling issues involving unlawful assembly. Protecting freedom of assembly can be relegated by police and courts to second place behind protecting the peace and tranquillity of the community. In the 1960s, in a series of decisions involving organised public protests against racial segregation in southern and border states, the US Supreme Court threw out breach-of-the-peace convictions involving African Americans who had participated in peaceful public demonstrations. For example, in *Edwards v. South Carolina* (372 US 229, 83 S. Ct. 680, 9 L. Ed. 2d 697 (1963)), the Court held that the conviction of 187 African American students for demonstrating on the grounds of the state capitol in Columbia, South Carolina, had infringed on their 'constitutionally protected rights of free speech, free assembly, and freedom to petition for redress of their grievances'.

In *Adderley v. Florida* (385 US 39, 87 S. Ct. 242, 17 L. Ed. 2d 149 (1966)), however, the Supreme Court declared that assemblies are not lawful merely because they involve a political issue. In this case Harriet L. Adderley and other college students had protested the arrest of civil rights protesters by blocking a jail driveway. When the students ignored requests to leave the area, they were arrested and charged with trespass. The Court held that '[t]he State, no less than a private owner of property, has power to preserve the property under its control for the use to which it is lawfully dedicated'.

In general, a unit of government may 'reasonably' regulate parades, processions, and large public gatherings by requiring a licence. Licences, however, are not meant to be denied based on the political message of the group. People who refuse to obtain a licence and hold their march or gathering may be charged with unlawful assembly.

Australia

A contemporary Australian enactment of the unlawful assembly law is the New South Wales Crimes Act. Section 545C states that whoever knowingly joins an unlawful assembly or continues in it shall be taken to be a member of that assembly, and shall be liable to imprisonment for up to six months. Under that provision, any assembly of five or more persons whose common object is by means of intimidation or injury to compel any person to do what the person is not legally bound to do or to abstain from doing what the person is legally entitled to do, shall be deemed to be an unlawful assembly. The NSW Police Commissioner can also apply to a court for an order prohibiting an assembly under the Summary Offences Act, section 25.

In some jurisdictions, the offences of riot and unlawful assembly are covered by the same provisions. In the Australian state of Queensland, Section 61 of the Criminal Code states:

> 61 (1) When 3 or more persons, with the intent to carry out some common purpose, assemble in such a manner, or being assembled, conduct themselves in such a manner, as to cause persons in the neighbourhood to fear on reasonable grounds that the persons so assembled will tumultuously disturb the peace, or will by such assembly needlessly and without any reasonable occasion provoke other persons tumultuously to disturb the peace, they are unlawfully assembled.
> (2) It is immaterial that the original assembling was lawful if, being assembled, they conduct themselves with a common purpose in such manner in subsection (1)
> (3) An assembly of 3 or more persons who assemble for the purpose of protecting the house of any 1 of them against persons threatened to break and enter the house in order to commit an indictable offence therein is not an unlawful assembly
> (4) When an unlawful assembly has begun to act in so tumultuous a manner as to disturb the peace, the assembly is called a riot and the persons assembled are said to be riotously assembled.
> A person who takes part in an unlawful assembly is guilty of a misdemeanour.
> The maximum penalty for the offences of riot and unlawful assembly is imprisonment for one year.

In some Australian states, unlawful assembly remains a common law offence. In Victoria, it is a common law offence for there to be an assembly of three or more people with an intent to commit a crime by open force, or with intent to carry out any common purpose, whether lawful or not, in such a manner as to give reasonable people in the vicinity reasonable grounds to fear a breach of the peace.

Also, in that state, section 10 of the Unlawful Assemblies and Processions Act 1958 make it an offence to take part in a parade or procession, including a political demonstration, relating to 'differences between any classes' or 'calculated to provoke animosity between Her Majesty's subjects'. There is imprisonment for up to one month for failing to obey a magistrate's order to disperse. This charge has been rarely used, but retains a power for a government to outlaw a political protest.

Events surrounding the Asia-Pacific Economic Cooperation (APEC) summit in Sydney in 2007 provided a case study of the operation of the NSW provisions, as well as special legislation introduced for the APEC meeting. In two special sittings, the NSW Supreme Court sanctioned two key measures – a police ban on the proposed route of the main protest march and the police listing of 'excluded persons' who could be detained for entering designated parts of Sydney.

Justice Michael Adams granted an application by Police Commissioner Andrew Scipione for an order preventing the 'Stop Bush Coalition' from holding a march through the city, even though the planned route went no closer than a kilometre from any APEC venue. As a result, the march was confined to just three blocks, between Town Hall station and Hyde Park.

Before the hearing even began, in a display of defiance of judicial authority, Commissioner Scipione had declared that police would stop marchers at a new blockade along the intended route, regardless of the court's ruling.

In court, Justice Adams voiced disquiet over the police application, and the fact that it was delayed until the last minute. He said it could be seen by some people as evidence of a 'police state' and cause in itself to protest. 'There's no question that there would be many people in the community, and I'm not talking about most, but many, who would resent the extension of such powers to the police, even for such a limited period of time' (Wright 2007).

Nevertheless, he ordered the march route changed after the commander of the NSW Police Public Order and Riot Squad, Chief Superintendent Stephen Cullen, warned of 'horrendous consequences' if protesters came anywhere near the newly-announced blockade.

Cullen told the court: 'Police lines will come under attack and a full-scale riot is probable ... Based on my research, experience, current intelligence and evidence from internationally similar events – more recently G20 in Melbourne – I have absolutely no doubt that minority groups will engage in a level of violence not previously experienced in Sydney' (Wright 2007)

This testimony proved to be totally false. The march saw no large-scale clashes between police and protestors, despite repeated police attacks and acts of provocation. The dire predictions cannot be explained as the product of a police mindset. Cullen's claims reflected weeks of efforts by Prime Minister John Howard, NSW Premier Morris Iemma and federal Labor leader Kevin Rudd to depict APEC protesters as 'violent' and 'ferals'.

In effect, the court order gave the police a green light to herd demonstrators into a narrow entrance into Hyde Park, and refuse to allow them to leave the cordoned-off section of the park once the march ended. In the name of protecting 'public safety', those participating in the demonstration, young and old, were corralled into a crowded corridor in a manner calculated to cause alarm and trigger clashes with police.

Justice Adams's ruling underscored the extent of the power in the hands of the police and the judiciary to prohibit any public assembly. Under section 25 of the NSW Summary Offences Act 1988, the Police Commissioner can apply to the court for such an order, without giving any reason, and the court can grant the application, also without giving any reason.

On 6 September, in an exceptional late-night session, a three-judge Court of Appeal panel of the NSW Supreme Court dismissed a legal and constitutional challenge by four men listed by police as 'excluded persons'. The four, Dan Jones, Paddy Gibson, Dan Robbins and Tim Davis-Frank, objected that the blacklist violated the rules of natural justice, as well as the Australian Constitution's implied right of freedom of political communication (*Padraic Gibson v. Commissioner of Police* [2007] NSWCA 251).

Section 26 of the state's APEC Meeting (Police Powers) Act 2007 gave the police Commissioner power to compile an 'excluded persons list' of people he was satisfied 'would pose serious threats to the safety of persons or property (or both) in an APEC security area'. Those blacklisted could be excluded or removed from any APEC 'declared area', rendering them liable to immediate arrest and likely to be charged with related offences such as resisting arrest.

The police were not required to give 'excluded persons' any notice, let alone a hearing, or even inform them that they were on the list. Nor was there any appeal to a court. These measures clearly breached the principles of natural justice, or procedural fairness, which specify that government agencies must give members of the public a chance to be heard and respond to adverse accusations before making any decision against them.

However, the presiding judge, Justice Margaret Beazley ended the proceedings without even hearing from the defendants, the NSW and federal attorneys-general. She declared: 'This case was not a strong one'. At one point during the brief hearing, Justice David Ipp said: 'This sounds like Alice in Wonderland'.

In a summary judgement, delivered verbally, the court held that the banning of a limited number of potentially dangerous people from a protest, in a limited area, for a limited amount of time, served the 'legitimate end of responsible government'. The sweeping aside of basic civil liberties was thus dismissed as necessary for 'responsible government'. Although the judges spoke of limited numbers of people and areas, the APEC Act set no such limits. The judges stated:

> The Court is satisfied that the provisions under challenge here are appropriate to achieve the end of public safety and the safety of leaders of other countries and their accompanying parties who are present in Australia for the APEC meeting. It is relevant and significant that the legislation does not prohibit public protests by any person including persons on an '*excluded persons list*'. Rather, it provides for the potential exclusion of persons on the '*excluded persons list*' for a limited

period in designated areas. The ability to engage in protests and any other form of political communication both before, during and after the APEC period in any other part of the city or indeed, any other part of the State of New South Wales, is unaffected. We consider, therefore, that there is no disproportionate effect on any burden of communication. (*Padraic Gibson v. Commissioner of Police* [2007] NSWCA 251, [10-12])

Apparently, at least 27 people were on the list of 'excluded persons'. Their names were leaked to the media and their pictures splashed over the pages of the Sydney *Daily Telegraph*. But the Act allowed any number of people to be banned, even thousands. Moreover, section 6 of the Act gave the state Police Minister the power to designate any area within metropolitan Sydney as an 'additional declared area', on the advice of the police commissioner that it would 'substantially assist in promoting the security or safety of an APEC meeting'.

Although these powers lasted only during the 'APEC period' – 30 August to 12 September 2007 – similar provisions could be imposed for any future political event. The NSW Supreme Court's ruling confirmed earlier Australian High Court decisions that the so-called implied constitutional right of political free speech can be easily swept aside. A government only has to insist that a ban on protest or other political activity is needed for a purportedly legitimate purpose, such as public safety (see, for example, *Levy v. Victoria* (1997) 189 CLR 579, where an anti-duck-hunting activist failed in a bid to invoke the implied freedom to defend his right to protest on location during the shooting season).

The power to deprive 'excluded persons' of their freedom of expression was just one of the extraordinary measures in the APEC Act. Others included stop and search powers, seizure of any items prohibited by regulations, and powers to issue directions, erect checkpoints, cordons and roadblocks, close roads and remove vehicles. The police Commissioner could declare 'restricted areas' within APEC zones, preventing anyone from entering without 'special justification'. Even if a person were unaware that they had entered such an area, they could face up to six months' imprisonment, or two years if they possessed a 'prohibited item'.

A presumption against bail applied to people charged with various offences, including assaulting a police officer, effectively giving police the power to lock people up without trial for the duration of the APEC period. Police were explicitly given the right to use 'reasonable force', which could mean shooting to kill. Orders made under the Act could not be challenged in any court of law (APEC Meeting (Police Powers) Act 2007 (NSW) ss. 5–23, 32, 37, 38).

Associated Offences

Many other so-called minor offences exist that can be used against those whose political activities are deemed to be a threat to society. They include obstruction, trespass, offensive conduct, besetting, breach of the peace, assault, resisting or hindering a member of the police force. Many and various statutory offences have been created in each jurisdiction. Such offences are notoriously open to selective or discriminatory enforcement by police and the courts. Behaviour that would otherwise be lawful, such as participating in a street protest or making a politically-charged speech, can be criminalised by police and prosecutorial judgements about what constitutes 'offensive' conduct or what amounts to a 'breach of the peace'. Police tactics can also provoke resistance, which can then be exploited to make arrests. Breaches of these provisions, despite their nominally minor character, can have serious legal and political consequences.

Numerous examples could be given to illustrate the potentially far-reaching implications of prosecutions for such offences. Two British cases stand out. In May 1926, amid the turmoil surrounding that month's general strike, Shipurji Saklatvala, a Communist Party MP, was arrested on a warrant charging him with inciting the public to commit a breach of the peace during a May Day speech in London's Hyde Park, in which he called upon the army to 'revolt and refuse to fight'. Insisting on his right to free speech, Saklatvala refused to be bound over, and was jailed for two months. The Speaker of the House of Commons dismissed a subsequent appeal by a fellow MP for parliamentary privilege to protect Saklatvala (Ewing and Gearty 2000: 201).

In 2010, five supporters of the Islamic fundamentalist organisation Islam4UK, who chanted anti-Army slogans at a military parade in Luton in March 2009, were convicted of using abusive words. The slogans chanted included 'British Soldiers go to Hell', 'British Soldiers Murderers', and 'British soldiers, baby killers'. The demonstrators were charged under the Public Order Act 1986 for using threatening, abusive or insulting words or behaviour likely to cause harassment, alarm or distress and given two-year conditional discharges and each ordered to pay £500 costs. At the same time, Home Secretary Alan Johnson banned Islam4UK and its 'parent' organisation, al-Muhajiroun, under anti-terrorism legislation and made membership a criminal offence punishable by up to 10 years in jail. Two other offshoots of al-Muhajiroun, al-Ghurabaa and The Saved Sect, were already proscribed. Islam4UK cancelled a subsequent anti-war march through a village, the scene of military 'repatriation ceremonies', in which hearses carrying the coffins of soldiers killed in Afghanistan drove from a local airbase down the main street to a nearby morgue (Mitchell 2010).

During the hearing of the five demonstrators, lawyers acting on their behalf argued that their action was 'a legitimate protest on a matter of important public debate, conducted with the knowledge of the police, and that the defendants were entitled to exercise their fundamental right to freedom of expression'. They submitted that the European Convention on Human Rights protected the right of the demonstrators 'to say what they had, and that the criminal prosecution was not justified as a proportionate interference with that right'. During the court proceedings, one of the accused, Shajjadar Choudhury, said: 'To shout the truth in a street is not an insult. We were highlighting the truth.' Another defendant, Munim Abdul explained: 'We chose our words carefully. We did not intend to distress or alarm anyone. The banners were saying they are murderers. We meant the entity of the British Forces are a murdering entity. We meant they are killing people when there is no justification. The war was illegal. Anyone that kills was a murderer.' Abdul told the court that Amnesty International had recorded many cases of abuse and that the soldiers were called 'baby killers' because of the indiscriminate bombing of towns and villages.

Luton District Judge Carolyn Mellanby rejected these arguments, ruling: 'I have no doubt it is abusive and insulting to tell soldiers to "Go to hell" – to call soldiers murderers, rapists and baby killers. It is not just insulting to the soldiers but to the citizens of Luton who were out on the streets that day to honour and welcome soldiers home.' The ruling represented an erosion of free speech and the democratic right to oppose the wars in Afghanistan and Iraq. In effect, free comment can be declared illegal simply because someone finds it upsetting. Following the verdict, defence lawyer Sonal Dashani quoted Voltaire's dictum: 'I disagree with what you say, but I will defend to the death your right to say it … If you believe in freedom of speech you have to accept that some things will be said that you will like and some things will be said that you will not like' (Mitchell 2010).

A study of 'political trials' in Australia in the 1930s found almost 900 cases in which left-wing activists were arrested for 'minor offences' such as vagrancy, bill-posting, leafleting, disobeying police instructions, unlawful demonstrations, disturbing public order, malicious damage, theft, assault and resisting police. More than 90 per cent of defendants were convicted (Douglas 2002b). A further study of the 1945 to 1955 period in Australia pointed to the regular use of judicial contempt charges against trade union officials associated with the Communist Party, as well as 210 arrests for 'political' public order offences. The most frequent charges were offensive behaviour, assaulting police, resisting arrest, obstruction and demonstrating without a permit, with a conviction rate of 83 per cent (Douglas 2007).

Chapter 9
Emergency Powers, Martial Law and Official Lawlessness

It is beyond the scope of this present work to examine in any detail the powers to suppress political dissent and other perceived threats to the state that arise under emergency legislation. Nor can this volume deal with the even more arbitrary measures involved in declarations of martial law. Only a brief reference can be made to another issue: governments have also been known to resort to lawless actions, such as assassinations, renditions, torture, reprisals and military or paramilitary violence.

Nevertheless, attention must be paid to these matters. The historical record has demonstrated close interconnections between such semi-legal or extra-legal mechanisms, and prosecutions for crimes against the state. Time and again, resort to these kinds of measures has augmented or enhanced the utilisation of the criminal law. This has occurred on several levels. Emergency legislation may make it easier procedurally to prosecute for offences such sedition and mutiny. This may establish political and legal precedents for application long after the emergency has subsided. On another level, actions by governments, security agencies and police may be calculated to provoke outraged political opposition and resistance that can then be dealt with by criminal prosecutions.

Hence, it is essential, in order to provide an accurate picture of the role of crimes against the state, to consider, at least in outline, the operation of some of these executive powers and to review some relevant historical experiences. As hopefully will become clear, it would be artificial to assess the part played by crimes against the state in isolation from the capacity of governments to activate other extraordinary measures.

Emergency Legislation

To deal adequately with the emergency powers legislation that the countries under examination have in place, or have adopted in periods of war or alleged emergency, would require an entire book by itself. Numerous studies already exist of emergency powers in various jurisdiction (e.g. Bonner 2007, Lee 1984), but a wider and more historical analysis remains to be undertaken.

Britain

Britain has been portrayed as a bulwark of the 'rule of law', most notably by Dicey (Dicey 2005). But its history, including that of the twentieth and twenty-first centuries, has been characterised by the repeated adoption of emergency powers. These measures were implemented not only during both World War I and World War II but also in peacetime, particularly against industrial action and left-wing political activity, as well as in Ireland.

The Defence of the Realm Acts 1914–15, which initially authorised the making by the executive of regulations of the most far-reaching kind, were passed in wartime and conferred powers for the duration of the war only. But these powers were invoked for broader purposes than the war effort, in particular to suppress industrial action and political opposition, including to the war itself. The measures were applied to socialist opponents of the so-called 'Great War' who indicted the war as an essentially capitalist conflict over markets, trade, profits and colonial possessions, and suggested that workers should reject nationalism, fraternise and unite with their fellow workers in a common struggle against the nation-based wealthy elites.

Moreover, many of the powers were retained after the war. Thus, the Emergency Powers Act 1920 gave the United Kingdom government power to declare an emergency by proclamation in certain peace-time circumstances. These provisions were invoked 12 times during industrial and political unrest, notably during the 1926 general strike and the 1970–4 period of discontent that eventually led to the defeat of the Heath government (Walker and Broderick 2006: 39).

During the 1920s, the usual practice was to have draft regulations prepared to be promulgated whenever necessary. These regulations were largely based on the Defence of the Realm Regulations 1914 ('DORA Regulations') (Young 1976: 32). There is no reason to believe that this practice has been discontinued. Sweeping emergency powers, including the making of regulations that override Acts of Parliament, were re-adopted in the Civil Contingencies Act 2004 (see below).

By regulation 42 of the 1914 DORA Regulations, it became an offence to cause mutiny, sedition or disaffection among the civilian population. This provision was used to suppress political and industrial unrest on Clydeside. A particular victim was the British Socialist Party leader John MacLean, who was jailed in 1916, and again in 1918, for anti-war speeches (Ewing and Gearty 2000: 57). MacLean was initially sentenced to three years' penal servitude for allegedly making inflammatory statements against conscription and encouraging the Clyde workers to strike. At one meeting, police reported that he said: 'Workers are being made slaves to suit the bloody British capitalists, which was pure Kaiserism and Prussianism' (Ewing and Gearty 2000: 77–8).

MacLean was released after 14 months, only to be arrested again in 1918, accused of 'making statements likely to prejudice recruiting and cause mutiny and sedition among the people'. The essence of his crime was to urge workers to follow the example of the October 1917 Russian Revolution by taking control of the Glasgow city chambers, the post office and the banks. Addressing the jury, the Lord Advocate said there was nothing in the law, as then framed, to prevent people talking about socialism 'however inappropriate it might be, but there came a time when such discussion of social questions became seditious' (Ewing and Gearty 2000: 79–80). MacLean was sentenced to five years' jail, but released several months later, then imprisoned again before his death in 1923 (Ewing and Gearty 2000: 80).

Taken as a whole, the regulations gave the civilian and military authorities vast powers to restrict civil liberties. These included freedom of assembly and association (either by banning meetings or authorising a police presence at them), freedom of the press (by censoring or suppressing newspapers) and personal liberty (by internment or deportation for behaving 'in a manner prejudicial to the public safety or the defence of the Realm') (Ewing and Gearty 2000: 61–2). The courts proved to be reliable enforcers of the measures, regardless of the impact on rights and liberties traditionally regarded as enjoying the protection of the common law. A study of the emergency measures adopted in Britain found that 'there is not a single case of significance in the Law Reports of legislation passed between 1914 and 1945 to restrict personal and political liberties being restrained in its scope by the judicial power of interpretation' (Ewing and Gearty 2000: 29).

How these powers were perpetuated under the Emergency Powers Act 1920 was demonstrated by widespread arrests of members of the newly-formed Communist Party in 1921. Emergency Regulations 1921, initially made after the declaration of a state of emergency in response to the national lockout of coal miners, closely resembled the wartime regulations (Ewing and Gearty 2000: 106). Regulation 19 dealt with incitement to sedition or mutiny (of the armed forces, police forces, fire brigades or civilian population), as well as actions designed to impede essential services. Regulation 20 authorised the Home Secretary and, if authorised by the Home Secretary, magistrates and police chiefs, to ban public meetings and processions on the grounds that a meeting would give rise to 'public disorder' or a procession would lead to a breach of the peace or promote disaffection. Other regulations gave police wide powers of arrest, search, entry and seizure, including to arrest without warrant anyone who 'acts to endanger the public safety' or is suspected of any offence against the regulations (Ewing and Gearty 2000: 106–7).

More than 50 communists were arrested while the regulations were in force, many for sedition. One was arrested for suggesting at a public meeting that the King be put to work in the mines 'with his shirt off' and 'do the same work as the miners'. Another was arrested for discouraging trade unionists from signing up as reservists because '[y]ou workers have nothing to lose. Now is the time to throw over the rotten Government system and the capitalist class' (Ewing and Gearty 2000: 107–8). The culmination was the arrest of the Communist Party's general secretary, Albert Inkpin, under regulation 19 in connection with the publication of the Theses and Statutes of the Communist International. This prosecution challenged the very programmatic basis upon which the party had been established. Inkpin was found guilty and sentenced to six months' hard labour, and his conviction was upheld on appeal (Ewing and Gearty 2000: 109–12).

The 1926 General Strike saw the longest declaration of a state of emergency under the Emergency Powers Act, lasting some six months (Ewing and Gearty 2000: 155–213). Again, the regulations closely resembled the wartime provisions. Between the nine-day General Strike and the end of the miners' lockout in December 1926, hundreds of miners were jailed. Altogether, 3,304 people were charged under the regulations, with the bulk of the cases relating to 'damage to property', 'seditious speeches and literature' and 'disrupting supplies' (Ewing and Gearty 2000: 197–8).

Examples of the punishments handed out by magistrates included a man sentenced to three months' hard labour for pulling a government notice off a wall. A miner was jailed for three months for advising workers not to enlist as special constables. A trade unionist was sentenced to three months' hard labour and a £50 fine for telling workers 'what he conceived to be their duty to their trade union'. Teenage pickets were jailed for a month (Ewing and Gearty 2000: 198). Many people were arrested for producing or distributing Communist Party publications containing 'seditious matters' or 'false rumours' (Ewing and Gearty 2000: 202–4). Marxist books were confiscated and one leader of the Young Communist League was jailed for three months for distributing a leaflet in a mining area calling for mass pickets to stop scabs (Ewing and Gearty 2000: 207–8). Public meetings and marches were banned on a widespread basis. At one point, the Home Secretary informed parliament he had invoked a ban on communist meetings, while acknowledging that he had no legal authority to do so (Ewing and Gearty 2000: 204–5).

Alongside the use of the emergency powers came some extraordinary uses of ordinary criminal law offences and judicial powers. Among the estimated 1,000 Communist Party members arrested was Shipurji Saklatvala, a Communist Party MP. As mentioned in the previous chapter, he was charged with inciting the public to commit a breach of the peace during a 1926 May Day speech in London's Hyde Park, in which he called upon the army to 'revolt and refuse to fight'. Saklatvala refused to be bound over, and was jailed for two months (and the Speaker of the House of Commons dismissed a subsequent appeal by a fellow MP for parliamentary privilege to protect Saklatvala) (Ewing and Gearty 2000: 201).

World War II again saw resort to emergency powers. Provisions included 'corruption of public morale', 'foment opposition' to the war and 'cause alarm or despondency', as well as wide-ranging internment powers (Ewing and Gearty 2000: 401). This regime gave rise to the House of Lords ruling in *Liversedge v. Anderson* [1942] AC 206, which demonstrated the judiciary's willingness to accept wide-ranging use of the powers, including for mass detentions without trial. The issue arose from the internment of people suspected of being of 'hostile origin or association' under regulation 1B of the 1939 Defence Regulations, made under the Emergency Powers (Defence) Act 1939. After parliamentary objections to the initial form of the regulation, it was redrafted to require the Secretary of State to have a 'reasonable cause to believe' certain facts before exercising the power. This formulation was thought to impose an objective test but, after a series of legal challenges, the Home Office declined to file affidavits to justify internments.

By a majority of four to one, the House of Lords upheld this practice, effectively interpreting 'reasonable cause' as merely requiring a belief in such a cause.

Lord Atkin dissented on the basis that some evidence was essential if the proper, objective meaning was to be given to the regulation. He commented that on the majority's interpretation, the Secretary of State enjoyed 'an absolute power which, so far as I know, has never been given before to the executive' (*Liversedge v. Anderson* [1942] AC 206, 226). Atkin commented that in the case he had heard arguments that 'might have been addressed acceptably to the Court of King's Bench in the time of Charles I' and that his colleagues had responded in a manner that was 'more executive minded than the executive' *Liversedge v. Anderson* [1942] AC 206, 244). Atkin's dissent was a narrow one, however. All he sought was the filing of a pro forma Home Office affidavit, of the kind he had accepted in the previous case of *Greene v. Secretary of State for Home Affairs* [1942] AC 284. Ewing and Gearty concluded that Atkin's observations pointed to 'successive judges' ability to absorb official illegality and turn it into part of the common law' (Ewing and Gearty 2000: 398).

These provisions are far from being of purely historical interest. Similar powers were created for peacetime in the first decade of the twenty-first century. The Civil Contingencies Act 2004 substantially replaced the Emergency Powers and Civil Defence legislation (Walker and Broderick 2006: 63–80, 153–88). It empowers 'Her Majesty' by an Order in Council (in ordinary times, this means the senior cabinet ministers) to issue sweeping emergency regulations in any event that 'threatens serious damage to human welfare' or 'serious damage to the environment' or 'war or terrorism, which threatens serious damage to the security of the United Kingdom' (section 19). These regulations can, inter alia, 'enable the Defence Council to authorise the deployment of Her Majesty's armed forces' and 'make provision (which may include conferring powers in relation to property) for facilitating any deployment of Her Majesty's armed forces' (section 22(3)(l) and (m)).

Under the Civil Contingencies Act, emergency powers can be triggered whenever the governing authorities, namely Her Majesty in Council, are 'satisfied' that an emergency has occurred, is occurring or is about to occur. The regulations can suspend, modify or override any other Act of Parliament, with the sole exception of the Human Rights Act (Walker and Broderick 2006: 44–5). Even statutes regarded as essential to civil liberties and basic constitutional rights, such as the Magna Carta 1297, the Bill of Rights 1688, the Parliament Acts 1911–49 and the Representation of the People Act 1983, can be swept aside (Walker and Broderick 2006: 192). Regulations can last for up to 30 days, and can be renewed. They must be laid before parliament 'as soon as is reasonably practicable' and shall lapse after seven days unless both houses of parliament approve them, but in the meantime their effect is immediate. Moreover, even these limited provisos would mean little if parliament could not or did not meet. In addition, the Secretary of State has the power to rule whether an event or situation poses a threat to human welfare, and to amend the Act itself, subject to subsequent parliamentary approval.

Although the Blair government presented the Act as one concerned primarily with responding to disasters, the 2003 Queen's Speech specifically referred to terrorism, and the proposal was also driven by concerns about civil unrest, including the eruption of fuel price protests and pickets outside oil refineries in 2000 (Walker and Broderick 2006: xiii, 47). The definitions of emergency are extensive, considerably wider than the previous provisions under the 1920 Act and allow for politically 'interventionist stances' toward potential crises (Walker and Broderick 2006: 63–76). Possible threats to 'human welfare' extend to 'damage to property' and disruption to supplies, communications or transport. No criteria are provided for the key tests of 'serious damage to human welfare' and 'war or terrorism, which threatens serious damage to the security of the United Kingdom'. 'Serious' is not defined, nor is 'security'. Ministers are given powers to specify that certain situations or events are emergencies.

Once an emergency has been declared, the authorities can assume 'almost boundless power' (Walker and Broderick 2006: 161). They can, among other things, prohibit assemblies, ban movement, create offences, deploy the armed forces and confer emergency powers on any individual. There are no specific powers of arrest or detention without trial, but the Act's sponsors refused to rule out such detention, which the courts have in the past been prepared to accept, even in peacetime 'civil emergencies' (see *Attorney-General of St Christopher, Nevis and Anguilla v. Reynolds* [1980] AC 637).

In a briefing on the legislation, Liberty (the National Council for Civil Liberties) called it 'the most powerful piece of peacetime legislation ever proposed in the UK' and warned that 'it seeks to grant the Government unprecedented powers to make emergency regulations which are unavailable under existing laws'. Liberty expressed concern that 'it is in times of emergency that citizens' fundamental rights are at greatest risk' (Liberty, *Liberty's second reading briefing on the Civil Contingencies Bill in the House of Lords*, June 2004: para 4). Liberty also noted that the government had shown an increased willingness to declare an emergency, citing the declaration of a 'technical' emergency following the September 2001 attacks in the United States. This declaration enabled the government to derogate from article 5 of the European Convention on Human Rights, thereby permitting detention without trial under the Anti-Terrorism Crime and Security Act 2001 (Liberty: para 5).

One detailed study of the Civil Contingencies Act described it as 'the most powerful and extensive peacetime legislation ever enacted', containing within it 'the tools for dismantling civil society', with 'the potential to inflict terrible damage on the constitution of the United Kingdom' (Walker and Broderick 2006: 188, 214). The authors also drew attention to the slim likelihood of any effective parliamentary or judicial review of actions taken under emergency powers. In effect, the legislation provides the framework for extra-constitutional and dictatorial forms of rule, backed by military force.

British government and military policy assumes that considerable powers exist to mobilise armed troops internally to deal with a variety of threats to 'public safety' or 'order'. The 2005 Ministry of Defence document, *Operations in the UK,*

The Defence Contribution to Resilience, sets out policy guidelines for Military Aid to the Civil Power (MACP). It states:

> Based under common law, MACP is the provision of military assistance (armed if appropriate) to the Civil Power in its maintenance of law, order and public safety, using specialist capabilities or equipment, in situations beyond the capability of the Civil Power. (Ministry of Defence 2005: 4–1)

According to the guidelines, the legal basis for instructing Armed Forces personnel to provide MACP in the UK can be one, or a combination, of the following:

- Section 2 of the Emergency Powers Act 1964 (plus the Emergency Powers (Amendment) Act (Northern Ireland) 1964) enables the Defence Council to issue instructions to undertake 'work of urgent national importance';
- Part 2 of the Civil Contingencies Act 2004 empowers the Queen or a Senior Minister, in particular circumstances, to issue emergency regulations which can in turn enable the Defence Council to deploy the Armed Forces;
- A common law tenet indicates that citizens should provide reasonable support to the police if requested to do so. All members of the Armed Forces have a duty to provide the support normally expected of the ordinary citizen. The same common law tenet enables a Defence Minister to direct the Armed Forces, on a case by case basis, to provide specialist support to the police.
- Queen's Regulations place an additional duty on military commanders to act on their own responsibility without a request by a civil agency where 'in exceptional circumstances, a grave and sudden emergency has arisen, which in the opinion of the Commander demands his immediate intervention to protect life or property'.

Thus, the guidelines assume or assert that alongside specific statutory provisions, there are potentially far-reaching common law and prerogative or executive powers to justify armed interventions. These can be invoked to deal with 'a varying range of criminal and malicious activities'. The request procedures envisage MACP operations for criminal investigations and major events (Ministry of Defence 2005: 4–2, 4B–2).

The Ministry of Defence suggests that the Emergency Powers Act and the Civil Contingencies Act 'provide a stronger basis for' MACP activity than the common law. It insists that the common law imposes a duty on every citizen, including service personnel, to assist in the enforcement of law and order when requested, where it is reasonable to do so, and that this requirement forms the 'main basis for the MACP mechanism'. However, the guidelines state that this duty is 'difficult to formulate and cannot be relied upon in all circumstances to provide a legal basis for a response, especially if commanders use it without Defence Council authorisation' (Ministry of Defence 2005: 4–2).

The Ministry of Defence's reference to the common law duty to provide military aid being 'difficult to formulate' points to the uncertain scope and character of this power and the associated legal rights and liabilities of called-out service personnel. As noted in Chapter 2, the last judicial guidance on this subject was provided in 1832 in *R v. Pinney* ((1832) 170 ER 962). The mayor of Bristol and nine aldermen were unsuccessfully prosecuted by the Attorney General for breaching their common law duty to assemble a sufficient force to put down three days of riots. A military major had advised the mayor that it would be 'imprudent to put arms in the hands of young troops'. But in the related case, *Charge to the Bristol Grand Jury,* Lord Tindal insisted that soldiers had a duty, as citizens, on their own authority, to do their utmost to 'put down riot and tumult'. Two officers who had refused to order the troops to fire without a magistrate's sanction were found guilty of neglect of duty, causing one to commit suicide (Babington 1990: 84).

In the 1890s, a parliamentary committee endorsed the common law duty. The 1893 *Report of the Select Committee on the Featherstone Riots* said resort to military assistance must be the 'last expedient' of the civil authorities, but when such a call was made, 'to refuse such assistance is in law a misdemeanour' (Babington 1990: 122–32).

Apart from the Queen's Regulations, *Operations in the UK* makes no mention of the prerogative powers of the Crown. The relationship between these and the asserted common law tenet remains unclear. The royal prerogative powers are vast in scope – they are said to cover any situation not otherwise dealt with by statute – and effectively unreviewable by the courts (*Burmah Oil Co. Ltd. v. Lord Advocate* [1965] AC 101; Whelan 1985: 287).

In *Chandler v. Director of Public Prosecutions* ([1964] AC 763, 800), Lord Hodson stated:'The Crown has, and this is not disputed, the right as head of State to decide in peace and war the disposition of its armed forces'. In *Burmah Oil Co Ltd v. Lord Advocate* ([1965] AC 75, 100), Lord Reid said: 'There is no doubt that control of the armed forces has been left to the prerogative ... subject to the power of Parliament to withhold supply and refuse to continue legislation essential for the maintenance of a standing army'.

It is remarkable that, some three centuries after the struggle for parliamentary and civilian supremacy over the British monarchy – and in a political system that professes to be democratic – the power of the government to call out the military is said to rest on vestiges of regal authority. In the words of two scholars, the prerogative power to control disorder 'is a dangerous mystery unwarranted in a democratic society' (Whelan 1985: 287).

Ordinarily, the Defence Council, which consists of military leaders as well as government ministers and officials, exercises the prerogative powers on behalf of the Crown. The council is based in the Ministry of Defence and is normally chaired by the Secretary of State for Defence.

These powers and arrangements operate above and beyond the Civil Contingencies Act. That is, they can be instigated without any formal declaration of a state of emergency under the Act (Walker and Broderick 2006: 251). Taken as a whole, considerable legal powers are said to exist to authorise calling out the troops to deal with a wide variety of alleged threats to society, including civil unrest, industrial action and acts of terrorism, and these measures have been augmented by the 'almost boundless power' that can be asserted under the 2004 Act.

Historically, governments and other authorities have been willing to exploit vague and elastic phrases such as 'emergency', 'essential' and 'security' to act without clear legal authorisation and, if necessary, obtain retrospective indemnity. Seven Indemnity Acts were passed in Ireland between 1796 and 1800 to protect the authorities against legal liability for their unlawful acts (Lee 1984: 222). Another illuminating example was the British government's media announcement during the 1926 General Strike:

> All ranks of the Armed Forces of the Crown are hereby notified that any action which they may find is necessary to take in an honest endeavour to aid the Civil Power will receive, both now and afterwards, the full support of His Majesty's Government. (Whelan 1985: 289–90)

A further case was Attorney General Sir Hartley Shawcross's advice during the 1949 docks strike about the dubious legal enforceability of the emergency regulations:

> I do not think that matters ... I have advised that this risk should be taken and that the Regulations should cover matters on which action is required without due regard to the niceties of the law. In an emergency the Government may have, in matters admitting of legal doubt, to act first and argue about the doubts later, if necessary obtaining an indemnification Act. (Whelan 1985: 289–90)

Shawcross's contempt for the 'niceties of the law' demonstrates the tendency of governments to discard the 'rule of law' in the face of perceived political or industrial threats to the stability of the ruling establishment.

Although the 1974 Heathrow operation was officially justified as a precaution against terrorism, the legal authority of the government to use the army was not clear (Lee 1984: 211). The editor of the *Criminal Law Review* proposed that resort be had to the royal prerogative to address the legal vacuum: 'If on a future occasion the legal powers of police and soldier prove inadequate, reliance may, in the last resort, have to be placed on the Royal Prerogative governing emergencies. That power, with its requirements of compensation, may be an acceptable means of filling in gaps in statutory and common law powers' (Lee 1984: 211–12).

United States

In the United States, a President has substantial leeway, both as chief executive, charged with seeing that laws are faithfully executed, and as Commander in Chief, to mobilise the armed forces. The Supreme Court has made it clear that the President does not require express Congressional or statutory authorisation to exercise such powers. If an emergency threatens the freedom of interstate commerce, transportations of the mails or some other federal government responsibility, he may call upon 'the army of the Nation, and all its militia ... to brush away the obstructions' (*In re Debs*, 158 US 364 at 381).

Such rulings have left the way open for increasingly aggressive assertions of presidential, executive and prerogative powers to use military personnel and resources against civilians, flying in the face of the clear intent of the Constitution. In effect, the role of Commander in Chief has been transformed from a guarantor of civilian supremacy over the military, to an instrument for utilising the armed forces against civil unrest and political dissent.

Constitutional presidential authority has been asserted to provide a broad basis for the mobilisation of military forces under the banner of homeland security. Particularly since 2001, the White House has asserted that the executive powers of the President and his position as Commander in Chief support wide-ranging exceptions to the Posse Comitatus Act, which generally prohibits the domestic use of the armed forces. Defense Department regulations assert another 'constitutional' exception to the Act, founded on the 'inherent right of the US Government ... to ensure the preservation of public order and to carry out governmental operations ... by force, if necessary'.

The Civil Disturbance Statutes (10 USC, sections 331–5) allow the president to call up the armed forces and the National Guard (state militia) to suppress challenges to the political order, including insurrections, 'domestic violence', unlawful obstructions, combinations, or assemblages, and 'rebellion against the authority of the United States'.

The Department of Defense Directive 3025.12, 'Military Assistance for Civil Disturbances (MACDIS)' provides for far-ranging use of the military against civil unrest:

> The President is authorized by the Constitution and laws of the United States to employ the Armed Forces of the United States to suppress insurrections, rebellions, and domestic violence under various conditions and circumstances. Planning and preparedness by the Federal Government and the Department of Defense for civil disturbances are important due to the potential severity of the consequences of such events for the Nation and the population ... The President has additional powers and responsibilities under the Constitution of the United States to ensure that law and order are maintained. ('Military Assistance for Civil Disturbances [MACDIS],' Department of Defense Directive, No. 3025.12, 4 February 1994: 3)

DoD 3025.12 also states: 'Under reference (r), the terms "major disaster" and "emergency" are defined substantially by action of the President in declaring that extant circumstances and risks justify Presidential implementation of the legal powers in those statutes'.

In addition, the National Security Presidential and Homeland Directive (NSPD 51, HSPD 20) was promulgated in 2007. In the event of a 'catastrophic emergency', which the President can declare without congressional approval, NSPD 51 would institute virtual martial law under the authority of the White House and the Department of Homeland Security. It would suspend constitutional government under the provisions of Continuity in Government, leaving extraordinary powers in the hands of the President and Vice-President. 'Catastrophic emergency' is loosely defined as 'any incident, regardless of location, that results in extraordinary levels of mass casualties, damage, or disruption severely affecting the U.S. population, infrastructure, environment, economy, or government functions'. 'Continuity of Government' is defined as 'a coordinated effort within the Federal Government's executive branch to ensure that National Essential Functions continue to be performed during a Catastrophic Emergency'.

Australia

As mentioned in Chapter 3, emergency powers were adopted in Australia during both world wars, and were used to suppress socialist and anti-war opinion. One study of the World War II national security legislation pointed out that it closely resembled its World War I equivalent, as well as the similar legislation in Canada, New Zealand and the United Kingdom (Douglas 2003).

The punitive use of these regulations against opponents of the war and conscription provoked several political confrontations during World War I. In 1915, a prominent International Workers of the World (IWW) leader, Tom Barker, was convicted of publishing posters likely to prejudice recruiting. He was charged under New South Wales state War Precautions Regulations. A magistrate ruled that a poster with the words, 'Workers, follow your masters, stay at home' was prejudicial to recruitment, and, in effect, sentenced Barker to 12 months' jail. Amid protests, his conviction was quashed on appeal, with the court ruling that the state regulations were invalid in a field covered by federal law. The following year Barker was convicted again, this time under federal regulations, and his appeal was dismissed. As discussed in Chapter 4, his jailing triggered threats of IWW retaliation, including acts of sabotage, which were then cited as evidence in the 1916 seditious conspiracy trial of the Sydney Twelve. In a bid to defuse discontent, the Governor-General cut Barker's sentence by nine months, and he was released after four months (Turner 1969: 16–17, 37–8).

There was a further controversy when the Australian High Court lent direct support to the use of the regulations to suppress dissent in a 1918 case. Ernie Judd, a member of the NSW Labor Council, the state's peak trade union body, was convicted under the War Precautions Act 1914–15 (Cth) for successfully moving an amendment to a Labor Council resolution on the war effort. In the wake of the 1917 Russian Revolution, Judd's amendment set out the basis of socialist-minded opposition to the war, as well as the union movement's grievances against the conduct of the war. His amendment concluded:

[We] refuse to take part in any recruiting campaign, and call upon workers of
this and all other belligerent countries to urge their respective governments to
immediately secure an armistice on all fronts, and initiate negotiations for peace.
(Turner 1969: 217–8)

On appeal, the High Court unanimously rejected Judd's objection that the War
Precautions Act required prosecutions to be personally authorised by the Attorney-
General. Despite clear words in the Act forbidding indictments other than in the
name of the Attorney-General, the judges delivered brief judgements simply
declaring that the Act left the matter in the hands of the executive government.
Only Justice Isaac Isaacs offered any explanation, saying the legislation

allowed the Executive to take steps for the safety of the Commonwealth and of
the Empire which might be of a very drastic character, and the enforcement of
regulations made under that Act might involve a great deal of discretion on the
part of the public authority. (*R v. Judd* [1919] HCA 9, (1919) 26 CLR 168)

Judd was later convicted on two further counts under the Act – for making anti-
war statements during public meetings in the Sydney Domain. On one occasion,
he said the fight of the Australian working class was not in France but 'right on
the job'. On another, he invoked Christ's command: 'Thou shalt not kill' (Turner
1969: 218).

During World War II, wide-ranging powers were again conferred upon the
executive by the National Security Act 1939–40. Section 5 authorised the
Governor-General to make regulations for securing the public safety and the
defence of the Commonwealth and for prescribing all matters necessary or
convenient for the more effectual prosecution of the war. The Australian High
Court upheld the validity of section 5 in *Wishart v. Fraser* ([1941] HCA 8; (1941)
64 CLR 470), where Justice Dixon emphasised the open-ended breadth of the
judiciary's interpretation of wartime powers. He and fellow judges unanimously
dismissed an argument that section 5 was unconstitutional because the subject
matter handed over to the executive was so wide or uncertain that the legislation
was not a law with respect to the defence power or any other head of legislative
power in the Constitution. Justice Dixon stated:

The defence of a country is peculiarly the concern of the Executive, and in war
the exigencies are so many, so varied and so urgent that width and generality are
a characteristic of the powers which it must exercise.

Under the National Security Regulations, the federal government banned
communist publications, outlawed the Communist Party of Australia and the
Trotskyist Communist League of Australia, and authorised police raids of offices
and homes to enforce those proscriptions by seizing documents and arresting party
members. Three members of the Trotskyist movement – Jack Wishart, Gil Roper

and Allan Thistlewayte – were imprisoned for up to eight months for possessing or circulating dissenting material (Greenland 1998: 96–104).

The verdict in *Wishart v. Fraser*, where Wishart challenged his conviction in the High Court, demonstrated the extent to which these powers were employed to silence and punish socialist opponents of the war. In essence, the judges unanimously upheld the imprisonment of Wishart for propagating the analysis of the Fourth International, the international Trotskyist movement, that the war was an imperialist one – that is, fought between the major world powers for economic and strategic supremacy – and for advocating the election of soldiers' committees to establish democratic control over the armed forces.

In another remarkable case, *Francis v. Rowan* ([1941] HCA 6 (1941) 64 CLR 196), the High Court unanimously overturned a magistrate's acquittal of Rowan on a charge, under the same National Security (General) Regulations, of endeavouring orally to influence public opinion in a manner likely to be prejudicial to the efficient prosecution of the war. Without a single dissent, the court reversed the verdict of the magistrate, who interpreted the word 'endeavour' in the regulations as requiring a conscious intention on the part of the accused to influence public opinion in the manner that the regulation prohibited. That is, the magistrate insisted on the normal criminal law requirement that the necessary intent, or mens rea, be proved.

Rowan's offence had been to address an anti-conscription public meeting and express a definite political opinion – that the war was being fought in the interests of the ruling capitalist elite. According to Acting Chief Justice Rich, the speech attacked 'the government, [Prime Minister Robert] Menzies and his followers'. The Acting Chief Justice quoted sections of Rowan's speech at some length, including the following excerpts:

> The men in control of this country form a minority government which is controlled by the big combines and industries and monopolies in this country, who by reason of their smoothness of tongue and suave manners have tricked the people of this country and have lulled them into a sense of false security. Also because I know that the people of this country have been tricked and robbed and forced into things by false statements and promises which have never been carried out. I consider it my duty to speak to you tonight to oppose conscription which Menzies and his followers wish to introduce into this country … men like Essington Lewis and other leaders of the big combines are preying upon the working class the same as the people in France and in every country in the world; the same little clique praying upon the masses.

The magistrate ruled that Rowan had not endeavoured to influence public opinion in a manner prejudicial to the efficient prosecution of the war, but the High Court judges insisted that such an intent was not necessary for guilt. In the words of Williams J: 'The offence would be committed if the statements he [Rowan] made were capable of influencing public opinion in the forbidden direction irrespective of any mens rea on his part'.

It was a highly political ruling. Not only did it effectively outlaw expressions of opposition to the Menzies government; it prohibited reference to the economic class interests involved in the war. The judgements revealed concern that articulating anti-government and anti-capitalist sentiment could undermine public support for the war. Justice Williams found it objectionable that:

> [T]he defendant was making a number of statements calculated to create mistrust in the minds of his hearers as to the bona fides of the Government, suggesting that it was a minority government acting in the interests of one class of the community to the detriment of the general public, that it had fascist tendencies and that the army under its control would be more of a menace than an asset to the country.

At the same time, Justice Williams asserted that war made necessary a different approach to civil liberties. 'In time of war the necessity to protect the safety of the realm is paramount and must take priority over individual rights,' he stated. This proposition suggests that courts should allow almost unlimited power to the executive to override traditional legal principles in periods of war or other alleged emergency.

In a study of the use of the World War II legislation, Douglas observed that some of the behaviour covered by the offences created by the national security regulations would also have constituted sedition (Douglas 2003). As seen in Chapter 6, seditious purposes under the then Crimes Act 1914 (Cth), sections 24A to 24E, included exciting disaffection against British, Dominion and Australian governments. However, for prosecutions, the emergency regulations had several advantages. First, defendants in sedition cases had a right to opt for trial by jury – a basic legal right enshrined in the Australian Constitution for indictable offences – and juries might be sympathetic to anti-war sentiment. By contrast, defendants charged under the wartime regulations were tried summarily. Second, there was no need to prove that statements were actually likely to arouse disaffection; only that they were calculated to do so. Third, there was no 'good faith criticism' defence under the regulations. A fourth advantage could be added. As illustrated by *Francis v. Rowan*, there was no need to prove any intention to cause disaffection.

Douglas estimated that during World War II, governments approved the prosecution of at least 69 people, primarily communists, with some pacifists, fascists and a lone Jehovah's Witness (Douglas 2003). Of these, 61 were tried, and 28 were jailed. However, a wider number of arrests were made, accompanied by 'massive' police raids and the seizure of literature. The Communist Party and the Trotskyist organisations were forced to dismantle and secret their printing presses away.

Despite the severity of these measures, Douglas argued that wartime political repression was limited, with a degree of official tolerance toward anti-war opinion.

However, he noted that enforcement was constrained by political considerations, most importantly governments' need to secure the support of the Labor and trade union movement. Another major factor was the Communist Party's backflip to fervently support the war effort after the Nazi invasion of the Soviet Union in June 1941; from that point onward, prosecutions were rare. Douglas summarised the political sensitivities related to the trade unions as follows:

> Unions were willing to work with the government, but the price of cooperation was recognition of union sensitivities. Thus, union papers were treated more favourably than communist papers, notwithstanding that they sometimes published very similar articles. Communist union leaders could say certain things as union leaders, which they could not say as communists. Following the banning of the CPA, planning for raids proceeded on the basis that no prominent union officials were to be targeted. (Douglas 2003: 113 footnotes omitted)

These political considerations are revealing. Far from offering any guarantee of official tolerance, they point to the politically calculating and discriminatory character of the application of such emergency powers.

New Zealand and Canada

Extraordinary wartime measures were also imposed in other British-derived legal systems, notably in Canada and New Zealand.

In New Zealand, during World War II, dozens of communists were prosecuted for making or publishing subversive statements, most of whom received prison sentences, and numerous pacifists were arrested under the Emergency Regulations for holding illegal meetings and for publishing subversive literature. Overall, in 1940, there were 59 charges of making or publishing subversive statements, of which nine were heard in the New Zealand Supreme Court, where only one was acquitted. As in Australia, courts in Canada and New Zealand usually approached the regulations on the basis that, in wartime, executive powers were to be given a broad construction (Douglas 2003).

Likewise in Canada, the War Measures Act of 1914 conferred extreme powers on the federal government, allowing it to effectively rule by decree when it perceived the existence of 'war, invasion or insurrection, real or apprehended'. During both world wars, the Act was used to issue detailed regulations limiting the freedom of Canadians of foreign descent. In World War II, by early 1940, two communist papers were banned and 64 people arrested for offences under the subversion regulations, of whom 19 were imprisoned. The Communist Party of Canada and 14 associated bodies were declared illegal in 1940, and more than 100 communists were interned. Hundreds of Jehovah's Witnesses were also arrested and large numbers of people were prosecuted for making statements prejudicial to the war effort (Douglas 2003).

In 1988, the powers contained in the War Measures Act were replaced by the Emergencies Act. It conferred extraordinary powers on the federal Cabinet, allowing it to govern by decree when it perceives the existence of 'threats to the security of Canada', including acts of serious political violence or activities aimed at overthrowing the system of government.

The Act was invoked to authorise a military intervention in a domestic crisis in October and November 1970, when a state of 'apprehended insurrection' was declared to exist in Québec and emergency regulations were proclaimed in response to two kidnappings by the separatist Front de Liberation du Quebec (FLQ) (Maloney 1997: 138–9).

Under the emergency regulations, the FLQ was declared an illegal organisation, normal liberties were suspended, and arrests and detentions were authorised without charge. Ultimately more than 12,000 troops were deployed in full battle order for a show of force to the citizens of Montreal. Airborne forces were brought in to conduct special operations, while soldiers conducted cordon and search operations jointly with Quebec provincial police. Over 450 persons were detained in Québec, most of whom were eventually released without the laying or hearing of charges.

In all, ten shots were fired, all warnings, without casualties. It could easily have been worse. At one point, Prime Minister Trudeau directed the Vice Chief of Defence Staff to place 'tanks on all the bridges in Montreal and men all over the city to show these pipsqueaks who has the power'. When troops arrived in Ottawa without Rules of Engagement and sought advice from the RCMP on what to do when approached by unknown individuals, they were told 'shoot them, but let us know afterwards so we can clean up the situation' (Lerhe 2004: 10).

The Emergencies Act permits the Canadian government to rule by executive orders and regulations in any 'national emergency', which is defined broadly as 'an urgent and critical situation of a temporary nature' that 'seriously endangers the lives, health or safety of Canadians' or 'seriously threatens the ability of the Government of Canada to preserve the sovereignty, security and territorial integrity of Canada'. Four kinds of emergency are provided for: public welfare (natural disasters), public order (internal security), international (external threats to security or territorial integrity) and war (war or other armed conflict, real or imminent). Considerable scope exists for domestic military intervention under the other three headings, but 'public order emergencies' explicitly relate to suppressing certain types of political opposition.

A public order emergency, covered by Part II of the Act, is one that arises from 'threats to the security of Canada' as defined by the Canadian Security Intelligence Service Act. Section 2 of that statute refers to espionage, sabotage, foreign influenced activities, 'acts of serious political violence' for the purpose of achieving a 'political, religious or ideological objective' within Canada or a foreign state, and activities 'directed toward or intended ultimately to lead to the destruction or overthrow by violence' of the Canadian system of government. Although the definition exempts 'lawful advocacy, protest or dissent', unless linked to any of the proscribed activities, the section leaves open considerable scope for emergency rule directed against various forms of political dissent, particularly if they can be depicted as potentially violent.

Once a public order emergency has been declared, the Governor in Council (normally on behalf of the federal cabinet) can issue far-reaching orders, including banning public assemblies, stopping travel and seizing control of public services, and imposing summary convictions for up to six months of imprisonment. There are no unlimited search and seizure powers, previously available under the War Measures Act, for a public order emergency, but they remain for an international emergency. Emergency powers can last initially for 30 days and be continuously renewed. Ministers and other personnel exercising emergency powers 'in good faith' are protected from personal legal liability, although government liability and compensation remain. Parliamentary scrutiny is weak and belated: either House of Parliament can revoke an emergency declaration, but only after a delay of at least seven sitting days (Emergencies Act, ss 3, 16–26, 47–8, 58–9).

The statute states that it does not confer on the government the power to detain, imprison or intern Canadian citizens or permanent residents 'on the basis of race, national or ethnic origin, colour, religion, sex, age or mental or physical disability' (Emergencies Act, s 4). This proviso, however, does not preclude detention on political or ideological grounds, nor does it apply to non-citizens without permanent residency status.

One limitation on use of the Act, compared to its predecessor, the War Measures Act, is that under section 25(3), the Governor in Council cannot declare a public emergency unless requested by a province, or the emergency extends to more than one province. For that reason, there have been calls from within military and police circles for the Act to be amended (Lerhe 2004: 17).

Forcese states that it is doubtful whether the Act could be used, as the War Measures Act was in October 1970, to abridge fundamental civil liberties. He explains that the Act's preamble says that the 'special temporary measures' are subject to the Charter of Rights and Freedoms, the Canadian Bill of Rights and 'must have regard to the International Covenant on Civil and Political Rights, particularly with respect to those fundamental rights that are not to be limited or abridged even in a national emergency' (Forcese 2008: 124). However, such preambles are not legally binding and the Charter of Rights and Freedoms and the Bill of Rights provide no secure protection of basic rights in the context of an alleged national security emergency (Head 2009).

Martial Law

British-derived law has also been prepared to support recourse to the imposition of martial law, which is, in essence, the suspension of law altogether. Martial law declarations can pave the way for setting loose extensive military powers, including the right to summarily try and execute individuals, in order to put down civil unrest. After the final defeat of the absolute monarchy in 1688 and up until the nineteenth century, martial law was regarded as an emergency suspension of the rule of law, strictly confined to cases of necessity in times of war, not in times of peace when ordinary courts were open (Hale 2000: 26–7, Capua 1977). Yet, this view seemed to shift somewhat during the nineteenth century.

At the beginning of that century, Blackstone conceded that the rules regarding the power to declare martial law were unclear and capricious. Writing in 1809, he said martial law was 'built upon no settled principle, but is entirely arbitrary in its decisions'. Indeed, it was 'in truth no law but something rather than allowed as law, a temporary excrescence bred out of the distemper of the state' (Blackstone 2001: 413). Writing toward the end of the nineteenth century, however, Dicey asserted that the right to invoke martial law is 'a right inherent in government' (Dicey 2005: 543–5). Dicey, who is best known as a proponent of the concept of 'rule of law', said the term martial law was most accurately 'employed as a name for the common law right of the Crown and its servants to repel force by force in the case of invasion, insurrection, riot, or generally of any violent resistance to the law' (Dicey 2005: 288). It was a 'right, or power' that was 'essential to the very existence of orderly government, and is most assuredly recognized in the most ample manner by the law of England' (Dicey 2005: 155, citing *R v. Pinney* (1832) 5 Car & P 254).

Halsbury's Laws of England states that martial law applies 'when a state of actual war, or of insurrection, riot, or rebellion amounting to war, exists' (Hailsham 1973: vol 8(2), para 821). Other authorities contend that a modified form of martial law can be declared in cases of internal insurrection or disorder that is beyond the power of the civil authorities to quell, applying the same test of necessity as applies to 'military aid to the civil power' (Wade and Phillips 1970: 409, Dicey 2005: 543). It seems to have been accepted that martial law allows the creation of military tribunals to administer summary justice (Ewing and Gearty 2000: 362–3).

Doubt exists as to the legal basis of martial law. It is said to be either an example of a common law right to employ force to repel force or, alternatively, a royal prerogative (Hailsham 1973: vol 8(2), para 821). Despite this fundamental uncertainty, the Privy Council in the 1902 *Marais* case on appeal from the Cape Colony, extended the doctrine of martial law to apply even where the ordinary civilian courts were still sitting (*D F Marais v. The General Officer Commanding the Lines of Communication and the Attorney-General of the Colony* [1902] AC 109). Martial law has been somewhat loosely described as 'the right to use force against force within the realm in order to suppress civil disorder' (Heuston 1964: 152). This formulation could justify dictatorial measures.

According to de Smith (a leading late-twentieth century authority on English constitutional and administrative law), if martial law arises, it is generally thought that the officer commanding the armed forces will become all-powerful and his actions 'non-justiciable and, for the time being, absolute, subject only to consultation (if this is feasible) with the civil power' (de Smith 1981: 511). 'Non-justiciable' means that the courts have no power to scrutinise the lawfulness of the actions taken.

How these propositions might apply in practice can be assessed from the experiences of British rule in Ireland, which provide a case study of the operation of martial law in the twentieth century. The first instance was triggered by the Easter 1916 Rebellion. The nationalist uprising was short-lived, lasting five days in Dublin, while the insurrection never even got off the ground elsewhere. Officially, 124 Crown forces were killed, and 388 injured in the five-day counter-insurgency operation, compared to 180 civilians killed and 614 wounded (Ewing and Gearty 2000: 338–9). The Lord Lieutenant, Lord Wimborne, proclaimed an immediate state of martial law in Dublin city and county. Under this authority, the British army commander-in-chief in the region, General Friend, swiftly issued martial law regulations that imposed a curfew and declared that any civilian carrying arms was liable to be fired upon without warning.

A day later, martial law was extended across the whole of Ireland, with British Prime Minister Asquith informing parliament that General Sir John Maxwell was being 'given plenary powers under martial law over the whole country'. By War Office instructions, Maxwell was empowered to 'take all such measures as may in his opinion be necessary for the prompt suppression of insurrection in Ireland' (Ewing and Gearty 2000: 339, 339n). A further proclamation brought into operation an emergency regulation that contemplated two types of military justice, a general court-martial and a field general court-martial, to try anyone charged with offences against the Defence of the Realm Regulations then in force throughout the UK. These tribunals, which sat in secret, could impose the death penalty, where the intention of the accused was to assist the enemy, and, in other cases, prison sentences up to life imprisonment (Ewing and Gearty 2000: 341). In the first few weeks of May 1916, 3,419 suspected Sinn Fein sympathisers were arrested by the military under internment and other emergency regulations, 188 civilians were tried by courts-martial, 90 death sentences were passed and 15 people were executed (Ewing and Gearty 2000: 342).

No effort seems to have been made to challenge the legality of the executions, but one bid to challenge the closed-door conduct of the hearings was dismissed unanimously by a seven-member King's Bench court. Lord Chief Justice, Viscount Reading considered that, having regard to the army commander-in-chief's opinion that it was necessary for public safety and the defence of the realm to exclude the public and the media, it was 'abundantly clear' that the in camera proceedings were lawful. The readiness of the judges to dispense with the legal principle of open courts was voiced most vehemently by Justice Darling. He declared that it would have been 'grotesque' to invite 'the public to come and hear witnesses give evidence against rebels with whom a great many of that same public sympathised (*R v. Governor of Lewes Prison, ex parte Doyle* [1917] 2 KB 254, 272, 274). One month after its proclamation, martial law was extended indefinitely. It was never formally revoked by proclamation, but simply ceased to apply when not judged essential by the UK government (Ewing and Gearty 2000: 339n).

Military tribunals re-emerged in Ireland in 1920, under the Restoration of Order in Ireland Act of that year, accompanied by an official policy of covertly authorised retaliation or reprisals. Entire towns were wrecked in revenge for the killing of army officers by the Irish Republican Army, and troops fired indiscriminately into a Dublin football crowd, killing 14 men, women and children in Ireland's first 'Bloody Sunday' (Ewing and Gearty 2000: 358–60). Three weeks later, martial law was proclaimed once more, covering the four south-western counties. Two days after Lord French's declaration, the military commander-in-chief, Sir Nevil Macready, issued his first martial law proclamation. This made into capital offences, triable by the military, the unauthorised 'possession of arms, ammunition, or explosives', the wearing of military apparel and the harbouring or assisting of any rebels who were 'levying war' against the king. Within martial law areas, which soon included four further counties, a policy of 'official reprisals' was vigorously followed (Ewing and Gearty 2000: 360–1). Some confusion ensued, because the ordinary courts continued to function, alongside courts-martial operating under three distinct systems: martial law, the Defence of the Realm Consolidation Act 1914 and the Restoration of Order in Ireland Act 1920.

The willingness of the courts to legitimise martial law was demonstrated in three Irish King's Bench Divisional Court cases (*R v. Allen* [1921] 2 IR 241, *R (Garde) v. Strickland* [1921] 2 IR 317 and *R (Ronayne and Mulcahy) v. Strickland* [1921] 2 IR 333). The first involved John Allen, who was sentenced to death by a military tribunal for possessing a revolver, ammunition and an IRA publication, entitled 'Night Fighting'. Giving the unanimous decision of the court to uphold the sentence, even though it would not have been possible under the ordinary law or even the emergency legislation, Chief Justice Molony declared:

> It is the sacred duty of this Court to protect the lives and liberties of all His Majesty's subjects, and to see that no one suffers loss of life or liberty save under the laws of the country; but when subjects of the King rise in armed insurrection and the conflict is still raging, it is no less our duty not to interfere with the officers of the Crown in taking such steps as they deem necessary to quell the insurrection, and to restore peace and order and the authority of the law. ([1921] 2 IR 241, 242)

In that case, there was no challenge to the government's proclamation of the existence of a state of war, or to its claim that such a state of disorder existed when Allen was arrested. The court ruled that it was 'clear on the authorities that when martial law is imposed, and the necessity for it exists, or, in other words, while the war is still raging, this Court has no jurisdiction to question any acts done by the military authorities' ([1921] 2 IR 241, 269). Relying upon the 1902 precedent set by the Privy Council in *Marais*, the court held that the continued functioning of civilian courts in the martial law areas did not affect the legality of the military tribunals. And the lack of availability of the death penalty for these offences under the ordinary law was an objection 'rather for the consideration of Parliament than for this Court, which cannot, durante bello [during war], control the military authorities, or question any sentence imposed in the exercise of martial law' ([1921] 2 IR 241, 272). Allen was duly executed four days later, together with five others (Ewing and Gearty 2000: 364).

In the first *Strickland* case, death sentences imposed on seven men for levying war against His Majesty were challenged through writs of habeas corpus and certiorari on the basis that the military tribunal that had tried them had been improperly constituted. Chief Justice Molony asserted that the court had 'the power and the duty to decide whether a state of war exists which justifies the application of martial law' ([1921] 2 IR 317, 329). But the court agreed with the military's assessment and therefore would not 'interfere to determine what is or what is not necessary' ([1921] 2 IR 317, 332). On the same day, in the second Strickland case, the court rejected an objection that the power to declare martial law had been 'surrendered or released' by the *Restoration of Order in Ireland Act*. In a one-page judgement, Chief Justice Molony and his fellow judges simply dismissed the submission as having 'no foundation in law' ([1921] 2 IR 333, 334).

Another judicial ruling, handed down in mid-1921, did call the continued application of martial law into question. *Egan v. Macready* ([1921] 1 IR 265) was a further challenge to a military court's death sentence, this time for possessing ammunition. Significantly, the case was heard following the partition of Ireland, after sweeping electoral victories in the south for Sinn Fein and amid the announcement of a truce between the British forces and the IRA (Ewing and Gearty 2000: 365–6). Possibly influenced by the truce, Ireland's Master of the Rolls, Charles O'Connor, ruled that the power to declare martial law had been removed by the adoption of the Restoration of Order in Ireland Act – the very proposition rejected by Chief Justice Molony's Irish King's Bench court two months earlier. Master of the Rolls O'Connor insisted that the 'claim of the military authority to override legislation, specially made for a state of war, would seem … to call for a new Bill of Rights' ([1921] 1 IR 265, 275). He cited the then very recent House of Lords judgement in *Attorney General v. De Keyser's Royal Hotel* [1920] AC 508, which ruled that legislation could preclude the operation of prerogative powers by evincing an intention to cover the relevant field.

Master of the Rolls O'Connor's judgement led to an extraordinary confrontation with the military. General Macready refused to obey the habeas corpus order, and another in a similar case decided by O'Connor on the same day. The judge issued writs of attachment against the general and his deputy, as well as the governor of the prison where the men were held, declaring that their obstruction amounted to a 'deliberate contempt of Court – a thing unprecedented in this Court and the whole history of British law' ([1921] 1 IR 265, 280). The Crown argued that it had the right to hold the prisoners pending an appeal. General Macready threatened to 'arrest anyone, including the Master of the Rolls himself, who attempted to carry out the service of the writs'. A constitutional crisis was only averted when the government decided to release the men, telling parliament that the decision was 'based solely upon the existing situation in Ireland' and 'not due to any decision given by a Civil Court in Ireland', since the courts had 'no power to over-rule the decisions of Military Courts in the martial law area' (Ewing and Gearty 2000:

367). It seems that the government was driven by concerns about not upsetting the truce negotiations, rather than respect for the rule of law.

To say the least, the O'Connor affair left unresolved the claim for the primacy of martial law and indeed called into question the principle of civilian control of the military. Moreover, a prominent constitutional scholar cast doubt on O'Connor's ruling, saying it 'has not met with approval' and appears 'to depend upon the view that the right to use martial law is a prerogative right' rather than 'simply an extension of the ordinary common law power to meet force with force' (Heuston 1964: 159).

In summary, even if the ordinary courts have jurisdiction to decide whether the state of disorder warranted martial law, there is no precise and settled body of law for answering that question, which seems to depend on judging whether order could only be restored by handing over power to the military authorities. If the courts decide that martial law is warranted, then the military's actions will be unreviewable, at least until the courts decide that the disorder has been pacified. Legal action could be brought against the military for manifestly unreasonable conduct and possibly for unnecessary use of force against people or property, but the law is unclear (de Smith 1981: 512). In de Smith's opinion, the legal uncertainty is academic in any case, because indemnity legislation would almost certainly be passed to exonerate those who acted in good faith to suppress an uprising (de Smith 1981: 514). The British parliament passed such an Act of Indemnity to cover the 1920 declaration of martial law in areas of Ireland (Rowe 1985: 200).

In Australia, martial law was invoked several times during the nineteenth century against convicts, Aborigines and workers (Lendrum 1977, Windeyer 1979). Governor King declared martial law in 1804 in New South Wales to suppress an 'Irish insurrection'. Many participants in the revolt were tried by court-martial and a number were hanged (Lendrum 1977: 40). Another NSW Governor, Darling, rejected the urging of his Attorney-General to declare martial law in 1826 to use the military against Aborigines who were resisting seizures of their lands. Darling was of the view, however, based on advice from the British Secretary of State, Lord Bathurst, that he that he could use troops against Aboriginal people without such a declaration, as if they were 'open enemies' against whom war could be declared (Lendrum 1977: 42).

Two of the most barbaric declarations of martial law came in 1828 and 1830, when Governor Arthur of Tasmania mobilised troops to drive Aborigines from settled areas. Arthur twice invoked martial law even though Aboriginal retaliation against their dispossession had taken the form of isolated attacks, not a general war (Lendrum 1977: 41, Calder 2008: 127–50). In 1840, Governor Gawler of South Australia cited martial law, although not formally declared, as well as the war of law, as the legal justifications for the summary execution of two Aboriginal people rounded up by troops in the Coorong area, near the mouth of the Murray (Lendrum 1977: 29, 34). As late as 1867, British authorities sent regulations to the Australian colonies providing for declarations of martial law, although it seems that these regulations were not put into practice (Clark 2007: 17, citing *Proposed Rules on the Subject of Martial Law*, SAPP No 107 of 1867).

In his work, *Emergency Powers*, Lee 'hazards a guess' that the power to resort to martial law continues in Australia as a creature of the common law. Despite the uncertainty involved, Lee considers that, while legislation is generally preferable, the doctrine of martial law should not be buried 'for in the face of an extraordinary crisis it may come in useful … it may be better to rely on a "shadowy, uncertain, precarious something" than nothing at all' (Lee 1984: 224). This argument would seem to justify dispensing with the rule of law. The words quoted by Lee are taken from a nineteenth century English judgement, where Chief Justice Cockburn stated: 'Martial law when applied to the civilian is no law at all, but a shadowy, uncertain, precarious something, depending entirely on the conscience, or rather on the despotic and arbitrary will of those who administer it' (*R v. Nelson and Brand* (1867) F Cockburn Sp Rep 86).

Official Lawlessness

In the name of defending the state, governments or official security agencies may engage in unlawful acts of surveillance, harassment, violence or intimidation. These may also include wars of aggression, military interventions, coups, assassinations, renditions and torture. It appears that such practices grew in the first decade of the twenty-first century. Considerable evidence has been produced of such crimes being committed from 2001 onward, both domestically and abroad. It is not possible to investigate or review these operations here. But it is important to note that those allegedly affected by these crimes have faced considerable difficulties in bringing law suits seeking to prosecute or obtain redress for such conduct. Courts have dismissed legal actions on various grounds, including 'state secrets' doctrines invoked by the government accused of being responsible. Two American cases decided in 2010 illustrate this development. One concerned the use of 'renditions' to secretly transport prisoners to locations in other countries where they could be tortured. The other involved the targeted assassination of people indentified as terrorists.

In the first decision, the US Ninth Circuit Court of Appeals in a 6–5 en banc ruling dismissed a lawsuit by five victims of the Central Intelligence Agency's 'extraordinary rendition' program against Jeppesen Dataplan, a unit of Boeing. The ruling relied upon the 'state secrets' doctrine advocated by the Obama administration. The American Civil Liberties Union brought the suit, charging that defence contractor Jeppesen Dataplan knowingly facilitated the renditions, also known as 'torture flights', by providing flight planning and logistical support to CIA personnel. The suit, *Mohamed v. Jeppesen Dataplan*, Inc. (9th Cir. – 8 Sept. 2010), sought to expose a web of connections between top executives of defence corporations, foreign intelligence agencies and the US government.

The Ninth Circuit's ruling argued that 'there is precious little Jeppesen could say about its relevant conduct and knowledge without revealing information about how the United States government does or does not conduct covert operations'. On this basis, the court dismissed the case. Earlier, a three-judge panel of the Ninth Circuit had ruled against the Obama administration. Writing for the panel, Judge Michael D. Hawkins wrote that the 'state secrets' doctrine advocated by the administration 'has no logical limit'. The judge noted: 'As the Founders of this Nation knew well, arbitrary imprisonment and torture under any circumstance is a gross and notorious act of despotism'.

The Obama administration sought review of Hawkins' decision, which was overturned by the entire Ninth Circuit, in a judgement authored by Judge Raymond C. Fisher. While couching his opinion in the language of 'balancing' national security against individual liberties, Judge Fisher concluded, '[c]ourts must act in the interest of the country's national security to prevent disclosure of state secrets, even to the point of dismissing a case entirely' (Savage 2010).

In another 2010 decision, Federal District Judge John D. Bates dismissed a lawsuit that challenged the Obama administration's policy of targeted killings of individuals around the world, including US citizens. The administration had placed the name of US citizen Anwar Al-Aulaqi on a 'kill list', permitting any of the US government's military or intelligence agencies to carry out his assassination. Al-Aulaqi was reported to be in Yemen. The CIA had launched a cruise missile at a meeting Al-Aulaqi was attending there, but the intended victim survived.

In *Al-Aulaqi v. Obama* (DDC 7 Dec. 2010), the American Civil Liberties Union (ACLU) and the Center for Constitutional Rights (CCR) filed a lawsuit on behalf of Al-Aulaqi's father, Nasser Al-Aulaqi, challenging the targeted killing program. The Obama administration argued that the President had the power to order the killing of an American citizen without a trial or judicial review, despite this being a clear violation of international law and the US Bill of Rights. The Fifth Amendment to the US Constitution states: 'No person shall be ... deprived of life ... without due process of law'. The administration further argued that the case should not be allowed to proceed because it threatened to reveal 'state secrets'.

Judge Bates, in his ruling, acknowledged that the case raised 'stark' and 'perplexing' questions. He asked (at 2): 'Can the Executive order the assassination of a US citizen without first affording him any form of judicial process whatsoever, based on the mere assertion that he is a dangerous member of a terrorist organization?' However, Bates concluded that the case could not proceed because Anwar Al-Aulaqi's father, Nasser Al-Aulaqi, lacked legal standing to bring the case.

This ruling implies that in order for the targeted killing program to be challenged, the persons marked for death must appear themselves in the courts of the country that is trying to assassinate them. Bates included in his opinion a passage suggesting that in light of Anwar Al-Aulaqi's political and religious views, he should not be entitled to the protections of the US Constitution. The judge wrote that Al-Aulaqi has 'decried the US legal system and suggested that Muslims are not bound by Western law'. Accordingly, Bates wrote, Al-Aulaqi would not 'likely want to sue to vindicate his US constitutional rights in US courts'.

Judge Bates dismissed Al-Aulaqi's claims under international law because the doctrine of 'sovereign immunity' prevents the government from being the target of certain lawsuits without its express consent. Bates held that a judicial evaluation of the Obama administration's assassination program would involve a 'political question' not subject to judicial review. Bates indicated that in light of his other rulings dismissing the case, it was unnecessary to decide whether the 'state secrets' doctrine applied.

Chapter 10

Conclusions

A range of conclusions can be drawn from this study. The main propositions, with some pertinent examples, can be stated as follows:

1. Legal neutrality is a myth. Alongside murder, the offences examined in this book are the most serious in the criminal law. They exist, and are administered, to defend the existing state structure and socio-economic order against perceived political threats. Lord Chief Justice Holt may have expressed this role crudely in *R v. Tutchin*, when he said: 'If people should not be called to account for possessing the people with an ill opinion of the government no government can subsist' (see Chapter 6). Nevertheless, that is the approach that has generally prevailed to this day. Instructing the jury in the trial of Henry Hunt and other organisers of the fatal 1819 St Peter's Fields meeting, a British judge said the banners carried by participants, objecting to 'taxation without representation' and being 'sold like slaves' were evidence of a seditious conspiracy and unlawful assembly. 'Is the telling a large body of men they are sold like slaves likely to make them satisfied and contented with their situation in society?' he asked rhetorically (see Chapter 1). In a 1962 decision, the English House of Lords judges ruled that, as a matter of law, the 'interests of the State' are determined exclusively by the government of the day, at least where the issues at stake concern the deployment of the armed forces (see Chapter 5).

2. Above all, crimes against the state are directed at radicals, anti-establishment activists and revolutionary socialists, and the support they seek to win among ordinary people. The fear of revolt from below, and ultimately of social revolution, has driven the historical development of the law. In handing down decisions, judges have made contemptuous references to the alleged gullibility or stupidity of poorer people, or warned that members of the 'lower classes' are particularly susceptible to criticisms of governments and the existing order. Many outcomes have been animated by this inherent political bias. Thus, Tom Mann and fellow anti-war syndicalists were convicted of inciting mutiny in 1912, while more overtly mutinous Tory and military opponents of Irish Home Rule were not prosecuted (see Chapter 4). Left-wing Socialist Party members were convicted of 'criminal anarchy' for advocating mass political strikes in *Gitlow*, and leaders of the US Communist Party were jailed for advocating the 'principles of Marxism-Leninism', while members of the Ku Klux Klan were not convicted for fomenting racialism(see Chapter 2). Australian Trotskyists were jailed in World War II for inciting disaffection among soldiers by arguing that the war was being waged in the interests of the business elite and urging soldiers to elect committees to watch their officers(see Chapter 4).

3. Political non-interference is another myth. Governments have repeatedly intervened to direct arrests and prosecutions against those perceived to be political dangers to the ruling establishment. Thus, British Attorney General Sir Douglas Hogg (later Lord Hailsham) personally recommended to Cabinet the arrests on sedition charges of 12 leading members of the Communist Party of Great Britain in 1925, the year before the 1926 general strike (see Chapter 6). President Franklin D. Roosevelt was consulted by his Attorney General before the 1941 Smith Act arrests were launched against the leaders of the Trotskyist Socialist Workers Party for opposing World War II as an inter-imperialist conflict(see Chapter 2). Australian Prime Minister Robert Menzies personally ordered the 1960 sedition prosecution of Brian Cooper, a 24-year-old former junior officer in the Australian colonial administration of Papua New Guinea, for 'exciting disaffection against the government' by encouraging local people to demand independence (see Chapter 6).

4. The right to popular revolution, embodied in the American Revolution of 1776, has been reduced to a nullity. While judicial lip service has been paid to free speech and the right to espouse revolution in the abstract, any actions or advocacy directed toward a specific goal based on a social uprising have been severely punished. In effect, according to judicial interpretation, the US Constitution, while it may recognise a 'right' to revolution, also recognises the 'right' and 'duty' of governments to put down actual rebellions. Thus, US Supreme Court Justice Douglas, after citing Abraham Lincoln's passionate declaration that people anywhere have the *right* to rise up, and shake off the existing government, immediately commented: 'Of course, government can move against those who take up arms against it. Of course, the constituted authority has the right of self-preservation' (see Chapter 3).

5. Serious offences relating to the protection of the state are revived in times of economic, social and political turmoil. Offences thought to be redundant have been resurrected to deal with freshly perceived subversion. In Britain the long disused 1797 Mutiny Act was resuscitated just before World War I to deal with anti-war and syndicalist opposition (see Chapter 4). In 2006, a United States federal grand jury issued the first indictment for treason against the US since 1952, charging an American-born Muslim for aiding an enemy of the US by appearing in videos in which he spoke supportively of al-Qaeda (see Chapter 4). A sedition prosecution was conducted in New Zealand in 2006, the first since 1942. A court found Timothy Selwyn guilty for issuing a statement calling for acts of civil disobedience to protest against the government's foreshore and seabed legislation (see Chapter 6).

6. Political choices are made by governments and prosecuting authorities as to which offences to pursue. This has happened historically, producing both long-term shifts and short-term changes. From the eighteenth to the nineteenth century, there was a marked turn from the use by the authorities of seditious libel to prosecutions for unlawful assembly, reflecting a fear of the rising level of mass political consciousness after the Peterloo Massacre of 1819 and in the development

of the Chartist movement (see Chapter 1). During the Vietnam War, as powerful domestic opposition began to develop to it, one method of silencing dissent – prosecutions for espionage or sedition – gave way to other means, including surveillance, harassment, disruption and secrecy, exemplified by the illegal counter-intelligence program (COINTELPRO) (see Chapter 2). One of the most controversial Australian sedition cases was the 1916 prosecution of the 'Sydney Twelve' for seditious conspiracy. It followed the withdrawal of the treason felony charges against them, evidently out of government concern that prosecuting an offence thought to carry the death penalty would backfire politically in the campaign for a conscription referendum (see Chapter 4).

7. Many overlaps exist among crimes against the state, allowing the authorities to selectively apply their provisions. As the Canadian Law Reform Commission noted in 1986, that country's provisions were marked by overlapping, inconsistency, excessive complexity and detail, and uncertainty as to scope and meaning, as well as out-of-date features, over-criminalisation and possible violations of the Canadian Charter of Rights and Freedoms (see Introduction). Likewise, the Australian Law Reform Commission's 2006 report on sedition found significant overlaps between the offences of sedition, treason and treachery (see Introduction).

8. The scope and discretionary reach of crimes against the state is increased by a range of ancillary measures. These include conspiracy and complicity, and incitement and advocacy, as well as 'preparing' and 'attempting'. For example, following some narrowing of sedition law by the courts, the offence of seditious conspiracy developed at the end of the eighteenth century, and came to prominence during the great working class struggles of the first half of the nineteenth century. Some notable cases include the trials of those who conducted the meeting at St. Peters Field, Manchester, that was the subject of the Peterloo massacre. [Chapter 6]. During the Vietnam War, a series of conspiracy trials were directed against anti-war activists, although most prosecutions failed because of lack of evidence, unlawful government surveillance or reversal on appeal. Politically, these cases backfired because they gave invaluable publicity and moral authority to the defendants. [Chapter 2]. In one of the major 2005-2010 terrorism trials in Australia, a conspiracy charge effectively widened the scope of the terrorism laws. It allowed Islamic men to be convicted on circumstantial evidence for doing things that are legal in themselves – such as expressing opposition to the invasions of Afghanistan and Iraq, viewing jihadist videos and buying various commonly-used chemicals. [Chapter 7].

9. Further ancillary weapons are provided to the authorities by so-called minor offences. Provisions such as 'breaching the peace' and 'public disturbance' and 'offensive behaviour' can be used to trigger more serious charges or legal consequences. In 1926, amid the turmoil surrounding that year's general strike, a British Communist Party MP was arrested for inciting the public to commit a breach of the peace during a May Day speech in London's Hyde Park, and jailed for two months (see Chapter 8). In Seattle in 1999, some 50,000 people protested against a World Trade Organisation meeting, objecting to corporate power, environmental

damage and violation of human rights. In order to clear a path for the delegates, more than 600 people were arrested, and detained, but generally without charges being filed. Many misdemeanour charges, mostly for 'failure to disperse', were dropped. In 2003, a US federal judge ruled that the police lacked probable cause to arrest the protesters. (see Chapter 8). Studies of 'political trials' in Australia in the 1930s, 1940s and 1950s found hundreds of cases in which left-wing activists were arrested, and almost universally convicted, for 'minor offences' such as vagrancy, bill-posting, leafleting, disobeying police instructions, unlawful demonstrations, disturbing public order, malicious damage, theft, assault and resisting police (see Chapter 8).

10. Prosecutions for crimes against the state, even if unsuccessful in producing convictions, have wider investigatory and chilling impacts. In 1794, although all the three British treason trial defendants were acquitted, the trials intimidated the radicals, nearly all of whom retreated from active politics. Moreover, to remedy the perceived gap that the failed treason trials revealed in its legal armoury, the Pitt government introduced the 1797 Incitement to Mutiny Act to provide severe punishments, including the death penalty, for this crime (see Chapter 4). During the 'Red Scare' in the US in the early 1920s, more than 200,000 people were placed under surveillance, more than 4,600 were arrested – virtually every known communist – and some 3,000 non-citizens were deported. Thirty-two states outlawed displays of the Red Flag. In 1919–20, at least 1,400 people were arrested under such legislation, with some 300 convicted and sentenced to jail terms of up to 20 years. The New York legislature expelled its five Socialist Party members on the grounds of being unpatriotic and disloyal. Five months later, all five were re-elected, signalling growing public opposition to the political witch-hunt, which then began to collapse (see Chapter 2). Australia's 1949–50 sedition prosecutions, and other threatened prosecutions, became vehicles for wider political, surveillance and prosecutorial campaigns against the Communist Party of Australia, and for permitting extensive operations by the intelligence and police services, including frequent search and seizure raids on party members. These efforts reached crescendos during Prime Minister Robert Menzies' 1950–51 failed bid to ban the party (see Chapter 6).

11. Prosecutions, trials, convictions and sentences are affected by political calculations. Often, they can be determined by political factors, as much as by legal formulations, interpretations and considerations. Thomas Paine's 1792 sedition trial for writing *Rights of Man* was delayed and he fled to France in the intervening months, apparently with the blessing of the government, which was afraid that Paine might use his trial as a political platform. By the time he was declared guilty, Paine was in France. Nevertheless, crowds of supporters greeted Paine's lawyer as he emerged from the court after the verdict and pulled his carriage through the streets of London. Across the Channel, Paine himself was fêted as a hero, granted citizenship and made a representative to the National Convention (see Chapter 1). During the 1965 Los Angeles riots, some 3,927 people were arrested but only 732 were eventually imprisoned, illustrating the potential for riot law to be used for

mass roundups, arbitrary arrests and dubious trials (see Chapter 8). In Australia, after the Eureka Stockade of 1854, 13 rebel miners were prosecuted for treason, but all were acquitted by juries who refused to be intimidated by a government – supported by the judiciary – intent upon securing convictions. The first miner to be acquitted was carried around the streets of Melbourne in triumph by over 10,000 people (see Chapter 3).

12. Anti-terrorism laws have provided governments and security agencies with new arsenals, capable of being deployed against anti-war and anti-government dissenters, as well as against supporters of foreign struggles against despotism. In 2008, with the agreement of the Attorney General, a member of a Women's Peace Camp was placed on trial for a terrorist offence for conducting a peaceful anti-nuclear missile protest at an Atomic Weapons Establishment (see Chapter 7). In 2010 the US Supreme Court upheld 6–3 a provision of law making it a federal crime to 'knowingly provide material support or resources' to a listed 'foreign terrorist organization', even if the 'support' consisted only of 'expert advice or assistance' for 'lawful, non-violent purposes'. The case concerned organisations working with two separatist groups, the Partiya Karkeran Kurdistan (PKK) and Liberation Tigers of Tamil Eelam (LTTE) (see Chapter 7). In Australia, a series of terrorism prosecutions have relied heavily on citing the defendants' political and religious views – particularly opposition to the invasions of Afghanistan and Iraq – as proof that they were intent on terrorist retaliation (see Chapter 7).

13. Courts have invariably permitted the executive government to determine the content of 'the interests of the state' or 'national security'. Judges have dismissed attempts by anti-war or other protestors, and leakers of government secrets, to argue defences based on their beliefs in the public interest, not matter how sincere. Such defences have been rejected, even when it is argued that the government's conduct violates domestic or international law. In Britain in 1985 a civil servant was prosecuted for leaking documents which showed that the government had provided incorrect information to parliament about the sinking of the Argentinean ship *Belgrano* during the Falklands War. The trial judge directed the jury that the 'interests of the state' were the interests according to the recognised organs of government and the policies as expounded by the government of the day. Nevertheless, the jury found the accused not guilty (see Chapter 5). In the US, during 2005, three nuns were jailed for between 30 and 41 months for attempting a 'citizen weapons inspection' and symbolic disarmament of a Minuteman III nuclear missile silo. The federal judge barred the jury from hearing international law and Nuremberg defences, adopted a sweeping definition of 'national defense', and prohibited the sisters from speaking about the moral and legal justification for their actions. An appellate court upheld the rulings, and added that there was no 'constitutional privilege' for a citizen to interfere with military facilities, even if they were illegal (see Chapter 5). This tendency has been strengthened in the 'war on terror' since 2001, as illustrated by the arguments of three Australian scholars that that the very *political* character of the power to proscribe terrorist organisations, and the calculations involved in exercising it, made it appropriate

for the executive, not the courts, to hold that power. The authors cited high-level judicial support for their approach, referring to the 2004 English House of Lords case where Lord Nicholls of Birkenhead referred to 'the heavy burden, resting on the elected government and not the judiciary, to protect the security of this country and all who live here' (see Introduction).

14. International human rights law provides little reliable protection against the application of offences against the state, regardless of any violation of basic democratic rights. International law reserves to the national state the power to override even the most basic legal and democratic rights in alleged emergencies or dire challenges to the stability of the state. In the Universal Declaration of Human Rights, the International Covenant on Civil and Political Rights (ICCPR), and other related instruments, such as the European Convention on Human Rights and Fundamental Freedoms and the UK Human Rights Act, the listed civil and legal rights are mostly subject to far-reaching exemptions, including 'national security' and 'public safety' (see Introduction).

15. The coming period may see greater use of offences against the state. This is particularly possible if the global financial crisis that surfaced in 2007–8 leads to mass protests against austerity measures and other social upheavals of the kind witnessed in Greece, Ireland, France, Spain and Britain in 2010. There were indications of a shift, with the advent of the Obama Administration in the United States in 2009, to broaden the concept of 'security'. Instead of terrorism, economic and political instability became the primary focus of concern (see Introduction).

16. From all the above considerations, it is suggested that defence campaigns and legal presentations should not focus only on evidentiary and legal issues. Arguments of law may well be crucial in certain circumstances, but success with even these legal points is often bound up with developments in the sphere of public opinion and other political factors. As outlined by James Cannon in the 1941 Smith Act trial in the US, those on trial should 'utilise to the fullest extent each and every legal protection, technicality and resource available to us under the law and the Constitution' but resist the advice of lawyers not to 'use the courtroom as a forum to popularise the principles of our movement' (see Chapter 3). There is no doubt that political factors played a decisive part in ultimately exposing the anti-Irish Republican Army 'miscarriage of justice' cases of the 1970s to 1990s, including the *Birmingham Six, Guildford Four and Maguire Seven* (see Chapter 7). The same can be said of the eventually unsuccessful 1968 Chicago Democratic Convention conspiracy trial, which transformed the defendants into national celebrities, and the US Supreme Court's 6 to 3 refusal to grant the Nixon administration an injunction to stop the publication of the Pentagon Papers in 1971 (see Chapter 2). In Australia, it was the 'court of public opinion' and the courageous actions of a barrister in leaking police interview transcripts that led to the dropping of a terrorism charge against Dr Mohamed Haneef in 2007 (see Chapter 7)

17. Further research in this field needs to be guided by an approach that takes into account the socio-economic, historical, political and other elements outlined

above. Some empirical studies have disclosed patterns of connection between the legal and historical-political tendencies in different locations and periods, but more systemic and generalised investigations are called for (see Introduction). In particular, further assessment is required of the use of emergency powers, executive authority, military measures and outright lawlessness by governments (see Chapter 9).

Bibliography

ABC (Australian Broadcasting Corporation) News (2011). 'Men acquitted over ASIO documents leak'. February 8, 2011 [Online]. Available at http://www.abc.net.au/news/stories/2011/02/09/3133701.htm [accessed 2 May 2011].

Ackroyd, P. (2001) *London: The Biography*. New York: Doubleday.

ACLU (American Civil Liberties Union) (2008) 'ACLU v. NSA: The challenge to illegal spying' [Online]. Available at: http://www.aclu.org/national-security/aclu-v-nsa-challenge-illegal-spying [accessed: 11 May 2010].

ALRC (Australian Law Reform Commission) (2006) *Fighting Words – A Review of Sedition Laws in Australia*. Canberra: Commonwealth of Australia.

ALRC (Australian Law Reform Commission) (2010) *Secrecy Laws and Open Government in Australia*. Canberra: Commonwealth of Australia.

Amnesty International (2002) *Amnesty International's Concerns Regarding Post September 11 Detentions in the USA*. London: Amnesty International.

Australian Press Council (2005) Submission [Online]. Available at: http://www.aph.gov.au/senate/committee/legcon_ctte/terrorism/submission/sub143.pdf [accessed: 2 December 2005].

Avrich, P. (1984) *The Haymarket Tragedy*. Princeton, NJ: Princeton University Press.

Babington, A. (1990) *Military Intervention in Britain: From the Gordon Riots to the Gibraltar Incident*. London: Routledge.

Bacevich, A. (2002) *American Empire: The Realities and Consequences of US Diplomacy*. Cambridge, MA: Harvard University Press.

Barrell, J. and Mee, J. (eds) (2006) *Trials for Treason and Sedition 1792–1794*. 8 vols. London: Pickering and Chatto.

Bell, J.B. (1993) *The Irish Troubles: A Generation of Violence 1967–1992*. New York: St. Martin's Press.

Bentham, J. (1967) *A Fragment on Government*. Oxford: Basil Blackwell.

Berger, T. (1981) *Fragile Freedoms: Human Rights and Dissent in Canada*. Toronto: Clarke, Irwin & Company.

Bills, S. (1988) *Kent State/May 4: Echoes Through a Decade*. Kent, OH: Kent State University Press.

Birkinshaw, P. (2001) *Freedom of Information: The Law, the Practice and the Ideal*. London: Butterworths.

Blackstone, W. (2001) *Commentaries on the Laws of England* (edited by Morrison, W.). London: Routledge-Cavendish.

Blair, D. (2009) Annual Threat Assessment of the Intelligence Community for the Senate Select Committee on Intelligence [Online]. Available at: http://www.dni.gov/testimonies/20090212_testimony.pdf [accessed: 7 May 2009].

Blom-Cooper, L. (1997) *The Birmingham Six and Other Cases.* London: Duckworth.

Blum, W. (2002) *Rogue State: A Guide to the World's Only Superpower.* London: Zed Books.

Boasberg, J.E. (1990) Seditious libel v. incitement to mutiny: Britain teaches Hand and Holmes a lesson. *Oxford Journal of Legal Studies* 10(1), 106–21.

Bonner, D. (2007) *Executive Measures, Terrorism and National Security.* Aldershot: Ashgate.

Braddock, J. (2006) An attack on democratic rights: New Zealand man jailed for sedition. *World Socialist Web Site*, 25 July 2006 [Online]. Available at: http://www.wsws.org/articles/2006/jul2006/sedi-j25.shtml [accessed: 5 December 2010].

Bramall, E. (1985) The place of the British army in public order, in Rowe, P. and Whelan, C. (eds) (1985) *Military Intervention in Democratic Societies.*

Brief for the Prosecution against Henry Seekamp (1854) [Online]. Available at: http://eureka.imagineering.com.au [accessed 9 November 2009].

Burns, D. (1992) *Poll Tax Rebellion.* Oakland, CA: AK Press.

Butler, M. (ed.) (1984) *Burke, Paine, Godwin, and the Revolution Controversy.* Cambridge: Cambridge University Press.

Calder, G. (2008) Routing a rebellion or crushing a crime wave? Proclaiming martial law and a call-to-arms in Van Diemen's Land, 1828–1830'. *Legal History* 12, 127.

Cannon, J. (1999) *Socialism on Trial.* Sydney: Resistance Books.

Capua, J. (1977) The Early History of Martial Law in England from the Fourteenth Century to the Petition of Right. *The Cambridge Law Journal* 152.

Caputo, P. (2005) *13 Seconds: A Look Back at the Kent State Shootings.* New York: Chamberlain Bros.

Carlson, P. (1983) *Roughneck: The Life and Times of Big Bill Haywood.* New York: W.W. Norton and Co.

Chafee, Z. (1954) *Free Speech in the United States.* Cambridge, MA: Harvard University Press.

Chaliand, G. and Blin, A. (eds)(2007) *The History of Terrorism: From Antiquity to al Qaeda.* Berkeley, CA: University of California Press.

Clark, D. (2007) *Principles of Australian Public Law.* 2nd edn. Sydney: LexisNexis Butterworths.

Clark, M. (1978) *History of Australia.* Vol. 4. Melbourne: Melbourne University Press.

Clements, C. (2006) *Inquest into the Death of Mulrunji.* Brisbane: Office of the State Coroner [Online]. Available at: http://www.justice.qld.gov.au/courts/coroner/findings/mulrunji270906.doc [accessed: 24 June 2010].

Coady, T. and O'Keefe, M. (eds) (2002) *Terrorism and Justice: Moral Argument in a Threatened World.* Melbourne: Melbourne University Press.

Collier, C. and Collier, J.L. (2000) *Slavery and the Coming of the Civil War*. New York: Benchmark Books.

Congressional Research Service (2010) Criminal prohibitions on the publication of classified defense information. **6** December 2010 [Online]. Available at: http://www.fas.org/sgp/crs/secrecy/R41404.pdf [accessed: 20 December 2010].

Cooper, B. (1961) The birth-pangs of a nation. *Overland* 20, 31–6.

Crowley-Cyr, L. (2005) Mental illness and indefinite detention at the minister's pleasure. *University of Western Sydney Law Review* 9, 53.

Deane, P. (1979) *The First Industrial Revolution.* Cambridge: Cambridge University Press.

de Smith, S. (1981) *Constitutional and Administrative Law.* 4th edn. London: Penguin/Longmans.

Dewar, M. (1997) *The British Army in Northern Ireland.* London: Arms and Armour Press.

Dicey, A. (2005) *Introduction to the Study of the Law of the Constitution.* Boston: Adamant Media Corporation.

Doughty Street Chambers (2008) Victory for free speech and the right to protest – peaceful anti-nuclear protestor acquitted of terrorist offence [Online]. Available at: http://www.doughtystreet.co.uk/news/news_detail.cfm?iNewsID=281 [accessed: 30 November 2010].

Doughty Street Chambers (2009) Refugee cleared of terror charges [Online]. Available at: http://www.doughtystreet.co.uk/news/news_detail.cfm?iNewsID=313 [accessed: 30 November 2010].

Douglas, R. (2001) Keeping the revolution at bay: the unlawful associations provisions of the commonwealth crimes act. *Adelaide Law Review* 22, 259–97.

Douglas, R. (2002) Saving Australia from sedition: customs, the Attorney-General's department and the administration of peacetime political censorship. *Federal Law Review* 30, 135.

Douglas, R. (2002b) Let's pretend? Political trials in Australia, 1930–39. *UNSW Law Journal* 25, 33.

Douglas, R. (2003) Law, war and liberty: the World War II subversion prosecutions. *Melbourne University Law Review* 27, 65–116.

Douglas, R. (2005) The ambiguity of sedition: the trials of William Fardon Burns. *Australian Journal of Legal History* 9, 227.

Douglas, R. (2007) Cold war justice? Judicial responses to communists and communism, 1945–1955. *Sydney Law Review* 29, 43.

Edelstein, J. (2002) The Prasad affidavits: proof of facts in revolutionary legitimacy cases. *Sydney Law Review* 24, 57–88.

Engdahl, D. (1985) Foundations for military intervention in the United States, in Rowe and Whelan (eds).

Engels, F. (1977) *The Origin of the Family, Private Property and the State.* Moscow: Progress Publishers.

Ewing, K. and Gearty, C. (2000) *The Struggle for Civil Liberties: Political Freedom and the Rule of Law in Britain 1914–1945*. Oxford: Oxford University Press.

Farrer, W. and Brownbill, J. (2003) The city and parish of Manchester: Introduction, *The Victoria History of the County of Lancaster – Lancashire. Vol. 4*. London: University of London and History of Parliament Trust.

Feldman, D. (2002) *Civil Liberties and Human Rights in England and Wales*. Oxford: Oxford University Press.

Fitzgerald, R. (2002) *The People's Champion*. Brisbane: Queensland University Press.

Forcese, C. (2008) *National Security Law, Canadian Practice in International Perspective*. Toronto: Irwin Law.

Four Corners (2004) Trust and Betrayal. ABC television broadcast 1 November 2004 [Online]. Available at: http://www.abc.net.au/4corners/content/2004/s1229543.htm [accessed: 30 November 2010].

Fraser, M. (2005) A betrayal of trust and liberty, *The Age*, 20 October 2005 [Online]. Available at: http://www.theage.com.au/news/opinion/a-betrayal-of-trust-and-liberty/2005/10/19/1129401313656.html [accessed: 4 April 2011].

Freeman, M. (2001) *Lloyd's Introduction to Jurisprudence*. London: Sweet and Maxwell.

Fricke, G. (1997) The Eureka Trials. *Australian Law Journal* 71, 59–69.

Fritz, C. (2008) *American Sovereigns: The People and America's Constitutional Tradition Before the Civil War*. Cambridge: Cambridge University Press.

Gellhorn, W. (1960) *American Rights: The Constitution in Action*. New York: Macmillan.

Gibbon, E. (2003) *The Decline and Fall of the Roman Empire*. New York: Modern Library.

Gill, C. (1913) *The Naval Mutinies of 1797*. Manchester: Manchester University Press.

Goldstein, R. (2006) D'Aquino, linked to Tokyo Rose broadcasts, dies. *New York Times*, 27 September 2006.

Greenland, H. (1998) *Red Hot: The Life and Times of Nick Origlass*. Sydney: Wellington Lane Press.

Greer, S. (1983) Military intervention in civil disturbances: the legal basis reconsidered. *Public Law* 573.

Hailsham, L. (ed.) (1973) *Halsbury's Laws of England*. 4th edn. London: LexisNexis Butterworths.

Hale, M. (2000) *The History and Analysis of the Common Law of England*. Union, NJ: The Law Book Exchange.

Halsbury (1976) *Laws of England*. 4th Edition. Oxford: Butterworths.

Hamburger, P. (1985) The development of the law of seditious libel and the control of the press. *Stanford Law Review* 37, 661.

Hamill, D. (1986) *Pig in the Middle: The Army in Northern Ireland 1969–1985*. London: Methuen.

Hancock, N. (2002) *Terrorism and the Law in Australia: Supporting Materials*. Canberra: Parliament of Australia (Department of Parliamentary Library, Research Paper No. 13).

Hansard (1912) [Online]. Available at: http://hansard.millbanksystems.com/commons/1912/may/30/mr-tom-mann-mitigation-of-sentence [accessed: 9 November 2009].

Harlow, C. and Rawlings, R. (1992) *Pressure through Law*. London: Routledge.

Hay, D. (1975) Property, authority and the criminal law, in Hay, D. et al., *Albion's Fatal Tree*. London: Allen Lane.

Head, M. (1979) Sedition – is the Star Chamber dead? *Criminal Law Journal* 3, 89–107.

Head, M. (2001) A victory for democracy? An alternative assessment of *Republic of Fiji v. Prasad. Melbourne Journal of International Law* 2, 535–49.

Head, M. (2002) Counter terrorism laws: a threat to political freedom, civil liberties and constitutional rights. *Melbourne University Law Review* 26, 666.

Head, M. (2004) Another threat to democratic rights: ASIO detentions cloaked in secrecy. *Alternative Law Journal* 29, 127.

Head, M. (2004b) ASIO, secrecy and lack of accountability. *Murdoch University Electronic Journal of Law* 11.

Head M. (2007) The political uses and abuses of sedition: the trial of Brian Cooper. *Legal History* 11, 63–78.

Head, M. (2007b) *Evgeny Pashukanis: A Critical Re-Appraisal*. London: Routledge-Cavendish.

Head, M. (2009) What the Haneef Inquiry revealed (and did not). *Alternative Law Journal* 35.

Head, M. (2010) *Marxism, Revolution and Law. The Lively Debates of Early Soviet Russia*. Saarbrucken: VDM.

Head, M. and Mann, S. (2009) *Domestic Deployment of the Armed Forces: Military Powers, Law and Human Rights*. Farnham: Ashgate.

Hennessy, P. (1985) Whitehall contingency planning for industrial disputes', in Rowe and Whelan (eds).

Heuston, R. (1964) *Essays in Constitutional Law*. 2nd edn. London: Stevens.

Hobsbawm, E. (1964). 'The machine breakers' in *Labouring Men: Studies in the History of Labour*. London: Weidenfeld & Nicolson.

Hoffman, B. (1998) *Inside Terrorism*. New York: Columbia University Press.

Hollingsworth, M. and Fielding, N. (1999) *Defending the Realm: MI5 and the Shayler Affair*. London: Andre Deutsch.

Hope, R. (1979) *Protective Security Review Report*. Canberra: Australian Government Publishing Service.

Ingraham, B.L. (1979) *Political Crime in Europe: A Comparative Study of France, Germany and England*. Berkeley, CA: University of California Press.

Jeffery, K. (1985) Military aid to the civil power in the United Kingdom – an historical perspective', in Rowe and Whelan (eds).

Kaufman, I. (1951) Judge Kaufman's statement upon sentencing the Rosenbergs. University of Missouri–Kansas City [Online]. Available at: http://www.law. umkc.edu/faculty/projects/ftrials/rosenb/ROS_SENT.HTM [accessed 24 June 2008].

Keelty, M. (2009) Law enforcement contribution to national security. National Security Australia 2009 speech, 23 March 2009 Sydney [Online]. Available at: http://www.afp.gov.au/media/national_media/national_speeches/2009/law_ enforcement_contribution_to_national_security [accessed 3 April 2009].

Keen, P. (1999) *The Crisis of Literature in the 1790s: Print Culture and the Public Sphere*. Cambridge: Cambridge University Press.

Kelsen, H. (1946) *General Theory of Law and State*. Cambridge, MA: Harvard University Press.

Kershaw, I. (1998) *Hitler, 1889–1936: Hubris*. London: Allen Lane.

King, D. (1859) *The Life and Times of Thomas Wilson Dorr*. Boston: published by the author.

Kish, J. (1995) (edited by D. Turns) *International Law and Espionage*. The Hague: Martinus Nijhoff.

Kyer, C. (1979) Sedition through the ages: a note on legal terminology. *University of Toronto Faculty of Law Review* 37, 266.

Laing, N. (2005) Call-out the guards – why Australia should no longer fear the deployment of Australian troops on home soil. *University of NSW Law Journal* 28, 507.

Laqueur, W. (1999) *The New Terrorism: Fanaticism and the Arms of Mass Destruction*. New York: Oxford University Press.

Law Reform Commission of Canada (1986) *Crimes Against the State*. Working Paper 49. Ottawa: Law Reform Commission of Canada.

Lee, H. (1984) *Emergency Powers*. Sydney: Law Book Company.

Lendrum, S. (1977) The 'Corrong Massacre': martial law and the Aborigines at First Settlement. *Adelaide Law Review* 6, 26.

Lenin, V.I. (1918) The proletarian revolution and the renegade Karl Kautsky, in Lenin (1971) *Selected Works 3*. Moscow: Progress.

Lerhe, E. (2004) Civil military relations and aid to the civil power in Canada: implications for the war on terror, CDAI-CDFAI 7th Annual Graduate Students Symposium, RMC, October 29–30, 2004 [Online]. Available at: http://www. cda-cdai.ca/symposia/2004/Lerhe,%20Eric-%20Paper.pdf   [accessed: 15 August 2008].

Lobban, M. (1990) From seditious libel to unlawful assembly: Peterloo and the changing face of political crime c.1770–1820. *Oxford Journal of Legal Studies* 10, 3, 307–52.

Lynch, A., McGarrity, N., and Williams G. (2009) The proscription of terrorist organisations in Australia. *Federal Law Review* 37, 1–40.

Macintyre, S. (1999) *A Concise History of Australia*. London: Cambridge University Press.

Maher L. (1992) The use and abuse of sedition. *Sydney Law Review* 14, 287.

Maher L. (1994) Dissent, disloyalty and disaffection: Australia's last Cold War sedition case. *Adelaide Law Review* 16, 1.

Maloney, S. (1997) Domestic operations: the Canadian approach. *Parameters* (US Army War College Quarterly), Autumn 1997, 135–52.

Mandela, N. (1995) *Long Walk to Freedom*. Boston: Little, Brown and Company.

Manning, R. (1980) The origins of the doctrine of sedition. *Albion* 12, 99.

Martyn, A. (2002) The right of self-defence under international law – the response to the terrorist attacks of 11 September. Australian Law and Bills Digest Group. Canberra: Parliament of Australia.

McClelland, R. (2010) Counter-terrorism trial sentences. Media release. 15 February 2010 [Online]. Available at: http://www.attorneygeneral. gov.au/www/ministers/mcclelland.nsf/Page/MediaReleases_2010_ FirstQuarter_15February2010-Counter-TerrorismTrialSentences [accessed 22 December 2010].

McGarrity, N. (2010) 'Testing' our counter-terrorism laws: the prosecution of individuals for terrorism offences in Australia. *Criminal Law Journal* 34, 92.

McPherson, J. (1990) *Abraham Lincoln and the Second American Revolution*. New York: Oxford University Press.

Ministry of Defence (1999) *The British Army in Northern Ireland – The Armed Forces in Northern Ireland*. London: Ministry of Defence.

Ministry of Defence (2005) *Operations in the UK: The Defence Contribution to Resilience*. London: HMSO.

Mitchell, P. (2010) Anti-Islamic measures in Britain threaten democratic rights. *World Socialist Web Site*. 19 January 2010 [Online]. Available at: http://www. wsws.org/articles/2010/jan2010/isla-j19.shtml [accessed 22 December 2010].

Molony, J. (1989) *Eureka*. Melbourne: Melbourne University Press.

Morreau, P. (2007) Policing public nuisance: the legacy of recent events on Palm Island. *Indigenous Law Bulletin* 6, 9.

Moysey, S. (2008) *The Road to Balcombe Street: The IRA Reign of Terror in London*. Binghamton, NY: Haworth.

Murray-Smith, S. (1961) Black men – and a white conscience. *Overland* 20, 32.

Neumann, F. (1942) *Behemoth, The Structure and Practice of National Socialism*. London: Victor Gollancz.

North, D. (1998) *The Heritage We Defend*. Detroit: Labor Publications.

North, D. (2004) *The Crisis of American Democracy: The Presidential Elections of 2000 and 2004*. Oak Park, MI: Mehring Books.

Note (1969) Legislation and riots: interaction. *Brooklyn Law Review* 35, 472–85.

Packer, H.L. (1962) Offenses against the state. *The Annals of the American Academy,* 339.

Paine, T. *Writings of Tom Paine*. Vol. 2 (1779–1792), 36 [Online]. Available at: http://www.scribd.com/doc/5695/Writings-of-Thomas-Paine-Volume-2-17791792-the-Rights-of-Man [accessed: 4 April 2011].

Pashukanis, E. (1978) *Law and Marxism: A General Theory*. London: Ink Links.

Penner, N. (1988) *Canadian Communism: The Stalin Years and Beyond.* Toronto: Methuen.

Pietrusza, D. (2007) *1920: The Year of Six Presidents.* New York: Carroll & Graf.

Posner, R. (2006) *Not a Suicide Pact: The Constitution in a Time of National Emergency.* Oxford: Oxford University Press.

Priest, D. and Arkin, W. (2010) Monitoring America. *Washington Post* [Online]. Available at: http://projects.washingtonpost.com/top-secret-america/articles/monitoring-america/ [accessed 22 December 2010].

Public Record Office Victoria (2003) Eureka on trial [Online]. Available at: http://www.prov.vic.gov.au/eureka/state_treason_trials.htm#5 [accessed 10 November 2009].

Reid, R. (1989) *The Peterloo Massacre.* London: William Heinemann.

Roberts, S. (2001) *The Brother: The Untold Story of the Rosenberg Case.* New York: Random House.

Robertson, G. (1993) *Freedom, the Individual and the Law.* London: Penguin.

Robertson, G. (2005) *The Tyrannicide Brief: The Story of the Man who sent Charles I to the Scaffold.* London: Chatto & Windus.

Ross, J. I. (2003) *The Dynamics of Political Crime.* Thousand Oaks, CA; Sage.

Rowe, P. and Whelan, C. (eds) (1985) *Military Intervention in Democratic Societies.* London: Croom Helm.

Rowland, D. (2004) Data retention and the war against terrorism – a considered and proportionate response? [2004] JILT (*Journal of Information, Law and Technology*) 27.

Ruddock, P. (2004) A new framework: counter terrorism and the rule of law, address to the Sydney Institute, 20 April 2004 [Online]. Available at: http://152.91.12/www/MinisterRuddockHome.nsf/Alldocs/RWPB046617DB0869 [accessed: 29 June 2004].

Rushton, P. (1973) The trial of the Sydney Twelve: the original charge. *Labour History*, 53–7.

Sagarin, E. (1973) Introduction, in Proal, L., *Political Crime.* Montclair, NJ: Paterson Smith.

Salvatore, N. (1984) *Eugene V. Debs: Citizen and Socialist.* Champaign, IL: University of Illinois Press.

Sands, P. (2006) *Lawless World.* London: Penguin.

Saul, B. (2006) *Defining Terrorism in International Law.* Oxford: Oxford University Press.

Savage, C. (2010) Court dismisses a case asserting torture by CIA. *New York Times*, 8 September 2010 [Online]. Available at: http://www.nytimes.com/2010/09/09/us/09secrets.html. [accessed 22 December 2010].

Senate Committee (2002) Evidence to Senate Legal and Constitutional Committee, Parliament of Australia, Inquiry into the Security Legislation Amendment (Terrorism) Bill 2002 and Related Bills. *Official Committee Hansard*, 8 April 2002.

Schmalleger, F. (2002) *Criminal Law Today.* Upper Saddle River, NJ: Prentice Hall.

Schmid, A., Jongman, A., et al. (1988) *Political Terrorism: A New Guide to Actors, Authors, Concepts, Data Bases, Theories, and Literature*. New Brunswick, NJ: Transaction Books.

Schneir, W. and Scheir, M. (1973) *Invitation to an Inquest: Reopening the Rosenberg "Atom Spy" Case*. Baltimore: Penguin Books.

Schrecker, E. (1998) *Many Are the Crimes: McCarthyism in America*. London: Little, Brown and Company.

Sevastopulo, D. (2009) Intelligence chief warns of security threat. *Financial Times*. 13 February 2009.

Shalom, S. (1993) *Imperial Alibis: Rationalizing US Intervention After the Cold War*. Boston, NJ: South End Press.

Solnit, D. and Solnit, R. (2008) *The Battle of the Story of the Battle of Seattle*. Oakland, CA: AK Press.

Spector, M. (1931) The defendants before the docks in Canada. *The Militant*, 5 December 1931[Online]. Available at: http://www.marxists.org/history/canada/socialisthistory/Docs/TrotOrigin/1931Trial/Trial6.htm [accessed: 12 February 2010].

Stent, W. (1980) An individual v. the state – the case of B.L. Cooper. *Overland* 79, 60–8.

Stephen, J. (1883) *A History of the Criminal Law of England*. New York: Burt Franklin.

Stevens, R. (2010) Police-state tactics against protesters in Britain [Online] Available at: http://www.wsws.org/articles/2010/dec2010/pers-d13.shtml [accessed: 17 December 2010].

Stone, G. (2004) *Perilous Times: Free Speech in Wartime*. New York: Norton.

Sutton, M. (1994) *Bear in Mind these Dead: An Index of Deaths from the Conflict in Ireland 1969–1993*. Belfast: Beyond the Pale Publications.

The 9/11 Commission (2004) *The 9/11 Commission Report*. Washington, DC: Government Printing Office.

The Age (2007) APEC blacklisters lose court challenge. September 6, 2007. [Online]. Available at: http://www.theage.com.au/news/National/Police-await-court-action-for-APEC-four/2007/09/06/1188783407820.html [accessed: 4 April 2011].

The Australian (2010) US staff 'told to spy on friend and foe'. 30 November 2010, 2 [Online]. Available at: http://www.theaustralian.com.au/news/nation/us-staff-told-to-spy-on-friend-and-foe/story-e6frg6nf-1225962959401 [accessed: 30 November 2010].

The Times (2010) Cossor Ali found not guilty of failing to pass on airline bomb plot information [Online]. Available at: http://www.timesonline.co.uk/tol/news/uk/crime/article7051241.ece [accessed: 30 November 2010].

Thompson, E.P. (1966) *The Making of the English Working Class*. New York: Vintage Books.

Torr, D. (1944) *Tom Mann*. London: Lawrence & Wishart.

Trotsky, L. (1975) *Terrorism and Communism*. London: New Park Publications.

Trotsky, L. (1997) *Writings of Leon Trotsky 1929. New York: Pathfinder Press.*

Tucker, R. (1975) *The Lenin Anthology*. New York: W.W. Norton and Co.

Turk, A.T. (1984) Political crime, in Meir, R.F. (ed), *Major Forms of Crime*. Beverly Hills, CA: Sage.

Turner, I. (1969) S*ydney's Burning (An Australian Political Conspiracy)*. Melbourne: Heinemann.

United Kingdom House of Commons (1951) *Parliamentary Debates*, 21 March 1951, 2410 (Herbert Morrison, Secretary of State for Foreign Affairs).

United Kingdom. Parliamentary Papers (1893) *Parlt Papers*, Vol. 17, (1893–4).

United States v. Ardeth Platte (2005) US Court of Appeals Tenth Circuit, 17 March 2005 [Online]. Available at: http://www.ca10.uscourts.gov/opinions/03/03-1345.pdf [accessed: 30 November 2010].

Vallely, P. (2002) The Airey Neave files. *Independent*, 22 February 2002 [Online]. Available at: http://www.independent.co.uk/news/people/profiles/the-airey-neave-files-661625.html [accessed: 12 May 2009].

Von Doussa, J. (2005) Presentation at Forum on National Security Law and Human Rights [Online] Available at: http://www.hreoc.gov.au/about_the_commission/speeches_president/20051101_forum_on_national_security_laws_and_human_rights [accessed: 2 December 2005].

Wacks, R. (2009) *Understanding Jurisprudence*. London: Oxford University Press.

Wade, E. and Phillips, G. (1970) *Constitutional Law*. 8th edn. London: Longmans.

Walker, C. and Broderick, J. (2006) *The Civil Contingencies Act 2004: Risk, Resilience and the Law in the United Kingdom*. Oxford: Oxford University Press.

Whelan, C. (1985) 'Military intervention in democratic societies: the role of law' in Rowe and Whelan (eds).

Williams, G. (1961) *Textbook of Criminal Law*, 2nd edn. London: Stevens.

Willams, G. (1971) The king's peace: riot law in its historical perspective. *Utah Law Review* (1971), 240–58.

Williams, G. (2001) Republic of Fiji v. Prasad: Introduction. *Melbourne Journal of International Law* 2, 144.

Windeyer, V. (1979) Certain questions concerning the position of members of the Defence Force when called out to aid the civil power, in Hope (1979), Appendix 9.

Winterton, G. (2003) The *Communist Party* Case, in Lee and Winterton (eds), *Australian Constitutional Landmarks*. Cambridge: Cambridge University Press.

Wise, D. (2003) *Spy: The Inside Story of How the FBI's Robert Hanssen Betrayed America*. New York: Random House.

Witcover, J. (1989) *Sabotage at Black Tom: Imperial Germany's Secret in America, 1914–1917*. Chapel Hill, NC: Algonquin.

Wright, T. (2007) A funny thing happened on the way to APEC... *The Age*, 8 September 2007 [Online]. Available at: http://www.theage.com.au/news/in-depth/a-funny-thing-happened-on-the-way-to-apec/2007/09/07/1188783490462. html?page=fullpage#contentSwap3 [accessed: 4 April 2011].

Wulf, M. (1972) Commentary: a soldier's First Amendment rights: the art of formally granting and practically suppressing. *Wayne Law Review* 18, 665–82.

Yeates, A. (2007) A 'foolish young man, who can perhaps, be straightened out in his thinking': the Brian Cooper Sedition Case. *Australian Historical Studies* 129.

Young, T. (1976) *Incitement to Disaffection.* London: Cobden Trust.

Zeidan, S. (2006) Desperately seeking definition: the international community's quest for identifying the specter of terrorism. *Cornell International Law Journal* 36, 491–2.

Index

Aborigines, use of martial law against 268–9
abusive words 244–5
Adams, John 37–8
advocacy of government overthrow 47, 48, 50–52, 54–6, 76–81, 89–91, 158–60
see also subversive advocacy
advocacy of law violation 60–61
advocacy of republicanism 101
advocacy of terrorism 13
advocacy of violence 60
affray 9, 221–36
Afghanistan, intervention in 18, 61–3, 127, 138, 143, 164–5, 182–7, 214–20, 245
Africa, sedition cases 156
aid to the civil power
see Military aid to civil power
aid to the civil community
see Military aid to the civil community
allegiance 99–100, 103
American Civil War 10, 37, 39–41, 73
American Declaration of Independence 38, 56, 65
American Revolution 26–8, 39, 42, 65–6, 70–4, 274
Amnesty International 17, 185
anarchists 31, 42, 45, 47, 116
ancient origins of treason law 24–6
ancillary measures 275
anthrax attacks 9
anti-conscription 31, 32–3, 36, 37, 44, 57–61, 148
anti-nuclear protests 140–41, 143–4, 197–198
anti-Semitism 45, 49
anti-terrorism laws
see counter-terrorism legislation

anti-war activities 31, 32–3, 37, 44, 58–61, 62–3, 79–81, 119–24, 125–31, 140–44, 197–8
armed forces
see military call-out powers and troops, use of
arson 32–3, 106, 145, 231
Asia-Pacific Economic Cooperation summit Sydney 2007 241–3
Assange, Julian 3, 126–7, 184
assassination, government by 269–71
assisting the enemy 163–6
atomic weapons 131–4
attempt 9, 24–5
Australia
Asia-Pacific Economic Cooperation summit Sydney 2007 241–3
Australian Defence Force 17
Australian Law Reform Commission 1, 9, 177–9
Australian Security Intelligence Organisation (ASIO) 134, 137–8, 177–9, 204–5, 207, 213–20
Communist League 124, 258, 260
Communist Party 32–5, 90–93, 169–77, 258, 260, 276
Communist Party case 34, 91–2, 170
Constitution
implied freedom of political communication 242–3
counter-terrorism legislation 11–13
Eureka Stockade 32, 81–5, 149, 277
executive powers 257–61
historical experiences 32–5
sedition cases 166–79
'Sydney Twelve' case 32, 90, 106–7, 123, 145, 166–8, 257, 275
terrorism cases 212–20

Australian Security Intelligence
    Organisation (ASIO) 134, 137–8,
    177–9, 204–5, 207, 213–20

Bali bombing 137–8
Bentham, Jeremy 68
Berger, Victor 46
besetting 243–5
Birmingham Six 187–8
Black, Hugo 51–6
Blackstone, William 67–8
Blair, Dennis viii, 4
'Bloody Code' 7
'Bloody Sunday' 116–17, 266
Bolsheviks 45–7
Boston Five conspiracy trial 57, 122
Brandeis, Louis 45–7, 60
breach of the peace 221, 236–45, 250
bribery 1, 8
Britain
    'Bloody Code' 7
    Chartist movement 21, 22, 28–9, 153,
        225–6, 275
    Civil Contingencies Act 31–2, 248,
        251–5
    Communist Party 31, 111–16, 154–6,
        237, 249–50, 274
    Defence of the Realm Regulations 248
    docks strike 1949 16, 255
    Emergency Powers Act 248–55
    English Civil War 25, 26, 65–70,
        75–6, 150–51, 221
    General Strike 1926 16, 155, 248, 250,
        255, 274
    'Glorious Revolution' 1688 25, 26,
        149–51
    Guildford Four 187–8
    Heathrow airport, troops at 17, 31, 255
    historical experiences 21–32
    Human Rights Act 14, 15–16
    Incitement to Disaffection Act 1934
        31–2, 115–18
    Incitement to Mutiny Act 1797 30–31,
        108–15, 155–6
    Ireland, British rule 31, 116–18, 154,
        264–8
    Mansfield doctrine 224–5
    military callout laws 251–5

'miscarriage of justice' cases 187–8,
    278
National Unemployed Workers
    Movement 31, 111–16, 237
Official Secrets Act 127, 129–31,
    140–41
Peterloo Massacre 1819 21, 22, 28,
    153, 225, 273, 274, 275
regicides, trials of 75–6
Treachery Act 99–100
Treason Act 1351 96–7
Zinoviev letter affair 154–5
Brown, John 102
Burke, Edmund 26
Bush, George W. 17, 38, 61–3, 185
    assertion of executive powers 62–3
    'war on terrorism' 17, 38, 61–3, 185

Cambodia, US invasion of 17, 57
Canada
    Bill of Rights 263
    Charter of Rights and Freedoms 9,
        15, 263
    Communist Party 35, 93–4, 261
    emergency powers 261–3
    Law Reform Commission 8–9
    Quebec crisis (1963–70) 35, 262
    Winnipeg general strike 1919 35, 93
Cannon, James 77–81, 278
capitalism, development of 65–8
Caribbean, sedition cases 156
censorship 41
Central Asia 18
Central Intelligence Agency (CIA) 58,
    126, 185–6, 269
Charles I 1, 26, 75–6, 151
Chartist movement 21, 22, 28–9, 153,
    225–6, 275
Chicago Democratic Convention
    conspiracy trial 58, 231–2, 278
Chifley, Ben 34, 170–71
chilling impact of prosecutions 276
Churchill, Winston 30
Civil Contingencies Act 31–2, 248, 251–5
civil disobedience 8, 36, 144, 147
civil liberties 11, 19, 37, 39, 48, 50, 57–63,
    249–71
civil rights movement 58

civil unrest viii, 22, 252–6
civil–military relations 31, 58, 267–8
civilian supremacy, principle of 31, 58, 267–8
class society and conflicts 5–7, 23
'clear and present danger' doctrine 43–8, 50–56, 60–61, 111, 124, 158–9, 170, 173
Clinton, Bill 128, 185, 202
Clinton, Hillary 126
COINTELPRO counter-intelligence program 58, 61, 275
Cold War 2, 32–4, 50–56, 103, 170–79
collective bargaining 86
commodity exchange 7
Communist League of Australia 124, 258, 260
Communist Party of Australia 32–5, 90–93, 169–77, 258, 260, 276
Communist Party of Canada 35, 93–4, 261
Communist Party of Great Britain 31, 111–16, 154–6, 237, 249–50, 274
Communist Party USA 50–56, 58, 132–4
communists 47, 48–56
complicity 9
concealment 9
conscription 31, 32–3, 41–3, 57–61, 106, 116, 119–20
conspiracy 9–10, 24–5, 32–3, 45, 50–51, 54, 57–61, 77–81, 83, 106–7, 131–4, 155–6, 230
    Boston Five conspiracy trial 57
    Chicago Democratic Convention conspiracy trial 58, 231–2, 278
    overt acts requirement 54
contempt (legal) 8, 56, 84, 114, 232
control orders 92, 209–210
corruption 1, 8
counter-terrorism legislation 11–13, 31, 35, 147, 160, 181–220, 277–8
coups 71–4, 269
criminal anarchy 47
criminal law vii, 4, 7
criminal libel 8
criminal syndicalism 47

death penalty 7
Debs, Eugene 37, 41, 44, 118–20

defence campaigns, political character of 278
democracy 2, 6, 45–6, 70
    façade of 6, 70
democratic rights 4, 6, 15
deportation 42–3, 61
desertion 100
destruction of military facilities 141–5
detention 61, 73, 92, 181, 196–7, 207–10, 250–52
    see also internment
dictatorship 6, 7, 252
    see also totalitarianism
diplomatic immunity 127, 129, 137
'domestic violence' 256
Douglas, Roger 34–5, 89–91, 176
Douglas, William 51–6, 65–70, 81, 158, 274
draft dodging 8
    see also conscription

Eastman, Max 42
economic crimes 1, 125, 128
economic espionage 125, 128
economic sabotage 139–40
effectiveness, doctrine of 72–4
Eisenhower, Dwight 103, 133
Ellsberg, Daniel 59–60
emergency 47
emergency, state of
    see state of emergency
emergency powers 16–17, 31, 40–41, 73, 116, 122–4, 196–7, 247–63
Emergency Powers Act (UK) 248–55
Engels, Frederick 5–6, 53, 78
English Revolution 25, 26, 65–71, 75–6, 150–51, 221
entrapment 213–18
equality 6, 67, 70
espionage 2, 3, 8, 41, 118, 125–38
    economic espionage 125, 128, 142–4
Espionage Act (US) 3, 37, 41–8, 59–61, 118–20, 127, 132, 144
Eureka Stockade 32, 81–5, 149, 277
European Convention on Human Rights and Fundamental Freedoms 14, 15–16, 127–8, 196–7, 244, 252, 278

exception, state of
    see state of exception doctrine
executive power 11, 14, 16–17
    see also prerogative powers
exploitation of labour power 5
extra-legal measures 247–71

Falklands War 130
fascism 6, 48–9, 99
Federal Bureau of Investigations (FBI) 37,
    58, 61–3, 77, 126, 131, 185–6
feudalism 65–7, 71
Fiji, coups in 74
flag desecration 60
Ford, Gerald 57, 103
Fox's Libel Act 152
Fraser, Malcolm 187
freedom of assembly 6, 236–45, 249–69
freedom of association 11, 181
freedom of expression 4, 6, 10, 11, 57–61,
    113, 236–45
French Revolution 24, 26–8, 67–8, 97–9,
    152

Gaddafi, Muammar 130–31
Germany 6, 11
    fascism 11
    Reichstag Fire 11
global financial crisis viii, 4, 63, 278
Goldman, Emma 41
good faith, defence of 89–91, 105, 162,
    164–5
government intervention in prosecutions
    vii, 1, 112–15, 155–6, 170–71,
    177–9, 274–5, 276–7
Great Depression (1930s) 4, 32–3, 63,
    169, 237–8
Grenada, invasion of 74
Guantánamo Bay 61–3, 187
Guildford Four 187–8
Gulf War 1990–91 35, 177

habeas corpus 10, 37, 40–41, 62–63, 98,
    181, 196–197, 267
Haneef, Mohamed 207, 210–212, 278
harbouring suspects 9
Hay, Douglas 7
Heathrow airport, troops at 17, 31, 255

heresy 22
high treason 1, 32, 75–6, 82–5, 95–6, 107
hindering police 244
Hitler, Adolf 11
Hobbes, Thomas 66–7
Holmes, Oliver Wendell 43–6, 60, 119
Hoover, J. Edgar 47–8
Howard, John 138, 204–7, 212
Hughes, Billy 32, 90, 106–7, 145, 166
human rights 70–74
human rights legislation 14–16, 70–74,
    127–8, 251–2
humanitarian aid 105, 202–4

ideology of justice 7
incitement 9, 45, 54, 58, 108–24, 153
Incitement to Disaffection Act 1934 (UK)
    31–2, 115–18
Incitement to Mutiny Act 1797 (UK)
    30–31, 108–15, 155–6
indemnities from legal liability 16, 255,
    268
India, sedition cases 156
industrial action 6, 30, 167
inequality 67, 70
insubordination 41, 44, 49, 119–24
insurrection 2, 3, 42, 65–94
intelligence agencies viii, 4, 10, 18, 170,
    185–6
'interests of the state' 125, 130, 140–41,
    273, 277–8
International Covenant on Civil and
    Political Rights 14–16, 17, 185,
    263, 278
international law 14–16, 61–3, 70–74,
    128, 143–4, 271, 278
International Workers of the World 32–3,
    90, 107, 122–3, 139, 145, 166–8,
    257
internment without trial 50, 116, 250–51,
    265–8
investigate, power to 56
Iraq, intervention in 18, 61–3, 127, 143,
    164–5, 182–7, 214–20, 245
Ireland, British rule 31, 116–18, 154,
    264–8
    'Bloody Sunday' 116–17, 266
Ireland, British troops to 31, 116–18

Irish Easter 1916 uprising 99
Irish Republican Army 31, 99, 116–18,
    184, 187–8, 266–8, 278
Italy 6

Jefferson, Thomas 28, 39
Jehovah's Witnesses 49, 153, 260, 261
Johnson, Lyndon 56, 58, 62, 231
judiciary, role of 13–14, 249

Keelty, Mick viii, 4
Kelsen, Hans 72–4
Kennedy, John 59, 103
Kent State University shootings 17, 37, 57
King, Martin Luther 57, 231
Korean War 34, 50–56, 132–3, 176
Ku Klux Klan 60, 158

labour power, exploitation of 5
lawlessness, official 247, 269–71
Learned Hand, Billings 42, 51
legal immunities
    see indemnities from legal liability
legal neutrality, myth of 273
legal positivism 72
Lenin, Vladimir 6, 50, 78, 92, 124
lethal force, against civilians
    see also reasonable and necessary force
Libya 130, 198–9
Lincoln, Abraham 10, 37, 40–41, 68, 274
Locke, John 27, 65–7, 69
'Lord Haw-Haw' 109
LTTE (Liberation Tigers of Tamil Eelam)
    202–4, 220, 277
Luddites 139–40

McCarthy, Joseph 103
McCarthyism 37, 50–56
MacDonald, Ramsay 112, 115
MacLean, John 248–9
McPherson, James 39–40
Magna Carta 62, 66
Maguire Seven 187–8
Maher, Laurence 34–5, 170
Malaysia 2
Mandela, Nelson 138–9, 181–2
Mann, Tom 30, 109–11, 273
Mansfield doctrine 224–5

Maori land claims 36, 148
martial law 6, 16, 30, 39–40, 150, 225,
    247, 257, 263–9
Marx, Karl 53, 78, 92, 121
Marxism 50–56, 66, 70, 79, 91–2, 149,
    273
Marxist legal theory 5–7
media censorship
    see censorship
Menzies, Robert 34, 91–2, 170–79,
    259–60, 274, 276
Middle East 18
military callout powers 17, 28–32, 36,
    81–5, 223–5, 229, 251–71
'Military aid to civil power' 253–4, 256–7
military coups
    see coups
military exercises 31
military intelligence agencies 58, 62
military law 121
military recruitment, interference with 41,
    44–5, 49, 57–61, 108–24, 155–6
military tribunals 40–41, 264–8
military–civil relations 31, 58, 267–8
minor offences 243–5, 275–6
'miscarriage of justice' cases 187–8, 278
misprision of treason 102
money-laundering 1
Montesquieu, Charles-Louis 56
Mussolini, Benito
mutiny 30–31, 41, 44, 49, 108–24
    Home Rule Bill for Ireland 111
    Incitement to Mutiny Act 108–9
    'Invergordon Mutiny' 1931 115
    Nore mutiny 1797 108–9
    Spithead mutiny 1797 108–9
My Lai Massacre 122

'national defence' 142–4
'national security' 2, 4, 8, 10, 13, 23, 32,
    123–4, 125–45, 197, 252, 277–8
National Security Agency (US) 58, 62
National Unemployed Workers Movement
    31, 111–16, 237
natural law 67–70
necessity, doctrine of 70–74
New Zealand
    emergency powers 261

Maori land claims 36, 148
sedition cases 36, 148, 156, 176
World War I sedition charges 35–6,
    148
World War II subversive document
    case 148
Nixon, Richard 17, 57–61, 103, 231–2,
    278
Nuremberg principles 143–4
Nuremberg Trials 122

Obama, Barack 4, 38, 62–3, 202, 270–71,
    278
obstruction 243–5
obstruction of justice 8
offensive conduct 243–5
official lawlessness 247, 269–71
official secrets 3, 125–38
Official Secrets Act (UK) 127, 129–31,
    140–41
oil 18
overlapping offences 275

pacifists 31, 143–4
Paine, Thomas 2, 26–8, 149, 152, 276
Papua New Guinea 35, 177–9, 274
    secessionist agitation 35, 177–9, 274
parliamentary privilege 75
Pashukanis, Evgeny 7
Paterson, Fred 32–3, 149, 169
Pearl Harbor, attack on 48
Pentagon Papers 59–69, 278
'people smuggling' 1
perjury 1, 8
Peterloo Massacre 1819 21, 22, 28, 153,
    225, 273, 274, 275
petty offences 1
    see also 'public order' offences
Pitt, William 86, 97–9, 108–9, 152
PKK (Partiya Karkeran Kurdistan) 202–4,
    277
police 29–30, 225–7, 236–45
    establishment in Britain 29–30, 225–6
    powers to ban demonstrations 227,
        236–45
political calculations 1, 9
political crimes 8
political dissent vii, 3, 8, 44, 61

political instability viii, 4
political power 7
politically motivated violence 147–79
Posner, Richard 10, 60
posse comitatus doctrine 224–5
Posse Comitatus Act (US) 256
postal bans 41–2
prerogative powers 17, 254–6, 264–9
    see also reserve powers, emergency
        powers
preventative detention 181
press censorship
    see censorship
private property 5, 7
property rights 67
proscription of organisations 11
prosecutorial discretion 9
public defence campaigns 81–5, 118
'public emergency' 14, 15–16
'public order' offences 4, 222, 233,
    236–45, 250–51, 275–6

Quebec crisis (1963–70) 35, 262

rebellion 8, 10, 32, 65–94
Red Scare 1919–20 46–8
redress, law of 68
    see also revolution, right to
Reed, John 42
regicides, trials of 75–6
Reichstag Fire 11
religious freedom 49
rendition 61–3, 269–70
republicanism 101
reserve powers
    see prerogative powers
resisting arrest 8
revival of old offences 274
revolution, punishment of 65–94
revolution, right to 26–8, 56, 65–85, 158,
    274
revolutionary legality, doctrine of 70–74
revolutions, role in history 65–6, 70–74
Rights of Man 2, 26–8, 149, 152, 276
riot, offence of 9, 58, 221–36
    conspiracy to 230
Riot Act 30, 221–6, 233, 235
riots 28–9, 46, 57, 221–36

Bristol riots 1832 28–9, 254
Featherstone Colliery riots 29, 109,
    254
Gordon riots 1781 224–5
Haymarket riot 1886 232
Los Angeles riots 1965 276
Palm Island riot 222
Seattle anti-WTO riots 229, 232–3
Toronto riot 2000 223
US urban riots 1960s 57, 230–31
Robertson, Geoffrey 75–6
Roman law 24
Roosevelt, Franklin 37, 48, 80–81, 103,
    274
Rosenberg, Ethel and Julius 131–4
Ross, Jeffrey 7
rout, offence of 226, 230
    see also riot
royal prerogative powers
    see prerogative powers
'rule of law' 17, 19, 248, 255, 264, 269–71
Russian Revolution 31, 35, 41–8, 66, 87,
    93, 154, 248, 257

sabotage 2, 8, 125, 138–45
    economic sabotage 138–9
Scandalum Magnatum 22, 25, 150
Schmitt, Carl 11
secret information
    see official secrets
security
    see national security
sedition vii, 1, 2, 8, 21, 27, 28, 32–6, 37–9,
    49, 53, 82, 87–94, 97–9, 113–14,
    121, 147–79
    early history 24, 148–56
    private prosecution 157
    sedition trials of 1790s 26–8, 97–9
    seditious conspiracy 22, 32–3, 153–4,
        157–60, 166–7
    seditious libel 21, 22, 25–6, 82,
        150–53, 157
    US Sedition Act 37–9, 77–81
Seekamp, Henry 32, 149
self-preservation, right of 65–70
Sharkey, Lance 33, 174–6
Sharpeville Massacre 139
slavery 39–40, 73, 102

smuggling 1
social contract 66–70
Socialist Party of America 37, 43–7,
    118–20
Socialist Workers Party (US) 37, 48, 58,
    77–81, 121–2
socialists 30, 44–8, 66, 70, 118–20, 149,
    273, 276
socio-economic order 5
sovereign immunity 271
Soviet Union 33, 50–56, 131–4, 170–77,
    261
Spain 6
Spanish Civil War 116
Spinoza, Baruch 56
Spock, Benjamin 57, 122
spying for foreign power 99–100, 125–45
Stalinism 54
Star Chamber 25, 148–51, 221
state apparatus 5–7
state of emergency 31, 139, 249–69
state of exception doctrine 11
'state secrets' doctrine 269–71
Stone, Geoffrey 37–62
strikes 6, 30, 31, 35, 46, 57, 89, 109–11
    Australian miners' strike 1949 91–2,
        170
    Boston police strike 46
    British docks strike 1949 16, 255
    British general strike 1926 16, 155,
        248, 250, 255, 274
    British miners' strike 1912 109–11
    British miners' strike 1974 31
    New Zealand general strike 35
    Seattle general strike 46
    US mineworkers strike 46
    US steelworkers strike 46
    Winnipeg general strike 1919 35, 93
    see also industrial action
students 56–61
subversion 2, 3
subversive advocacy 49, 60, 158–60
subversive documents 148
superior orders defence 122
surveillance 10, 18, 56–63, 186, 269
Sydney Hilton Hotel bombing
'Sydney Twelve' trial 32, 90, 106–7, 123,
    145, 166–8, 257, 275

syndicalists 30, 32–3

tax evasion 1, 8
terrorism 2, 3, 10, 61–3, 137–8, 159,
        181–220, 251–5
    advocacy of 13
    counselling terrorism 13
    definition of 7–8, 12–13, 18, 183–4,
        188–9, 199, 205–6
    praising terrorism 13, 194–5
    'terrorist organisation' 13, 86, 87, 92–3,
        188–9, 210
    membership of 13
Thailand 2
'Tokyo Rose' 103
Tolpuddle Martyrs 86
torture 10, 61–3, 269–70
totalitarianism 2, 6
trade secrets 128
trade unions 29–30, 86
treachery 9, 99–100, 105–6
Treachery Act (UK) 99–100
treason 1, 2, 8, 22, 32, 42, 75–6, 81–5,
        95–108, 150, 159
    allegiance requirement 99–100, 103
    ancient origins 24–6
    defined by US Constitution 101–3,
        159
    early Germanic law 24
    high treason 1, 32, 75–6, 82–5, 95–6,
        107
    misprision of 102
    petty treason 95, 107
    revival of 95
    Roman law 24
    Treason Act 1351 (UK) 96–7
    treason trials of 1794 26, 97–9
treason felony 32–3, 100–101, 106–7
trespass 197–198, 243–5
troops, use of 6, 28–32, 36, 81–5, 223–5,
        229, 251–71
Trotsky, Leon 6–7, 78
Trotskyism 37, 48, 54, 77–81, 123–4, 258,
        273, 274
Turner, Ian 107, 166–8

UK Human Rights Act 14, 15–16
United Kingdom

    see Britain
United Nations 126, 183–4
United States
    Alien Act 42
    Alien Registration Act
        see Smith Act
    American Revolution 26–8, 42, 65–6,
        70–74, 274
    Boston Five conspiracy trial 57, 122
    Bush Administration 17, 38, 61–3, 185
    Central Intelligence Agency (CIA) 58,
        126, 185–6, 269
    Chicago Democratic Convention
        conspiracy trial 58, 231–2, 278
    Civil War 10, 37, 39–41, 73
    COINTELPRO counter-intelligence
        program 58, 61, 275
    Communist Party 50–56, 58, 132–4
    Constitution 10, 270, 274
        Bill of Rights 15, 270
        Definition of treason 101–3
        Fifth Amendment 132, 201, 270
        First Amendment 10, 42–63,
            119–22, 158–60, 201, 238–40
        Fourth Amendment 233
    Declaration of Independence 38, 56,
        65
    Espionage Act 3, 37, 41–50, 59–61,
        118–20, 127, 132, 144
    Federal Bureau of Investigations (FBI)
        37, 58, 61–3, 77, 126, 131, 185–6
    historical experiences 37–63
    Kent State University shootings 17,
        37, 57
    National Security Agency 58, 62
    Obama Administration 4, 38, 62–3,
        202, 270–71, 278
    Posse Comitatus Act 256
    Presidential powers 255–7
    Red Scare 1919–20 46–8
    Sedition Act 37–9, 43, 77–81
    Smith Act 48–51, 54–6, 76–81, 120,
        147, 278
    Socialist Party 37, 43–7, 118–20
    Socialist Workers Party 37, 48, 58,
        77–81, 121–2
    USA PATRIOT Act 38, 61–3,
        199–204, 206

War with France 37–9
Watergate 57, 60
Universal Declaration of Human Rights 70
unlawful assembly 9, 21, 221–3, 236–45
unlawful associations 35, 85–94
unlawful oaths 86
unlawful orders 122
urging violence 162–6
USA PATRIOT Act 38, 61–3, 199–204, 206

Vietnam War 17, 35, 37, 56–61, 103, 121–2, 176, 231, 275
vigilante groups 42
violence, politically motivated 147–79
violence, urging 2
violent disorder, offence of 223, 226–7, 234

Wall Street, interests of 42, 43
Wall Street crash 169

'war on terrorism' 1, 3, 17–19, 37–38, 61–3, 86, 103, 138, 147, 159–60, 181–220, 277–278
wartime powers 248–69
Washington, George 102
Watergate 57, 60
weapons of mass destruction 9, 10, 18, 62–3, 200
'whistleblowing' 125–38
WikiLeaks 3, 126–7, 184
wilful damage 148
Wilson, Woodrow 41, 45, 118
working class 6, 21, 22, 27–31, 33, 56–61, 65–6, 109–11, 149, 169, 176, 224–6, 273
World War I 32–3, 37, 41–8, 122–3, 127, 141–2, 145
World War II 2, 32, 37, 48–50, 91, 116, 123–4, 132

Zinoviev letter affair 154–5